BARRIER-FREE THEATRE

Including Everyone in Theatre Arts
— in Schools, Recreation, and Arts Programs —
Regardless of (Dis)Ability

SALLY BAILEY

Idyll Arbor, Inc.

39129 264th Ave SE, Enumclaw, WA 98022 (360) 825-7797

ISBN: 9781882883783

Printed in the United States of America

Library of Congress Cataloging-in-Publication Data
Bailey, Sally D.
    Barrier-free theatre : including everyone in theatre arts-in schools, recreation, and arts programs-regardless of (dis)ability / Sally Bailey.
        p. cm.
    Includes bibliographical references and index.
    ISBN 978-1-882883-78-3 (alk. paper)
    1. People with disabilities and the performing arts. 2. Drama in education. I. Title.
    PN1590.H36B348 2010
    791.087--dc20

                                                2010024365

Contents

Acknowledgements

Much of the information that is included in this book came from my experiences with over 1,000 children, teens, and adults with and without disabilities who I have had the privilege to teach and observe in drama classes, theatre productions, and summer camps at the Texas School for the Deaf in Austin, Texas; Bachman Recreation Center in Dallas, Texas; Appel Farm Arts and Music Center in Elmer, New Jersey; the Bethesda Academy of Performing Arts (now Imagination Stage) in Bethesda, Maryland; Ivymount School in Rockville, Maryland; special education classrooms in the Montgomery County, Maryland, public school system; Fillmore Arts Center in Washington, DC; Hartwood House Residences in Alexandria, Virginia; the Barrier-Free Theatre of the City of Manhattan's Parks and Recreation Department in Manhattan, Kansas; the Super Summer Creative Arts Camp at Kansas State University; and my K-State students and our Manhattan community guests during my 10 years of teaching Drama Therapy with Special Populations at K-State. I must thank each and every one of them for teaching me how to structure a drama class, how to mediate conflict, how to listen for what is *really* happening between people and what is *really* needed to make a given situation successful. In addition, I thank them for sharing their creativity, hard work, and joy. Without them there would be no book — they are my source material and my inspiration.

I am also grateful for the generosity and support which I have received from my students' parents over the years. Without their belief in the power of the arts and their understanding of the value of our work together, the artistic and educational work their children accomplished would not have happened. Of these parents, I must single out a few leaders: Joyce Glenner, who personally rounded up the majority of actors who joined my first performing company as a fledgling Arts Access Director in Bethesda; Claudia Segal, who first introduced me to the concept of "seeing the child and not the disability"; and Jane Gibson, who believes that every city and town in America should have their own Barrier-Free Theatre.

Thanks also go to the executive directors, artistic directors, program directors, camp directors, special education teachers, and other employers who have had the vision to hire me to bring accessible arts programming into their classrooms or organizations. This thanks extends to the administration and faculty of the Communication Studies, Theatre, and Dance Department at Kansas State University who had the vision to continue the drama therapy program begun by Dr. Norman Fedder, my predecessor at Kansas State, after his retirement, and hire me.

I did not want this book to reflect my voice alone. Theatre is, after all, a communal art. We need to work together to put on the show and to change the world. This book includes essays from a number of colleagues, including Tim Reagan, Cindy Bowen, Lisa Agogliati, Patti Woolsey, Caleen Sinnette Jennings, Elizabeth van den Berg, Jade Gingerich, Marie Schick, Jeanie Hayes Hatch, Suzanne Richard, and Mandy Hart. They attest to the possibility of learning to become an inclusive teacher/director/therapist and in the process each discovered that barrier-free classrooms and rehearsals made them better communicators for all their students. Also represented are the voices of former students and parents, including Chammi Rajipatirana, Molly Work, Kim Smith, Claudia Bocock, J.P. Illamarendi, Mary Ann McNally, Joyce Glenner, Karen Martel, and Ken Moore. They speak directly to the power of drama to change lives.

The photographs in this book were taken by a number of caring and sensitive individuals who were able to really see, feel, and capture the delight of the participants in class and on stage. Their work has allowed you to have a glimpse of the fun you can have when you start your own Barrier-Free program. Thanks go to John Carter, Alan Honey, Keith Jenkins, Lea Ann Rosen, Pam Stokes, Patricia Theriault, and Allison Walker.

For over ten years I submitted *Barrier-Free Theatre* to publishers of disability, special education, education, and theatre books. All of them passed on it, because, as they said, they couldn't figure out who would want to buy it. Whenever I replied, "Twenty percent of the population has a disability of some kind and they have many family members, caregivers, teachers, therapists, and others who would like to see them express themselves better and participate in the life of the community! Everyone who teaches theater or directs plays sooner or later will work with actors who have identified and unidentified disabilities, special education teachers will want to learn how to bring drama into their classrooms in order to bring their material to life, parents of children with disabilities want their children included in public programming, and recreation leaders, social workers, counselors, and therapists need a tool for including and empowering their clients." But my arguments were not heeded until I approached Tom Blaschko and Idyll Arbor. I am so very grateful for his vision, understanding, and willingness to publish *Barrier-Free Theatre*. It takes courage to believe that individuals who are often looked down on and dismissed as un-able might 1) have the desire to participate in the arts and 2) have the ability to do so.

Above all, thank you for buying this book, for believing in the power of theatre to heal, and for believing that all people have a right to be included in the arts — barrier-free!

Prologue:
A Saturday's Rainbow Adventure

My Saturday's Rainbow drama class went on a trip to Cape May. Early in the morning, we boarded a minibus and headed out to the sea coast. After about two hours, we finally arrived.

We rolled down the dock and up the gangplank of Captain Meriwether's cruiser. The Captain shouted, "Welcome aboard!" and started up the engine of his boat. In a twinkling we were off for the high seas.

The seagulls called out to each other as they flew around above our heads. The water beneath us was clean and blue. Gentle waves lapped against the side of the boat. We rounded a bend in the coastline and entered a protected cove. The Captain turned off the motor and dropped anchor. There in the middle of the cove was what we had come to see — the dolphins of Cape May. Everybody threw on their bathing suits and jumped into the water, splashing and playing and talking to the dolphins. We had a great time!

Around 3:00 PM the sky started to cloud over and everyone reluctantly swam back to the cruiser. Sam and Phillip didn't want to get back on board. They tied their surfboards to the side of the boat so they could float back with us. The Captain started the cruiser and we left the dolphin cove, sadly waving goodbye to our new-found friends.

Suddenly a horrible squall came up. The rain started softly, but quickly built into a torrential storm with thunder and lightning. Sam and Phillip were knocked off their surfboards!

"Men overboard!" shouted the Captain.

"Help! Help! We're drowning!" cried the boys as they struggled to stay above the surface of the waves.

Joey and Amos jumped off the side of the board and swam to save their friends. Everyone else heaved two huge life preservers into the water and pulled the four boys to safety. Everyone was relieved that Sam and Phillip were saved. We all cheered for Joey and Amos, the heroes of the day.

As suddenly as the storm came up, it dispersed. The sun came out from behind the clouds and the seagulls began to sing again. When we pulled into the dock at Cape May, everyone was still excited about the rescue at sea. No one wanted to go home.

"Surf's up!" shouted Sam and grabbed his surfboard. He started out for the breakers on the beach at a run. Everyone else grabbed their boards and paddled out behind him. Just at the right moment, we all hopped on our boards and caught a big wave to ride back in.

"Wipe out!" screamed Amos and suddenly everyone was rolling around in the surf, laughing and shouting in delight.

After that we had to dry off and begin our journey home. When we arrived back at Saturday's Rainbow, everyone agreed that they had had a great day — one they would remember forever!

I shared this incredible adventure one Saturday morning with ten children who were in wheelchairs. We never left the drama room and we never got wet. We went on our journey solely through our imaginations, creating the environment around us with our voices and pantomimed action, yet the whole experience was as real to us at the time as it seems now in my description. When I think back to that day, intellectually I know that throughout the trip ten drama students were sitting in wheelchairs in a circle on a brown carpet in an elementary classroom, but in my mind's eye, I see ten smiling, laughing children wearing colorful bathing suits, sporting gorgeous tans, standing on surfboards, and riding a wave in the summer sun. And I know when they think back to that same Saturday morning, they see the same thing, too.

This is the power of the imagination in action. Whatever you want to do, you can do. Whatever you want to be, you can be. No one can limit you. No one can stop you.

Introduction: How I Learned to Make the Arts Accessible

The year 1987 brought change for me. I had a Master of Fine Arts degree in drama and had worked in professional theatre in a variety of technical, administrative, and artistic positions for 13 years. I loved theatre, but felt I wasn't using it to touch people's lives in a real and meaningful way. I left my job as assistant artistic director of the Shakespeare Theatre at the Folger in Washington, DC, and began looking for a way to do this.

In February I found the address of an organization called the National Association for Drama Therapy. "This sounds fascinating," I thought. "I think this is what I've always wanted to do." I wrote to them for more information. The NADT office forwarded my query letter and résumé to Jan Goodrich, one of the Registered Drama Therapists in the DC Metropolitan area. Jan felt the best way to find out about drama therapy was to experience it, so she offered me an internship with her at Second Genesis, a long-term residential therapeutic community for recovering alcoholics and drug addicts.

Drama therapy is an experiential form of psychotherapy that uses drama processes and theatre products to treat emotional disorders, learning difficulties, geriatric issues, and social maladjustments. Drama therapists are trained in theatre arts, psychology, psychotherapy, and drama therapy. They use a wide variety of techniques, including but not limited to theatre games, improvisation, role-play, puppetry, masks, gestalt and psychodrama techniques, and theatre productions as means of

1

emotional and physical integration for clients. Most drama therapists work with groups although some work with families, couples, or individuals.

In drama therapy I discovered an exciting path that led through the familiar dramatic landscape I loved but approached it from a more meaningful, socially conscious angle. Through the medium of drama I saw people grow, heal, and learn how to connect with themselves and others. I knew I needed to make the transition into the field of healing arts.

Up until this time my training had been in theatre, primarily directing and playwriting. I earned a Bachelor of Fine Arts degree in directing from the University of Texas at Austin and a Master of Fine Arts degree in directing and playwriting from Trinity University at the Dallas Theater Center. During my education I had had a little experience working with children and adults with special needs, but no formal training in special education or adaptive drama. As an undergraduate and afterwards for a short time as a teacher's aide, I volunteered with the drama club at the Texas School for the Deaf in Austin. There I learned sign language and some of the rudiments of theatre of the Deaf.

In graduate school at the Dallas Theater Center, I assisted Mark Medoff when he came to direct *Children of a Lesser God* for the 1980-81 theatre season. Because I knew how to sign, he turned the direction of the minor deaf characters (Orin and Lydia) and all of the deaf and hearing understudies over to me.

Later that summer, I directed a barrier-free production of *The Butterfly*, an Iranian morality tale, at the Bachman Recreation Center in Dallas. The Bachman Center, which had just opened, was a state-of-the-art recreation facility for people with disabilities, designed to be totally accessible. The actors in the production were mostly adults, children, and teens with disabilities and a few non-disabled adults. Teens with disabilities built the costumes and set and served as technicians for the show. The entire project was the last in Dallas funded by federal CETA grants, which had been cut by the Reagan administration.

The disabilities of cast and crew included intellectual disabilities, deafness, learning disabilities, epilepsy, cerebral palsy, and a wide variety of physical disabilities. This was my first experience with any condition other than deafness. It was a big change and a big challenge. There are patterns of communication that work well with deaf actors but that are confusing for actors who have intellectual disabilities. Nevertheless, the production came together and was beautiful and heartfelt.

Patsy Swank, a writer for the *Dallas City Paper*, said that she went to the performance "because it was the climax of the twelve-week Summer Youth Employment Program, and I felt dutiful. So much for fatuousness. What I saw was a delightful adaptation…Sally Bailey…had directed a beautifully paced piece that was sharp, funny, sad and endearing without ever approaching sentimentality." In addition to our performances at Bachman, we took the show on tour to White Rock Lake, a park on the other side of town, to perform in their Bath House Cultural Center. This was very exciting for cast and crew. Patsy Swank, now our fan, came back to see the show again.

The most moving experience I had during this production and the one that probably most motivated me to later work with people who have disabilities happened with my lead actor in *The Butterfly*. Billy was in his early 20s and had been diagnosed with mental retardation. When he was born, the doctor told his parents that their son was so profoundly retarded that when he grew up he would not be able to learn how to "read a stop sign or to know what the lights on a traffic signal mean." They did not believe the doctor; instead, they believed in their son. They supported him and insisted that he have as many opportunities to grow and learn as he could.

When I came into the director's position for the show, Billy had already been cast by the producers as the Spider, the powerful villain of the barn who ensnares the Butterfly and promises to spare her life if she captures other creatures for him to eat. The Spider has a good number of lines in the first and last scenes of the show and is a presence in the background throughout. If he is not credible, the play will not work, because his threatening presence motivates all the action. I was very nervous that this young man, pleasant though he was, would not be able to memorize the lines. An occasion of great dramatic irony (and my first lesson in not listening to society's expectations) was the rehearsal at which all the actors were scheduled to be off book (theatre parlance for having your lines memorized so you don't have to read from the script). The only actor who knew his lines was Billy! His parents had practiced with him at home and he knew them inside out. I was relieved but still skeptical.

"Well," I thought, "memorizing the lines is great, but acting them will be another hurdle."

However, it turned out that Billy took direction really well. At one rehearsal I told him that whenever the other characters in the barn had scenes and he was watching from his spider's web, he had to be in character: thinking and feeling about what was happening. He had to pretend to be the Spider from the moment the curtain went up to when it went down. When the Butterfly was convincing the insects to come back to the web, he should be pleased or excited and hungry. Each time she decided not to lure the innocent creatures to their deaths, he should feel angry or frustrated and even hungrier. Two days later I glanced from the scene in progress to the Spider's web upstage and I saw the most incredible concentration coming from Billy, who as the Spider was hanging on to and reacting appropriately to every word being said by the Butterfly.

At the curtain call opening night Billy's parents were in tears. They had never been so proud. They tried to give the credit to me, but it didn't belong to me; it belonged to Billy and to them. Billy had worked hard and they had worked hard with him. They had never given up their belief in his strengths and his ability to succeed and he believed in their belief. It was a great lesson for me. Billy and his parents were my first teachers in how a disability doesn't need to hold anyone back.

In the spring of 1987 I met Gail Humphries, the Artistic Director, and Bonnie Fogel, the Executive Director, of the Bethesda Academy of Performing Arts (BAPA) in Bethesda, Maryland. BAPA was not an academic school, as the name suggests, but a not-for-profit arts organization that offered drama, dance, and singing classes to children and teens in the Washington metropolitan area. Classes and rehearsals were held after school, in the evenings, and on Saturdays. The teachers were professional artists — actors, directors, musicians, and dancers — who taught on a part-time contractual basis. Students' tuition covered sixty percent of the cost of operations and the rest of the budget was made up through donations from individuals, corporations, foundations, and local and state governments.

Founded in 1979, BAPA had recently gone through an amazing growth spurt under the leadership of Gail and Bonnie. The Board of Directors had developed its first mission statement, which committed the organization to integrating the arts into the lives of all children in the community. BAPA was reaching out to a sizable portion of the DC metropolitan area, attracting students from Montgomery County (Maryland), the District of Columbia, and Northern Virginia. However, one segment of each of these communities was not being served — young people who had disabilities.

Research into public-school population statistics at the time revealed a total of 39,471 students with special needs enrolled in the combined public schools of the metropolitan area. In addition, there were over 30 private, independent schools specializing in educating students with special needs. Bonnie had been made aware of BAPA's lack of attention to these students by close friends who had children with disabilities. Their typically developing children attended BAPA classes and thoroughly enjoyed their experiences, developing creatively, emotionally, and socially as they had fun learning about the arts, but their disabled children were unable to participate because there were no adaptations in place to accommodate them by leveling the playing field.

Lack of a special-needs program did not mean that children with disabilities never took BAPA classes. From time to time, students with mild learning disabilities or attention deficits were included in classes. Often there were positive results. One mother wrote:

> Our son, age 13, attends a special school for children with learning disabilities. He has always been active and involved in drama at school, but was always shy about pursuing his interest in a mainstream [sic] setting because of his reading disability. We were thrilled that he could be mainstreamed in BAPA's Improvisation class in the fall. It was the perfect transition for him and improved his self-confidence beyond our greatest expectations. We had never seen him so comfortable and sure of himself on stage.

However, when students who had disabilities took classes, there was rarely communication between parent and teacher about the special needs involved. Sometimes ignorance can be bliss because the student gets treated like everyone else, but it can also be a time bomb waiting to go off. Several teachers, unaware one of their students had dyslexia, reported bizarre emotional outbursts when that student was asked to read a scene or a monologue out loud in class. Caleen Sinnette Jennings, one on the finest acting teachers on contract, had one such experience. A student who had been a delight the whole semester suddenly started "bouncing off the walls" when she handed him a script. Other teachers, uninformed when students had attention deficits or emotional problems, could not understand why their normally orderly class had become chaotic. Dance teachers, unaware that a student's confusion between right and left was due to learning disabilities, would leave class totally frustrated at being unable to communicate what to them was a very simple concept.

Bonnie heard these stories after classes when the disheartened teachers returned to the cramped little office that everyone shared. Sometimes the teachers blamed themselves. Sometimes they blamed their students. Rarely did it occur to anyone that this situation involved a disability that could be addressed with a little bit of accommodation.

Physical access was another bone of contention. An embarrassing situation occurred during one of the performances of the spring musical. The father of one of the actresses couldn't get his wheelchair through the front doors! The building, an old public school that was being rented out to several non-profit organizations, had been built before accessible architecture was required. Here was a patron who had paid tuition for his daughter to be in the performing company and bought tickets for his family to go to the show, but he couldn't get in to see her. Luckily, the custodian took out the removable doorjamb between double doors at the front of the building, which created an entrance wide enough for the wheelchair to pass through, and disaster was averted.

I was hired as BAPA's Special Needs Director in January 1988. My first six months were to be spent primarily on research, publicity, and curriculum development, but I also taught two pilot creative drama classes after school at Ivymount, a private school in Rockville,

Maryland, for students with multiple disabilities. Since I had no formal training in special education or disability, I began researching drama with special populations. I found a few books, but most of them were vague — long on inspiration and encouragement, short on detailed information and specific interventions.

I fell back on creative drama and improvisation texts that offered lots of specific suggestions for activities. Nellie McCaslin's *Creative Drama in the Classroom and Beyond* and Nancy King's *Giving Form to Feeling* were my bibles. However, in trying out material in my pilot classes, I found that many tried-and-true drama games, such as mirror exercises, did not work well with my Ivymount students.

I researched disabilities. This avenue of inquiry was not entirely fruitful either. I found only a few books that were written in non-technical terms and had information that could be applied to the drama classroom. However, I started to gain a few insights into why certain activities had succeeded with my students and others had failed miserably.

I also formed a Special Needs Steering Committee made up of parents of children with disabilities, special education teachers and administrators, individuals who had disabilities, therapists, and other experts in the disability field. The committee's suggestions and encouragement guided me through the rough times and kept me on track. My favorite quote was from the principal of a special needs school who said, "Our job is work our way out of a job by creating an environment in which everyone can succeed."

In trying to cover all possible levels of experience and combinations of students and encourage inclusion in "regular" classes as soon as possible, I devised a program that would provide introductory, intermediate, and advanced experiences. Process-based classes were needed for those who were not ready to perform and performance-based classes were needed for those who were. I felt peer classes were important to offer to beginners, to build their artistic skills and self-confidence so they could succeed when included in "regular" classes later on. The resulting program had four basic components: special-needs classes, inclusion in "regular" BAPA classes and performing companies, performing companies that purposely mixed students with and without disabilities, and outreach classes at other locations.

As time went on and I learned more, I decided that the term "special needs" had negative connotations, thus the name of the program needed to be changed. The issue wasn't that certain students had special needs because, if you think about it, we all have special needs of one kind or another; the issue was that certain students needed to have access to the arts. With the support of Barbara Hardaway, one of the BAPA Board members and a polio survivor, I was able to convince the Board to change the name from Special Needs Program to Arts Access Program and my position from Special Needs Director to Arts Access Director.

In the ten years that I worked as BAPA's Arts Access Director, the program grew dramatically from two outreach classes for thirteen students to six onsite and ten outreach classes for 99 students to 20 classes for over 250 students, and so on, exponentially, each year. Many students enjoyed so much success that they came back again and again until they aged out of the program. Up to that point BAPA had never offered programming for anyone over the age of 18. My students' parents begged for programming to be created for their now young adults because they didn't want to stop doing drama and there was no other performing arts organization in the area that welcomed them into their programming. Of course, we began offerings for young adults.

At this point I realized that the community needed another stepping stone beyond BAPA to full inclusion in the arts level of access. Jade Gingerich, a colleague who worked as Director of Employment Policy for the Maryland Department of Disabilities, was also a singer/actress/director who frequently participated in community theatre productions. When she saw the work my performing companies were doing and realized the strides the actors (many of whom she had known personally for years) were making each season in their confidence, artistic skills, and social abilities, she decided the next step was a community theatre which had as its goal creating inclusive theatre. It could then serve as a role model for other community theatres, so they could also learn how to become inclusive. Jade created the Paradigm Players, which functioned under the auspices of BAPA's non-profit status for its first production of *Godspell* in order to get start-up funding from the Maryland Developmental Disabilities Council. You can read more about the Paradigm Players in the sidebar Jade has written in Chapter 10.

Parents responded enthusiastically to the growth they saw in their children after participating in the program:

> "[As a result of Creative Drama class] Betsy's verbal communication improved (her willingness to express herself). Betsy got an *A* in Oral Expression on her report card."

> "Jacob seems to have improved his ability to approach and work/play with other children. We know he enjoyed the classes and missed them when they were over. He asked several times on Saturdays why we weren't going to drama class."

> "Freddie has a really big imagination but didn't really know how to channel it. The drama class helps him have direction. He doesn't have a lot of physical abilities so this gives him an outlet for his creative imagination. He has no other after school activities at all that he enjoys."

> "Jane, a non-handicapped [*sic*] child, gained a lot from the experience [of being in the Pegasus Performing Company]. Basically, it taught her something about perspective — to be grateful for all she does have — when something in her life doesn't go perfectly smoothly. It was a little anxiety provoking, but she felt she gained from choosing to do this."

The staff and faculty began to widen their teaching horizons as students with disabilities joined their classes. When faced for the first time with including a student with a disability, most faculty members were fearful and hesitant. Some had no personal or professional experience with disability. They were afraid of not knowing what to do or say, afraid of the reaction of the typically developing children in the class, and afraid of what their own emotional reactions would be. Part of my job became providing them with information and support so they could succeed and gain confidence.

When I first approached Tim Reagan, one of the most popular and skillful creative drama teachers, with the idea of including a boy who had Down syndrome in one of his classes, his reaction was typical. His eyes glazed over and his breathing froze for an instant. After a short pause, he said, "But I don't know how…" Experience changed that fear and lack of expertise. He enjoyed it so much that he began using the arts as a one-on-one intervention with children who had pervasive developmental disorders, under the supervision of child psychiatrist Dr. Stanley Greenspan. Later, Tim became a Registered Drama Therapist himself. You can read his description of his first experiences including children with disabilities in "regular" classes in Chapter 12.

I learned through trial and error. It is not a cliché to say that experience is the best teacher — it is the plain truth. I don't know all the answers but I try to ask the right questions and I try to pay attention to what is going on in front of me. There is no chart to go to which tells you what is the right or wrong thing to do in any given situation; there is only an honest, open, problem-solving process that includes teacher, student, and parent. I never feel afraid to ask for help or for more information. Above all, I listen to what my students are telling me — they are the real experts on what they need in relation to adaptations, content, and form of their dramatic experiences and expressions.

In 1999 I was hired as an assistant professor of theatre at Kansas State University in Manhattan, Kansas, inheriting the position and program in drama therapy created by Dr. Norman J. Fedder. We met when we were both board members for the National Association for Drama Therapy, he as Central Region Chair and I as Membership Chair. He knew he was going to retire in the next few years and was looking for someone who had a Midwestern sensibility, a love of teaching, and skills in drama therapy, creative drama, and playwriting (the courses he taught at KSU). He asked me to come out to Kansas one summer to teach a weeklong intensive drama therapy course to see how I liked it and how his students liked me. It was a good match.

I am now an associate professor with tenure. I love teaching. I love mentoring young drama therapists and expanding the field. I love providing training to students in pre-medicine, pre-mental health, and education who in the course of their careers will be working with individuals who have disabilities. However, I miss my clients tremendously: both the students from BAPA and my recovering drug addicts at Second Genesis (I had inherited the drama therapy position there from my mentor Jan Goodrich when she retired). I still get emails and letters from students and parents inviting me to birthday parties, commitment ceremonies, plays, and graduations. No matter how far away they are, they will always be in my heart.

The good part is that I still do drama with people who have disabilities. The year I moved to Manhattan, the City Parks and Recreation Program was in need of a director for its Barrier-Free Theatre program. This program was not in existence by chance as it had been created at the insistence of Jane Gibson, a former BAPA arts-access parent, who moved to Manhattan in the mid-1990s. After her son's positive experience with theatre, she strongly believed that each community in America needed its own barrier-free drama program.

Each year I direct the Barrier-Free Theatre Company, comprised of adults with developmental and physical disabilities, Kansas State students, and volunteers from the community, as they create an original one-act play through improvisation. I also inherited "Drama Therapy with Special Populations," a class created by my predecessor "Doc" Fedder over twenty-five years ago, in which teens and adults from the community who have disabilities come to Kansas State once a week to do creative drama with Kansas State students. Drama class is the highlight of their week.

The stories in this book are true. They are examples of real events and real people. In most cases, the names of students have been changed, but the details of the experiences have been reported accurately. In a few cases, former students, now young adults, have written essays about their experiences and requested that I use their full, real names for their bylines and any description referring to them in the text. Since they are consenting adults and young professionals themselves, I have honored their requests.

Whether you work in the arts, education, recreation, therapy, or rehabilitation, this book will help you incorporate drama and the other arts into the lives of individuals who have disabilities. For theatre professionals, general background information about disabilities has been included with definitions, origins, characteristics, and developmental and educational issues that may affect the teaching of drama. Most of this will already be familiar to special-needs professionals.

For special-needs professionals, basic information on how to teach drama has been included. Most of this will already be familiar to theatre professionals.

Specific ideas for adapting basic drama, playwriting, and play-directing techniques for student/actors with various disabilities will be useful for both groups. Chapter 1 explains why the arts are important to all people so that you can explain why to others who may not understand. Chapter 2 explains why the arts are specifically helpful as educational and therapeutic tools for people who have special needs and introduces the ugly issue of stigma.

Chapter 3 deals with physical disabilities and how to make physical accommodations. Chapter 4 describes common cognitive disabilities and how to make program accommodations for them.

Chapter 5 describes how to set up an effective class environment, how to function well as a teacher and as a class assistant, and how to manage behavior problems. Chapters 6 and 7 present how to plan an effective lesson and contain specific activities with rationale for how to create adaptations. This will empower you to take any activity and find a way to change it to fit the strengths and avoid the weaknesses of your students/actors.

Chapter 8 covers puppetry, a dramatic activity that can be a wonderful introduction to performance, particularly for shy or inexperienced actors. Chapter 9 explains how to create original plays that are tailor-made for the strengths and talents of your group. Chapter 10 discusses various ways of making play rehearsals accessible to all.

Chapter 11 details the many ways drama and the arts can be incorporated into the school curriculum to enhance the learning of academic subjects as well as emotional intelligence. Learning differences and Howard Gardner's Theory of Multiple Intelligences are discussed at length.

Chapter 12 offers many examples of how inclusion can be made successful in classrooms and performing companies and how all students benefit from working together through the arts.

At the end of each chapter I have listed books and resources that I highly recommend. They will add to your knowledge in each area and help you move forward with even more support and background. Many of these did not exist when I wrote *Wings to Fly: Bringing Theatre Arts to Students with Special Needs*, the precursor to this book.

Drama students and teachers come in both sexes, so in the interest of non-sexist language, I have alternated the use of male and female pronouns by chapter to avoid awkwardness or confusion.

My hope is that you will find this book an empowering tool that allows you to open the world of drama and other arts to all of the people you work with. Francis Hodge, my directing professor at the University of Texas at Austin, always talked about the need to give actors wings to fly. The purpose of this book is to give you, the drama educator/practitioner, the wings you need to help your students fly.

1. The Need for the Arts

Whenever I talk to people about the need for the arts in our lives, I get one of two reactions. Either the person understands the integral value of the arts and is tuned in to the wide range of contributions they make to our lives or she sees the arts as pretty-but-useless frills that can easily be done without. These reactions have nothing to do with the individual's intelligence, cultural background, or educational level. They originate from whether or not the person has had a positive personal experience with the arts.

If you are reading this book, you are undoubtedly in the former category. You understand that the arts are more than just a pleasant way to while away some free time. What you may not know is how to explain why the arts are important to those who are not supporters. Your boss or your coworkers may be in this category. The head of a foundation to which you are applying for a grant may be in this category. If you are attempting to integrate the arts into any kind of program, at some point you will be faced with justifying what you are doing. This chapter and the next will help you to do that.

What are the Arts?

Art is communication — as simple, and as profound, as that.

An artist takes human feelings, thoughts, and ideas and gives them form through symbols that other human beings understand. In the words of David Lewis-Williams (2002), "…the making of art is a social, not a purely personal, activity. Art serves social purposes, though it is manipulated by individual people in social contexts to achieve certain ends. Art cannot be understood outside its social context" (p. 44).

An artist is a person who expresses some facet of her experience through the medium of an art modality. A few artists are highly trained professionals who earn their living through making art, but they are not the only people who can be called artists. The truth is that we are all artists because at one time or another we have all expressed ourselves through the arts. If you have ever sung a song, danced a jig, drawn a picture, written a rhyme, or acted out your version of an event, you are an artist because you have communicated to someone else through art.

The conglomerate term *the arts* refers to the five major forms (modalities) that artists have developed as modes of communication: visual art, literature, music, dance, and drama. In all art forms the artist's communications are expressed symbolically through the same basic artistic elements: line, shape, color, texture, time, rhythm, movement, space, silence, and sound. Language, another symbolic form of communication, can also be an ingredient in art, in spoken or written form.

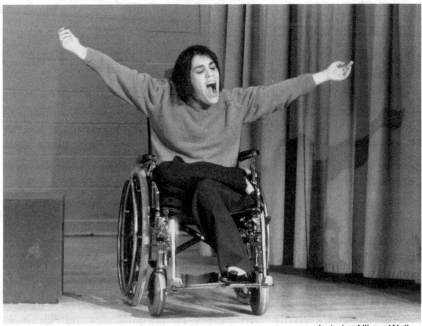

photo by Allison Walker

Figure 1: If you have ever sung a song, danced a jig, or drawn a picture, you are an artist.

The Arts and Culture

Since the Upper Paleolithic Period, 35,000-45,000 years ago, the arts have been used by all human societies as a means of sharing complex information between people and as a container in which to hold culture and pass it on to succeeding generations. In his book *The Creative Explosion*, John E. Pfeiffer points to the necessity of sharing more complex information as part of the reason for the growth in language and art. He says that this growth exploited the human brain's natural ability to form and remember images:

> When it comes to transmitting information, vision is the predominant sense, not just the viewing of real objects in the outside world, but also the inner sort of viewing... There is something amazingly real about the images we see with our mind's eye. The unique and distinctive patterns of real-life objects are somehow projected via the optic nerve onto layers of neurons in the brain... The ability to form images serves memory well... Add action to high imagery and memorability increases further... Even more helpful is some sort of emotional commitment, the addition of meaning to the imagined incident (pp. 215-217).

The arts were part of the basic fabric of prehistoric life because they helped our ancestors make meaning of their existence, which, in turn, helped them function better in their day-to-day living. Pfeiffer (1982) says, "Art in the broadest sense evolved rapidly, and changed rapidly, in response to changes in the structure of society. Ultimately, it became an essential aspect of prehistoric living, as essential as subsistence and reproduction for the survival of the human species" (p. 18).

Early religious rituals and rites of passage consisted of music, dance, painting, sculpture, and dramatic ceremonial re-enactments of natural events. The arts taught our ancestors how to behave for survival in a dangerous world. They also eased the anxiety caused by the mysterious forces of nature and death. Prehistoric storytelling preserved religious traditions in the form of myths and preserved actual events in the form of epic poetry. Legends and folk tales were passed down orally from generation to generation until the invention of writing (Harrison 1913; Lewis-Williams 2002; Mithen 1996; Pfeiffer 1982).

The same is true of the period of human existence we call "historic time." Much of what we know about all cultures that have come before our own is preserved in their surviving works of art. In fact, the civilizations, ancient and modern, which we remember as great are considered so because of the ideas they captured and passed on to us through their music, statues, paintings, poetry, and plays.

The arts are the most effective media for carrying on a dialogue about current cultural concepts and values, because art creates visual, auditory, and visceral images that humans respond to sensorially, emotionally, physically, and intellectually. An excellent example of this is Langston Hughes' poem "Harlem" from *Montage of a Dream Deferred*, which is reproduced below. Take the time to read it through slowly and pay attention to how it affects you.

> **What happens to a dream deferred?**
> Does it dry up?
> Like a raisin in the sun?
> Or fester like a sore —
> And then run?
> Does it stink like rotten meat?
> Or crust and sugar over —
> Like a syrupy sweet?
> Maybe it just sags
> Like a heavy load.
> Or does it explode?

Through words, Hughes creates images that evoke visual pictures in the mind as well as stir up memories of tastes, smells, textures, temperatures, weights, actions, and emotions — all to effectively capture the essence of an intolerable situation and communicate it to an audience who will be able to recognize it, avoid it, change it, or in some other way take an action in relationship to it. Lorraine Hansberry read Hughes' poem and wrote the play *A Raisin in the Sun,* which attempts an answer to the question asked by the original work of art. Other artists have read the poem or seen the play (or movie) and have responded with their own artistic expressions furthering the dialogue. Community leaders have responded with actions that have changed and will continue to change the original situation that inspired the verse.

The ultimate power in a work of art lies in its symbolic nature. It may originate as a response to one specific event, but because it is metaphor, it can speak to another situation that involves similar feelings, thoughts, or ideas. The legacy of "Harlem" is not limited to the situation of racism against African-Americans; there are many analogous human situations for which the poem's images work symbolically. A complex idea, in this case the feelings created when a righteous dream is blocked by society, is carried in images that are easier to remember and respond to than a long, logical, verbal explanation.

The arts continue to serve as excellent cultural teaching tools. They can be used to teach each society's young about the morals, values, and structures of that society. If a society's dramas show the struggle to resolve conflicts fairly and peacefully, the lessons learned in those dramas will be used by members of the audience to resolve their own conflicts. If a society's dramas show the resolution of conflict through violence and force, those are the resources that will be passed on.

The power of the arts as a cultural teaching tool can be used to continue the status quo or to change it. This is why totalitarian governments like to control the arts and why "subversive" artists, such as Czech playwright Vaclav Havel, get into trouble when they use them to express their criticisms. Both sides understand that plays, books, films, graphic images, three-dimensional forms, and poetry can reach the hearts and minds of people and be used to carry on a dialogue that can ultimately change the political system!

Because contemporary arts are in forms that exist physically and last over time, they will be used, just as art of ages past, to pass today's ideas, concepts, and history on to future generations. What our descendents will know about us will be what surviving artworks tell them.

The Arts and the Individual

So far this discussion has talked about the arts in a macro view, from the larger point of view of world history, culture, political systems, and power. But if we don't come from a family that goes to the theatre or reads great books out loud to each other or hangs famous images on our walls, do the arts really have a personal impact on our lives? The answer is an unequivocal "Yes!"

The arts are developmentally among the first learning tools that every child naturally uses to teach herself. In a sense, we are hardwired to become artists, just as we are hardwired to learn language. Jean Piaget, the Swiss developmental psychologist, spent his life studying how children develop into symbol making/manipulating adults. He identified

photo by Lea Ann Rosen

Figure 2: Arts projects provide opportunities to practice making decisions.

a developmental sequence of stages through which all of us normally progress as we grow (Ginsburg & Opper 1969). Infants and young children explore their immediate environment through their senses and through physical manipulation of their bodies and objects outside of themselves. At the outset of this first stage, the sensorimotor stage, they don't have the capacity for representational thought and memory, the ability to retain a mental image of objects or events. However, the neurons and neural connections in their brains are growing at an incredible rate, so that by the time children reach the preoperational stage, around age two, they are ready to develop the ability to understand, create, and use symbols. Piaget called the play of this period symbolic or representational play. This is where language and the arts come in.

Give a very young child a pencil, crayon, paint, sand, clay, or any other material that can make a mark or be formed into a shape, and she will begin making lines, shapes, and forms with it. Adults devalue this process by calling it *scribbling* or *making a mess,* but it is a very important, beginning part of the sensorimotor learning process that leads into the preoperational stage. The child is manipulating and experimenting with her environment. She continues to scribble because it is enjoyable to effect change, to be in control of a process, *to make something in the world.*

Over time, a child who is allowed to scribble progressively begins to make more and more recognizable shapes. Somewhere along the way, the artistic (symbolic) communication process has started. She is now taking in sensory information, processing it, responding to it emotionally and intellectually, and transforming that image and her response to it into a representational form outside herself. Eventually, she will discover that her feelings can be given form, too. If she feels angry, she can express it by drawing an angry sky. If it makes her feel happy when she sees a flower on a sunny day, she can paint it in a manner that expresses that happiness. Another important aspect of art-making is sharing. Children always share their drawings and creations with their parents. This is not just a bid for attention. This is a way of communicating an experience they have had in a more complete way than simple words can express.

Our young artist can take what she drew and show her mother her interpretation of what she saw in the backyard and how she felt about it.

Imitation begins in the sensorimotor period. The child copies behavior she sees the people around her doing, often in the guise of a game, but ultimately for the purpose of understanding what that action is all about firsthand through her own body. Deferred imitation, the ability to remember and imitate an action at a later time, follows several months later, after the child has developed the concept of object permanence — the understanding that an object still exists even when it isn't in your sight.

In his book *Play, Dreams, and Imitation in Childhood* Piaget reported a wonderful example of deferred imitation. One day he saw his daughter Jacqueline watch another child have a temper tantrum in the playpen. Up until that time she had never seen a temper tantrum or thrown one herself. However, the very next day while in the playpen, she decided to try out the kicking, stamping, and crying actions she had observed the day before. Piaget noted that she imitated the actions of the temper tantrum she had seen in a very deliberate manner, as if checking out how each movement felt and what response it would elicit (Ginsburg & Opper 1969).

Current brain research has discovered the neurological underpinnings of imitation. Research by Rizzolatti and Iacoboni in the 1990s on the brains of monkeys revealed that certain neurons (mirror neurons) fire when a monkey performs a specific motor action and when it is watching another monkey perform the same action (Iacoboni 2008; MacDonald 2003; Restak 2003). Similar results have been found in human subjects: the same regions of the brain lit up (were active) on a brain scan when the person was watching movements she would imitate or actually imitating the movement (Restak 2003). This suggests that the ability to learn through imitation is another hardwired trait.

Mirror neurons may be the basis for the development of empathy as well. Neuroscientists Sarah-Jayne Blakemore and Jean Decety say, "By simulating another person's actions and mapping them onto stored representations of our own motor commands and their consequences, it might be possible to estimate the observed person's internal states, which cannot be read directly from their movements. This simulating system could also provide information from which predictions about the person's future actions could be made" (Restak 2003 p. 35). It is still unclear if imitation is required to understand expression or if imitation is an empathic response to observed emotion (MacDonald 2003).

Once a child has reached the preoperational stage, she begins using symbolic or dramatic play to explore and learn more about the world. In symbolic play children recall actions they have seen and explore them through pretending; that is, they use their imaginations to explore their experiences in a new way — through drama. Instead of just imitating the actions they have seen, they improvise on them. They begin asking the question, "What if...?" Often they use symbolic play to take on adult roles they have seen. Through experimenting with more mature, diverse roles, they extend their role repertoire and learn new behaviors and coping strategies.

I remember setting up a tea party for my dolls when I was three. I laid my great-grandmother's china demitasse cups out at each place around my wooden play table and invited Raggedy Ann, Poppa Bear, and Momma Bear to join me. I can remember being very polite to my guests and carrying on a very serious conversation with them as I handed around imaginary cookies and poured water into their cups from my plastic teapot. This was not my first tea party. I had been given a small set of plastic dishes when I was one or two. I'm sure I remember this specific tea party so vividly because it was a special occasion. I had begged my mother for days to be able to use the beautiful, delicate, little cups and saucers from my great-grandmother's house. They were antiques and my mother was concerned that I would break them, but finally she gave her permission. I took great care of the teacups, which didn't get broken and in fact are currently in the china cabinet in my dining room.

My tea parties were examples of symbolic play. I had never seen my mother have a tea party. She never drank tea; she only drank coffee. She had never had a formal gathering of friends in for tea or coffee, which I might have copied. I was imagining something I had never seen, but had been told about, so I made up the situation as I went along.

As children develop their play skills, they become capable of playing with other children. In 1933 Margaret Parten proposed progressive stages of play development: solitary, parallel, associative, and cooperative (Garvey 1990). An example of solitary play would be my tea party with my dolls. Parallel play, which begins as early as age two years, is essentially solitary play in the general vicinity of another child. The children don't interact with each other; they tolerate each other's activity in proximity. If they do interact with each other, chances are they won't have the social skills for the give-and-take necessary in group play and conflict typically develops. They also don't have the attention spans to stay with and develop the play, so as a child becomes distracted, any beginning group play is broken off. I made the mistake once of trying to enact "The Three Little Pigs" with a group of two- and three-year olds. We never made it past the house of straw.

Between the ages of three and four, children start to acknowledge each other in play, perhaps talking about what they are doing, sharing toys, or engaging in shared monologues about what they are doing. This is associative play. They are interacting, they might even be playing the same games, but they aren't playing it *together*.

Cooperative play, which involves true interrelating, develops around the ages of four or five. This form of play requires more sophisticated abilities of communication and negotiation as well as higher degrees of patience and attention. Even then, in the beginning, disagreements and fights can break out. I can remember at age four going to my mother in tears because the girl who lived two doors down had come into my basement and interrupted a game of House that my best friend Eileen and I were playing with Eileen's younger brother and sister. The neighbor stopped the game by inviting everyone, except me, over to her house for Kool-Aid and cookies. When they all left, I was devastated. My mother said it was a lesson in life.

Later on, at seven or eight, I can remember coming home furious, slamming the door to my bedroom, and throwing myself down on my bed in tears on a day when nobody wanted to play the game *I* wanted to play. I hadn't been willing to compromise and neither had they. Another lesson.

Piaget felt that the highest or most mature form of play was game play, which involves interacting according to objective rules, often in competition and often in teams. In order to successfully follow the rules, take turns, play fair, handle working with team members, and deal with winning and losing, a child must reach a certain level of emotional control, ego strength, and cognitive maturity. This usually begins when children are six or seven and they enter what Piaget termed the developmental stage of concrete operations.

The Russian psychologist Lev Vygotsky believed that dramatic play was a major tool for children in developing the emotional-regulation skills that make learning and socialization possible. Recent research by Elena Bodrova and Deborah Leong that incorporates Vygotsky's theories has shown that young children who experience dramatic role-play embedded in their daily classroom activities develop abilities to internalize rules and expectations, inhibit impulsive behavior, focus their attention, verbalize their thinking processes, and work together cooperatively and maturely. They plan their play, "thinking as they are talking," and then act out the scenario that they have planned (Diamond, Barnett, Thomas, & Munro 2007).

I believe, as do Howard Gardner (1973) and R. Keith Sawyer (1997), that game play is not a *higher* form of play; it is just another type of play that uses different cognitive structures, such as reversibility and holding two points of view simultaneously. It develops out of the role-taking skills rehearsed through symbolic play. Extended symbolic (dramatic) play, which children become very skilled at by the age of four and five, is not *simple* or even *primitive*; it requires a very sophisticated use of imagination, language skills, awareness, concentration, imitative skills (both verbally and bodily), and social interaction abilities (Garvey 1990; Sawyer 1997).

Unfortunately, dramatic play as a formal and informal tool for learning is extinguished in children as they enter elementary school. Instead of harnessing and exploiting this natural, active, interactive, perspective-taking, learning method, educators traditionally focus on passive educational methods through which they strive to develop logical and systematic reasoning processes that are geared toward abstract thought. Just at the point that students master the ability to engage in cooperative play, learning becomes solitary. Students sit separately at desks and listen to lectures or work on individual learning assignments, reading and writing out answers to questions in workbooks. In reading groups students take turns reading out loud — active, but parallel, work. Most of the time when the teacher asks a question, it is meant to be answered simply and neatly by one student with one correct answer; convergent, not divergent, thinking is valued. Rarely are questions designed to promote messy, noisy classroom interaction and debate.

Dramatic play is relegated to recess or after-school times and deemed appropriate only for recreational purposes up to about the age of eight. "Play" becomes a word associated with being a "baby." As boys get older, they are channeled away from dramatic expression into sports activities, a form of game play that teaches the hierarchical structure and behavioral traditions of the American workplace. Girls continue with dramatic play a little longer, but they, too, eventually give it up as "childish." Soon they grow into adolescents and adults who have forgotten how to play and have lost touch with their innate abilities to express themselves through the arts.

The Arts and Play

The word *play* has a frivolous connotation in contemporary American culture. Children are immature and play; adults are responsible and work. In reality, play in all its forms is a significant ingredient in many aspects of life from recreation and interpersonal relationships to education and work. Play serves as the stepping-off place for the creative process; all of the arts are forms of play (Huizinga 1950).

Play is not something people do just to waste or fill time. It is a *bona fide* activity that provides a sense of rest and refreshment for the players. It involves the senses and the emotions. It is often interactive, deepening the relationships of participants. It can serve as a superlative stress reliever.

All play — even informal, improvisational play — is a structured experience guided by spoken or unspoken rules (Garvey 1990; Johnstone 1989; Sawyer 1997 & 2003). For play to come alive, participants must buy into the rules and willingly suspend disbelief. This allows the transformation of here-and-now reality into a pretend-play space, both of which exist simultaneously side by side (Garvey 1990; Winnicott 1971).

Playing is fun and enjoyable, but also a means of teaching life skills. It can open up new areas of experience for exploration and examination. In infancy, games of Peek-a-Boo teach object permanence. Making funny faces together introduces babies to nonverbal communication, which in human societies is done primarily through facial expression. Patty-Cake develops hand-eye coordination. As children grow older, they begin to learn through imitation, social games, sports, and dramatic play.

Games and imaginary play provide situations for acceptable, appropriate physical contact with others. Patty-Cake, Ring-Around-the-Rosy, and Tag teach how to touch in a non-threatening, playful manner. Appropriate social contact is also provided for through play. Team members and opponents get to know each other better through playing games and then sharing about the experience afterwards. Many people use the arts, social games, and sports as reasons for making social contact. Community theatres, bridge clubs, and bowling leagues are often initiated by friends who want an excuse to get together.

Play enhances spontaneity and joy. There is a sudden rush of excitement as the pace of a game picks up and all the players focus on the outcome of the roll of the dice, the turn of the card, or the pitch of the ball. Whatever the outcome, the players must be ready to jump in with the next appropriate response to keep the game moving forward. When the right response comes to the fore, the feeling of meeting the challenge of the moment is exhilarating!

Play provides an outlet for many other emotions as well. Children acting out the Grimm's fairy tale "Snow White and the Seven Dwarves" will feel anger at the evil queen, fear of the Hunter who is assigned to cut out Snow White's heart in the forest, sorrow at Snow White's apparent death from the poison apple, and delight in her reawakening at the end of the story. To borrow the slogan of a major television network, play provides us with "the thrill of victory and the agony of defeat."

Play also involves the paradox of the imagination. Dramatic play happens simultaneously in real time and in imaginary time, in real space and in imaginary space. British psychoanalyst D.W. Winnicott (1971) called this real/imaginary time/space overlap the transitional space. The realm of the imagination stretches our minds as we exist in this magical place of make-believe and in-between.

Understanding the difference between real and non-real is crucial to identity formation and the ability to relate to others. Part of this is interwoven with the development of the self. Object-relations theorists, particularly Margaret Mahler and her colleagues, theorize how a child develops a self from undifferentiated newborn to separated child to individuated adult. In their view, the newborn does not understand the separation between her and the rest of the world. She has no sense of boundaries, believing that everything outside of herself is part of herself. As far as she knows, her cries and desires control the universe. But as she has life experiences, some enjoyable, some disappointing and frustrating, she begins to understand that she is a separate being. Physical boundaries exist between herself, other people, and the objects in her environment (Irwin: In Schaefer 1993).

However, acknowledging physical boundaries is easy compared to recognizing other, more invisible psychological and social boundaries that exist between people. Each growing child must learn to make differentiations regarding emotions, thoughts, personal history, and belief systems. Young children often have the mistaken notion that others know what they are thinking. Sometimes they aren't sure which thoughts and feelings are their own and which belong to other people. A little girl begins to cry and her younger brother starts to cry, too. He's not just imitating his older sister's tears. He recognizes her upset feelings and, not able to separate them from his own feelings, begins to feel upset himself.

One way to resolve this confusion of boundaries is through play, where feelings and roles can be tested, explored, and evaluated in a safe, non-threatening imaginary setting. Through interactions and observations in play the child begins to recognize that others don't always respond the same way she does. She can't control them and they can't control her, but they can work together and share experiences.

Our technological age has added another aspect to the confusion between real and non-real, between fact and fiction. Television broadcasts the "news" which is fact; entertainment which is fiction; and docudrama and "reality" TV shows which are blends of both. Watching television, children and adults both sometimes find it hard to tell the difference.

Fact and fiction both hold truths for us, but those truths need to be understood in different ways. Picasso said, "Art is the lie that reveals the truth." Fact actually happened; it makes a statement about "what is" or "what was." Fiction didn't actually happen, but could have happened; it asks the question, "what if?" Facts are to be accepted as true. To accept fiction, one needs to willingly suspend disbelief and enter the zone of play and make-believe: the transitional space.

One could think of fiction as a simulation that runs on minds rather than on computers (Oatley 2002). It can be used to understand emotions, situations, psychological processes, and points of view of others without actually having to *really* experience it oneself. Books and movies provide this vicarious experience, but so does dramatic play. In fact, dramatic play creates an even more effective simulation because it is embodied, not just mental!

Playing out imaginary stories helps children understand the truth of fiction — how it can be experienced, processed, and believed. In the moment of dramatic play, a child can stand in Cinderella's shoes and experience her emotional situation *as if* it were really happening. And yet, it is not. Any moment her mother can open the back door to call her into the house for dinner, interrupting the fictional reality. Through these play experiences, children begin to learn that the imaginary often seems real, but can be left behind with a simple refocusing of the attention away from the transitional space. This separate reality created in play is called the "play frame" or the "dramatic frame" by play theorists and other social scientists (Sawyer 1997).

The experience of acting as a fictional character in play makes the explanation of the fictional roles taken on by actors on TV much clearer to a child. Parents can explain that an actor played the part of the scary monster, just as the child played the part of the wicked witch when she and her friends acted out "Hansel and Gretel." The actor wasn't a real monster and the child wasn't a real witch; both pretended to be something that they really weren't. The difference between fictional violence and real violence can be explained in a similar manner pointing out that with real violence there are irreversible consequences to people and in fictional violence actors aren't really hurt.

The greatest boon of play, particularly dramatic play, is that it allows players to try out new behaviors and ideas in safety — without risk to life, limb, or social prestige (Sternberg & Garcia 2000). If a player makes a mistake in a game and is put "out," she hasn't died; she's merely lost a turn. If she loses the game, she can play another. If she tries out a new role and doesn't succeed at it, she hasn't failed "for real." She can stop, reevaluate the make-believe situation, and play the role out in a different way. In this sense, because it offers the opportunity to experience real feelings and situations in a safe and imaginary environment, play becomes rehearsal for life.

The Arts and Education

Until they go to school, children use all their senses to learn in a hands-on, physical manner. They naturally explore the world and express their feelings and ideas through dramatic play, movement, song, drawing, and other untutored forms of the arts. When they enter school at four, five, or six, unless they are in a Montessori or Waldorf program, they are usually thrown into an educational setting that doesn't exploit these powerful tools.

As mentioned above, the American system of public education focuses primarily on the dissemination of information through teaching methods that are abstract rather than concrete, passive rather than active, solitary rather than participatory, and limited in terms of sensorimotor stimulation. Students listen to the teacher talk in front of the room. They are told *about* information rather than experiencing it for themselves.

Teaching through the arts offers students the opportunity to continue learning and communicating through all of their perceptual channels. They can use their senses of sight, hearing, touch, smell, taste, and kinesthesia for receiving and processing information and for expressing themselves. This doesn't mean they won't develop abstract reasoning skills; starting from where they are in a developmental sense will enhance the development of other cognitive processes. Gardner (1991) and other developmental psychologists (See: Crain 1985) make a strong case that when one cognitive stage begins, the skills and abilities developed in previous stages do not disappear, never to be used again. In fact, most people continue to rely primarily on the skills of previous stages, one reason why some students never really let go of preoperational concepts and move fully into concrete and formal operations (Gardner 1991).

Learning through the arts becomes active and interactive because the whole person — senses, emotions, cognitions, and body — becomes involved in generating an active response outside of the self (a painting, a poem, a performance) to the information taken in. A student who crams facts and figures soon forgets the answers, but a student who has an experience with the material makes that information part of herself and will remember it for years because it has been deeply encoded into long-term memory and has attained personal meaning for her (Jensen 2000).

Experiences in the arts engender complex and subtle cognitive modes of thought that "fosters flexibility, promotes a tolerance for ambiguity, encourages risk taking, and depends upon the exercise of judgment outside the sphere of rules" (Eisner 2002, p. 35). In other words, working in the arts requires the ability to "think outside of the box" and generates divergent thinking. Rarely in life when we are faced with complex problems, particularly interpersonal problems, is there only one possible solution. There are usually dozens, but we do not have practice generating a variety of answers because that is not how we are taught to think about problems in school.

One of the big "buzz words" in education in the late 1990s was "Emotional Intelligence" (Goleman 1995). We will talk more about specific ways the arts can generate emotional intelligence in Chapter 11. Suffice it to say here that the arts require us to get in touch with our emotional responses, whether we are creating art or experiencing it as an audience member. The more familiar we are with our own emotions and the larger an emotional vocabulary we develop, the more aware we become of ourselves and others, the clearer we can communicate, and the better we can negotiate and problem-solve. An upward spiral of growth around the mastery of our own emotions and understanding of interpersonal psychology begins.

Education, the Arts, and Work

One of education's biggest concerns is to prepare students for taking their places in the workforce after they leave school. Every adult must be able to work in some capacity in order to earn enough money to buy food, shelter, clothing, items of personal hygiene, and a few of the luxuries of life. Businesses are concerned about finding workers who have the appropriate skills to succeed on the job. The workplace has changed at a tremendous rate over the last century. There are fewer factory jobs and more jobs in technology and service sectors. Factory jobs required manual skills and the ability to follow directions given by a superior. "Job categories and definitions were often narrowed to improve efficiency. Jobs were designed to give workers little or no discretion in their movements and workers were not expected to use their intellect or judgment in performing work...a high volume, standardized product and a labor force that was trained to perform small and repetitive tasks [developed as a result]" (Parks 1995, p. 21). Current jobs stress independent as well as team-based problem-solving and people skills. This trend in the workplace is projected to continue into the 21st century.

To get a more specific handle on the seismic change in workforce employment, here are statistics from the U.S. Census Bureau (2001). At the turn of the 20th century approximately 38% of the workforce was involved in farming, 38% was involved in mining, manufacturing, and construction, and 31% was involved in service By the end of the 20th century less than three percent were farmers, 19% were involved in manufacturing, mining, and construction, and 78% were involved in service (U.S. Census Bureau 2001, p. 3). Obviously, the skill set required of workers in the 21st century needs to be different across the board.

What businesses identify as competencies (thinking skills) they want in their workers are

1. The ability to manage resources: setting priorities, managing money and materials, and managing people.
2. The ability to work with other people on the job.
3. The ability to acquire and use information.

4. The ability to synthesize knowledge from one situation or system to another.
5. The ability to deal with new technology. (SCANS, 1992, p. xiv).

These skills are not covered in current school curricula, they have not been prioritized by the "No Child Left Behind" Act, nor are they taught through current traditional "talk and chalk" teaching methods. However, these skills *can* be achieved through the arts.

Working in the arts, particularly the performing arts, is a great way to teach time management. Performing artists constantly deal with deadlines. Musical instruments must be practiced every day. Dancers must work out daily to keep their muscles in shape and their technique sharp. Actors in a play must learn lines and movement patterns on time. Sets and costumes must be built and in place by opening night. When it's time for the curtain to go up, every facet of the presentation must be ready. You cannot come out before the show begins and say to the audience, "Sorry, folks, we only know the lines for Act One, so we'll only do part of the play," or "We didn't finish all the costumes, so just imagine the princess is wearing a beautiful ball gown instead of blue jeans."

Management of resources is another skill an artist uses every day. Because designers and technicians have to work within a budget to create sets, costumes, and props, the art of stagecraft has been developed to include many clever tricks that make the audience believe they are seeing something that really is not there. The walls of a house on stage might *look* like solid brick, but in reality it's only muslin fabric stretched across a wooden frame and painted to create the illusion of brick. The pirate's treasure chest might look like it's filled with gold doubloons, but in reality they are only old poker chips sprayed with gold-colored paint.

The performing arts, in particular, stress interpersonal-interaction skills. An actor, musician, or dancer must learn to work *with* others toward the creation of a common goal: the performance. Drama, which often involves the re-creation of real-life situations and relationships, is especially useful for developing the ability to work with and understand others. The ability to share and to negotiate solutions to problems is crucial in the workplace and in the rehearsal hall. In addition, the more clearly a person can communicate with words and actions, the less frequently others will misunderstand her — and the more often she will be able to understand the communication of others.

The process of creating art involves flexibility, spontaneity, and the ability to adapt to change. Each line that an artist puts on a piece of paper requires assessment and adjustment to the overall creative plan. Each moment on stage must be brought to life anew by the performer each time it is performed. Mishaps or mistakes in a performance must be dealt with by the actor, dancer, or musician without stopping the show or letting the audience know that anything went awry. If you forget your line or dance step, you improvise something that makes sense and does not throw off the other performers until you remember the next thing you are supposed to do or say. If they are doing their job, they'll improvise something in return that will help get you back on track!

Improvisation in life and in art is important; inflexibility and rigidity will kill the ability to be expressive and creative in any art form, interpersonal relationship, or problem-solving situation. Improvisational acting games train students to respond quickly and appropriately to incoming verbal and nonverbal messages from others, a skill that any salesperson, teacher, or personnel manager needs to have. Improvisation also teaches approaching life and work in a flexible, playful manner rather than in a stressful, tense one.

Communication is inherent in the arts. And the ability to make connections — between one idea and another, between one person and another — is inherent in communication. Assessing information and synthesizing it are the first steps in the artistic process. The information comes in and is internally evaluated. Connections and comparisons are made within the artist between the new information and the old. A new response is generated and the artist must formulate a way to express that new idea. Here we have practice in information assessment and synthesis, two of the thinking skills mentioned above as necessary for workers to develop.

In addition to all of this, the arts teach the rewards of completion. A student who works hard and finishes her art project, whether it is a painting or a performance, has a finished product in the end — something she has made, can be proud of, and which says something about her. The feeling of accomplishment that comes with completion is one that cannot be understood until it is experienced. Once it is experienced, the student learns that the effort and sacrifice involved in working on a project is worth it. Job satisfaction, self-discipline, and taking pride in your work are no longer just abstract ideas; they become meaningful in personal terms.

The final outcome of an experience in the arts is the development of self-esteem. When a student finishes a project, overcoming all the challenges, obstacles, and frustrations along the way, she starts to feel good about herself. Connections of new knowledge are made inside. Connections of recognition and appreciation are made between herself and others. She sees that she can contribute something which others in the community value. She can feel personal growth and sense her own potential. This creates the motivation to keep on going and keep on growing.

Recommended Reading

Bodrova, E., and Leong, D. (2006). *Tools of the Mind: The Vygotskian Approach to Early Childhood Education, 2nd Edition.* Upper Saddle River, NJ: Prentice-Hall.

Brown, S. (2009). *Play: How It Shapes the Brain, Opens the Imagination, and Invigorates the Soul.* New York: Avery.

Dewey, J. (1958). *Art as Experience.* New York: Capricorn Books.

Dissanayake, E. (1992). *Homo Aestheticus: Where Art Comes From And Why.* Seattle, WA: University of Washington Press.

Eisner, E. W. (2002). *The Arts and the Creation of Mind.* New Haven, CT: Yale University Press.

Goleman, D. (1995). *Emotional Intelligence: Why It Can Matter More than IQ.* New York: Basic Books.

Iacoboni, M. (2008). *Mirroring People: The New Science of How We Connect with Others.* New York: Farrar, Straus & Giroux.

Jensen, E. (2000). *Brain-based Learning, Revised Edition.* San Diego, CA: The Brain Store.

Pink, D. H. (2006). *A Whole New Mind: Why Right-Brainers will Rule the Future.* New York: Riverhead.

2. Disability and the Arts

The arts can greatly enhance every aspect of our lives: education, work, play, relationships, and identity formation. Because they are so basic and so life-affirming, the arts open up new avenues for stimulation, communication, and growth. If this is true for people who don't have disabilities, it is equally so for people who do.

Disabilities — whether physical, cognitive, or emotional — cause a great deal of frustration in the lives of those who have them. Full participation in community life can be sometimes blocked by obstacles created by the disability itself, lack of accommodation, or prejudicial attitudes by others. Design barriers can limit access to transportation and buildings along with access to the programs and work opportunities held inside those buildings. Traditional educational systems don't always answer the needs of people who learn in alternative ways. Due to the nature of the disability or lack of accommodations in the community, the range of choices a person with a disability is able to make, from educational level and career to living situation and lifestyle, can be limited. Faced with a myriad of frustrating and confining situations, a person who has a disability can easily become focused on what he cannot do, instead of what he can do or on the possibilities and potentials for which he can strive.

The arts break through barriers and limitations. They offer participants many possibilities and options for the successful expression of feelings and ideas. Difficulty on one level of perception or communication does not negate enjoyment or participation on another. In fact, the arts may provide stronger channels for self-expression for a person with a disability than non-artistic media can. For example, someone who has difficulty expressing himself in words because of a speech disorder or a learning disability may be able to express himself clearly through pantomime or dance. A student who can't write about something that happened to him might be able to act it out or sing about it and experience the same or even a higher degree of expression.

If an individual can experience success, be valued for his ideas, and have his feelings validated, his self-confidence and self-esteem begin to grow. When attitudes about the self change for the positive, people begin to feel their obstacles are surmountable. Choices multiply. Life becomes filled with excitement and joy.

Making friends and sharing experiences create a sense of belonging to the community as a whole. The individual feels as though he has the right to exist and enjoy life alongside everyone else. To be acknowledged for artistic creations leads to the desire to contribute more — to self, family, friends, and the community.

Government figures regarding specific disability conditions vary widely, but statistics indicate that about 49.7 million people or 19.3% of the U.S. population have some form of disability (U.S. Census 2000). These figures indicate a significant number of community members who could benefit from participation in recreational arts programming or through the integration of the arts into the curriculum but who may at present be excluded. Arts and recreation programs are passing up important opportunities to boost attendance and income as well as to generate goodwill. Educational institutions and rehabilitation services are missing out on powerful tools to build their clients' self-esteem and motivation for self-sufficiency and for learning important academic, life, and job skills. Even for adults who have been out of the education system for years, the arts can be a powerful motivational force to unlock creative potential that has long lain dormant.

Specific Skills Drama Develops

Each art form helps student artists develop specific skills. A look at some of the skills that drama enhances shows how participation in theatre arts might benefit a person who has a disability.

Listening

Drama builds listening skills. There are many opportunities for practicing listening skills in a drama classroom. Directions to games must be listened to in order to play. Stories must be heard before they can be acted out. While acting out a scene, each actor must listen to the others in order to know when to say his line. In the case of improvisational acting, the actor must listen in order to know what to reply to a scene partner.

In an academic classroom it might be difficult to listen if you are not interested in the subject being taught or if what is being said is hard to

photo by Keith Jenkins

Figure 3: Drama provides opportunities for self-expression.

grasp. However, in a drama classroom listening leads to fun. If the student can listen, he can participate and is rewarded with an enjoyable experience, such as a fun game, an interesting imaginary experience, positive attention from the teacher and others in the group, or the feeling of doing a job well.

In addition to reinforcing the practices of listening, of attending to the human voice, and processing directions being spoken, drama teaches *what* to listen for. There are many tone-of-voice exercises that actors play to develop vocal expressiveness. Listening to the manner in which others are speaking teaches students to recognize emotion and meaning in the human voice apart from the literal content of the words. This can be a crucial skill that students who have Asperger's disorder and other developmental disabilities need to practice repeatedly in order to master. There are also action/reaction exercises that teach how to respond appropriately to what another actor is communicating vocally, emotionally, and physically. Even deaf students can participate in these kinds of exercises because emotional meaning and intent put into the voice show up in facial expression and body language.

Eye Contact

Many children who have cognitive disabilities, depression, or low self-esteem have difficulty making eye contact with others. Eye contact is part of listening and receiving information from others. It is also part of sharing information with others about what you are thinking and feeling. Being able to make eye contact with another person, at least in our American culture, enhances trust as well as communication.

There are many drama games that stress eye contact and therefore develop the ability to use it on stage and in real life. Many trust and non-verbal communication exercises require eye contact, as do action/reaction exercises. Mirroring and other follow-the-leader exercises encourage students to really look at each other. On stage as in real life, actors usually look at each other when they are talking unless there is a strong dramatic reason to look away. Students working on improvisational or scripted scenes can be encouraged to hold eye contact in rehearsal and performance. Once these habits are introduced through an enjoyable and meaningful experience, students begin to feel more comfortable making eye contact with others and they will naturally carry over its use into relationships at school and home.

Awareness of the Body in Space

Many children with special needs have difficulty understanding how their physical bodies take up space; without this knowledge they can end up intruding on others around them. They are often unaware that each person has "personal space," an invisible area around the body into which others may not come without permission (Somers 1969). The boundary for personal space is different for each person. Some people need a lot and some need just a little. Personal space needs can change depending on one's mood or physical health. People in happy, exuberant moods often need less personal space than they do when they are sad or angry. Likewise, people who are sick or in pain often need more personal space than they do when they are feeling well.

If someone breaks the boundaries of your personal space without your permission, you will most likely feel threatened. The threat will be experienced as more intense if the boundary is broken by a stranger or acquaintance than by a close friend or family member. More personal space is typically required if the other person you are interacting with is taller or larger.

Awareness of personal space is a cultural concept that is taught non-verbally. Children normally learn it through observing their parents as they interact within the family and in the world. People in some cultures (for example, those in Mediterranean or Latin American regions) like to get closer to others with whom they are interacting. People in other cultures (for example, those in Britain and Northern Europe) prefer more distance between interactants. One reason for these differences is that differing amounts of the other person's body are typically observed when communicating in those cultures. Latin and Mediterranean cultures like to focus on the face; Anglo-Saxon, Germanic, and Scandinavian cultures like to focus on the entire person from head to toe; and Americans are somewhere in the middle. To get the appropriately sized view of another person, you have to stand a certain distance away from them (Marsh 1988; Somers 1969).

There are four zones of interaction: the intimate, the personal, the social, and the public. In the U.S. the intimate zone, for family, lovers, and close friends, is within eighteen inches of oneself. The personal zone, for friends and less intense interactions with those we let into our intimate zone, is between one-and-one-half feet and four feet. The social zone, which is for acquaintances and business associates, is between four and twelve feet. Finally, the public zone, for strangers and brief encounters, is twelve feet and over. (Marsh 1988)

In every culture children who have special needs may miss out on information that is taught non-verbally because their attention is occupied with other emotional, physical, or information-processing demands. They need to have their attention drawn specifically to these behaviors in order to realize they need to observe them. For them the importance of these behaviors must be reinforced by verbally explaining them as well.

Sometimes students are aware of their needs for their own personal space, but not the needs of others around them. Lack of awareness of body- and personal-space boundaries can lead to personal misunderstandings and fights. One child may innocently stretch out his arm and unknowingly invade the space of the child next to him. This child whose space has been invaded gets upset and aggressively hits out at the invader. Within seconds both are rolling around on the floor, punching each other.

Drama is a good training ground for developing awareness of personal-space boundaries. A child can be encouraged to be aware of how he uses his body and how his body can take up more or less space by expanding or contracting. Shape-shifting or body transformation games stress changing your physical self into other animals or objects, both large and small, and moving in different ways. Slow-motion/fast-motion games enhance the awareness of how your body moves through space and at which speeds you have more or less control.

Once a student understands how his body inhabits the space around him, he can develop better control over his body and begin to learn how it interacts with other bodies in space. Many movement games teach spatial relationships and body control. Others teach how to touch appropriately and in a non-aggressive manner. (See Chapter 7 for a few examples of these.) The zones of proximity can be demonstrated to visual learners by drawing a chart similar to a target, with the self in the middle as the bull's-eye and the zones as concentric rings radiating out from the self. The basic personal-space bubble can be enacted by having students move around the room while holding hula-hoops around them to represent their personal space. The goal of an activity like this is to practice giving others enough room to get by.

Physical Coordination

Balance, hand-eye coordination, and gross motor skills can be refined through movement and social games as well as through pantomime and acting activities. Practicing a physical skill for its own sake can get boring. Think of how hard it is to stick to a daily exercise regimen! It is often easier to improve a skill if you are focused on a fun objective instead of on the skill itself. All drama games have a stated dramatic goal, but develop many subskills along the way. Begin to consciously look at games and activities to find these subskills.

A good example of this is the game Elbow-to-Elbow. The leader calls out different body parts: elbow-to-elbow, head-to-knee, and heel-to-toe. Each student must connect one of his body parts with the body part of another student. The overall dramatic goal is to get actors to work together and contact each other cooperatively. While they are doing this, they are also learning about body parts, making decisions, becoming aware of themselves in space, developing balance, using gross muscles, coordinating body placement, socializing with each other, and much, much more.

Physical Expressiveness

Social science researchers have identified that only about seven percent of our communications are delivered through the actual words we say (content, text), while 38 percent of meaning comes through tone of voice and 55 percent comes through body language, including facial expression (Marsh 1988). Drama classes address these skill areas directly. Much of actor training focuses on learning how to clearly use and control the body and voice in nonverbal ways. This fits perfectly with the needs of children with disabilities who, for various reasons, require help developing these skills.

Drama activities stress using the body in a physically expressive manner. A neutral body communicates nothing. A tense body communicates tension, worry, and anxiety. A relaxed body can communicate any emotion the actor wants to express. Guessing games and transformation games require actors to use their bodies in different ways to communicate an idea to others. Pantomime necessitates that actors imitate an action as clearly as possible. Creating a character different from oneself encourages expressing emotions in different ways and exploring how other people move and express themselves.

Facial Expressiveness

The face is an important part of the body. For humans it carries more emotional information than any other part. In fact, communication begins with the face. From the moment of birth, babies are hardwired to make contact with the human face and look into their mothers' eyes (MacDonald 2003). Faces are very elastic, having forty-four muscles that can create between 10,000 and 15,000 facial expressions (Blum 1998; Ekman 2003). A facial expression can mask what a person is feeling or express it honestly. Because of this, particular attention is often paid to developing facial expressiveness in drama.

Some children with special needs don't know how to express what they are feeling through their faces. Others may have difficulty reading the expressions in others' faces. Children who have been abused tend to interpret ambiguous expressions as anger (Restak 2003). Working with facial expressiveness in drama class develops ease and appropriateness of expression as well as the ability to interpret the true meaning of facial expressions in others. Communication becomes clearer on many levels and, as a result, misunderstandings happen less often.

Verbal Expressiveness

In addition to non-verbal, physical expressiveness, drama deals with expressing ideas and feelings in sound and words. The most obvious way drama can enhance verbal expressiveness is by training students to speak clearly and understandably. But many other aspects of verbal expressiveness exist: the ability to articulate ideas in words and learning to understand and express feelings and meaning through the appropriate use of tone of voice.

Most drama classes involve spoken feedback from the teacher and the participants to help performers improve their skills. This encourages the development of critical thinking and the ability to put ideas and concepts into words. The best use of feedback is when teachers encourage students to formulate constructive criticism which identifies what the performer did that was effective and why, along with identifying the aspects of the performance that could be improved with ideas about how that might be accomplished. Criticism without support and encouragement causes the recipient to shut down. More will be discussed about how to introduce this concept in Chapters 5 and 6.

Every verbal communication contains two messages: the text (the actual words spoken) and the subtext (the emotional undertone and intention of the words). Subtext can support and enhance the text, it can give away an underlying message not inherent in the words alone, or it can totally change the meaning of the words spoken. In every day living we use subtext all the time. For example, you could say, "She's my best friend" four different ways and each time communicate a different emotional meaning. By the way you use your tone of voice and through the stress put on different words in the sentence, you might mean "She is my friend," "She's not my friend; she's my enemy," "I can't stand her," or even "She's a cute kid, but she follows me around constantly and I wish she'd leave me alone."

Subtext is another one of those cultural constructs that are taught non-verbally through observation and imitation. Consciously working on developing these skills helps students who have missed out on social learning become able to use their tone of voice and interpret it better. As communication becomes clearer, misunderstandings will happen less often.

Identification and Naming of Emotions

Through improvisation students can learn to identify emotions and translate them into words. Everyone needs to learn how to do this, but children who have disabilities sometimes have particular difficulty finding words to express what is going on inside. Improvisational drama can help students practice this. Expressing how a character in a fictional context feels can provide a student with enough emotional distance to be able to sort through feelings and choose appropriate words for them. Describing what you just experienced during an exercise can be the beginning of describing emotions that you feel in real-life situations.

Focus and Concentration

Focus and concentration are crucial skills for an actor to develop in order to create an exciting performance. The more an actor can concentrate and focus on his lines, characterization, emotions, movement, stage business, and the other actors on stage, the closer to the dramatic truth of the moment he will come. A low-energy performance during which an actor daydreams or wanders aimlessly about the stage without connecting with the other actors is boring.

Special-needs students may lack focus and concentration for a variety of physical, emotional, or cognitive reasons. Focusing on drama games and activities, which are of short duration but create intense, enjoyable feelings, allows the student to begin to learn how to focus his attention. The immediate positive feedback from his body, his emotions, the teacher, and his fellow students reinforces focused behavior and encourages him to pay closer attention to what is going on in and outside of the classroom.

As students move on to more advanced dramatic work, such as improvisation, scene study, or performance, they have more opportunities to hone concentration abilities. An improvisational scene stops dead in its tracks if an actor stops paying attention to what is going on. It jumps around and becomes confusing if the actors cannot concentrate on the conflict. When rehearsing a scene from a play that has been memorized, an actor must listen for his cue before he can say his line. If he is not paying attention, he will miss his part and the play will stop!

Memory Enhancement

The brain has multiple memory systems; each deals with remembering different types of information (Cozolino 2002). School often focuses on the use of rote memorization, a form of semantic memory that deals with encoding and retrieving facts. However, other systems that encode information differently can also be used for learning: episodic, autobiographical, somatic, perceptual, emotional, and behavioral memory. A number of these forms of memory embed information within sequential narrative structures. Roger Schank and Tamara Berman (2002) propose that "most of the knowledge we use in our day-to-day lives is stored in our memory structures as stories. Some of the stories are our own past experiences that we mentally structure as stories... Others are stories we hear from outside sources" (p. 287). Drama is, by nature and form, stories that are acted out, narratives that are embodied and performed rather than read. This means that facts and concepts that are embedded within stories will be learned and remembered more effectively by children who have strengths in these types of memory.

> It remains somewhat of a mystery why narrative text is so easy to comprehend and remember. Perhaps it is because the content of narrative text has such a close correspondence with everyday experiences. Perhaps it is because the language of oral conversation has a closer similarity to narrative text than other discourse genres. Perhaps it is because there are more vivid mental images. ...Researchers have not yet provided a satisfying answer to the question of why narrative has such a privileged status in the cognitive system (Graessner, Olde, & Klettke 2002, p. 240).

Another discovery about learning and memory is that information learned in connection with an intense emotion is often retained better than information that is presented in a non-affective (that is, boring, unemotional, and unimaginative) manner (Jensen 2000). In order not to traumatize students, educators should strive for that intense emotion to be a pleasant one. Unpleasant emotions and traumatic events cause stress in learners and stress can interfere with memory formation (Cozolino 2002). Stress reactions cause the secretion of cortisol and other stress hormones that pump up the "fight-or-flight-or-freeze" reaction of the body. Sustained exposure to stress and resultant stress hormones can cause damage to the brain in a number of ways that lessen the ability to create new memories and access old ones. Jensen (2000) reports that sarcasm, negative or harsh criticism, and put-downs increase abnormalities of heart rate. In contrast, positive challenge and enjoyment of the learning process releases endorphins ("feel-good" peptide molecules that create a "natural high" in the body), promoting higher-quality learning. "The ideal state for learning attention is a balance of high serotonin and cortisol/adrenaline." (Jensen 2000, p. 125). Jensen presents evidence that cortisol alone creates a negative stress reaction while cortisol with adrenaline creates a positive stress (or eustress) reaction. For most children with and without disabilities, drama is experienced as a very enjoyable way to learn because their imaginations, creativity, and senses of humor are engaged in the process.

Stress Release

Students with disabilities often experience high levels of stress, either because of the academic frustrations caused by learning differences, the accessibility frustrations caused by physical disabilities, or the emotional frustrations caused by stigma, rejection, and not fitting in socially. Drama and other arts are excellent avenues for reducing stress and relieving frustration because they involve the participant simultaneously in physical, emotional, and mental activities that either divert them from the stress or allow them to vent the feelings caused by the stress. Distraction is one of the best ways to release negative feelings caused by stress (anger, worry, anxiety) because it's hard to remain unhappy when you are having a good time (Goleman 1995). The body relaxes, the mind lets go of the upsetting thoughts, and one's emotions make a transition to positive engagement, enjoyment, and hope. As one of my college student reports about her Creative Drama class at Kansas State:

> In an incredibly stressful semester, it helped immensely for me to go to a class where I could play, interact with people, or listen to a story. This was true even on days when I initially wasn't really all that eager to go to class. Creative drama gave me a chance to take a breather, to forget about all my other stresses and classes and pressures... You go to class and are engaged in a fun yet challenging class, and you come out refreshed, having interacted socially with wonderful people (Myers 2005).

Self-Control and Patience

Daniel Goleman says, "There is perhaps no psychological skill more fundamental than resisting impulse. It is the root of all emotional self-control, since all emotions, by their very nature, lead to one or another impulse to act" (1995, p. 81). Drama can enhance students' self-control and patience because the payoff — having fun — is worth waiting for and gratification, while not always immediate, is soon. Most theatre games involve some kind of turn-taking. Students who have little patience can be started out with games in which everyone acts at once so no turn-taking is involved. Then they can move to interacting and turn-taking in pairs. Often these types of games have "roles" or actions for both partners to do simultaneously; they just take turns in which role they play. Turn-taking can later be stretched to larger and larger groups where there is more waiting time before getting to your turn. If respect for and interest in the other class members is being reinforced (all part of developing good audience behavior), students will be focused on observing, enjoying, and/or critiquing each other's performances and they will not become bored.

In order to act out a story, one has to sit and listen to it first, and since listening to a story is pleasant and often exciting, students can usually remain attentive. One effective storytelling technique for overactive or impatient listeners is to make a story interactive. Students can join in on repetitive lines like "Little pig, little pig, let me come in," during "The Three Little Pigs" or they can pantomime motions the character is doing from their seats, such as Aladdin rubbing the magic ring and the magic lamp. The more one is able to practice being patient, the better one gets at it.

Flexibility, Problem-Solving, and Risk Taking

The ability to be flexible is crucial in order to get along with others and solve the many different problems that come up in life. In trying to cope with physical, relational, or educational situations that seem to be out of their control, many children with special needs can become very rigid and inflexible in the choices that they are willing to make. They stop taking risks and limit themselves to a narrow range of behavior that may or may not be appropriate for the moment.

For example, a child who has difficulty controlling his body movements because of cerebral palsy could develop an inflexible need to always be in control of every personal interaction. Things have to go his way or no way at all. If he is not able to call the shots, he might whine, complain, protest, have a temper tantrum, or refuse to participate. Obviously, these are not productive coping strategies. No one can always control other people's behavior. Sometimes you get your way and other times you do not.

Another child might have had a bad experience riding on a bus and refuse to take public transportation ever again. This will cause difficulties for him when he becomes an adolescent and, later, an adult. If he is unable to drive a car and cannot afford to go everywhere by cab, this inflexible practice may limit his ability to get around independently and even to hold a job.

In drama class students have the opportunity to try out different roles and behaviors in a safe situation. Different strategies for solving a problem can be acted out and the pros and cons of each evaluated and discussed. Changing points of view on a situation through role reversal often helps students open up their personal perspective on a specific problem or on their general orientation toward life. Just the experience of standing in another's shoes for a little while teaches flexibility and opens up the possibility that other choices do exist and might be considered.

Social Interaction

Sometimes children who have disabilities have poor group-interaction skills. One reason for this is that they may not have enough opportunities to practice them. They may live isolated lives compared with children who do not have disabilities. They might spend a great deal of time in the hospital or at their doctors' or therapists' offices. They might have to ride the bus for many hours to get to their special school. They might not be accepted by other children in the neighborhood and thus miss out on opportunities for social play. They might have to spend extra time doing homework each day in order to succeed academically.

Even in regular education classes, school time is rarely devoted to the development of social skills. Each child sits alone at his desk doing his assignment and is permitted to talk with friends only during lunch or recess. A few teachers are beginning to use group learning methods in which a number of students work together to create a project or solve a problem, but interactive learning is not the norm. Some schools have

photo by John Carter

Figure 4: Improvisation teaches communication and social interaction skills.

done away with recess in order to devote more time to studying. This further limits socializing opportunities.

Drama classes offer many chances for students to practice working with others constructively and to make friends. The drama teacher is responsible for creating a non-competitive forum where each student is encouraged to do his best and to support others in doing their best. Sharing feelings and ideas, taking turns, and being generous and kind to each other should be stressed over perfecting performance skills. Theatre is first and foremost a communal art. Those involved must work together. Contrary to the media stereotype of the *prima donna* or *diva*, truly successful artists base their work and interactions on mutual respect.

One positive experience can make a big difference in the life of a child. One mother said of her emotionally disturbed son's experience in a creative drama class, "We believe Jacob has made progress this year in his social skills and his ability to express his feelings and that drama class has a lot to do with it." You can read more about Jacob in the Epilogue at the end of the book.

A wide variety of group experiences are available for students in a drama classroom. The entire class might act something out together in a parallel fashion, expressing different versions of the same idea side by side without interacting. The teacher might lead the group in a transformation game where everyone changes from elephants to monkeys to thorn bushes. The whole group might play an interactive game like Elbow-to-Elbow. Individuals can take turns getting up in front of the group and pantomiming different activities or singing a song. Partners can work together on games and exercises. Small groups can invent an improvisational scene or play a game in which they have to work together to solve a problem. In each type of group experience, students have the opportunity to make positive contact with others, to give and take ideas, to resolve conflicts, and to make friends.

Self-Esteem and Self-Confidence

Self-esteem and self-confidence are often in short supply among children who have disabilities. Because they are different from other children in their neighborhood or school and because they may not succeed in typical academic, athletic, or social settings — main arenas of childhood and adolescence — they may not feel good about themselves and may doubt their abilities. Drama is a self-esteem and self-confidence builder. Through dramatic experiences in classes and performances, students can share the creative, vulnerable, and unique aspects of themselves with others. They can explore who they are, experience success, and begin to feel proud of themselves.

Optimism and Positive Outlook on Life

The end result of all of the personal growth, success, and skill development that can result from a drama experience is a new, more optimistic outlook on life. Martin Seligman (1991) believes that individuals can chose to view the world and think in optimistic or pessimistic terms. Optimism is associated with positive outlook, hope, health, an action orientation toward life, internal locus of control (belief that you can make a difference), and the ability to face setbacks by believing they are only temporary, taking on the challenge again and trying harder. Pessimism is associated with depression, giving up, self-blame, helplessness, low immunity, and external locus of control (belief that others control you and it does not matter what you do). Optimism and pessimism can be self-fulfilling prophecies. By their active nature, dramatic activities teach internal locus of control. The success that students can experience in a drama class can demonstrate to them that they possess many abilities and strengths instead of only the deficits and weaknesses that may have been highlighted by academic or athletic failures.

===============================

Kids Next Door
Marie Schick, MA, RDT

Where can you be a courtroom judge, dance to the Macarena, and help homeless children? In a drama therapy group, of course! Kids Next Door is a drama therapy program for adolescents with Asperger's Syndrome, Autism Spectrum, and Non-verbal Learning Disorders. The groups provide a therapeutic and supportive community with activities related to self-sufficiency, peer relationships, and community service. Program objectives focus on three areas: 1) Individual: increasing self-awareness and sufficiency; 2) Group: establishing peer relationships; and 3) Community: experiencing a greater sense of belonging. There are weekly boys and girls groups as well as a weekly joint co-ed group. Experiences occur both in the group room and in the community.

For this population, goals related to self-regulation, communication skills, relationship development, and generalization of skills include: 1) managing and expressing strong emotions, such as frustration, anger, embarrassment; 2) managing anxiety about change, new experiences, or meeting people; 3) communication skills, such as non-verbal communication, conversation exchanges, and reading social cues; 4) greater social interaction with peers; and 5) self-awareness and reflection, as well as articulation of needs and advocacy.

Related to individual and group goals, some of the issues we have addressed in the Boys Group are playful rough-housing/"fooling around" versus verbal and physical teasing. During one session, the boys were completing a collage of their painted handprints. Between two boys, Ryan and Devin, who had struggled with teasing each other for several weeks, verbal teasing escalated to smearing paint on each other's clothes. When confronted with their behaviors by the leader and the group members, Ryan stated that he was just "fooling around" and that Devin acted wrongly and should be punished. However, the remaining group members, having observed Ryan and Devin's behavior on this and other occasions, knew that the boys disliked and frequently teased each other. A third boy, Jack, stepping between Ryan and Devin, quickly joined the discussion, "Wait, wait. Let's hear both sides of the story and then we can decide who should apologize."

And we turned it into a drama: a spontaneous courtroom evolved with two defendants seated on either side of the judge, holding a paint roller as a gavel, and a jury seated opposite; the group leader and assistant, to help guide the drama, become court reporters providing commentary. The boys, familiar with courtroom dramas and excited by our real life story, arranged the furniture in the room, assumed their roles, and began. The courtroom was a natural choice with its structure and roles to fairly review the situation and determine an appropriate solution. Both Ryan and Devin, enrolled as "defendants," managed and appropriately expressed their strong emotions of anger and frustration (another group goal) through the drama, while the other group members experienced feelings of empathy toward their peers. The group's goals of self-awareness and reflection played greatly into both Ryan and Devin's individual experiences but also the judge and jury's thoughtful consideration of the situation and solution. Not only did the group's courtroom create a forum to openly address Ryan's frequent insistence that he's "fooling around," the boys addressed the broader issue of playful roughhousing between friends and teasing, verbal and physical, that is otherwise motivated, both of which are recognized components of their group dynamic.

Besides using more traditional drama therapy methods, such as personal/group storytelling and role-playing, other techniques have included: developing a group magazine, self-portraits through digital photography, individual and group art projects, shopping, sports and games at the park, cooking lessons, and money management. We have addressed peer pressure and bullying, personal safety, lying/stealing, health and nutrition, making healthy eating choices, physical fitness, and personal hygiene and self-care.

The Kids Next Door drama therapy program provides endless opportunities for individual learning, growth, and expression; the development of peer relationships, mentoring, and shared group experiences; and the connection, through interaction and involvement, to the greater community. Yes, we share our personal stories. Yes, we role-play scenarios and solutions. And, yes, we learn how to buy movie tickets at the theatre, shop for groceries and cook a simple meal, read maps and ride the subway, and dance with a friend — for a good cause — on a Friday night.

================================

Dealing with Stigma

One issue that consistently rears its ugly head whenever a person with a disability is involved is stigma: the belief that someone is less than human because of a discredited difference (Goffman 1963). Stigma leads to negative stereotypes, prejudice, and discrimination. It creates a situation of "us normals" against "them abnormals," whether in connection with physical, cognitive, emotional, social, ethnic, religious, economic, or other forms of difference from the norm or dominant group. Having a disability compartmentalizes one as different, as *dis*abled rather than able, as outside the norm; it creates, as the subtitle of Goffman's landmark book on the subject indicates, a spoiled identity.

On one hand, we can't help but recognize and categorize any difference. That is the way the human brain learns: through accommodation and assimilation (Ginsburg & Opper 1969). In fact, the ability to quickly categorize is how we survive! The amygdala, a structure in the limbic system in the brain, has a fast-reacting emotional circuit that allows us to recognize anything novel or out of the ordinary before it hits our conscious awareness in order to prepare us to act immediately for our self-preservation. This is backed up by a more slowly reacting circuit that goes through the pre-frontal lobes to the cortex of the brain, which evaluates whether the person, object, or animal that we have encountered is really dangerous or not. At the point this difference becomes conscious, we create a category based on whatever it was that we noticed that was "different," and we take action (LeDoux 1998). Often we stigmatize anyone or anything that is in a different category than we are. We do not *have* to stigmatize what is different, but we often do. The original sorting process, "same-as-me" versus "different-from-me," becomes the default position. To *not* stigmatize after someone is categorized takes conscious effort.

It is not fun to be the target of stigma. Stigma generates feelings of being rejected, unwanted, tainted, dirty, and bad. Does that mean people who stigmatize others are "bad people?" No. The unfortunate truth is that we *all* stigmatize people who are different from us until we learn through experience what it is we have in common with that different person or group of people — and until we learn that whatever was different will not harm us.

For thousands of years people who had leprosy were stigmatized and isolated from society in leper colonies. Leprosy is a disfiguring disease caused by a bacillus that attacks the nerves and skin. The belief was that lepers rotted slowly away and that by being near a leper, one could catch the disease. Not until the 20th century did scientists discover that leprosy is only mildly contagious and that ninety percent of people are immune to it (Eyman 1987). Another false belief about leprosy was that it was an incurable, terminal condition. In actuality, leprosy does not cause death and medical science has recently discovered a cure. We now know that leprosy does not "rot" the body; it kills the nerves, thus people who have the disease often burn, cut, or wound themselves without knowing it. When they get infections, they do not feel any pain and they then develop gangrene that causes the loss of fingers, toes, noses, and other extremities. The scales that develop on the skin before the disease is treated or the scars that remain after the disease is cured remind those of us without the condition of decay and death. Unless we are educated about what has happened and we can get past the sight of the physical blemishes that remain, we will continue to stigmatize the person who had leprosy. Unfortunately, this stigmatization — "once a leper, always a leper" — is common all over the world. Many people who have recovered from the disease refuse to leave their "leper colonies" to return to society for fear of maltreatment (Callo 1987).

When people thought leprosy was highly contagious, were they wrong to isolate those who had it? No. They were trying to preserve the health of the community based on the information they had about the disease. However, it was wrong to treat people who had leprosy as unclean outcasts. Even if they had been contagious and terminal, they still deserved to be treated with respect and care.

A psychological byproduct of being the object of stigma is that the recipient tends to internalize the stigma and believe the truth of the negative attributes that are assigned to him by others (Goffman 1963). This can be readily seen in many people with disabilities who give up participating in the community because they feel they will not be welcomed. Recently in my Drama Therapy with Special Populations class Maggie, who has Down syndrome, was asked by her Kansas State partner why she always talked about playing inside at home and never talked about going outside to play. The answer was, "I can't go out. Look at me — I'm retarded. Nobody wants me around." This was not said so much in anger as in acceptance of the "obvious" fact that "of course" no one would want to spend time with her since she was "defective." Maggie is an incredibly creative person, very much fun to be around, so warm and energetic that I cannot imagine *not* wanting to have her around, but she has felt stigmatized and has internalized it.

Emma van der Klift and Norman Kunc (1994) identify four attitudes with which people with disabilities can be treated: *marginalization, reform, tolerance*, and *value*; the first three involve different "flavors" of stigma. The most oppressive is *marginalization*: segregating people with disabilities in colonies, workshops, institutions, special schools, and so on, so they are kept away from the rest of the community. In our own American society, many people diagnosed with mental retardation and mental illness were warehoused almost exclusively in state institutions until the 1960s (Mackelprang & Salsgiver 1999). Sometimes marginalization involves killing to get "them" out of the way, as in Nazi Germany, or sterilizing "them" so they cannot reproduce. Despite many years of work by activists, marginalization of many kinds still happens.

A second response is reform. Reform says, "You are not okay as you are. You need to change and be 'rehabilitated' so you can look and act like everyone else and then you can be assimilated into society with the rest of us." If who you are intrinsically isn't good enough, how can you feel accepted and wanted?

If someone with a difference cannot be reformed or marginalized, then they are often tolerated. At first blush tolerance sounds pretty good, and it is certainly an improvement on the first two options; however, tolerance, in the van der Klift-Kunc model, usually involves a certain amount of patronage and condescension. Tolerant people tend to talk down to others who have intellectual and developmental disabilities as if they are babies or shout at individuals who use wheelchairs as if they can't hear. Tolerant people are the ones who grab the blind person and drag him across the street before asking if he even wants to cross the street.

The ideal response is to genuinely value people who are different: seeing diversity in all its forms (ethnicity, disability, socio-economic background, etc.) as normal and positive, not "other" and "politically correct." This kind of approach truly puts people on an equal footing, welcomes them fully to the table, and appreciates the qualities they have that are unique as well as the many they have in common with the rest of humanity. Making the shift to this final response takes a lot of honesty, soul-searching, and a willingness to think consciously about how you relate to others. Will you always think, say, and do the right thing? No, but in time, with practice, you'll begin to start to "see the person and not the disability."

In a recent discussion about stigma and helping that came out of a discussion of the van der Klift-Kunc Model, Sierra Gottlob, one of my K-State students, had this to say:

> Helping another person should be viewed as a form of teamwork involving the helper and the helped. In an ideal world, helping and teamwork would be synonymous. Everyone should be working towards the same goal and helping should be part of that rather than a distraction from it.

It is crucial that helping professionals — therapists, drama teachers, special educators, drama therapists, administrators — take a serious look at how they relate to clients/students/actors who have disabilities and evaluate which of the responses to difference is their baseline response. If you do not respond with valuing, you need to work on making the shift to it in your heart and mind. Without that stance, there is no way to develop a healthy relationship with another person — with or without disabilities! In addition, if you refuse to take that approach, all of your clients/students/actors who do not have disabilities will read your behavioral and attitudinal clues and will model your example in their interactions with the clients/students/actors who do have disabilities.

I have come to believe that it is a moral responsibility to take an active stance in addressing any condescending, rejecting, dismissing, ridiculing, demeaning, or limiting treatment of someone who has a disability, whether the person doing the stigmatizing is a colleague, supervisor, or another student/client. This is not an easy task and cannot be done in a condescending, rejecting, dismissing, ridiculing, demeaning, or limiting way. Whenever I have tried to "give people back a taste of their own medicine," I have failed miserably. The person with the negative attitude does not realize he has one and is unaware of how he is coming across. Typically, he is just mirroring the attitude modeled for him by society, school, family, or supervisors. "Fighting fire with fire" doesn't work because he does not view his behavior as inappropriate; he just sees me as really rude and mean.

Stigmatizing people need to be educated in a gentle, kind way or they will shut down. In my classes at Kansas State University, I introduce the concept of stigma by having students fill out a survey (shown on the next page) of twenty disabling conditions listed in alphabetical order (Westbrook, Legge & Pennay 1993). They number the conditions from 1 (least stigmatizing) to 20 (most stigmatizing) and answer two questions: If you were to have any disability/medical condition, what would it be and why, and what disability/medical condition would you most not want to have and why. I do not share individual results with the class; I compile the scores and the comments anonymously and share them with the class, asking them to compare their answers with the results of the same survey given to six different cultural groups (Westbrook, Legge & Pennay 1993). The results are always interesting food for discussion and introspection, especially when paired with questions for journaling, such as:

- Which conditions do all the cultures rate similarly?

  Why do you think this is?

DISABILITY SURVEY

Please rank the following disabilities/medical conditions from what you consider to be the LEAST stigmatized (1) to the MOST stigmatized (20) from 1 through 20. The list* is in alphabetical order.

_____ AIDS   _____ Epilepsy

_____ Alcoholism   _____ Facial Scars/Disfiguring

_____ Amputated arm or leg   Birthmarks/Burns

_____ Arthritis   _____ Heart Disease

_____ Asthma   _____ Mental Retardation

_____ Blindness   _____ Multiple Sclerosis

_____ Cancer   _____ Paraplegia

_____ Cerebral Palsy   _____ Psychiatric Illness

_____ Deafness   _____ Stroke

_____ Diabetes   _____ Stuttering

_____ Dwarfism

For the following two questions, you don't need to limit your choice to the list above:

1. If you were to have a disability/medical condition — which would you be *most* willing to have? Why?

2. If you were to have a disability/medical condition — which would you be *least* willing to have? Why?

*List from: Westbrook, M. T., Legge, V., & Pennay, M. (1993). Attitudes towards disabilities in a multicultural society. *Social Science & Medicine. 36*(5):619.

- Which conditions did your class as a group rate differently from the other cultures? Do you think these differences are because of:

  Your age (i.e., mostly young adults without children)?
  This is 2010 and not 1993?
  You are college students (better educated)?
  Your culture (typically Midwest, Kansan, American)?

- If your individual answers were different from the group's collective answers, why? Are you in some way different from the rest of the group in relation to:

  Personal experience?
  Educational background (different major, studying different subjects)?
  Where you were raised?
  Other?

I follow this with the assignment of reading first-person articles in which people with different kinds of disabilities talk about their experiences. Community members who have disabilities come into class once a week so we can do drama with them and get to know them as people. Class on Tuesday with our guests is followed by discussion on Thursday about what happened and how we can better address our guests' individual needs the next Tuesday, making them feel welcomed and wanted and creating a really fun time for all of us. I end the semester by having students write a reaction paper about stigma, describing their personal experiences as recipients as well as projectors of it and reviewing what they learned from their experiences during the semester.

Obviously, if you are not teaching a class or you do not have a "captive audience" of some kind, it is not possible for you to engage people in a thoughtful, long-term process like this. One of the recommended books at the end of the chapter, *Encountering Bigotry: Befriending Projecting Persons in Everyday Life*, includes a number of wonderful suggestions for dealing with stigmatizing individuals. In a nutshell, the authors recommend remembering that when one person stigmatizes another, it is usually the end result of strong feelings that have been generated in the stigmatizer by the other person's difference. These strong feelings usually are based on past history and are unconscious. To get rid of those feelings, the stigmatizer projects them out onto the person who they view as responsible for "creating" the feeling — resulting in prejudice, discrimination, and stigmatization.

When faced with someone who has a disability, many people feel helpless, vulnerable, sad, angry, and awkward, along with a variety of other uncomfortable feelings. They may be reminded of their own mortality or feel guilty that they are "okay" and this other person is "not." They may not know what to do to help "make him better," when really the person just wants to be accepted for who he is right now.

We each need to learn to become responsible for owning our own feelings and for dealing with them in a non-hurtful, non-projective manner. When we see others mishandling those same types of feelings, we can help them by acknowledging how they are feeling and inviting them to listen to an alternative view, based on our own felt experiences — not those of the person who is being stigmatized, since you cannot speak for him, you can only speak for yourself. This means we must risk being vulnerable by sharing how we feel in a nonjudgmental way so that an authentic dialogue can develop in the here and now about the real issues underlying the projection. Will one conversation "cure" someone of projecting? Probably not, but it may begin the process of self-discovery for the projecting person and deepen the process for ourselves.

Recommended Reading

Condeluci, A. (1996). *Beyond Difference.* Boca Raton, FL: CRC Press.

Ekman, P. (2003). *Emotions Revealed: Recognizing Faces and Feelings to Improve Communication and Emotional Life.* New York: Henry Holt & Company.

Goffman, E. (1963). *Stigma: Notes on the Management of Spoiled Identity.* New York: Simon & Schuster.

Jensen, E. (2000). *Brain-Based Learning* San Diego, CA: The Brain Store.

Kunc, N. & van der Klift, E. www.normemma.com

Lichtenberg, P., van Beusekom, J., & Gibbons, D. (1997). *Encountering Bigotry: Befriending Projecting Persons in Everyday Life.* Lanham, MD: Jason Aronson, Inc.

Mackelprang, R. & Salsgiver, R. (1999). *Disability: A Diversity Model Approach in Human Service Practice.* Chicago: Lyceum Books.

Seligman, M. E. P. (1991). *Learned Optimism.* New York: Alfred A. Knopf.

3. Physical Disabilities

No two children learn in precisely the same way. One child may need to physically walk through the motions to learn a new skill, while another may learn better by watching a demonstration. Obviously, children with disabilities have learning styles that are just as unique as other children. However, particular disabilities present similar types of learning challenges; understanding how a specific disability may affect a child's behavior or her ability to learn can make it easier for teachers to help her benefit from a drama experience.

For the benefit of readers who do not have a background in special education, this chapter includes basic information on the characteristics of the most common types of physical disabilities. It also discusses some ways of accommodating these disabilities within the drama classroom and on stage. More specifics will be included in Chapters 5, 6, and 7, respectively describing how to run a structured drama class, how to develop a strong lesson plan, and how to adapt specific activities for students with special needs.

When offering a class or holding auditions for a peer group or an integrated group, include a line on your application form on which people can identify special needs. The line might say, "Please identify any disabilities, special needs, or medical conditions which the teacher should be aware of in order to make appropriate accommodations and serve you [your child] better." This indicates your interest and willingness to accept and work with all students. Without that line on the form, many students/parents will not share pertinent information. By the same token, some parents will not disclose information, even if you ask for it, because when they have disclosed special needs in the past, they have experienced rejection, and they fear you will stigmatize their child if they disclose information now. This can obviously create a dangerous situation if a student has a condition like epilepsy or diabetes and can set the student up for failure or frustration if she has an "invisible" disability, such as dyslexia, hearing loss, or attention deficit hyperactivity disorder (ADHD). If the line is left blank, you cannot read minds to know that accommodations will be needed, but do not assume that there are no needs to accommodate.

Types of Physical Disabilities

There are many different reasons why someone may need to use a wheelchair, walker, or crutches. Orthopedic disabilities — conditions that affect bone, joint, or muscle functioning — can be caused by paralysis due to spinal cord injury or brain trauma, cerebral palsy, osteogenesis imperfecta ("brittle bone disorder"), arthritis, spina bifida, or a neuromuscular disease, such as muscular dystrophy or multiple sclerosis.

Visual or hearing impairments can also be included among sensory disabilities, but in this chapter I am categorizing them with physical disabilities because they are often caused by a physical difference in eye or ear structure that interferes with the processing of sight or sound. Typically, the movement abilities of people with visual or hearing disabilities are normal but may be affected by the loss of sight or sound, for example, a balance problem could be connected to a hearing loss.

Many times a person who has a physical disability has normal cognitive functioning and normal or above-normal intelligence. Often she can be included in a regular drama class with a few changes in the physical environment to make the space more accessible and a few adjustments to your lesson plan to facilitate her interactions with you, the group, and the material.

Sometimes students with physical disabilities also have cognitive disabilities. In this case, refer also to Chapter 4, which contains information about cognitive disabilities and basic classroom adaptations for them.

There are no hard and fast rules that apply to everyone with any given diagnosis. Each individual will be affected in a slightly different way — emotionally, physically, and cognitively. Getting to know your student and her specific needs is more important than any advice this or any other book can give you.

Accessibility

The first thing you must do, long before a student with a physical disability signs up for a class, is to evaluate the accessibility of your building and classroom space. If a student cannot get in your front door, get around inside your building, use your restroom, or use your classroom equipment, she will not be able to avail herself of your services. Below are some suggestions for making your building, classroom, stage, and activities accessible.

Accessible Buildings

Many barriers can be removed at little or no cost. Sometimes it can be as simple as rescheduling a class from the second to the first floor or moving furniture around in order to provide a wider aisle for a wheelchair. Sometimes it is as inexpensive as adding a paper cup dispenser next to a water fountain or as easy as propping a door open with a doorstop or adjusting the automatic hinge on a door so it does not close as quickly (always check with your local fire marshal to be sure the prop or adjustment is acceptable, as the door in question may be a fire door).

Go through your building with the Checklist for Building Accessibility (see the Appendix) and evaluate where your facility is barrier-free and where it needs improvement. Ask adults in your community who have different types of physical disabilities to go through your building with you and point out the areas where they would have difficulty. They will find barriers that you, as a person without a disability, will not notice. Ask for suggestions on how to make changes cheaply and simply. People who deal with barriers every day have often developed quick, easy, common-sense solutions that someone who doesn't would never consider.

Design for Accessibility: A Cultural Administrator's Handbook, published by the National Endowment for the Arts, provides information to help you comply with Section 504 and the Americans with Disabilities Act (ADA), two federal laws dealing with accessibility, passed in 1973 and 1990, respectively. The *Handbook* addresses accessible design of buildings, mission, programming, administration, and staff. It can be ordered in hardcopy through the National Assembly of State Arts Agencies' website (www.nasaa-arts.org/publications/design_access. shtml) or downloaded for free in PDF format (www.arts.gov/resources/ Accessibility/DesignAccesibility.html).

Americans with Disabilities Act Accessibility Guidelines (ADAAG) and other free technical-assistance materials are available from the Architectural and Transportation Barriers Board (1331 F Street NW, Washington, DC 20004-1111; 1-800-USA-ABLE [voice and TTY]). They can be downloaded for free in PDF format (www.access-board.gov/pubs.htm) or ordered free in hard copy (www.access-board.gov/pol.cfm) in a variety of formats such as print, large print, Braille, or disc.

You can also contact the ADA information line (800-514-0301; TTY 800-514-0383) or go online (www.ada.gov). In addition, ten federally funded ADA and Information Technology centers can be found online (www.adata.org), which provide information, training, and technical assistance.

If money is a need in addressing accessibility at your facility, check out the Community Development Block Grant Report, which details how arts organizations across the country used federal funds to remove barriers and how to apply in order to make access improvements in your facility. The report is available on line (Webmanager; www.arts.gov/pub/access_pub.html) and from the Office of AccessAbility (Room 724, National Endowment for the Arts, 1100 Pennsylvania Avenue, NW, Washington, DC 20506; 202-682-5532).

You might find an architectural firm in your area that specializes in access issues, but before you hire them, make sure their consultant is truly an expert on accessibility and not just a good salesman. Your best bet in locating a reputable architectural consultant is to ask an independent-living center in your area. Independent-living centers are organized and staffed by people who have disabilities. If you are not sure how to find an independent-living center, contact the National Council on Independent Living (www.ilusa.com).

Accessible Classrooms

Let us assume that students with physical disabilities are able to get into your classroom or performing space. How well will they be able to function once they are there? Floor surfaces need to be considered. Wheelchairs don't roll well on thick pile carpets and have an equally difficult time moving over rough or uneven surfaces created by brick, tile, or textured linoleum.

Very slick surfaces or floors covered with slippery wax make walking dangerous for students who use walkers, crutches, or braces or who have a limp or balance problems. Ask the custodian to switch from regular to slip-resistant floor wax to provide more gripping action under foot. Doing this may cut down on slips and falls taken by other students as well.

Check your classroom for barriers that could impede a blind student. Any change in the floor level created by steps, thresholds, textures of floor surface, platforms, or transitions higher than one-quarter inch from one type of floor surface to another could cause a blind person to trip. Slick floor surfaces are dangerous for them, too. Carpet edges that are not tacked down could also cause tripping.

A blind person who uses a cane might have difficulty with a carpeted surface. A cane tapped against the floor surface provides aural and tactile information to its user about what is ahead. On a carpet the sound of cane taps are muffled and the touch of the cane on the surface is muted so sensory information is not as clear. Canes also provide information about objects that are in the way. However, they do not alert their user to objects that are protruding from the wall, such as fire extinguishers or coat racks. The cane will go along the floor, right underneath the object, indicating a clear passageway where none really exists, so remove protruding objects that do not have to be there and mark the ones that must remain by placing another object, such as a planter, chair, or trash can, on the floor underneath or to either side of it.

If you are doing writing, art, or any other kind of activity that requires the use of tables or desks, make sure the top surface is high enough for the arms of a wheelchair to fit underneath. For most wheelchairs, this means a clearance of thirty inches from the floor to the bottom of the tabletop. If your tables are not that high, check their legs; some tables have legs that can be extended. If legs cannot be adjusted, the table could be temporarily raised by placing equally thick objects, such as telephone books or blocks of wood, underneath all of the legs. Make sure that whatever you use will not slip out and pin the person in the wheelchair under the table.

For students who have muscular or motor impairments, adaptive scissors and other art equipment that require the use of less muscle strength or have firmer or larger hand grips can be purchased through special-needs equipment catalogs and supply houses. Pencils, pens, and other writing implements can have their grips enhanced or enlarged with inexpensive rubber additions from your local office supply store.

Place all equipment and materials to be used by a student who is in a wheelchair or who has limited mobility easily within arms' reach. She will not be able to stand up and reach across the table the same way typically developing students can. Blind students will also need materials placed within arms' reach and the location of each item verbally identified.

Some individuals who have low vision are very light-sensitive. For those who can see better with more light, increase the general lighting level in your classroom. Brighten dark spots or areas where there are potential hazards. If you are on a stage, be sure no lights are angled so that they glare into the eyes of a student who has limited mobility. If their chair or wheelchair is placed in the beam of the light, they may not be able to move themselves out of its path. A verbal student can tell you to move her, but a nonverbal student cannot.

If you can, keep the classroom free from distracting noises and white sound, such as that created by fans, furnaces, or air conditioners. Blind students need to clearly hear what is going on. Also bear in mind that hearing aids and cochlear implants will pick up white noise and sounds that hearing people with normal hearing automatically tune out.

In the same vein, be aware of the visual distractions in the room. Lots of competing colors or moving objects could be distracting or confusing to deaf students as well as to students with attention deficits. If you stand in front of a moving object, a deaf student who is naturally visually oriented will not be able to focus on you.

Accessible Stages

Most theatres have not been designed with wheelchair accessibility in mind. In most theatre designs, stages are raised above the level of the audience and are reached backstage and in front by stairs. Many backstage areas, such as dressing rooms, the lighting grid, and the light/sound booth, can often be reached only by ladders or stairs. This, obviously, creates barriers for students who have orthopedic disabilities.

If your organization's stage is inaccessible, some structural modifications are in order. Perhaps a temporary ramp can be borrowed or built to connect the stage in front or backstage with floor level. To be safe and usable by most wheelchairs, the ramps should be at least 36 inches wide and have not more than an 8.3 percent slope. In other words, for every twelve feet of horizontal run to a ramp, there should be only one foot rise. Ramps should have a railing or raised curb on any open side but not next to a wall, to prevent wheelchairs from rolling off.

A high stage will necessitate a long ramp. If space is limited, ramps can be built in an L-shape or with a switchback. Obviously, constructing a ramp of this type can turn into a major carpentry project. An alternative solution might be to rent or buy a mechanical lift to raise students who are in wheelchairs from one level to another.

During the 1980s and 1990s the Bethesda Academy of Performing Arts rented space in an old elementary-school building and had an accessibility problem with its stage that was corrected with a semi-permanent ramp. Brick walls surrounding the stage made it impossible to make renovations backstage without major structural changes. We were on a very limited budget as well. Faced with these limitations, Steve Holliday, our technical consultant, added a ramp across the front of the stage from left to right, parallel to the audience. As luck would have it, the ramp fit perfectly at the correct 8.3 rise from the floor stage right to a

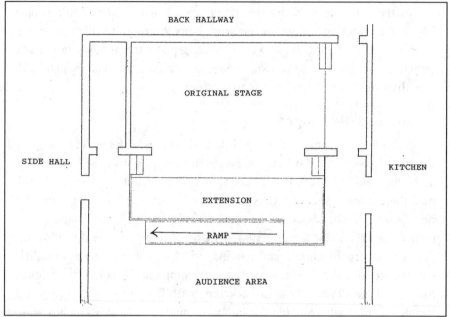

Figure 5: Modifications to the Academy stage.

small turn-around platform stage left. Actors who could not climb stairs could enter from the stage-right hallway at floor level and cross up the ramp onto the stage. If they needed to be on stage at the start of the performance or if they made their first entrance from backstage, they would go up the ramp before the show started to get into place.

The new ramp was greeted with great enthusiasm by students and faculty alike. Not only did it make the stage accessible to students with orthopedic disabilities, it made the stage easier to use by all students. Actors no longer had to worry about making an entrance from the audience in the dark and tripping on dimly lit steps. Dancers could dance up onto the stage. Small children could parade onto the stage, taking whatever size steps their little legs best managed. The new ramp added new levels to the stage, making it more theatrically dynamic and visually exciting. In various productions, the ramp became a hillside, a sliding board, a gangplank, and a hiding place. Later on, the direction of the ramp was changed to reach from down center stage out into the center aisle of the audience. This created a hanimichi-style ramp, like that used in Kabuki theatre in Japan, which juts out into the audience at a 45- or 90-degree angle.

In other theatre designs, ramps have been incorporated in other ways. The Bachman Lake Recreation Center in Dallas, Texas, specifically designed to be used by people with disabilities, solved the issue of stage accessibility by ramping the backstage left area down through a passage opening to the stage left hallway.

The Columbia campus of the Maryland School for the Deaf has an auditorium design based on ancient Greek amphitheatres. This creates a very exciting and accessible performance space. The stage is on the same level as the first row of the audience. The seating in the house is raked (raised in level, row by row) so the audience has an optimally unencumbered and dramatic view of the stage. The lobby at the back of the theatre is at the same level as the stage and is connected to it and the house by passageways on either side of the raked auditorium. The light/sound booth is backstage right on the same level as the stage floor. Actors and technicians can get around on stage and backstage easily because everything is on the same level.

Make sure that the architect or consultant who designs your theatre or modifications to it understands accessibility issues *and* the unique needs of theatre architecture. If she doesn't, have an expert in technical theatre look over her plans *before* you approve them and begin building. Theatres which are designed without an understanding of how actors, directors, and designers use theatre space end up with bad acoustics, poor audience sightlines, limited options for the flow of actor movement, little or no offstage wing space, no fly space above the stage for scenery and lights, and a myriad of other frustrating architecture problems.

Orthopedic Disabilities

Students who have orthopedic disabilities can participate in most of the typical activities done in the drama classroom. Focus on exercises that develop students' imaginations, verbal abilities, facial expressions, and physical expressiveness in the parts of their bodies that they *can* move.

Adaptive devices, such as wheelchairs, were invented to give people as much mobility as possible, not to keep them stationary. When acting out stories and scenes, let students move their wheelchairs around the room just as they normally would at home or on the playground. If a child has cerebral palsy or is paralyzed and is unable to move her wheelchair herself, an assistant can move it for her. There's no reason why Little Red Riding Hood can't go to her grandmother's house in her wheelchair or why the Big Bad Wolf can't follow her in his!

When guiding an actor in the creation of a character, place emphasis first on the development of the actor's emotional connection with the character and then on her ability to express herself through the dialogue with words and sound. You can include as much movement in scenes and games as your student feels comfortable with. Every student will be different. Some may feel very comfortable with their bodies and enjoy joining in a spirited aerobic warm-up for the upper body, a relay race, a pantomime game, or a wheelchair dance. Others may feel more inhibited. Gauge your use of movement by the ability and comfort level of the individual.

A wheelchair takes up more space than a body; therefore, the more wheelchairs in a classroom, the larger your classroom needs to be in order to accommodate wheelchair movement. Wheelchair traffic jams can be frustrating and collisions can be dangerous. Games, such as Come Along (see Chapter 7) are safe if there are only one or two wheelchairs in the circle; more than that and you can end up with massive collisions as students race to their places at the end of a round.

If you are uncertain what types of activities are safe or appropriate for your students, contact a physical therapist or a therapeutic recreation specialist in your area. For help finding experts in your area, contact Disabled Sports USA (www.dsusa.org), formerly National Handicapped Sports, which has more than eighty chapters and affiliates around the U.S., National Sports Center for the Disabled (www.nscd.org), the American Dance Therapy Association (www.adta.org), the American Physical Therapy Association (www.apta.org), the American Therapeutic Recreation Association (www.atra-online.com), or the National Therapeutic Recreation Society (www.nrpa.org).

photo by Lea Ann Rosen

Figure 6: Wheelchairs can become a taxi, carriage, or moveable throne.

Take a look at your repertoire of theatre games to see how you could adapt different activities in order to bypass your students' physical limitations. For instance, games, such as Come Along, Fruit Salad, or The Winds are Blowing, in which players sitting in a circle exchange seats, could be adapted so players change *places*. Places can be delineated on the floor with pieces of tape, and wheelchairs can be moved at the appropriate time to a new location in the circle.

If you can't figure out how to adapt a game or if the student's movement limitations would put him at a disadvantage to others in an inclusive classroom situation, do not play that game. There are hundreds of drama games! Choose one that stresses activities and actions that your student *can* do. Let everyone use their strengths to participate.

Although it is not necessary to do so, there are many creative ways to incorporate a mobility device into a story, play, or scene. A wheelchair can become the King's throne, the Queen's carriage, a horse, a machine, a boat, or an automobile. A walker can be transformed into a storefront for a merchant, moving camouflage that the hero or the villain hides behind, or a cage for a wild animal. Through imagination, crutches can be turned into a rifle, a battering ram, or the wings of a bird.

Cerebral Palsy

Cerebral palsy is a condition caused by damage to the brain before or during birth. It affects the brain's ability to control motor functions in the muscles. There are many specific causes, including pre-natal trauma, the mother's infection during pregnancy with German measles or another viral disease, lead poisoning, head injuries, and insufficient oxygen to the brain during birth. The major damage usually is caused by insufficient oxygen. Cerebral palsy's effects on movement and posture can range from mild to severe. It can affect the whole body or only one part of it, for example, only the arms, the legs, one side, or the top or bottom half of the body. A person with cerebral palsy also may have muscle spasms, involuntary movements, slurred speech, speech delays, and difficulty with sight, hearing, or other sensory perceptions.

Depending on the severity of the condition and the parts of the body affected by the disorder, Students with cerebral palsy might use a wheelchair, walker, or crutches — or they might be actively mobile and able to participate in any kind of physical activity. As with other orthopedic disabilities, adjust your class's movement activities to the specific abilities and interests of your students.

People who have cerebral palsy fall into the full range of cognitive processing abilities. Some have average intelligence, some have above average intelligence; and about twenty-five percent have cognitive disabilities. Don't assess your student's cognitive abilities on the basis of physical appearance, speech, or motor coordination. A person who has cerebral palsy can have speech that is so slurred or movements that are so spasmodic that she "appears" to be mentally challenged. However, the chances are that her mental functioning is completely normal. If you are unsure, ask the child's parents or check with her schoolteachers.

Slurred speech can pose a problem in dramatic production, since clear diction is important for the audience to understand what the actors are saying. Encourage your actor to take her time and form each word completely before going on to the next. A slower, clearer, and more distinct delivery of a line is better than a quickly delivered line that sounds muddy. The key to clear stage diction is enunciation of the consonants in words (Lessac 1967). Consonants create each word's sound-shape. Ending each word clearly with its final consonant (if it has one) will help separate the sound of one word from the next.

Many students who have speech difficulties regularly go to speech therapy. You might suggest the student work on her lines with her therapist. Working on a project that the student is excited and motivated about, instead of an abstract speech exercise, can often yield positive results on both fronts.

Understanding the subtext and the intention of the lines and then communicating it to the audience is ultimately more important for an actor than impeccable diction. Even if a student's lines remain slurred, the audience will understand most of what is happening by reading the actor's emotions, tone of voice, intensity, and relationship with the other characters. A good director can enhance the meaning of a scene by creating clear stage pictures and motivating the actors with blocking and stage business that express the dramatic action of the scene.

For those readers who are not theatre artists: *Stage pictures* are the pictures created by the actors' bodies in relationship to each other and to the stage setting. *Blocking* is the theatre term for movement by an actor on stage. *Stage business* refers to gestures, use of props, and other physical actions in addition to blocking which an actor uses to physically express her character. Stage pictures, blocking, and stage business are three of the tools the director has for expressing the *dramatic action* — what is emotionally happening between the characters in the play. *Dramatic action* ultimately moves the plot of the play forward (Hodge 1971).

One issue that can come up in relation to cerebral palsy is salivary overflow, commonly called *drooling*. Unfortunately, many people have negative reactions to drooling and this can cause problems when you are trying to help a student seek acceptance in a class in which positive social interaction is important. Drooling is associated with babies and immaturity. The physical reality is that no one has conscious control over her salivary glands. Most people are able to swallow saliva when it builds up in their mouths. Some people who have cerebral palsy, but not all, do not have this ability because of their motor-control difficulties. The saliva stays in their mouths, with nowhere else to go, building up until it comes dribbling out.

I have read a number of articles — some angry, some humorous — by individuals who have cerebral palsy and who involuntarily drool. They do not like drooling any better than anyone else does, but they accept it as a fact of their lives. Surgical solutions have been tried, but they do not offer great success rates. Barrier creams and pump devices have been invented, but they are not really practical. Speech therapists sometimes recommend chewing gum because the chewing action forces the chewer to swallow periodically. Sometimes a periodic, quiet reminder to "swallow" works.

The hygiene issue related to drooling must be addressed in a classroom or recreational situation. If you have a sink in your room, you could suggest to your student that she wash her hands before class or before a game that involves touching or holding hands. If you do not have a sink, you could keep moist towelettes or hand sanitizer available for everyone's use. The most practical solution, and the one that puts the individual in control of her own situation, seems to be for the student to carry a small towel or to wear a terrycloth armband to wipe away excess drips. If a student who has a drooling problem does not already use one of these methods, you might suggest one or keep a towel on hand for her to use while in your class.

Model accepting behavior for typically developing students. If you are "grossed out" or "turned off" by a student's drooling and show it, the other students will pick up on your attitude and mirror it. If you act as if it is not a big deal, they will probably begin to feel this way, too. You might be able to address the issue indirectly in a creative drama class by acting out a story, such as "Beauty and the Beast" or "The Ugly Duckling," which deals with outer ugliness and inner beauty. If you think drooling needs to be addressed more directly, for example, if fellow students are refusing to hold the student's hand or are making rude comments, sit down and have an open discussion about the situation. Ultimately, you and your students must learn to look beyond the physical appearance and accept the person inside.

Spina Bifida

Spina bifida is the most common birth defect and is comes about because of a neural tube defect early *in utero* which results in incomplete closure of the spinal column. Many causes for this condition have been proposed (among them, abnormal metabolism or deficiency of the vitamin folic acid, the mother's elevated body temperature during the first trimester of pregnancy due to fever or hot baths, obesity) but for most cases of spina bifida, no cause is known. Sometimes surgery is required to repair the condition at birth. Depending on the type of spina bifida (where the neural tube defect is), a person who has spina bifida may have mobility impairments which require the use of crutches, a walker, or a wheelchair because there is usually paralysis and sensory loss below the defect. Bladder and bowel problems may be present and must be addressed with catheters and/or colostomies. Some people have hydrocephalus, a condition in which fluid doesn't drain out of the brain into the spinal cord. This must be corrected surgically very early in life with placement of a shunt, an internal tube that sends the fluid down into the abdomen, or the person will experience brain damage and become mentally impaired. Eighty percent of people who have spina bifida have normal to above-normal intelligence, but many of them have learning disabilities which involve difficulties with proprioception (awareness of the body in space) and problems with motor skills, attention, memory, and organization. Typically they are very socially adept and good with words but poor in math and have difficulty with eye-hand coordination and writing (Lollar 2001). See Chapters 4, 5, 6, and 7 for adaptation techniques to use with learning disabilities.

Many people who have spina bifida have severe allergies to latex, possibly due to undergoing many necessary medical procedures involving the use of rubber gloves and other sterile equipment containing latex. People can be exposed to latex when products that contain rubber come in contact with skin or mucous membranes of the eyes, mouth, or other parts of the body or microscopic latex particles are breathed in through the nose or mouth. If food is handled by someone wearing latex gloves or if a catheter or colostomy bag is changed by someone wearing latex gloves, an allergic reaction can happen. Symptoms of an allergic reaction are watery and itchy eyes, sneezing, coughing, or wheezing, rash or hives, swelling of the windpipe, difficulty breathing, and possibly life-threatening anaphylactic shock. Products to avoid in a drama classroom are balloons; rubber bands; elastic in costumes, clothing, or masks; beach toys; Koosh balls; art supplies, such as molding clay, Play Dough, and acrylic paint; latex or rubber gloves; and adhesive bandages, such as Band-Aids (Meeropol 2001). Because of the medical dangers involved in such serious allergic reactions, unless told otherwise, stay on the safe side and assume your student does have a latex allergy.

Osteogenesis Imperfecta

Osteogenesis imperfecta (OI) is a rare disorder, but I include information on it because I have had a number of students with OI who have had great talent and found great emotional outlet in drama. OI is a genetic disorder, inherited through a dominant gene or a spontaneous mutation, which causes bones and teeth to be brittle and break easily. Often people with OI are of short stature because their bones don't grow to full length and, even if they did, they wouldn't be strong enough to support a tall body. Depending on their bone strength, people with OI may be able to walk by themselves or may need to use crutches, walkers, braces, wheelchairs, or some combination of assistive mobility devices. You will see your students with OI in lightweight casts, slings, splints, or braces when bones break as they inevitably will do. Many people with OI have loose joints and poor muscle development in arms and legs, a barrel-shaped rib cage, spinal curvature, and triangular face. Some people bruise easily. The whites of their eyes could have a blue, gray, or purple tint instead of being white. Their voices tend to remain high-pitched because of small lung capacity, which creates a lack of vocal resonance. Respiratory problems occur frequently. They may also have hearing loss due to fixation or fracture of bones in the ear.

As a teacher, your first impulse will be to want your students with OI to remain immobile so they don't get hurt. However, people with OI need physical exercise to build bone and muscle strength. While participating in games such as a relay race or Red Rover would be very dangerous, participating in Pass the Sound/Pass the Movement,

Machines, or other games where people move but don't touch each other, would be fine. Don't push or pull a limb or bend it into an awkward position, but gently touching someone with OI (with their permission, of course) is usually okay.

Diabetes

Insulin is necessary for the body to turn glucose, which has been obtained from what we eat, into energy that the cells of the body can use for food. In diabetes the insulin-producing cells in the pancreas either cannot make insulin (type 1) or cannot make enough (type 2). Without enough insulin, glucose builds up in the blood because it cannot be used, so a person literally begins to starve to death. At the same time the excess glucose in the bloodstream can damage organs, such as the eyes, kidneys, lower extremities, and nervous system. Too much glucose can cause a person to go into a diabetic coma and too much insulin can cause a person to go into insulin shock; in either situation the person may die. To keep their insulin and glucose levels in balance, people who have diabetes have to frequently monitor their blood glucose levels, take insulin injections or oral medicine each day, and eat diabetic meals and snacks every day. There is a general belief that cases of type 2 diabetes are increasing in the U.S. population. If this is so, you may see more and more students who have diabetes in your classes.

A student who has diabetes should wear a medical-alert bracelet or band and should communicate with the group leader in advance about her condition and what to do in case of emergency. She may need to have a scheduled snack at some point during your class or rehearsal for her health and safety. Know what to look for in case of insulin shock or diabetic shock. In both instances, the affected individual often becomes confused and may not be able to communicate clearly what is wrong.

Symptoms of hypoglycemia (low glucose/high insulin) can occur if a student has missed a meal or a scheduled snack, isn't taking medications as prescribed, has exercised too much, is fatigued, or is seriously stressed. Her pulse will become strong and rapid; her breathing will be shallow; her skin will become pale and sweaty; she may report headaches, hunger, or dizziness, or feel faint; her body may tremble; and she may behave in a belligerent or confused manner. In fact, sometimes people who are about to go into insulin shock are often thought to be drunk or high because their speech becomes incoherent and their body lurches uncontrollably. The best intervention is to sit her down and perform the *ABCs* of first aid: check her *Airway* to make sure nothing is blocking her breath, make sure she is *Breathing*, and loosen her clothing to make sure she has adequate blood *Circulation*. Then have her eat something with high sugar/low fat content — hard candy, not a chocolate candy bar — or drink some juice. If she loses consciousness, call for medical help (911) immediately and do not try to feed her.

If she has hyperglycemia (high glucose/low insulin), her pulse will become weak and rapid; her breathing will become deep and she will sigh frequently; her skin will be flushed, dry, and warm; her breath will smell like a musty apple or nail polish; she will complain of nausea; and she will walk unsteadily. Sit her down and do the ABCs of first aid. Immediately call 911.

Keep some kind of sweet snack and water on hand whether you know you have a student with diabetes or not. You never know when you will need it. Also make sure you have access to a phone or cell phone in case any emergencies occur.

Blindness

In the United States, the term "blindness" is used to refer to vision of less than 20/200 in the better eye, even with corrective lenses. That is, when 20 feet away from an object, the person sees — at best — what someone with normal vision would see at 200 feet. Most blind people are not totally blind; they have varying amounts of visual perception. Some can see light but not defined shapes. Others are limited in their field of vision; for example, they may not have any peripheral vision, they may have macular degeneration that destroys the center of their vision, or they may not be able to see out of one eye. Terms for various visual impairments include: *partially sighted*, *low vision*, and *legally blind*. Blindness can be congenital or caused by glaucoma, diabetes, retinal disintegration, muscular disorders, cataracts, infection, or injury to the eye or optic nerve. The vision centers in the brain are in the occipital lobe at the back of the head. A blow to the back of the head that injures that area could also result in blindness.

People who are blind need lots of aural, tactile, and kinesthetic stimulation to make up for the visual information they miss out on. They learn how to structure their environment and remember spatial relationships so they can function independently. With encouragement to take risks, they can become confident, self-reliant, and independent.

Only five to ten percent of people who are blind learn to read Braille, the raised-dot system invented in 1824 by Louis Braille. Typically people who are born blind will be taught Braille in school. Older people who lose their sight do not always bother to learn a new way to read; instead, they often prefer recordings or large-print materials.

In the last ten years audio description has been incorporated into television programming, some movies, and theatre productions to help blind audience members understand the physical actions that happen which are not talked about. A chip can be put into a TV to pick up audio description; in movies and theatres a headset can be worn and live audio description is broadcast through it during the show.

Here's an example of how audio description works. Imagine the following scene: JoAnn and Bob are married and giving each other the silent treatment over a disagreement. JoAnn enters a room and walks past Bob, ignoring him and Bob sees her but does not talk to her. A blind person would have no idea what was going on in the silence. An audio description of that interaction might be, "Bob is sitting on the sofa reading a book. JoAnn enters and walks past him. Bob looks up from his book, sees her, and looks back down."

When you are teaching students who are blind, speak clearly and at a normal pace and volume level. There is no need to shout. Blind people are blind, not hard of hearing.

Remember that many nonverbal communication cues, such as facial expressions, shaking the head "yes" or "no," shoulder shrugs, and hand gestures, are visual communications that cannot be picked up without sight. You will need to verbalize these nonverbal communications. Many times when we speak to others or ask them to do something, we initiate the interaction with eye contact. You might look at Susie and say, "Go to the front of the room and perform your monologue now." A blind student will not know you are looking at her or talking to her unless you address her by name first. "Susie, go to the front of the room and perform your monologue now."

In a similar vein, a blind person will not know who is around her unless the individuals who are there identify themselves. While she may have a good memory for voices, do not rely on it or play "guess who this is." It is good manners to tell a blind person when someone is entering or leaving the group or the room. You might say, "Phil is walking over here. Hi, Phil." If Phil decides to leave, he should say goodbye or verbally indicate that he is leaving. If he forgets, you can say, "Bye, Phil," or "Phil just went over to the other side of the room."

Warn a blind person before you touch her. Tell her if you are reaching out to shake hands. If you think through what you normally do nonverbally and physically, and take the time to translate that into verbal communication, the blind person will know what is going on.

Often in drama, ideas and instructions are shared through demonstration of an activity rather than talking about it. Blind students will not be able to see your demonstration. You will need to translate your demonstration into words. If appropriate, you could have your blind students follow your demonstration through touch. For instance, if you were demonstrating how to play The Magic Tube, a pantomime game described in Chapter 7, and you were pretending that the tube was a spyglass, you could say, "I am putting one end of the tube up to my right eye and pretending that I am looking through it." Or you could allow the blind student to put her hands on the tube and you to feel the placement in relation to your body.

Many blind people report that their most frustrating and frequently occurring experience is sighted people jumping in to "help" before finding out if the help is needed or wanted. Always ask before you help. It may be that your student can get around fine on her own and does not need any assistance.

If a student has a cane, do not move it from where she has placed it, as she has put it easily within her reach and will need to find it later on. If your student has a guide dog, remember it is a highly trained assistant, not a pet. From the outset, tell your other students not to feed or play with it. If the children in the class are young and have difficulty understanding this concept, you could discuss other animals that have jobs to do and act them out.

If you do need to guide your student from one place to another, the proper way is to stand to one side, offer your arm, and allow her to hold your elbow. She will take her movement cues from the movement of your body. Pick a pace that is easy for her to follow — not too fast and not too slow. Describe obstacles coming up and how to proceed around them: turn right, turn left, step up, step down, etc. If right and left are confusing concepts say, "Turn in my direction" or "Turn in your direction." "This way" or "that way" does not mean a thing to someone who cannot see where you are looking or pointing. It is a good idea to describe distances in terms of number of feet rather than number of steps as people have different lengths of stride.

When you lead a blind person to a seat, do not push her down into it. Put her hand on the back or the arm of the chair and she will use that as her reference point. She can take it from there.

Do not feel awkward about using expressions that refer to sight like "See you next week" or "You're looking good today." Your use of language will not be interpreted as insulting or demeaning. People with visual impairments use those words and expressions, too. They know that you can see and rarely are envious of your ability.

Blind students need to feel as much a part of the class as possible. When other students are performing a scene or presenting an exercise in which physical actions happen, assign a sighted student or an assistant to quietly describe the physical actions to the blind student. Do not talk during the lines, but insert concise descriptions during the silences, as in audio description.

There are many drama games done sitting in a circle. Start with these while your blind students are getting adjusted to the class. This will help them locate all the voices within a configuration that is even and regular. All faces (and therefore all voices) will be facing into the center instead of away from each other (as in a traditional classroom set-up) so the blind student will be able to hear everyone clearly. Many games highlight and develop tactile and aural sensitivities. One of my blind students had hearing so acute that if another student made a noise to indicate his location, she could throw a ball directly to him.

Don't avoid activities that get students up on their feet and moving around. Blind people love to dance, pantomime, play movement games, and use their bodies just like sighted people do. Before you turn your students loose, however, make sure your acting space is open and free of obstacles. If your floor is carpeted, check to see that the edges lie flat and there are no loose strings to trip on. If your floor is waxed, be sure the surface is not too slippery.

When considering performance opportunities for blind students, many people jump to the conclusion that Readers Theatre is the perfect style of performance to use because the need to move on stage is curtailed. In Readers Theatre the actors sit on stage in chairs or on stools and read their lines instead of memorizing them. Readers Theatre is a great way to develop oral interpretation skills because the entire performance is created through the actors' voices. Like radio theatre, Readers Theatre relies on the audience's imaginations rather than the physical production to bring the story to life. Since little is performed visually, the entire play must be communicated through dialogue and sound. This type of theatre is an excellent challenge for any student of acting. It trains verbal dexterity and vocal variety. Remember, however, that not all blind people read Braille and, therefore, may have a difficult time reading their lines!

Acting involves the voice *and* the body. Limiting blind students to a non-moving style of theatre will limit the development of their acting skills. Blind actors have the ability to move as skillfully on a stage set as they do in their own homes. Spike (mark with tape) the position of the furniture on your stage so that each time you set up for rehearsal the spatial relationships are the same. Then give the blind actor time to explore the space and memorize the distance between objects.

Use sounds or lines of dialogue for cues in places where sighted actors would follow visual cues.

If your student reads Braille, you can type up scripts and assignments for her on a Braille typewriter. Computer programs exist which can print out on a Braille printer. If a blind student can read large print, the size of the script can be enlarged by changing the document's font size. Many people have a scanner, which eliminates the necessity of retyping scripts into a document. There is even a device, similar to a bar-code scanner in supermarkets, that can "read" print from a book out loud and transfer it to the computer.

Check with local support groups for the blind or schools for the blind to locate Brailling equipment or computer programs that can be rented, borrowed, or bought. Some organizations will do Braille translating for you for a fee, usually a combination of hourly rate for the time the project takes plus a charge per Braille page. If your student does not read Braille or if Brailling equipment is too expensive or difficult to find, scenes and monologue assignments can be recorded on tape or CD.

Deafness

Estimates place the number of Americans with a hearing loss of some kind at 28 million (NAD website 2005). The vast majority are hard of hearing, while about two million are deaf. Very few people are "stone deaf," meaning that they hear nothing. Most deaf and hard-of-hearing people can hear certain frequencies of sound but not others. Hearing loss may be present from birth or may develop at any time during a person's life, can range from mild to severe, and can be caused by heredity, birth defects, accident, or illness. The defect in the hearing process may be located anywhere in the auditory system from the eardrum through the cochlea to the auditory cortex of the brain.

Hearing aids amplify sound for certain types of hearing loss, but not for others. Beginning in the 1990s, cochlear implants began to be used in people who had hearing loss due to damage to their cochlea. Like hearing aids, this technology does not cure deafness but sometimes enhances the ability to hear. Cochlear implants tend to be more successful for people who were able to hear and understand language before becoming deaf (postlingual deafness) rather than for people who were born deaf (pre-lingually deaf) and never were able to use sound and language to develop their auditory cortex. Success with cochlear implants varies greatly from individual to individual.

Deafness is not connected to intelligence in any way. The National Association for the Deaf says that the term "deaf and dumb" originates with Greek philosopher Aristotle who felt deaf people were not capable of learning or of reasoned thinking. Needless to say, this is not so. There are all ranges of intelligence in deaf people, just as there are in hearing people. Later the term "dumb" came to mean "silent" or "mute." This is also a misnomer. Most deaf people have nothing wrong with their vocal cords. Many deaf people can speak with their voice. Even more speak with their hands via sign language (NAD website 2005).

The primary challenge of deafness is language development and communication. For all humans the early acquisition of language is essential for the development of thought and cognitive processes as well as essential for academic, vocational, and social success in life. *The Miracle Worker*, a play about deaf-blind Helen Keller, focuses on the struggle of a child who has no language and, therefore, has no clear method of communication or socialization. In the play Annie Sullivan, the teacher who finally breaks through the isolation imposed by Helen's sensory disabilities, says, "Language is to the mind more than light is to the eye…What is she without words? With them she can think, have ideas, be reached, there's not a thought or fact in the world that can't be hers" (Gibson 1960).

The human brain seems to be "hardwired" for the bulk of language development to take place between infancy and the age of five or six. This is why it is so easy for a young child to learn a second or third language and why that is so difficult for someone who is older. A hearing child picks up sound from the moment of birth and receives continuous aural sound and language stimulation. Even when people are not talking to her directly, she hears what is being said around her, absorbing a great deal of information about how people relate to each other and how the world works. A child who is born deaf, or who loses her hearing at an early age, misses that constant aural exposure. The appropriate substitute for deaf children is to receive constant visual language stimulation through signs, gestures, facial expressions, finger-spelling, or cued speech. Without language, deaf children become handicapped; with language — be it spoken, signed, cued, or written — deaf children can function as well as hearing children.

There has in the past been a great deal of controversy in the deaf community and between the deaf and hearing communities about the best way to teach language and communication to deaf children. For many years hearing educators insisted on oral communication, teaching children to speak and to speech-read. (Most hearing people are familiar with the term lip-read.) Sign language was forbidden in schools for the deaf. Many deaf adults tell stories about how they were punished when they were caught signing at school.

Oral communication has drawbacks. Only about thirty percent of the sounds of the English language are visible on the lips and fifty percent of them look identical. For example, the same lip shape is used for b and p; b is voiced while p is not.

Cued speech, developed in the late 1960s by Dr. R. Orin Cornett at Gallaudet College, is a system of hand shapes that represent all the different consonant and vowel sounds in the English language. Used as people speak to each other, cued speech signals clarify the visual similarity of lip shapes and solve the difficulty of speech-reading. Cued speech is sometimes the preferred communication choice of people who have lost their hearing after they have acquired spoken English.

A communication method preferred by many deaf people is sign language. American Sign Language (ASL) is a visual language developed by the deaf for the deaf. It was imported from France in 1817 by Thomas Hopkins Gallaudet, an American hearing educator, and Laurent Clerc, a French deaf educator who had taught for many years in schools for the deaf in France (Sacks 1989). Sign language is not a universal language; each country has its own unique system of signs and finger spelling. Because modern American and French sign languages share roots, they have many similarities, but because they have developed independently since the early 1800s, they also have differences.

Many ASL signs are based on natural gesture; they look like the action or object they symbolize. ASL syntax and grammar are as different from English as English is from Swahili. In ASL, sentences are structured with the time element first, followed by object, subject, and verb. Negatives and modifiers are placed after the verb. This contrasts with English grammar, which is structured subject-verb-object. For example, in English you say, "I'm going to the store now," but in ASL you sign, "Now store me go" or "Now store go me." ASL also has its own idioms and figures of speech. If someone does not get a joke in English you say, "You missed the boat." In ASL, you sign, "Train gone."

ASL is a visual-concept language involving the whole body: hands, arms, eyes, facial expression, body tension, and directional inclination. To read an ASL speaker, one needs to see from their waist to their head. One sign can be expressed in a wide variety of ways and each way takes on a different shade of meaning (Sacks 1989). In English this type of expression is offered primarily through word choice based on connotation (associated meaning) and tone of voice.

Finger-spelling supplements signs. In finger-spelling, each letter in a word is formed individually using the right or left hand. The word is literally spelled out for the viewer. However, as one begins to read finger-spelling, many frequently used words are perceived as moving shapes rather than as individual letters.

Signed English (SE), Seeing Essential English (SEE1), Signing Exact English (SEE2), Manually Coded English (MCE), and Pidgin Signed English (PSE) are all sign-language systems that involve deaf signs with English sentence structure. They are used most often by hearing people who sign and do not think in ASL or by teachers who are teaching correct English grammar.

As mentioned earlier, most deaf people are able to speak. However, even with many years of intensive speech therapy, a deaf person may have difficulty creating the same pitches, intonations, and tones that hearing people do. This is because part of the speaking process involves an ongoing self-monitoring of the voice. Many deaf people cannot hear how they sound and, therefore, cannot make those adjustments. Without the ability to self-monitor, their voices can sound flat or high or off-key. Many hearing people jump to the mistaken conclusion that this unusual sounding speech is a sign of low intelligence and treat the deaf person as if she is mentally defective. Knowing this chronic misunderstanding, some deaf people choose not to speak.

Deaf people have a whole culture of their own of which the hearing world is often unaware. In fact, many deaf people do not identify with their deafness as being part of a disability group; instead, they feel deafness puts them into a cultural minority. There is a lot of pride in Deaf culture. Deaf artists create Deaf poetry, drama, and prose. Many communities across the country have their own Theatre of the Deaf, which presents plays in a highly theatrical, visually poetic version of

ASL. More and more Deaf actors, such as Phyllis Frelich, Ed Water-street, Lou Ferigamo, Howie Seago, and Marlee Matlin, have crossed over into the hearing world and their talents show up on stage, film, and television.

Many devices have been invented that make functioning in the modern world easier for deaf people. The teletypewriter (TTY) sends typed messages via phone lines to other TTYs, which are found in many public places as well as in deaf homes. Email and instant messages have revolutionized deaf people's ability to easily communicate with each other and with hearing people. The TDI, a phone relay service, makes connecting between a TTY and a telephone possible. If the message is coming from a deaf person, she will contact the TDI operator via her TTY. The operator (who is hearing) will telephone the hearing friend and speak the message that the deaf friend has written. The hearing friend tells the operator her response, which is relayed by the operator via TTY to the deaf friend. It takes a lot longer than instant messaging, TTY, or regular telephone communications, but it works.

When a deaf student signs up for a drama class, the first thing to ascertain is which communication system she uses. A student who uses cued speech will not necessarily understand sign language and vice versa. If the teacher does not know the preferred communication system, it may be necessary to employ an interpreter. Contact an interpreting service organization in your area or the Registry of Interpreters for the Deaf (RID) which maintains a national list of certified interpreters. It may be possible to integrate deaf children into a dance or visual arts class without an interpreter as the subject matter is so visual and the teacher's verbal explanations so minimal, but drama classes, which tend to be more verbal, need to be interpreted.

An interpreter will translate the English spoken by the hearing people in the room into ASL for the deaf person and will translate ASL into spoken English for the hearing. The interpreter may also function as the deaf person's voice. When using an interpreter, always look at and speak directly to the deaf person. Do not talk to the interpreter. She is only there to facilitate the communication, not to interact in the situation. Interpreters follow their own code of ethics, which includes not inserting counseling, advising, or personal opinions into a conversation. They are required to "render the message faithfully, always conveying the content and spirit of the speaker using language most readily understood by the person(s) whom they serve." (RID 2005).

When teaching deaf or hard-of-hearing students, there are a number of things to keep in mind. First, use natural gestures and facial expressions as you speak. The more clearly you express yourself in a physical manner, the more you will communicate, not only to your deaf students but to all your students.

Stand where deaf or hard-of-hearing students can see your lips. Make sure that your face is in the light, not covered by shadows. If there is a window in the room, don't stand with your back to it. The shadow created by the light hitting your back will obscure your facial features. Stand facing the window or in a profile position to it so that the natural light can reach your face and hands.

Fluorescent lighting is very hard on the eyes. If possible, use a room with incandescent or natural lighting (skylight, windows). If you have windows, open the drapes and blinds to allow as much natural light into the room as possible.

Remember that deaf students cannot hear you. I know that sounds obvious, but I have watched hearing people forget this and yell at the back of a deaf person, then become enraged when the deaf person did not respond. When you speak, face the deaf person and make sure she is looking at you. If she cannot see that you are moving your mouth and looking at her, she may not know you are talking! You can get her attention by waving your hand or by tapping her gently on the shoulder.

When talking to a deaf person, you do not have to shout or exaggerate your speech. Doing so will distort the shape of your lips as you speak and will make speech-reading more difficult. Chewing gum or food will also distort your mouth as you talk.

Keep hands and other objects away from your face, so your facial features can be seen as you talk. Large hats will cover your eyes and obscure your facial expressions. Sunglasses will cover your eyes and make your emotional messages less clear.

When signing to a deaf person, stand between three and six feet away. At this distance you are close enough for her to see your face clearly and far enough away for her to take in your hands and the rest of your body. Standing too close will make it difficult for the student to take in the top half of your body, the area in which signs are made.

If a student speech-reads and has difficulty understanding what you are saying, it could be that you are using words that have letters that sound similar and are hard to distinguish from each other, for example, pig and big or dug and duck. Try rephrasing your sentence with different words. If the message still doesn't get across and an interpreter is not available, try writing a note.

If you are signing, be aware of the colors of the clothing you are wearing. Most signs are placed between the waist and the top of the head. In order for your hands to show up clearly as you sign, the colors on the top half of your body need to contrast with your skin color. For example, if you have light-colored skin, black, brown, dark blue, or purple would be good colors to wear. If you have dark skin, yellow, white, orange, or pastels would be best. Choose colors that are easy on the eye. Shocking pink, electric green, or shiny metallic silver would be hard to look at for a long period of time. Also, it is better to wear solid colors rather than plaids, stripes, or patterns.

Try to avoid creating sudden, loud sounds. Noises like balloon bursts, loud whines, or harsh buzzers may be of a frequency that could irritate a deaf or hard-of-hearing person's ears. Remember to also avoid white noise, as your voice will become lost in it for a hard-of-hearing person.

When explaining an idea to deaf students, it is often helpful to offer a number of examples to clarify what you are talking about. To a hearing student I might say, "Today we will do age pantomimes. Act out a character at a specific age and we will guess how old you are." To a deaf student I would say, "Today we do age pantomimes. Think of a person and pick an age: maybe very old, maybe very young, maybe baby, maybe fifteen, maybe thirty-two. I don't know. You decide. Act out how that person moves, walks, sits, whatever."

This kind of explanation contrasts with the way you would explain something to a student who had a cognitive disability. One or two well-chosen examples are enough for a person who has cognitive processing difficulties and cannot hold many items in short term memory. For a deaf student, many specific examples flesh out your concept and provide dimension to the idea you want to communicate. This approach mirrors the manner in which ASL expresses ideas. Often a series of signs listing many items in a category will be used instead of inventing a specific sign for that category. For instance, the word *crime* is described through the use of the signs for kill, stab, steal, etc. and the word *sports* might be expressed by signing baseball, football, basketball, etc.

Movement games, pantomime, and activities that stress visual, olfactory, kinesthetic, and tactile strengths will all work very well with deaf students. Many deaf people also have excellent rhythmic skills and enjoy dancing and making percussion music. They understand rhythm through visual rhythm and through vibrations that they can feel through the floor, the musical instrument, etc.

Place greater emphasis on visuality and physicality in your choice of exercises. For example, if you were doing a sensory awareness exercise with smells or textures, instead of having the student describe the experience in words, encourage her to translate it into movement. Have the student tell a story through pantomime or through a series of tableaux. This need to place emphasis on the physical is not because deaf people are not good with language, but because deaf theatre stresses the creation of visual images on stage. Deaf actors, therefore, need to develop the skills that they will use in their community and culture.

However, developing physical expressiveness alone is not enough; link all physical characterization work to an emotional base. For example, a successful pantomime of an old woman feeding birds in the park should recreate the old woman's feelings about the birds and being alone in the park, not just focus on technically reproducing her movements. No matter how brilliant her technique, an actor who is not emotionally connected to her work is boring to watch. Audiences want to feel there is a living, breathing, feeling human being beneath each character they see on stage.

If your class includes hearing and deaf students together, encourage your hearing students to communicate with their bodies and encourage your deaf students to improvise with words. When doing scripted or improvisational work, keep the action of the scene and all of the characters within the sightlines of the deaf actors. Whether they are speech-readers or signers, deaf actors won't be aware a line has been delivered if they cannot see it being said. By contrast, hearing actors can hear what is said even if they aren't looking directly at the speaker.

Incorporate sign language and sign-language games into your integrated classes. ASL is an excellent avenue for teaching the expressive use of gesture and how to make emotional-physical connections for hearing and deaf acting students alike. Signing teaches actors how to use their hands, arms, and face to express themselves in a natural way.

There might be an occasion when a deaf actor is cast in a speaking role. If so, she may need some diction coaching in order to be intelligible to audience members. See the earlier section in this chapter on working with students whose speech is slurred: focusing on consonant action should help. Practicing diaphragmatic breathing will help if she has problems with projection or breathiness. If the student receives speech therapy, she could work on her lines with her therapist.

Above all, don't fall into the stereotyped belief that because deaf students talk with their hands they will necessarily be experts at pantomime or movement activities and poor at verbal ones. I have met deaf people who could use their hands and bodies expressively and others who were physically unexpressive and inhibited. I have met deaf people who are extremely loquacious and I know others who are not. Deaf people are as individual and unique as hearing people. See the person, not the disability.

Recommended Reading

Bailey, S. D. & Agogliati, L. (2002). *Dreams to Sign*. Bethesda, MD: Imagination Stage.

Bauby, J.-D. (1997). *The Diving Bell and the Butterfly*. New York: Alfred A. Knopf.

Gibson, W. (1960). *The Miracle Worker*. New York: Samuel French.

Hockenberry, J. (1995). *Moving Violations: War Zones, Wheelchairs and Declarations of Independence*. New York: Hyperion.

Keller, H. (1990). *The Story of My Life*. New York: Bantam Books.

Kisor, H. (1990). *What's that Pig Outdoors? A Memoir of Deafness*. New York: Penguin.

Murphy, R. F. (1987). *The Body Silent.* New York: Henry Holt and Company.

Medoff, M. (1980). *Children of a Lesser God.* New York: Dramatists Play Service.

Sacks, O. (1989). *Seeing Voices: A Journey into the World of the Deaf.* Berkeley, CA: University of California Press.

4. Cognitive Disabilities

Cognition, the process of knowing, is one of the major functions of the brain and involves many processes, among them: perception, memory, language, judgment, concept formation, and decision-making. Cognitive disabilities interfere with the brain's abilities to process, organize, understand, store, recall, and use information.

The brain is a very complex organ. There are billions of neurons (brain cells) and as many as a quadrillion neurological connections that serve as pathways for information in each individual brain. No two individuals who have normal cognitive functioning process information in *exactly* the same way because no two brains are built identically.

> The brain's development is an "experience dependent" process, in which experience activates certain pathways in the brain, strengthening existing connections and creating new ones. Lack of experience can lead to cell death in a process called "pruning." This is sometimes called a "use-it-or-lose-it" principle of brain development. An infant is born with a genetically programmed excess in neurons, and the postnatal establishment of synaptic connections is determined by both genes and experience. Genes contain the information for the general organization...but experience determines which genes become expressed, how, and when (Siegel 1999, pp. 13-14).

Siegel (1999) believes that human connections and interactions shape the brain in many ways.

Because of the intricacy of the brain, cognitive disabilities disrupt brain functioning along a very large continuum. Different categories of disabilities, such as learning disabilities, intellectual and developmental disabilities, and attention deficits, indicate similarities in processing disturbances but the ability to function within each category varies greatly from one individual to another. As with physical disabilities, people who have cognitive disabilities need to be looked at as unique individuals.

The area of cognitive disabilities is perhaps the one approached with the most trepidation by novices. This may be due to lack of contact. Our educational system tends to segregate those who learn differently from those who learn "normally" into different classrooms and schools so they are not frequently seen or interacted with. While this may be done with the best intentions, this separation creates a free-floating suspicion in the minds of "regular" education students that these "special" education students are too different, too strange, and maybe even too dangerous to participate with everyone else. This prejudice is carried into adult life

photo by Patricia Theriault

Figure 7: People don't have to all be the same to learn to work together.

and usually there are few opportunities to test its validity.

Once you get to know someone who has a cognitive disability, you will begin to throw away those old stereotypes and fears and realize that he is just a person who processes information differently. He might need more time to understand or respond; he might have difficulty with abstract reasoning and need concrete examples in order to understand something new. Whatever his cognitive difficulties, he is still a person who needs and wants to express himself and to connect with other people. With your help, he can do this better.

This chapter reviews the characteristics of the most common cognitive disabilities and suggests some general ways of involving people who have them in drama. Later chapters include more information on adapting specific drama activities for them. Cognitive disabilities are not always easy to diagnose because a number of conditions share similar symptoms. Some people have more than one condition (for example, a person could be dually diagnosed with learning disabilities and obsessive-compulsive disorder). Because of these situations, you may find a student who fits under several profiles. What is most important is to address the difficulties each child displays and find the adaptations that even the playing field for him as an individual, making him feel comfortable and able to succeed in the class or production. I have included the most common diagnoses that you may encounter so you have a starting place for thinking about ways to help each of your students succeed.

Learning Disabilities

Learning disabilities (LD) is a catchall term for many different kinds of information-processing difficulties. If you have LD, your ability to learn, to communicate through spoken and written language, and to understand the world around you is affected. Sometimes there is a processing delay and it takes longer to put the message into the brain or to get a response back out. Sometimes the message gets scrambled and can't be understood or isn't understood well. In any case, information processing is the key. Intelligence is not affected in LD; most people with LD have normal to above-normal intelligence.

In human beings, data enters through the sense organs and travels to the brain, the information processing center, via the nerves through the agency of electrical impulses and chemical neurotransmitters. The brain sifts through, evaluates, and comprehends the data, then sends impulses via neurotransmitters, neuropeptides, electrical impulses, and hormones to the speech center and the fingers, face, legs, or whatever body part needs to respond. In LD the problem is not in the eyes, ears, skin, nose, balance sensors, tongue, vocal chords, nerves, or muscles; it is somewhere in the neuronal systems within the brain.

In his book *A Mind at a Time* (2002), Mel Levine identifies eight neurodevelopmental systems that work together and serve as tools for learning and applying what is learned in the creation of products: attention control, memory, language, spatial ordering, sequential ordering, motor, higher thinking, and social thinking. Dysfunctions within each of these systems, individually or in combination, show up as the symptoms we see and experience as LD.

No one has a perfect brain. In any given human body a number of connections are bound to be blocked, poorly developed, or disconnected. This means that the cognitive functioning of each individual will fall somewhere on a wide continuum. Viewed from this perspective, it is quite possible that almost everyone could be said to have some kind of LD. Individuals who are diagnosed with LD just happen to have dysfunctions in areas that obviously impede their learning in their culture.

Medical science doesn't know yet what causes most specific LD. Research indicates a wide range of possible origins including genetic inheritance; lack of enough oxygen at birth; alcohol, drugs, or nicotine ingested by the mother during pregnancy; lead poisoning; poor diet; allergies; high sensitivities to environmental chemicals; a tumor or lesion in the brain; lack of rich sensory stimulation in infancy and early childhood; poor attachment with the primary caregiver; damage from sudden vascular change, such as a stroke; or other injury due to brain trauma.

Dyslexia

Some learning disabilities have specific names. Dyslexia is the inability to process letters and words well, resulting from a deficit in the phonological component of language (International Dyslexia Association 2003). Abilities to read and spell are affected. When we speak, we combine phonemes (the sounds of speech) to create words. Many people who have dyslexia struggle to perceive the individual sounds in speech and have difficulty connecting them with letters, which represent the sounds but are arbitrary symbols. "In order to read, a child has to develop the insight that spoken words can be pulled apart into phonemes and that letters in a written word represent these sounds" (Lyons 2003, p. 7).

Difficulties with attention and working memory can also be involved in reading problems (Levine 2002) or timing-related visual or auditory processing issues connected with translating and sequencing the sounds with the symbols (Wolf 2007). Connections within the brain circuits used for reading are as important as the structures within the brain that do the actual processing of sound, language, and visuals. A disconnection between frontal (attention) areas and posterior (visual) language regions in the insula, area 37, or the left angular gyrus could interfere with the automatic processing that is necessary for fluent reading (Wolf 2007).

Educators used to think that dyslexia was primarily a visual processing disorder because students confused letters that look similar, but recent studies reveal that letter confusion is just a symptom of the root cause: the phoneme identification problem. Brain imaging indicates that areas in the back of the brain's left hemisphere (the inferior parietal lobe) are where phonemes are normally processed. Children who are dyslexic tend to have underactive left inferior parietal lobes (Windham 2004). Other areas in the frontal, temporal, and occipital-temporal regions of the left hemisphere of the brain, which are highly involved in typical readers, are not engaged in the brains of readers with dyslexia, who rely more heavily on their right hemisphere regions and their left occipital temporal region. This suggests that they are engaged in memorizing what they see rather than analyzing it (Wolf 2007).

Dyslexia is very much culture-bound. If we had no written language, we would have no dyslexia (Pennington 2003). Reading is not a "hardwired," natural ability, such as drama, dance, and language; there is no "reading center" in the brain. We must go to school for many years to train our brains to create new circuitry between parts of the brain that were originally designed to do other tasks (Wolf 2007). As mentioned in Chapter 1, the origin of the arts is estimated at 35,000-45,000 years ago. In contrast, reading and writing are only about 5,000 years old. The first writing systems were developed by the Sumerians (cuneiform) and the Egyptians (hieroglyphics) circa 3400-3100 B.C.E., but the Greek alphabet, which relates a single phoneme to a single symbol, was not invented until 800 B.C.E.

The number of people diagnosed with dyslexia varies from culture to culture depending on the complexity of the written language. English is a very difficult language: there are more than 1,100 ways that letters are used to symbolize the forty phonemes that make it up. In part, this is because through time the English language has incorporated words from many different languages. Additionally, in England during the 15th through 17th centuries the pronunciation of many vowels changed during what is historically known in linguistics as the Great Vowel Shift, but the spelling of words was not changed to match the new pronunciation (Post 2003). Languages that have more of a one-to-one relationship between sounds and letters have less dyslexia. For instance, Italian has 33 sounds, which are symbolized in only 25 letters or letter combinations. Italians have a very low number of people who are diagnosed with dyslexia. French is a bit more difficult, with 32 sounds expressed in 250 different letter combinations. There is some dyslexia found in French-speaking countries but not as much as in English-speaking countries (Kansas City Star 2001).

Written material can be made more "reader-friendly" for people with and without dyslexia by using a combination of upper case with lower case letters rather than all capital letters, using cursive letters styles or letter styles with serifs, using type styles that are short and fat rather than thin and elongated, including white space within and around words in proportion to the shape and thickness of the letter, and using equal rather than varied sizes of the spaces between words in a line of text. Clean first- or second-generation copies are much easier to read than faded, dirty, speckled fortieth-generation copies. All of these qualities help the shape of the letters and words stand out for visual processing (Post 2003).

Dysgraphia

Dysgraphia is difficulty *physically* encoding sound into a visual, kinesthetically produced symbol by means of writing, which involves the neurodevelopmental systems of attention control, active working memory, long-term memory of motor sequences, and motor control itself, particularly the graphomotor function. Mel Levine (2002) says that writing involves some of the most complex muscular manipulations. When the graphomotor system is not working, a person cannot keep his writing going at the same speed as his thoughts and it becomes very hard to express his ideas on paper. In addition, the writing output is usually indecipherable. Keyboarding instead of writing helps, as does the use of an audio recorder for assignments.

Dyscalculia

Dyscalculia is poor math ability. Math consists of many subskills that build on each other: addition, subtraction, multiplication, and division. Before you can successful move on to a more complex subskill, you must master the earlier, simpler ones (Levine 2002). No core deficit has yet been identified for math disabilities, although executive function skills, procedural and working memory, visuospatial skills, and attention control possibly contribute to the problem (Mazzocco & Myers 2003).

Dyspraxia

Dyspraxia refers to difficulty with both gross and fine motor skills, affects learning that involves sequencing, eye-hand coordination, eye focus and control, and spatial relationships, and often co-exists with dyslexia, dysgraphia, and dyscalculia. Control of the muscles involved in speech is affected with dyspraxia as well as those of the rest of the body. Difficulties in all these areas then affect social skill development, since children with coordination problems tend not to be as successful at playing games and sports or at conversation.

Auditory Processing Disorders

People with auditory processing problems can physically hear speech, but have difficulty sorting through sounds to make sense of what they hear. A student might be able to hear a teacher talking, but not be able to sort out her words from all the other sounds in the room. Normal auditory functioning allows us to focus on the speaker and block out the background noise. Without that ability the world becomes a confusing and chaotic place!

To help students focus on stories or aural presentations, bring in pictures and objects to make what is being said more visual and concrete. Keep background and group noise to a minimum; take turns talking so each person can hear what is being said. When giving instructions, demonstrate and then practice the actions of games or activities with the group as you describe them.

Visual Processing Disorders

Visual processing disorders affect how the brain interprets what the eyes see and can make it difficult to identify letters, symbols, colors, and shapes, such as confusion between *b* and *d* in reading. Students are easily distracted by all the visual input and do not know where to focus. They have difficulty judging distances when moving or standing still. Staying within the lines when writing or aligning the columns in math problems is hard for them. Reading along a line of print can often be accomplished only by using a straightedge. Copying from the board or a book to a sheet of paper is challenging.

When doing script work, you may need to use audiotapes or CDs to help this student learn lines and understand directions, as reading the printed word will be difficult. Make sure the environment is visually simple. If need be, take down bright posters or hide piles of colorful objects so your student can focus on the work and the other students. Choose games with limited movement or limited numbers of people moving at one time.

Sensory Integration Disorders

Students with sensory integration problems have difficulties integrating the information collected from the different senses. This could mean a dysfunction in the vestibular or balance system, the proprioceptive system (awareness of body position in space), tactile or touch system, visual, olfactory (smell), auditory (hearing), and/or gustatory (taste) systems. Results of sensory integration problems include difficulty with motor planning (sending signals from the brain to the body to take physical actions, both gross and fine), coordination, eye focus, and body awareness. This can affect attention span, ability to concentrate, behavior, learning, feelings of self-control and self-efficacy, or the ability to complete daily living skills, such as dressing, eating, and brushing one's teeth. Some people with sensory integration problems under-react to (need more) sensory stimulation, while others overreact (need less). Sensory integration problems can show up in people with LD, intellectual and developmental disabilities, and autism-spectrum disorders.

Dramatic Adaptations for LD

The good news is that despite these processing difficulties LD doesn't have anything to do with the child's intelligence. By definition, students with LD are of normal to above normal intelligence. Moreover, LD students can be gifted and talented in many areas. While LD can lead to failure in the academic classroom without appropriate teaching and support, many students with LD can express themselves more clearly through movement, sound, and facial expression than they can through words and can experience success through the arts. Suddenly, with an appropriate outlet for their feelings and impressions, they change from inarticulate balls of frustration into graceful, funny, focused, and eloquent actors and actresses.

Twelve-year-old Faye had so many emotions bottled up inside that sometimes she seemed ready to explode. She was not allowed to express these feelings in school or at home, and with no outlet, they became all the more intense when she did express them — with a vengeance — and then she got into trouble because she expressed them inappropriately.

When she signed up for my creative drama class, her teachers, her parents, and even the principal of Ivymount School told me, "You'll love Faye — she's quite dramatic." Their tone of voice communicated, "— and you're going to have your hands full!" As it turned out, Faye was not a handful — she was a total delight. As Faye, she had trouble saying what was on her mind, but as a character, she could play every shade of emotion that person was experiencing. In one session we acted out "Cinderella" three times. She went from playing the most long-suffering, mournful Cinderella I'll ever see, complete with real tears when she could not go to the ball, to the meanest, nastiest, most spiteful Evil Stepmother who ever walked the face of the earth, to a Fairy Godmother so loving and kind you wished she was your own.

Success is hard to come by in the academic classroom. There is only one correct way to spell most words. There is only one right answer to "What is the capital of Outer Mongolia?" Two plus two equals only four. In drama, however, there are many right answers and few wrong ones. In fact, for many improvisations and theatre games, the more answers you can generate, the better! How does the color red make you feel? Angry, happy, excited, energized, on fire, and hungry are all correct answers. There are many different ways to act out an old man, a butterfly, or a boy flying a kite, because those creatures behave differently in different situations.

In a drama class, students with LD have the opportunity to use an alternate, stronger method of expressing their ideas. If they are not so good with words, they can use sound and movement. If they are not very coordinated, they may be great with facial expressions. If they have difficulty reading but they can make up dialogue on the spot, they can become experts at improvisation. As long as they are expressing an idea the best way they can, they've succeeded. And they deserve applause.

When teaching students with LD, you many need to proceed at a slower pace than you normally would, so students have more time for processing what you are saying. If your normal speaking rhythm is fast, slow down a little. Take a pause now and then. Too much information given at one time can be confusing. Allow students to keep up with you.

Directions given all at once can be overwhelming. Students may not be sure which action needs to be done first, second, or third. Because of this sequencing confusion, they might forget one or more of the steps. Break instructions down into small steps and present them one at a time. For instance, instead of saying, "Everyone find a partner and line up by the window back to back," you might say, "Everybody find a partner." When everyone has a partner, say, "Bring your partner over here by the window." When everyone is on the correct side of the room, say, "Line up with your partner." After they are lined up, tell them to stand back to back.

Clarity in explanation is important. Choose one good example to get your point across rather than offering three or four different ones. If you were assigning a pantomime and said, "I want you to pantomime flying a kite. Think of all the different problems you might encounter: there might be no wind, there might be too much wind, your string might get tangled, your dog might run away with the kite, the kite might get blown into the branches of a tree…" you may be providing too many images for students to hold in their short-term memory. By the time they have visualized the first image, they may have forgotten what you said next. One clearly presented example can serve to get your point across just fine. "I want you to pantomime flying a kite. Let's imagine one problem you might have while flying a kite. Suppose there was no wind and you couldn't get the kite into the air. What might happen?" Have someone act out that situation. Then ask for students to think of other situations to act out.

Learning how to make choices is important, but offering too many options can be overwhelming and confusing. Present two choices instead of three or four. Instead of asking, "What would you rather do first — listen to a story, draw a picture, sing a song, or play a game?" ask, "Would you rather listen to a story or play a game?"

Exercises, examples, and activities should be as concrete as possible. Some beginning drama games that involve pantomime of "invisible" objects or manipulation of an imaginary concept are difficult for many students with LD. For example, Space Balls is a pantomime game in which an imaginary ball is created from the shape of your hands and the space in between them. The Space Ball is passed around the circle. Each player makes the Space Ball bigger or smaller or heavier or lighter before passing it on to the next player. Beginners with LD, having nothing concrete or real to focus on, often have difficulty manipulating the imaginary ball, keeping its shape, and following its progress around the circle. A more concrete pantomime game, such as The Magic Tube, which puts an actual object into the student's hand, will often be more successful. See Chapter 7 for more examples of how make abstract games concrete.

Teachers in academic classrooms often carefully structure the physical environment to help create order for sensory input that seems overwhelming and chaotic for students with LD. A child's desk may be divided into specific areas for specific supplies or types of work. Places in the classroom might be color-coded or labeled to delineate where books, supplies, and materials are to be kept. Work areas in the classroom are laid out in configurations that aid in concentration and give students a feeling of safety and containment. So they know what to expect, schedules are often consistent from day to day or carefully laid out for students at the beginning of each day.

A drama classroom is usually an open space without many of the physical structures that help students with LD define their boundaries and focus their attentions in the academic classroom. Usually there are no desks and often no chairs. Structure must be added for children who cannot create structure on their own. If students have difficulty sitting in a circle or staying in their own place while sitting, create a circle on the floor with colored tape and, if necessary, tape *X*s at intervals on the circle to indicate where each student should sit. Small carpet squares are also useful to delineate seating areas and can easily be moved and placed in different configurations in any part of the room. Chapter 5 provides more detail about how to structure the physical space, your lesson plan, and your teaching style.

Certain types of LD create specific challenges for the drama teacher. A student who has a reading or speech disorder should not be put on the spot to read a script out loud in class. If you must do script work, you could give out the script a week in advance so students can work on it with parents at home or with teachers in reading class or you could provide an advance copy of the script on tape and in writing so students can listen to it beforehand to familiarize themselves. If these strategies prove to be unsuccessful, you might want to forget about script work and focus instead on creating characters and scenes through improvisation.

Students who have auditory processing disorders may have difficulty understanding verbal directions or listening to stories. If a student does not seem to be getting your messages, it will be useless to raise your voice, as the issue is not one of volume. Provide visual images that support your verbal instructions. Write your directions on the board or explain your idea through a chart or diagram. Use gestures and physical demonstrations to clarify your meaning. Write homework assignments or class rules on a separate sheet of paper to be taken home. When telling stories, show pictures of the characters. If your students read well, you could use a picture book with large print and let them help you read it out loud. They will then be able to focus visually on the words and imagery that supplement the lack of auditory information.

After a run-through of a play, directors typically give their actors "notes" or comments on things to change or improve. Most directors give notes verbally and the actors write them down to review later. An actor with auditory processing problems or one with dysgraphia will have difficulty with this task. One option is to ask an assistant or another actor to write down your comments for him. Another possibility is to type up your notes for this actor after rehearsal and email them to him before the next rehearsal or give them to him at the beginning of the next rehearsal.

Speech and Language Disorders

Speech disorders involve difficulties producing speech sounds or problems with vocal quality. People who have speech disorders may have problems with articulation, pitch, volume, and/or quality of their voice. They may be unable to form certain consonant sounds, such as *l, r,* or *th*. Stuttering, a speech disorder that affects more than a million people in the U.S., interrupts the rhythmic flow of words as the speaker gets stuck on certain sounds. Speech and language disorders can be the only disability a person has or they could be coupled with other physical or cognitive disabilities. It has been estimated that one quarter of the students in special education programs in this country's public schools have some kind of speech or language disorder.

A language disorder involves inability or delay in understanding and/or using words in context. Brain imaging studies have indicated that children with speech delays may be processing language on the right side of the brain instead of on the left side where language centers are located (Windham 2004). A person with a receptive language disorder might see or hear a word, but not be able to understand its meaning. A person with an expressive language disorder may understand the word's meaning, but not be able to use the word himself. He may have difficulty with semantics (the proper use of words and their meanings) and generalize one word to mean many others. For instance, a person could use the word *chair* when referring to any kind of furniture. He may use inappropriate grammatical patterns like "Me go store" instead of "I'm going to the store." He may have a limited vocabulary or may develop language at a slower pace. He may have difficulty using pronouns appropriately, confusing *I, you,* and *she/he* when referring to himself and others. As a result of these language impairments, he may have difficulty understanding others, following directions, or expressing his ideas.

Give students who have speech and language disorders the opportunity to express themselves through pantomime and movement as much as possible. These are skills that they can use to supplement their vocal communication, and they need to develop them. However, allow them to use words whenever they can. They need practice in this mode of communication, too!

If a student has difficulty expressing himself in words, give him "wait time" — extra time to process and/or formulate what he wants to say. Do not say it for him or refuse to call on him when he has something to say. He will never learn how to express himself verbally, if he is not given a chance. Waiting for a response can be hard, if other students do not have language delays or if they have short attention spans. If other students show impatience, remind them that each person in class has a right to express his ideas and opinions and this particular student just needs a little more time to get his ideas out. If the class is involved in a go-around activity where each person says or does something in turn, you might be able to give the student with the delay more time to formulate his response by temporarily passing over his turn and coming back to him when he is ready.

If you have a student who stutters or has difficulty forming certain sounds, you can reword the difficult words in a script to make them easier to say. For instance, one of the characters in a play was named Penelope Pittstop. Two of the actors who had to say her name had trouble with the *p* sound. So we changed, "Yes, Ms. Pittstop," to "Yes, Ma'am."

Sometimes people who stutter find that they do not stutter when they are singing. Country singer Mel Tillis is a prime example of this. If your student enjoys singing, you could showcase his talents through a song rather than through a monologue or scene. Songs are actually highly emotional monologues put to music. A well-structured song, particularly one from a musical play, will have the same emotional and thought progression as any well-written dramatic speech. Through the song the character evaluates how he is feeling and what he is going to do about it, sometimes going through a character change or making an important decision by the end of the song. Good singers are emotionally connected to their material and act a song as well as sing it (Shurtleff 1980).

Other people, such as actor James Earl Jones, find that when they read poetry or memorize lines from plays, they do not stutter (Jones 2005). The rhythm inherent in a poem and the lines of most plays seems to create a flow that facilitates speech. It is possible that an actor who stutters might have difficulty improvising lines but not stumble over scripted, read, or memorized lines.

Attention Deficit Hyperactivity Disorder

Attention deficit hyperactivity disorder (ADHD) is a spectrum of cognitive-processing disabilities involving the attention systems of the brain, specifically in the frontal lobe, which causes deficits in concentration, working memory, and impulse control. Poor muscle coordination and poor spatial awareness frequently accompany ADHD. Neuroscientists believe that the brains of children with ADHD mature more slowly, with a lag of as much as three years (Schmid 2007). ADHD is not officially considered an LD, but it definitely affects the ability to learn.

ADHD used to be differentiated into two related disorders: attention deficit disorder (ADD), which involved symptoms of distractibility and an inability to focus attention on one thing for an extended period of time, and attention deficit hyperactivity disorder (ADHD), which added a hyperactive-impulsive component. However, in 2000 the American Psychiatric Association revised their definition and ADHD is now seen as one disorder with three subtypes: combined type, predominately inattentive type, and predominately hyperactive-impulsive type.

Children with ADHD seem to never stop moving around; adults who have it fidget constantly. Some experts believe that the hyperactive behavior displayed by people with ADHD is an unconscious attempt to stimulate their under-aroused nervous systems. Because of their impulsivity, many children with ADHD have difficulty inhibiting aggressive behaviors. In times of stress, they react instead of stopping and thinking things through. This often gets them into conflicts with peers, siblings, parents, and teachers. ADHD affects every aspect of a child's life, from sleep to work to play.

The National Institutes of Health estimates that three to five percent of school-aged children in the U.S. have some form of ADHD. Other studies estimate as many as 20 percent of children are affected (MacDonald 2003). About half of these children also have LD. Like people with LD, people with ADHD often have normal to above-normal intelligence. Co-occurring disorders can be conduct disorder, anxiety disorder, Tourette disorder, or a mood disorder. Experts used to believe that children "outgrew" ADHD by the time they became adults. This is now disputed, as more and more adults are being diagnosed, realizing when they think back to their childhood that they probably had it then, too (Hallowell & Ratley 1994). The percent of adults with ADHD is considered to be similar to that in children: five percent (Talan 2004).

Neuroscience is getting closer to discovering the underlying causes of ADHD. Brain scans indicate that the prefrontal cortex (particularly the right frontal lobes), the basal ganglia, and the cerebellum are underactive (MacDonald 2003; Pisano 2003). The pre-frontal cortex functions as an executive for brain functions, helping us to organize ourselves, focus, manage time, make decisions, and direct behavior (Talan 2004). Another study suggested that people who had ADHD and who had never been medicated had a significantly lower amount of white matter in their brains than people without ADHD and people with ADHD who had been on medication (Hathaway 2005). Two neurotransmitters, dopamine and norepinephrine, are thought to be involved. Brains of research subjects with ADHD had 70 percent more dopamine receptors than subjects without it (Kansas City Star 1999). Ritalin (methylphenidate), Strattera (atomoxetine), and other medications seem to help people with ADHD by increasing the concentrations of dopamine and norepinephrine in their brains, indicating a possible imbalance between transmitters and receptors. However, this could be a symptom and not a cause (MacDonald 2003; Talan 2004). It does seem that some ADHD is genetically linked, as the condition shows up repeatedly in some families, but similar symptoms can also seen in people who have experienced brain injury or have no family history of ADHD.

A person who has ADHD does not just have a short attention span; he has difficulty choosing *which* stimulus out of the thousands of stimuli in his immediate environment to pay attention to. In one particular moment, a boy with ADHD could be torn among the sound of traffic outside, the teacher's voice, the scratching of chalk on the blackboard, two girls whispering and passing notes behind him, the hum of the air conditioner, a fly buzzing by, the fragrance of roses on the teacher's desk, the smell of lunch cooking in the cafeteria, the odor of automobile exhaust, an itch from a mosquito bite, an ache from a skinned knee, the pinch from brand-new shoes, a scratchy tag in the neck of his T-shirt, the bright blue book bag sitting on the floor next to him, the writing on the blackboard, the writing on his paper, the writing and photos in his open textbook on the desk in front of him, all the different colors of the books in the bookshelf to his left, and so on. Everyone else in class is processing similar sensory information, but those who do not have ADHD are not being confused or distracted by it.

Doctors, educators, and parents deal with ADHD in a number of different ways. Behavior modification therapy is often a first line of defense for treating behavioral symptoms. The first step is to identify the target behaviors that need to be changed. Then an appropriate alternative behavior is chosen to be substituted for the inappropriate one. For instance, the targeted behavior might be "wandering around the room" and its substitute would be "sitting at your desk." A program is set up to provide positive reinforcements or rewards for the performance of the appropriate behavior. In the case of a student who tends to wander, the teacher might put a sticker on his behavior chart for every fifteen-minute interval during which he stays seated. Other frequently used positive reinforcers include food, tokens, points, money, privileges, or other kinds of treats. Choice of reward depends on age, interests, and motivation of the child as well as philosophy of the teacher or parent. In more elaborate reward systems, geared to develop impulse control, tokens or points are accumulated to be traded in at a later time for food, privileges, or toys.

Negative reinforcement for inappropriate behavior is accomplished through the removal of the positive reinforcers, removal of attention, and/or administering of an aversive or unpleasant experience immediately after the inappropriate behavior. Stickers could be removed from a chart, privileges could be lost, previously earned tokens could be taken away. However, positive reinforcement of behavior is considered more powerful than negative reinforcement.

Teachers and therapists teach students with ADHD specific problem-solving strategies for handling stressful situations, set clear behavior limits, and structure physical environments to help them focus and concentrate. If a child has a need to move around the classroom in order to learn, the teacher might accommodate this need by setting up two desks on opposite sides of the room between which he can travel during the day. This provides an outlet for movement needs within clear physical and psychological boundaries.

Some people are prescribed stimulant medications, such as Ritalin, to control their symptoms. If the dosage is correct, the result should be the ability to focus normally. However, finding the correct dosage for medication is not an exact science and dosage needs can change over time as a child grows. On the down side, side effects, such as drowsiness, irritability, dizziness, dry mouth, nausea, loss of appetite, insomnia, skin rash, headaches, and stomachaches are common and will, of course, affect the student's behavior.

Children who take medications to control ADHD usually take a dose in the morning before coming to school and may take one or two more doses later in the day. The peak effectiveness of the medication varies, even for the time-release forms. If the medication wears off before the next dose is given, symptoms will return quickly. This means that if your drama class is scheduled around the time your student's medication wears off, you are likely to notice a return of hyperactive or inattentive behavior.

If you know a child is on medication, alert parents if you notice behavior that indicates possible side effects or the medication wearing off. You may be providing them with important information they need to know. In the case of over- or under-dosage, they can ask their doctor for a medication adjustment. If the child is in the process of a change in medication or dosage, parents may need feedback on how the child is responding to the change or when the medication is wearing off.

If your class is at a time when parents do not want their child to be medicated (some parents like to limit the amount of time their child takes medication to school hours), you will have to deal with the ADHD behavior through behavior modification techniques alone. This often happens at summer camp or on weekends when children are on "medication holiday."

Children who do not have ADHD can also be very distractible and hyperactive or hyper-vigilant if they have any of a number of other conditions, such as attachment disorders, depression, anxiety, post-traumatic stress disorder, traumatic brain injury, hormonal imbalances, or from the effects of strong medications, such as steroids, for asthma or other medical problems. It is hard to stay calm and focused when you are worried about your physical safety and your emotional well-being or you just don't feel good! If you feel you can talk to the parents about your concerns, do. If you work in a school and suspect abuse, neglect, or even a clinical problem that parents are not open about dealing with, the principal of the school should be able to tell you the school policy on reporting and who you should speak with about your concerns. You could also check with the school nurse or the school psychologist. In order to be licensed, they are required to take courses specific to diagnosis and assessment for all of these issues. If you are not working for a school, there is usually an office within the department of social services or child welfare in your state that provides information on these types of questions.

Some children may have food allergies or chemical sensitivities that cause hyperactive behaviors. Children may be highly reactive to sugar, so be cautious when serving snacks or drinks. With the rise in obesity and diabetes in the population in general, serving any food item containing sugar is ill-advised. In addition, be aware that there are individuals with extreme allergies to nuts, wheat, food coloring, certain preservatives, or salicylates that naturally occur in numerous fruits and other foodstuffs. Children who have phenylketonuria (PKU), a disorder in which the amino acid phenylalanine cannot be processed by the body, must avoid sources of protein, such as meat, fish, poultry, milk, eggs, cheese, ice cream, legumes, nuts and many products containing wheat flour. In addition, they cannot eat or drink anything that contains the artificial sweetener aspartame, which contains phenylalanine.

The use of chemicals as ingredients in synthetic fabrics, building materials, art supplies, paint, pesticides, carpets, cosmetics, perfumes, and cleaning compounds has exploded in the last 60 years. Only 1,000,000 metric tons of chemicals were produced worldwide in 1930; as of 2003, 400,000,000 metric tons were being produced annually (EHP 2003). Chemicals can be ingested through the skin, the mouth, or the nose into the respiratory system, or through the nose directly to the brain through the olfactory and the trigeminal nerves.

If you wear perfume, aftershave, or scented lotion and you have a child who has ADHD, Tourette's disorder, or autism in your class, you might try an experiment to see if he is sensitive to the chemicals you are wearing. Wear the scent and notice if the student's hyperactivity increases when you stand close to him. Does the same behavior occur when you are not wearing the scent? Normally, awareness of a scent disappears over time as the person adjusts to an odor; however, if a chemical sensitivity is involved, the opposite occurs as the person continues to be affected by the odor (EHA 1998). Watch for heightened hyperactivity during art projects. If you are using paint, clay, or another art material to which a student is highly reactive, find an alternate material. Please also remember that strong odors can cause problems for some children who have asthma.

ADHD can be the most difficult disability to deal with in a drama classroom. A drama class is a focused group experience. Most of the time, everyone works together on the same activity. If one or two or all of the students are wandering aimlessly around the room or paying attention to 20 different things at once, the class cannot move forward. It stops!

I taught a creative drama class in which attention deficits were present in some form in all five children. Instead of seeming like a class of five, it seemed like a class of fourteen! Andrew wanted to make sounds with every object he touched. Michael wanted to explore every corner of the room over and over. Peter could not sit still for more than ten seconds. Angela alternated between drawing and traveling around the room in circles talking to herself. Georgia had questions about everything except what we were doing. My assistant and I spent so much time trying to capture everyone's attention and keep it focused that we did not accomplish much each session. Every week we evaluated what had worked and what had not and revised our teaching strategies. We had many small successes, but we never fully succeeded at getting the whole group to work together for more than a 15-minute stretch.

The key to working with children who have ADHD in a drama class is to provide as much structure as you can in the physical space and in the lesson plan. Rules must be clear, written down, simple, and visibly posted somewhere. Activities must be concrete, active, and exciting enough to hold their attention, but not complex enough to be frustrating or distracting. The opening or warm-up activity is crucial for capturing the children's attention and starting class off on the right foot.

Transitions between activities must be smooth, clear, and swift or your student with ADHD will become anxious or distracted in the unstructured time. You will then lose him to something more interesting in the room or he might act out his anxiety by creating a conflict with another student. Chapter 6 describes a number of ways to make strong transitions within a lesson plan.

When planning transitions, include the time before class officially begins and the time after class officially ends as transition times as well. A student with ADHD who arrives early may feel lost and unfocused. Involve him in a fun, productive activity to focus his attention. Drawing, modeling in clay, or playing with puppets, blocks, puzzles, or Legos are all excellent pre-class activities. Endings also have the potential for creating anxiety. A pleasant, calming, closing activity is crucial for setting up a smooth transition at the end of drama class to whatever is next. See Chapter 7 for suggestions for pre-class and closure activities.

Do not despair if it seems like your student is not paying any attention to you. Sometimes it only appears that way. One summer I taught at the Ivymount Day Camp, which is for children who have severe LD and ADHD. None of the children in the class of four- and five-year-olds seemed capable of focusing their attentions on anything or anybody. During Native American Week we had an "Indian Campfire" in drama. I told them three short Sioux legends about how the animals were created by the Great Spirit and we did our best to act them out. I thought they got a bit of what I said, but their counselors were sure the storytelling session had been a complete waste of time. The next day a Native American guest speaker came to share Native American crafts and costumes with the whole camp. The group's counselors were astounded when their campers very confidently started telling her — in detail — one of the legends I had told them the day before!

Epilepsy

Epilepsy is a disorder in which the brain's electrical rhythms become imbalanced or misfire, causing seizures. The vast majority of people who have epilepsy fall along the normal range of intelligence; however, someone who has had a seizure that went on for an unusually long time or a series of non-stop seizures can sustain brain damage. Some people experience an *aura*, advance warning that a seizure is imminent, which can be experienced in a number of different ways, such as a taste, a smell, nausea, or a feeling of fear.

There are several different kinds of seizures. The most dramatic are general (previously called grand mal) which involve the whole brain. Someone having a seizure of this kind will most likely lose consciousness, fall to the ground, and begin convulsing in repeated jerking (tonic-clonic) movements. It looks as though he is in great pain, but he is not. He cannot feel anything because he is unconscious. What he will feel when he wakes, however, will be any injury he sustains from his fall or during the seizure. Bladder or bowel control can be lost in the course of a seizure, which can be embarrassing.

Absence seizures (previously called petit mal) happen in a smaller area of the brain and often look like daydreaming or blank staring. They usually last for a very short time and the person who has them may not even be aware they happened. Other physical symptoms are blinking, mild twitching, chewing, turning of the head, or waving the hands.

During complex-partial seizures (sometimes called temporal lobe or psychomotor seizures) the person seems to go into a trance or sleepwalking state. He may have a conversation with you that does not make sense or walk around and engage in activities. He may seem like himself or he may seem like he has a totally different personality. After he comes out of the seizure, he will not remember what he did during it.

When having a simple partial seizure, a person does not lose consciousness, but may "see" or "hear" or "smell" things that are not there. He is not losing his sanity; a sensory area in the brain is stimulated by the seizure and creates internal sensations that are experienced as real.

Sometimes epilepsy can be controlled by medication and sometimes a person's seizures are intractable. This depends on the brain chemistry of the individual, not the type of seizure. Some people who have had difficulty with medication have an electronic device called a vagal nerve stimulator implanted in their brain which sends little shocks at timed intervals to stop seizures. The stimulator is connected through wires under the skin to a flat round battery implanted under the skin in the chest area. If a seizure starts, it can often be stopped by swiping a specially designed magnet across the battery to send an extra stimulation to the brain. People typically carry their magnet on a Velcro band around their wrist or belt buckle so it can easily be grabbed and swiped when a seizure starts.

If you have a student who has epilepsy, you may or may not know. Some people wear medical alert bands/jewelry and disclose their condition so others are prepared to provide assistance, if necessary. Others are so afraid of the stigma that has been associated with epilepsy that they will not disclose their condition for fear of being shunned. At various points in history people with epilepsy have been burned as witches, locked in insane asylums, exorcised by priests, or banished from their community.

If someone has a generalized seizure and falls to the floor, roll him onto one side and place something soft under his head so he does not hit it on the floor during the convulsions. Remove any dangerous objects that might be close by. Remain calm. Do the ABCs of first aid: check his *airways*, check to see he is *breathing*, and loosen anything that might restrict his *circulation*. Sit next to him on the floor and keep him on his side so if he throws up, he won't gag or inhale it. Do not be afraid to touch him and comfort him. When the seizure ends, he will slowly come back to consciousness. He may be groggy and confused. Tell him where he is, remind him who you are, and tell him he just had a seizure. You do not need to call medical help unless the seizure goes on for longer than five minutes. Check your watch when the seizure starts and time it. Do not try to gauge the length of time in your head because one minute of watching a violent seizure will feel to you, the person assisting, like 30 minutes.

For other types of seizures, sit with the person and hold his hand until he comes back to consciousness. If he is walking around, follow him to make sure he does not run into anything or trip and fall. Again, when the seizure is over, you will need to reorient him to person, place, and time, because he will be confused.

A person needs to be taken to the hospital after a seizure if it is the very first time he has ever had a seizure, if the seizure went on longer than five minutes, if he does not return to consciousness, if he hurt himself during the seizure, or if he is having a seizure due to a fever, diabetic shock, heat exhaustion, poisoning, or head injury, or if she is pregnant.

NEVER put anything into the mouth of someone who is having a seizure. He will not swallow his tongue because that is not physically possible. What can happen, however, is that you can get bitten or you can hurt the person you are trying to help.

Acquired and Traumatic Brain Injury

Acquired brain injury (ABI) and *traumatic brain injury* (TBI) are the names given to conditions created by disease and injury to the brain after birth. ABI is the larger category and includes such conditions as stroke, tumors, lack of oxygen (anoxia or hypoxia), encephalitis, or damage caused by epilepsy, as well as the categories incorporated into TBI. TBI refers specifically to injuries from external causes, such as gunshot wounds, or a blow to the head sustained in a motor-vehicle accident or in a fall or a fight. TBI in and of itself is the leading cause of death and disabilities in children and adolescents in the U.S. due to traffic accidents, sports injuries, falls, and abuse/violence at home and in the streets (KidSource Online 1997).

Each brain injury is unique because it could affect one or many systems in the brain. After the injury happens, it often takes time to figure out exactly what areas are permanently affected. Many of the physical, cognitive, sensory, and behavioral symptoms that are expressed can be addressed in similar ways as suggested in other places in this book; however, what is key to know is that a person with ABI or TBI often remembers what life was like for him before the accident. He must relearn many skills. He also must adjust to being physically, cognitively, and emotionally different in many ways — in a sense a different person — than he was before and this is not always an easy adjustment to make. So expect frustration, confusion, denial, and anger about the difficulties that come up. Patience, acceptance of the individual as he is now, and appropriate accommodations are what is needed.

Tourette's Syndrome

Tourette's syndrome (TS) is a neurological disorder, probably caused by a number of defective genes that interfere with the body's manufacture of the neurotransmitter dopamine. Unlike individuals with ADHD, who may not have enough dopamine in their systems, individuals with TS probably have too much or, at least, an extreme sensitivity to it. The end result is that their internal neurological processing connections are sped up. There also seems to be a malfunction in the "wiring" of the basal ganglia of the brain, which normally facilitates communication between the cerebrum (which handles motor responses), the cerebral cortex (which handles language, ideas, concepts, attention, and executive function), and the limbic system (which deals with emotions and memory). In a functioning system, desired actions can be expressed and undesired ones can be inhibited. The opposite happens in the TS brain. Unwanted behaviors are expressed as tics (Olsen 2004; Tuma 2005). None of this affects intelligence in a negative way; people with TS have normal to above-normal intelligence.

On the downside, TS causes uncontrollable muscular tics and twitches, extremely impulsive behavior, compulsive repetitions of words or actions, quick emotional changes, and unusual vocal noises, such as grunting, barking, repetitive throat clearing, or recognizable words that erupt spontaneously and erratically. Less than ten percent of individuals with TS have coprolalia, an uncontrollable urge to say obscene or socially inappropriate words (Tuma 2005). Motor and vocal tics can sometimes be slowed or eliminated by drugs, but they never totally go away. On the up side, people who have TS tend to be extremely quick-thinking, creative, spontaneous, bright, and fun-loving.

TS symptoms usually appear around age seven years. The worst symptoms are typically concentrated between ages ten and twelve, then they usually decrease. Only about twenty-two percent of adults with TS still have severe tics (Tuma 2005).

About 50 percent of people with TS also have symptoms of ADHD. Forty percent of people with TS have LD that may affect their ability to read, write, spell, or compute (Burd 1992). Be sensitive to this possibility when you are introducing written scripts to a class for the first time.

At least 50 percent of people with TS also exhibit symptoms of obsessive-compulsive disorder (OCD), a neuropsychiatric condition that compels a person to think a certain thought or to repeat a particular action over and over again. The compulsive action is a coping strategy to stop the obsessive thoughts, reduce anxiety, or prevent a feared event from happening. Examples of compulsive activities are repeated hand washing, turning the lights in the room on and off, or continually smelling, touching, or arranging an object. If students with OCD try to ignore or stop their obsessions or compulsions, they become very anxious and fearful. OCD symptoms can often be improved by treatment with cognitive-behavioral therapy (CBT) and some psychiatric medications, as can co-occurring conditions, such as ADHD, anxiety, or depression. Remember that drugs often have negative side effects, such as making the person sluggish, dull, and unable to concentrate or irritable, dizzy, or nauseated.

Individuals with TS can have poor fine- or gross-motor coordination, poor balance, difficulty telling the difference between right and left, and clumsiness due to perceptual-motor problems. Because of this, students may need extra help or extra time for practice when learning dance routines or playing movement games. They may also need assistance when participating in art activities that require highly developed fine motor skills.

Sensory integration problems — difficulty organizing and using sensations — may be present in some students with TS as well. On one side of the sensory processing spectrum, persons with TS may be over-reactive (hypersensitive) to the sensations of touch. This can cause them to have a lower threshold to pain and an intense dislike for the texture of certain fabrics, art materials, or food. They may react negatively to unexpected touch. On the other side of the spectrum, they can be under-reactive (hyposensitive) to touch. Under-reactive individuals may have a higher threshold to pain. They may also have difficulty discriminating differences in texture, which, in addition to tics and poor muscular coordination, may cause clumsiness when manipulating small objects or doing projects involving fine motor skills. They may also be unaware of how strongly they are touching or bumping up against other students who have normal sensory integration.

Some people with TS are hypersensitive to certain odors. If the odor is caused by something in the room, such as a new rug, remove it or open the windows to air the room out. If it is caused by a room deodorizer or cleaning compound that is regularly used, ask if the custodian of your building can switch to a fragrance-free product. If the smell is from your perfume or aftershave, avoid wearing that fragrance on the days you teach.

TS symptoms are often exacerbated by stress. Taking a test under a strict time limit, trying to suppress tics in order to fit in or not disturb others, or being teased or put on the spot will often increase tics or impulsive outbursts of aggressive behavior. Give your students as much time as they need to complete in-class assignments. Break down a large assignment into small, manageable segments. For instance, if you are assigning lines for a play, ask for the lines from scene one to be learned for one rehearsal and the lines for scene two for the next one, rather than requiring the whole play to be memorized on one day. Also, a number of small assignments that are due one at a time will seem less overwhelming.

As a rule, stress reduction strategies are not taught in academic classrooms, although they probably should be. However, drama classes are excellent arenas for learning and practicing them. Physical warm-ups, deep breathing, sensory awareness sessions, concentration games, progressive relaxation, and guided imagery exercises (see Chapter 7) are tried and true tools that professional actors use to release stress and help them deal with nervousness. You may find that any of these techniques, used at the beginning of class or before a run-through or performance, serves to relax *all* your actors and allow them to perform with more ease and enjoyment. In addition, these coping strategies will stand them in good stead in other stressful life situations.

The severity of motor and vocal tics comes and goes depending on the overall stresses a student is dealing with in his life and his current neurological state. He will have good days and bad days. A student with TS who is going through a severe period of tics may feel more comfortable if he knows in advance that if he feels the need, he may go out into the hall or to the bathroom or, if it is a nice day, outside.

Verbal tics sometimes generate stuttering, which can interrupt line delivery in a scene. Students with TS may talk very quickly or they may pause while struggling to find a way to say a difficult word to get around the stutter. They may also use loud or pressured speech that sounds unnatural or they may adopt funny voices. The best way to deal with these kinds of speaking difficulties is not to put additional pressure on the student. The tenser he feels, the worse his speech will become. Tell him he has all the time in the world to get the line out. Make the vocal rhythm an integral part of his character's speech rhythm. Give him a prop to manipulate or some kind of stage business for his character to do to take his focus off the problem.

Often tics and other symptoms are reduced when the body is in motion. Including some form of physical activity — a warm-up or a movement game — in your lesson plan may provide a positive outlet. If the need to move comes over a student during part of the class that does not involve moving, you could give him permission to leave the room for a short time to engage in some kind of brief physical activity.

Motor and vocal tics can be disconcerting to the teacher and other students. It is important to explain to the class from the outset what TS is — particularly that it is not "crazy" or "catching." The other students need to understand that TS symptoms are involuntary and are not being done on purpose, that the person who has TS has little voluntary control over them, and that teasing, staring, or nasty comments will only make the symptoms worse. This may be more difficult for the other students to accept if the tics seem malicious rather than innocuous in nature. For example, it will be harder for a class to accept a student whose tics involve kicking, spitting, or swearing than it will to accept a student who blinks his eyes or jerks his head to the side.

Punishing a student for tics that are disruptive or violent will not make the tics go away. In fact, it could make them worse. If you feel behavior management of any kind is necessary, focus on proactive strategies rather than reactive ones. Instead of responding with a consequence after something goes wrong, be on the lookout for potentially difficult or hazardous situations and intervene *before* the problem happens. For example, instead of playing a game that involves a lot of physical contact, such as Elbow to Elbow, which could cause a tactilely sensitive child with TS to strike out aggressively when touched unexpectedly, you could play a game, such as Pass the Sound/Pass the Movement, in which students invent and pass sounds and body movements around the circle but do not make physical contact with each other.

The best thing the teacher and other students can do is to ignore tics and other symptoms. Concentrate instead on the positive aspects of the student's personality and his creative contributions to class. As in any classroom situation, the teacher has the key role in modeling how to treat the student who has the disability. Ignoring TS symptoms and making positive comments about the student's class work will go a long way to help him and the other students appreciate his strengths.

Recently, the use of drumming circles and other rhythmic activities has met much success with people who have TS. Participants report relaxation and a lessening of their symptoms. A great warm-up for a class could be a drumming circle to get everyone in tune with each other. Drumming will create positive emotional and physical responses in all your students and teach them important lessons about rhythm and working together in an ensemble — skills all actors need to develop.

Students who have TS are usually highly verbal and intuitive which, along with their impulsive tendencies, makes them very adept at improvisation and games that require on-the-spot, spontaneous decision-making. You will probably find a student with TS to be the most uninhibited and imaginative student in the class.

While this impulsive quality can be his best asset as a drama student, it can also be his worst. Expect impulsive comments and behavior and do not be offended by them. You and everyone else in the class probably have the same impulses, but because your brain is able to inhibit them, you have the ability to *not* act on them. Your student with TS cannot, so sometimes inappropriate comments and actions pop out along with all his appropriate, creative ideas. Handle awkward situations with a sense of humor.

For more ideas about how to work in an integrated setting with a student who has TS, see the following essay by Elizabeth van den Berg and Caleen Sinette Jennings' essay in Chapter 11.

==========================

Including a Child with Tourette Syndrome
Elizabeth van den Berg

As the spring semester started, I was feeling confident about including students with special needs in my classes at BAPA. I had had a number of positive experiences with students who had learning disabilities or developmental delays. As always, the arts access director had given me a list of the students with special needs who she knew were registered and suggested ways to adapt my teaching approach to them. What we did not know was that this semester a crucial line had been left off the class registration form. This line asked if students had "any special or medical needs of which we should be aware."

I had a large group in one particular acting class — fifteen students — but felt I could handle them. In the first class we were standing in a circle doing some warm-up exercises when I heard a popping sound, like someone snapping gum. This is a "no-no" in my classes. I identified the culprit and informed him that gum was not allowed during class time.

Very abruptly he asked, "Can I talk to you?"

I was quite taken aback by his manner, but answered, "Sure."

He crossed the circle towards me, stopped right in front of me, and said, "You see, I have Tourette syndrome and sometimes I make strange sounds and noises. Pop. Pop. Pop."

"Oh," I answered. I was completely thrown. I had no idea what Tourette syndrome was. Here was a student, taller than I, behaving oddly and making strange sounds. Fourteen other students were watching me, waiting for my response. "Okay," I said, "Thanks for letting me know. Let's continue."

So I continued class with Gerald occasionally bursting out with a "Whee" or pop-pop-popping along. As soon as class was over, I cornered the arts access director. She was as surprised as I was because this student was new to BAPA, but she immediately reassured me, explaining what Tourette syndrome is and providing me with literature on it. I couldn't believe we had not been forewarned — that even with the special needs line left off the registration form, Gerald's mom had not felt it necessary to inform us of his condition.

Gerald was an excellent artist. Exploring his characters by drawing them first helped him to feel comfortable with his acting and the scenes he worked on. He was very upfront with his disability, but hardly made any sounds after that first class. He explained that they seemed to be more prominent when he was nervous, as he had been that first day.

As we got closer to our final presentation, he expressed concern about being nervous and making sounds during the performance. I explained we would help him be as prepared as

possible so that he would be less nervous. And if he popped
— so what?

Indeed, he did pop, but only once, and his character work
was very strong. Despite what for me was a rocky start
because I was not prepared, things turned out quite well.

====================================

Intellectual and Developmental Disabilities

Currently a transition is going on in terminology in relation to this
set of cognitive disabilities. In 2006 the American Association for
Mental Retardation voted to rename itself the American Association on
Intellectual and Developmental Disabilities, due in part to the stigma that
the term mental retardation has acquired in our culture. Since our culture
is currently in transition on the use of this new term, I have called this
section "Intellectual and Developmental Disabilities" and I will refer to
the conditions as IDD.

Many syndromes and conditions are lumped together under the
umbrella of IDD. Generally, people are considered to have IDD if they
score 70 or below on an IQ test before they are 21 years old. There are
over 200 known causes of IDD, including genetic abnormalities, birth
trauma, fetal alcohol syndrome, PKU, lead poisoning, tumors, and other
diseases — but for many there are no known causes.

Children who have IDD can learn but they learn at slower rates than
others. When she was in elementary school, Amy Turnbull, who has no
disabilities, described her older brother's learning abilities this way:

> I was five years old when my parents explained to me that
> my brother has mental retardation [sic]. They said that his brain
> works slower than other people, and it takes him a longer time to
> learn. They also said he could always learn things. I asked how
> Kate's [her younger sister] and my brain worked, and they said
> our brains work fast. I then asked if brains were like record play-
> ers with the slow and fast speeds. They said that Jay's brain
> works on the slow speed and our brain [sic] works on the fast
> speed. Jay might be slow and Katie and I might be fast, but all of
> us can learn.

In addition to taking in information at a slower pace, people who have IDD are generally very literal. They may need concrete, physical examples in order to understand abstract ideas. Looking at a demonstration of how to peel a potato and actually doing it while being guided by a teacher may make more sense to them than listening to a description or reading about how to do it. People with IDD may have difficulty generalizing information from one situation to another. For instance, they may learn how to peel a potato, but not make the connection that the same tool could be used in the same way to peel a carrot or an apple.

People with IDD can appear rigid and inflexible in their approach to solving problems because they lack the ability to generalize. If new information is suddenly added to a task they have learned or if a social interaction takes an unexpected turn, they may have a hard time thinking of an alternative solution. Even if another solution is offered, they may find it hard to try out.

Often students who have IDD need to proceed at a slower pace than other students. They may need to have instructions broken down into small, individualized steps. Each step needs to be presented one at a time. If you present too many steps, even simple ones, all at once, your student will have difficulty retaining them in memory and in sequence, especially if the task is brand-new. When you are explaining an idea, explain it simply. Over-explaining will be as confusing as providing too many steps. One good example will suffice, especially if you demonstrate it as well. Show it while you tell it. For example, when presenting the game The Magic Box, I put the box in the center of the circle and say, "Inside this box is any present you can imagine. I'll show you how it works. First, I decide what I would like to be in the box." I then pause and think for a moment. "Then I imagine it in my mind." Another moment. "Then, I open the box…" I take off the lid. "…and take my present out!" I pantomime lifting my object out of the box. "…and show you what it is." I might pantomime placing a ring on my finger. Then I ask, "What do you think I got out of the box?" They may say, "A ring!" I say, "That's right. Now show us what *you* would like to get out of the box." Each person takes a turn to show us what he imagines is in the box.

Many students with IDD have difficulty speaking clearly. Certain sounds may be hard for them to form. They may hesitate as they search for words. They may have trouble speaking fluently. Let students use as much or as little language as they feel comfortable with. If there are words in a play that are difficult to say, change them to ones that are easier. For example, if it is too hard for an actor to say, "Come here immediately," maybe it would be easier for him to say, "Come here right away" or "Come here now" or just "Come here."

Some students with IDD excel at verbal activities, others do not. If your students do not, there are plenty of drama games that emphasize sound and movement. Try rhythm games that incorporate music, pantomime, and dance. Focus your lesson plans on drama activities that they can do and they enjoy. See Chapter 7 for examples of drama games that work.

Don't assume that a student who has difficulty expressing himself through spoken language does not understand what is being said to him. Receptive language and expressive language use two different brain processes. He could understand everything you say but not have the ability to translate that understanding into words or to actually speak words back to you.

If you ask a question and do not receive a reply, it could be that your student knows the answer but is not sure how to say it or do it. He may need a little extra time to figure it out. You may have to spend time finding out what he understands, how he really feels about the situation, or what he wants to do. He may need you to rephrase the question so that it is more structured and less open-ended. For example, if a student looks upset and I ask, "What's wrong?" he may not be able to tell me. But if I ask him "Are you feeling sick?" he can respond with a "yes" or "no" (although he may still not understand the question). If "yes," he can tell me what hurts. If "no," I might try asking, one simple question at a time, if he is angry, confused, upset, tired, sad, unhappy, or any other specific emotion that seems appropriate to the situation and the nonverbal expression he is showing. If he says he is angry, I might ask who he is angry at or what made him angry. Slowly, but surely, I can get to the root of the problem using this kind of detective work.

Some people who have IDD and have speech difficulties have been taught sign language as an expressive-language alternative. Through signs or gestures, a student may be able to convey what he cannot say in spoken language. If you are having difficulty getting through with words, try a gesture or sign.

There is no need to have lower standards of behavior for students who have IDD. They can understand what appropriate and acceptable behaviors are. Explain your classroom rules clearly in the first session. State the behaviors you expect in positive, simple, clear words. Explain what the consequences will be if a rule is broken. See the section on Behavior Management at the end of Chapter 5 for more specific information.

Down Syndrome

Down syndrome (DS) is a common type of IDD. It is caused by a chromosomal mutation that results in forty-seven instead of the normal forty-six chromosomes in the cells of the person's body. People with DS tend to have similar physical characteristics: a distinctive, broad, round face with high cheekbones; close-set, almond-shaped eyes; small, low-set ears; and a flat bridge to their nose. Their tongues tend to be too big for their mouths, which makes speaking clearly difficult. Some individuals with DS have a condition known as *atlanto-axial instability*, a misalignment of the top two vertebrae of the neck. If overextended or flexed, these vertebrae can shift position and squeeze or sever the spinal cord, causing paralysis or death. Just to be safe, ask parents if their child has this condition before doing any kind of physical activity that puts stress on the neck!

People who have DS usually have very warm and loving personalities, so much so that actor Chris Burke often says he has "Up syndrome" instead of Down syndrome. They love hugs and dote on praise. However, this can make them easy targets for people who would take advantage of them. Drama is a great way to teach about important, appropriate social-contact boundaries that should exist with different kinds of people, such as family, close friends, fellow students, teachers, acquaintances, and strangers.

Sometimes, just like all of us, people who have DS get into bad moods. When they do, it can be difficult to get them out of it; they seem to go into a deep, dark tunnel with no light at the end. Teen-aged girls can be particularly moody. If a conflict develops between two students at these times, compromise can be hard to achieve. My best suggestion for dealing with DS stubbornness is using patience and gentle humor. Do not try to argue with them, as they will not take in what you have to say. Do not try to force the situation, as they will only dig in deeper. Be loving and understanding — and if that does not work, give the pouter some time by himself to cool off for a while. He will either get it out of his system — or not. If you are not able to jolly him back into a good mood during that session, do not shame or embarrass him — that could ruin your relationship permanently. If you give him some space, by the next session he will be back to his usual lovable self again.

Williams Syndrome

People who have Williams syndrome (WS) lack the elastin gene on chromosome 7, due to a spontaneous mutation in the sperm or egg. This deletion causes specific physical features, medical complications, and cognitive limitations as well as unusual strengths. People with WS tend to have similar elfin facial features: broad forehead, small upturned nose with depressed bridge, puffiness around the eyes, curly hair, full lips, full cheeks, widely spaced small teeth, small chin, and small head. They may have a star-like pattern in their irises. If I were to describe their overall personality, I would say "sunny but sensitive."

People with WS have difficulty with visual-spatial processing and visual-motor integration, but have excellent auditory-processing abilities. In addition to being auditory learners, they have a love of language and develop strong verbal abilities as well as an affinity for music. They love to sing and many learn how to play musical instruments. They are highly social and develop strong, positive relationships with peers and adults. They are able to easily express emotions verbally and nonverbally which makes them great candidates for drama class. I have found those with WS to be among the most delightful, enthusiastic, and fun students I have ever had. Because of their strong auditory abilities, they are able to learn lines from recordings. They will not enjoy art activities nearly as much as other students because of their visual-processing difficulties, but if you turn the activity into a social event, they will happily work with a partner on any project.

People with WS are very sensitive to loud, harsh sounds, particularly if the sound is sudden and outside their control. Their emotional sensitivity can lead to feelings of anxiety, so they need lots of emotional support and encouragement. Recent research has revealed that music — particularly listening to music and playing a musical instrument — can be used to decrease their anxiety and fears (Dykens, Rosner, Ly, & Sagun 2005).

Autism Spectrum Disorders

Autism, Asperger's syndrome (AS), and pervasive developmental disorders (PDD) are related neurological disorders included in autism spectrum disorders. These involve disturbances in a number of areas, including impairments in verbal and nonverbal communication skills and reciprocal/social relationships, severe sensory integration problems, and a limited repertoire of activities and interests, often associated with repetitive or stereotyped movements (Frith 2003). Autism is at the lower functioning end of the spectrum; many autistic individuals never learn to speak and prefer to form attachments to things rather than people. AS is at the higher functioning end; these individuals learn how to speak (sometimes with delays), but have difficulties with social interactions. PDD fits in somewhere in between with delayed language and a mixture of symptoms and levels of functioning.

For many years the causes of autism-spectrum disorders (ASD) were a mystery and few methods worked to reach people who had them. Currently, neuroscientists believe that many of the behaviors seen in these disorders are due to poor connections between certain areas of the brain, particularly the superior temporal sulcus, the orbitofrontal cortex, and the amygdala, which are perceptual, executive, and emotional centers that must work together to help us make social interconnections and understand each other in subtle, empathetic ways (Baron-Cohen 1997; Spice 2004). Simon Baron-Cohen calls this ability *mindreading* (theory of mind) and the lack of it, *mindblindness*.

Marco Iacoboni (2008) suggests that deficits in mirror neuron areas might be the cause of inabilities to relate to and understand emotion in others. He reports that "children with autism had much lower activity in mirror neuron areas in fMRI (functional magnetic resonance imaging) brain scans compared with typically developing children. Moreover, Mirella [the neuroscientist who ran the tests] found a clear correlation between activity in mirror neuron areas and severity of disease: the more severe the impairment, the lower the activity in mirror neuron areas" (p. 176).

At times, people with ASD totally isolate themselves — literally retreating into a world of their own. This may be partly because incoming sensory stimulation is overwhelming. To filter out the overload, they focus on one object or action in what is called *self-stimulating behavior* or *stimming*, such as spinning in circles, focusing on spinning objects, or flapping fingers in front of the face. Stimming calms a stressed person with ASD and helps him refocus; however, he cannot be allowed to retreat into it for a long time as he would totally tune out and not be able to learn!

Sometimes people with ASD prefer relating to mechanical objects instead of people. Day after day, a child may play exclusively with a vacuum cleaner or the Venetian blinds instead of interacting with other children in the play group. This tendency may be due to his strong visual system and his need to stay in control of his environment. Mechanical objects are guaranteed to do the same thing again and again while people change all the time.

Temple Grandin, an expert in animal science and autism who is herself a person with autism, believes that most people with ASD are visual rather than verbal thinkers. She says she thinks first in pictures and then must translate the pictures into words (Grandin 1995). This makes her manner of processing the world very different from those of us who transfer our thoughts into language as our major symbolic mode. Lev Vygotsky, the Russian developmental psychologist, believed that language and thought (which is internalized language) originally develop from social communication with others about objects and experiences into egocentric speech (when a child talks to himself out loud) and finally into inner speech (the soundless thought processes inside our heads) (Dixon-Krauss 1996). Somewhere in this transition the brain switches from relying primarily on visual processing to verbal processing. In 1988 Graham Hitch did a study on visual working memory in children and discovered that five-year-olds used mental images more often to remember information than ten-year olds, who relied primarily on words (Robertson 2002). Perhaps the difficulty with speech that many people with ASD experience is caused in part by their inability to move from that early social language to egocentric speech and then on to internal verbal thought; instead, they may stay stuck in the original visual and visceral thinking of infants.

In any case, people with ASD seem to be "right-brain thinkers." They tend to score high in fluid intelligence and in nonverbal thinking, such as visual, spatial, and pattern-making skills. They are not as strong in verbal intelligence, sound inference, logic, or understanding the sequential steps in problem solving. Often they are visual and kinesthetic learners. Some are adept at creating with their hands, but others have motor-planning difficulties (Grandin 1986). They need to use concrete symbols rather than abstract ones to make meaning. A visual image or another type of sensory image can come to represent a concept if it is associated with a related experience. For instance, Temple Grandin reports that the concept of the give-and-take of personal relationships only has meaning for her through the visual symbol of doors and windows (Grandin 1995, p. 34).

People who have ASD tend to be oversensitive to sights, sounds, smells, and touch. Loud or sudden noises can be painful to their ears and certain smells are perceived as very offensive (Grandin 1986, 1995). When in a state of sensory overload, they may need what Donna Williams calls the "mono-channel approach" — to block out all but one type of sensory input in order to pay attention (Grandin 1996). For instance, in order to listen to an announcement on the PA system in a busy bus terminal, a person with ASD might have to shut his eyes to tune out all the movement and visual stimulation. While many people — with and without cognitive disabilities — do well with multisensory teaching, this may be too confusing for someone with ASD. Simplify!

People with ASD can become obsessed with subjects that have deep, personal meaning for them. They might only want to read, talk, and think about dinosaurs, geology, or the Civil War. While this can interfere with socialization, because most other people do not want to talk only about one subject all the time, their interests and passions can be guided into constructive pathways to help them learn and make a solid connection with the world. For example, as an adolescent Temple Grandin became obsessed with cattle chutes and squeezeboxes. She pursued her obsession with the encouragement of several mentors and is now one of the world's foremost designers of livestock handling facilities (Grandin 1986, 1995).

Current interventions include a variety of behavior modification techniques: speech therapy, auditory training, sensory desensitization, drugs, and social skills training. Drama can be one of the best approaches and, in fact, was one of the first used. Hans Asperger, the German doctor who first described the condition in 1944, created an educational program for the boys he was treating which involved speech therapy, drama, and physical education. Unfortunately, the director of the program, Sister Viktorine, was killed in World War II, so we have no record of exactly how she used drama (Attwood 1998).

Drama classes are filled with variety. Even if a teacher sets up a basic, structured lesson plan that stays the same from week to week (for example, always beginning with a go-around, followed by a physical warm-up, followed by a drama game, a story, and the enactment of the story), the specifics within that structure will be different every week. Because individuals with ASD do not communicate and interact well with others, are easily over-stimulated, and prefer routine, participating in a drama class can be challenging for them. Sometimes the amount of sensory stimulation is too much to handle. Sometimes the level of social interaction is beyond their level of social ability. All the other students' movements, gestures, talk, and laughter can become so overwhelming that some students with ASD may shut down.

Angela, a student with PDD in one of my creative drama classes, could handle solitary and parallel play, but had difficulty participating in any activity that involved associative or cooperative play. She did not like to sit in the circle with the others and listen to a story (associative play), but she could sit at the table with the others and draw a picture on her own (parallel play). She had difficulty acting out the story with the other students (cooperative play), but she could go off by herself and act out the characters alone in another part of the room (solitary play).

Angela drew cats — only cats. In fact, she drew the same cat over and over and over again. She would not draw anything else. When asked to do so, she would put the crayon into another person's hand and say, "You draw it." She kept repeating, "You draw it, you draw it, you draw it," until the other person finally did. If the other person refused, she became very upset. Because she did not like to sit with the rest of the class while I told the story, I allowed her to go to the table on the other side of the room and draw. During these times there was nobody else to draw for her, so she drew cats. Even though it did not look like she was paying attention, she heard every word of the story.

One week Angela came in talking animatedly about "Goldilocks and the Three Bears," which we had acted out the week before. Before class she tried to get me to draw Goldilocks sitting on the three chairs. I decided to be stubborn and see if I could entice her to draw it herself. She would not, so I started class before a conflict could develop over the drawing situation. When the story started, as usual, she went over to the table and began to draw. She was unusually involved with her work. I was not telling the story that week — my assistant was — so at one point I meandered over to take a look at what she was doing. Lo and behold, she was drawing a very complex and detailed rendition of the chairs in "Goldilocks' and the Three Bears."

I was very impressed, but not as impressed as her mother, who informed me after class that this was the first time Angela had ever drawn anything other than a cat. From that class on, Angela stopped asking others to draw for her. A predictable pattern developed. Each week she would come in talking excitedly about the story we had acted out the week before. When I told the story for the current week, she would draw a picture of the characters from the previous week. How she was able to focus on her drawing and thoughts about last week's story and listen so closely to the current week's story, I don't know.

If a child who has autism takes your drama class, check out how much sensory stimulation is in your classroom. If there are lots of toys, props, or odds and ends lying around, clean them up or cover them up. Simplify the visual design of the room so it is not distracting. Limit the distracting sounds inside and outside the classroom, if you can. Avoid drama games that incorporate sudden, loud noises or busy physical gestures that would over-stimulate. If your student needs one-on-one help, make sure you have enough assistants in the classroom. Assign one particular assistant to stay with the student and, when necessary, redirect his attention to class activities by communicating in whispered, short, simply worded statements.

Check to see if the student is tactilely defensive. If so, the surprise of a friendly hand on the shoulder might make the student feel threatened rather than supported. If you or your assistant touches the student, a "deep-pressure touch" (a heavy, downward, or inward pressure) would probably be better tolerated than a light touch. Be careful to press, not to pinch. Deep pressure seems to stimulate the brain and create a sense of integration. Another calming technique is to gently, firmly, and slowly brush the person on the back of the hand, the arm, or the back with your hand or the bristles of a stiff plastic hairbrush. Some people wear heavy vests that create a calming pressure on the upper body.

The student needs to feel in control of the amount and type of stimulation he is receiving. Provide a quiet, safe place in the room, where there are few visual or auditory distractions and where he can go to get away from the group, if necessary. Warmth and deep pressure tend to decrease arousal and create relaxation. You could provide a mat or heavy quilt for the student to wrap himself up in or some big pillows or bean bag chairs he could burrow under. If he needs to spin, allow him to spin in his safe place.

Sherry Haar, a professor of apparel and textiles at Kansas State University, has created a line of therapeutic costumes to promote sensory integration, motor development, and cognitive skills. The thematic designs (bug and butterfly) of the costumes allow the child to use his imagination while practicing developmental skills. The costumes include a variety of textures, resistance bands, and weights important for stimulation of the tactile and proprioceptive senses. Fine motor skills are encouraged through manipulation of closures (zippers, buttons, snaps, and lacing) and objects (antennae and eyes on the helmet). Shapes in a variety of colors and sizes aid in cognitive development. The cape part of the costume encourages the child to "fly," thus promoting balance and other gross motor skills. See the examples below.

Eye contact should be discussed with someone who knows the student's needs and personality well. Eye contact is a very important communication skill people who have ASD need to develop, but looking into another's eyes could feel too painful and overwhelming, and then set off a temper tantrum. If you find that eye contact is not an overwhelming experience for the student and thus will not result in a meltdown, try to incorporate drama games that can help your student practice making eye contact in a fun way.

Body boundaries are another problem. Often people with ASD are not sure where their body ends and the chair they are sitting in begins (Grandin 1995). Movement exercises in which body boundaries can be explored can help work through this confusion. Movement in itself can be another calming/focusing technique. Engaging students for a short time in interactive hand games that involve patterns of clapping hands and other body parts can create a sense of calmness and a strong focus.

photos by Sherry Haar

Figure 8: Costumes by Sherry Haar to promote sensory integration, motor development, and cognitive skills.

Use lots of vocal variety and facial expression when talking to your student, even if he speaks in a flat voice and shows little expression. The only way to learn how to use clear, expressive communication is to have a clear model and to be encouraged to practice. Play drama games that will enhance vocal, facial, and body expressiveness. Practice gestures and sounds that will communicate emotions and ideas. Provide a place to learn give and take between the student and others in the class.

A lot of times people with ASD feel the rest of us are very strange beings. How we think and relate to each other does not make any sense to them. Temple Grandin says that while growing up she viewed many cultural customs, behaviors, and fashions as "ISPs" — interesting sociological phenomenons (Grandin 2002). Role-play can be the perfect way for people with ASD to learn social skills. They can practice putting themselves in another person's or character's shoes. This can be the first step toward understanding how the rest of the world feels, thinks, and relates, a way to develop theory of mind and to encourage the development of mirror neurons.

As much as possible, follow a similar routine in your lesson plan from week to week. Begin with an opening ritual that stays the same: raising the drama curtain, bringing down the curtain of silence, or singing a song of welcome. If there is a game that the students in class love to play, you could play it — at the same point in the lesson each week. Have students sit in the same place for stories. Always place the audience and performance areas in the same place. Keep the arrangement of the room the same.

If he is having difficulty participating in exercises, you might want to involve him in a technical aspect of the class. For instance, if you are using a CD player for music, you might ask him to run it for you. If your story needs sound effects, bring in rhythm instruments and other objects that can make sounds and let him be the sound effects person while the others act out the story. Students with ASD might enjoy being involved in the technical aspects of a theatre production: building the sets and props, running the sound or lighting board, working the fog machine, pulling the curtain, or doing some other aspect of backstage assistance.

If drama is not the right modality for a person who has ASD, suggest a dance, art, or music class. These might be a better place to start because there is less interaction with others and more parallel and associative play.

================================

Inside My Autism
Chammi Rajapatirana

[Chammi is a young man of Sri Lankan descent who loves to write poetry. He wrote this to explain his experience of autism. He learned to type using facilitated communication, but now can type independently. This essay was typed independently.]

Hidden inside my autism I am a normal person with abnormal sensory, especially auditory and tactile, perception. That I am able to function is entirely due to my Mom. Ideally I will escape from solitary life to lead a productive and stimulating life. Autism for me is a wounded, nightmarish monster living inside my body. Being healed I am sure will mean leashing this monster. I am saying my gifts will be released when my monster is leashed. Please understand I tread carefully. I must be wary of letting that monster break his leash.

Altering my hearing through listening therapy helped lessen my painfully sensitive ears. Pity my dear mom not get listening therapy [Tomatis Auditory Training] for me while I was young. Utilizing wonderful music, Helen, my listening therapist, massaged my ears. Listening to Gregorian chants was like wallowing in painful memories. Dusting off long ago hurts, I wept. My helpless, gullible, trying-to-help Pop and Mom sent me to Japan. I was inert in Japan. In this school I was hungry all the time. Inside, tortured with the pain of missing Mom, I slept inert. Good Mom loved me, tell Pop I terribly unlike myself. Best to bring me home. Gregorian chants led my heart out of thinking of that painful time. Nearly inward turned pain finally came out.

Truth is my auditory sense is quirky. Ignominious word, quirky. I mean that it is assessed by others as quirky. Hearing is all right. Could even be that I hear better than most. Sometimes I seem deaf. Guess I am quietly awaiting sissing sound to stop. Meant that sounds of words get drowned in the sissing of my ears. Tired of sissing sound. Appearing and disappearing, it frets me. Being in a house with high ceilings, like our friend Christine's house, my ears hear echoes. I just feel I should not live in such a house. Echoes are irritating.

My skin is currently separating from my youthful irritation of letting people touch me. People's touch feels hot. I am hostile to being hot. I yearn to be hugged but I feel I can't breathe when I am hugged. The smell of the other person overwhelms me. I think being hugged from behind is the answer.

Padding about [walking around] I think helps me organize my thoughts. Likely moving my body is needed to move my brain. Lifting my feet ostensibly lifts my thoughts.

I like to think about my eyes now. My vision ripples when I look for long at faces. I thought that was how everyone was, with rippling vision. Peeping at a book is the same. The script ripples. I look away instantly. When I look back I don't know if I am in the same place on the page.

Learning to speak is greatly hampered by my always numb lips. I like hot, spicy food to wake up my mouth. Learning to speak is important to me. I always like to talk instead of typing. Finally your thoughts need to be expressed through your own mouth. Uttered words unfortunately have a credibility that facilitated typing does not.

Awake again last night I tried to sort out my problem. My head was ringing and my body was pulsing with energy. Felt I was waiting to explode. Maybe retribution to dear Mom for giving me Chinese dinner. I find hard to figure out why I get like this often. Up to now no one has helped and Mom is getting really tired.

I like to live surrounded by loving family. Loved by family I know I am alive. Ultimately love is all I need.

I like to say I like toiling with Mom to figure myself out. Please try to politely ask other people with autism about their experiences. Be determined to waste no more time thinking everyone experiences his/her world the same way. My purpose is lost if you believe others are just like me. Great that I am able to speak to you even though I am far away.

===============================

Recommended Reading

Attwood, T. (1995). *Asperger's Syndrome: A Guide for Parents and Professionals*. London: Jessica Kingsley Publishers.

Davies, A. (2004). *Teaching Social Skills Through Acting*. Arlington, TX: Future Horizons, Inc. (techniques in this book are demonstrated on the DVD that accompanies Navigating the Social World by J. McAfee)

Grandin, T. (1995). *Thinking in Pictures and other Reports from my Life with Autism*. New York: Random House.

Grandin, T. & Barron, S. (2005). *Unwritten Rules of Social Relationships: Decoding Social Mysteries through the Unique Perspectives of Autism*. Arlington, TX: Future Horizons.

Haddon, M. (2005). *The Curious Incident of the Dog in the Nighttime*. New York: Doubleday.

Hallowell, E. M. & Rately, J. J. (1994). *Driven to Distraction*. New York: Simon & Schuster.

Levine, M. (2002). *A Mind at a Time*. New York: Simon & Schuster.

Martinovich, J. (2006). *Creative Expressive Activities and Asperger's Syndrome: Social and Emotional Skills and Positive Life Goals for Adolescents and Young Adults*. London: Jessica Kingsley Publishers.

McAfee, J. (2002). *Navigating the Social World: A Curriculum for Individuals with Asperger's Syndrome, High Functioning Autism and Related Disorders*. Arlington, TX: Future Horizons, Inc. (Book with accompanying DVD)

Moon, E. (2005). *The Speed of Dark*. New York: Ballantine Books.

Myles, B. S., Trautman, M. L., & Schelvan, R. L. (2004). *The Hidden Curriculum: Practical Solutions for Understanding Unstated Rules in Social Situations*. Shawnee Mission, KS: Autism Asperger Publishing Co.

Weiss, L. (1997). *ADD and Creativity*. Dallas, TX: Taylor Publishing Company.

Wolf, M. (2007). *Proust and the Squid: The Story and Science of the Reading Brain*. New York: HarperCollins Books.

Recommended Videos

Lavoie, R. "How Difficult Can This Be?" The F.A.T. (Frustration, Anxiety, and Tension) City Learning Disability Workshop. PBS Video.

Recommended Websites

American Association on Intellectual and Developmental Disabilities: www.aaidd.org

Autism Society of America: www.autism-society.org

Center for the Study of Autism: www.autism.org

Epilepsy Foundation of America: www.epilepsyfoundation.org

International Dyslexia Association: www.interdys.org

Learning Disabilities Association of America: www.ldanatl.org

National Center for Learning Disabilities: www.nlcd.org

National Dissemination Center for Children with Disabilities (NICHCY): www.nichcy.org

National Tourette Syndrome Association (TSA): www.tsa-usa.org

5. Getting Off To a Good Start: Basic Adaptations for the Drama Classroom

Many different types of drama classes can be offered, depending on the age of your students and the skills to be developed. The most common classes are creative drama, improvisational acting, and scene study. Other types of classes include puppetry, radio drama, mask drama, mime, voice and diction, acting for the camera, readers' theatre, Shakespearean acting, Greek theatre, and auditioning skills. All can be taught successfully and all have something of value to offer to people who have disabilities.

This chapter focuses on the general adaptations and issues that should be considered before embarking on any kind of drama class. Chapter 6 discusses specific issues related to creative drama and improvisational acting classes.

Classroom Space

The physical space in which a drama class is held will greatly influence the kind of work that is done in it. Your drama space should have as few physical barriers and visual distractions as possible. It should not be too large or too small. Gymnasiums and school cafeterias are usually too large. In these types of spaces students have difficulty settling down to work. They run around, shout, and generally behave as if they have suddenly been transformed into professional basketball players. They are not intentionally misbehaving; they are engaging in behavior appropriate for a large, open space designed for sports. They will have difficulty understanding that you want to use the space in a different way, and you will have a great deal of difficulty trying to persuade them to do so.

A drama space should be a quiet place without a lot of auditory distractions. If your space is not soundproof, ask neighboring classrooms if they will agree to do a quiet project at the same time you are doing drama. It is very hard to tell a story or create a character when you are competing with someone else's distracting noise — of course, you will be creating distracting noise for them!

Good acoustics are important in a drama room. If your students cannot hear well, they will have difficulty focusing on what is being said by the teacher or by others. Students with and without auditory processing problems will become distracted in a room full of live sound. Instead of moving out in one direction and being absorbed by the walls, floor, and ceiling, as it does when the acoustics are good, the sound continues to bounce off the surfaces in the room, creating a hollow, echoing effect. The source of voices becomes hard to determine and students are not sure where to focus. Poor acoustics are another reason why gymnasiums and cafeterias are not good choices as drama spaces.

A school stage would seem to be the first and best choice as a space for a drama class. This is not always the case. Young children and students who have low impulse control and are easily distracted cannot focus on the lesson because the space is too exciting. Instead, they want to hang on the curtains or run backstage to hide.

A stage is a formal performance space. Its best use is for rehearsals for formal presentations or for performance skills training. Holding a creative drama or improvisational acting class on stage can change the tone of the class from informal/experiential to formal/presentational. Working on stage, students tend to start performing *for* their classmates instead of improvising *with* them.

An open, medium-sized classroom is often the best place for a drama class. This kind of room provides an informal space in which students can express their ideas and engage in process-oriented work. If you are in a classroom filled with desks, push the desks out of the way to make an open space in the middle of the room.

A large carpet creates a warm, welcoming area on which everyone can sit together. If students have trouble staying in one place or understanding their physical boundaries, have them sit in chairs or on carpet squares. Masking tape can be put on carpets to mark seating or performing spaces, but check with the custodian first since ripping up tape will do more damage to some kinds of carpet than others.

Bright, even lighting is important so everyone can see the teacher and each other clearly. Fluorescent lighting can be distracting for people who have autism and those who have ADHD. Electrical current in North America runs at sixty cycles per second. This means that the current and lights being illuminated by it are being turned on and off 120 times per second. Incandescent lights usually do not flicker because the filament in the lamp glows even when the current isn't on, but fluorescent lights flicker. The flickering is usually not seen by the majority of people if it happens faster than fifty times per second; however, Temple Grandin reports that some people with autism are so sensitive to light that they can actually see the flickers that run at frequencies as high as 120 times per second, which can create confusion and visual processing problems for them (Grandin 2002). And there is evidence that other people's visual cortex may still respond to the flickering at low frequencies: office workers report more headaches and eyestrain with fluorescent lighting than with incandescent or natural light. In a study comparing normal subjects' reactions to low- and high-frequency (flickering as often as 60,000 times a second) fluorescent lights, Igor Knez (2005) reported that people under low-frequency felt less relaxed, less calm, less content, and less at ease. Photobiologist John Ott has done numerous studies on how light affects behavior. His videotaped studies of hyperactive schoolchildren showed a marked behavior difference between children in classrooms with standard fluorescent lights and those in classrooms with full-spectrum radiation-shielded fluorescents (Ott 1990).

Chances are that you teach in a building lit by standard, low-frequency fluorescent lights and there is little you can do to change it. However, if you notice that students are bothered by this type of illumination, you can supplement it by opening the blinds and curtains to let in as much natural light as possible. If children in your class are particularly light-sensitive, you could bring in additional incandescent light sources, full-spectrum or otherwise, to enhance the quality of light and cut down on the irritating consequences of the fluorescents.

Beware of activity rooms with lots of paraphernalia in them. A room filled with toys or sports equipment is too distracting! If your room is cluttered with many interesting objects, put them away before class. Tape butcher paper over tempting shelves. Cover table displays with fabric. It may take you ten or fifteen extra minutes to prepare for class each week and to restore the room to its original state afterwards but, believe me, it is worth it!

I taught an after-school drama class at a learning center for special education students. Initially we were assigned to the physical/occupational therapy room. It was filled with seesaws, bikes, balls, swinging ropes, and climbing apparatus of every kind. I was able to hide or camouflage everything except for the large wooden jungle gym in the corner. My students had a lot of problems with impulse control and they were drawn to that jungle gym like a giant child-magnet! I started out with a class rule that no one could climb it during class. That did not work. I set up a contract with them that stated they could play on it before class and at snack time, but not at other times. That did not work. They wanted to climb on it from the time they entered the room until the time they left. Finally, I had to switch the class to the library. While not without its distractions, nothing in the library came close to being as enticing as the jungle gym!

Teaching Personnel

Whether integrated or not, a drama class for students with disabilities needs to be run by at least two teachers. The lead teacher takes responsibility for planning the lesson and leading the class in most of the activities. In a creative drama class, she would usually be the one who tells the story and provides narration for the enactment of the story. In a performance-based class, she usually would direct the scenes of the play. In all cases, she is the one who keeps the class moving forward.

The lead teacher needs to be strong and firm. She must communicate clearly and be able to pace her explanations at the average speed the students process information. She must remain aware of the current interest and attention level of individuals and the group as a whole so she knows when it is time to end one activity and begin a new one. Patience, flexibility, and a sense of humor are perhaps the most valuable qualities a lead teacher can have.

The assistant teacher has an equally important role. She provides the support that allows the lead teacher to keep the class moving forward. She models appropriate behavior for the students. She refocuses the attention of wandering individuals onto the activity at hand. She assists students who need extra help or extra attention during class. One student might need help finding the bathroom. Another may have difficulty cutting with scissors. A third may fall and need help getting up. She provides disciplinary intervention. Two students might get into an argument and need to be separated. Someone might lose control and need to take a time-out. The assistant deals with most emergencies as they arise so the lead teacher can keep the class moving forward.

A good assistant is crucial. Without someone to handle the inevitable problems that arise on the periphery, the lead teacher, who is holding the center together, must stop to handle each and every problem. As soon as the class loses its guide and focal point, students' attentions begin to wander. Soon their bodies have followed their minds and they are all over the room involved in some activity other than the one everyone had previously been engaged in together. Once you lose a group's attention, it is not easy to get it back.

An assistant is also a handy dramatic resource. She can take on a role in a story that no one wants to play. If the group is working in pairs or in teams, she can fill in when there is an uneven number. When the class has been divided in two, she can become the leader for one group while the lead teacher works with the other. If there are more than two groups, she can circulate among the groups along with the leader. When a group is rehearsing a play, the assistant can act as the stage manager, help students who are not on stage learn lines, or rehearse a separate scene simultaneously.

photo by Lea Ann Rosen

Figure 9: An assistant models an activity for a student.

A good assistant stays focused on what is happening in class at all times. She participates in activities whenever she is not off on the side solving a problem or assisting someone who needs extra help. She needs to be friendly, firm, and retain her patience and sense of humor under fire.

Some teachers like to share the roles of lead and assistant teacher to team-teach together. This is fine as long as each knows which role she is playing at any given moment in the class. Trouble arises when the lead teacher stops to deal with a behavior problem and the assistant tries to take over the class, but isn't prepared to do so, or if both stop to deal with the problem and leave the class leaderless.

I watched this happen during rehearsals for a show at a camp for emotionally disturbed children. The counselors were so used to jumping in immediately to head off behavior disturbances that whenever one camper acted out, all three counselors would stop rehearsal and focus on her. The rest of the campers had to wait until the counselors got back to them. Since the campers had difficulty dealing with unstructured time, they ended up getting into trouble, too. A lot of time was wasted and not much work got accomplished. The campers started to hate rehearsal, not because they did not like drama — they insisted that they did — but because they did not like being set adrift by their group leaders.

Because of their specific needs, some students may need one-on-one help all the time. In this case, a class may need to have a second assistant who is specifically assigned to one particular student. Sometimes the one-on-one assistant can be a slightly older student who serves as a companion, buddy, or mentor. In each case, this one-on-one assistant needs to stay with the child at all times.

Some classes may need two or more assistants to help out generally. Assistants must work as a team. Rather than assigning each assistant to specific students, each one should usually work with every student. That way all the students get to know all the teachers and vice versa. Besides, there is no guarantee that two different students assigned to the same assistant might not need help at exactly the same time. What are the other assistants going to do? Twiddle their thumbs and watch while she tries to be in two places at once? That is not teamwork.

There are several qualities that are important in being a successful drama teacher or assistant. To begin with, a good drama teacher must know how to play and be spontaneous with her students. As mentioned in Chapter 1, drama is a form of play, and spontaneity is one of its major ingredients. Inflexibility and rigidity on the part of the teacher will kill the sense of play and creativity in students. However, having a playful approach does not mean the teacher should be childish, immature, or become one of the kids. The teacher is the facilitator of the dramatic experience and the referee for games and conflicts. Students need to know that the teacher is in charge and that she will create structure and set limits fairly.

Another important quality is the ability to create a safe, supportive atmosphere in which children can express their ideas and feelings without feeling judged, categorized, or caustically criticized. A good drama teacher focuses on the potential in students. She starts with where the student is, accepts that, and works on developing what could be. She does not try to destroy what is there and replace it with something else. Instead she uses the students' current skills and abilities as a starting point on which to build.

A third key quality is the ability to recognize and respond to magic when it happens. What I call *magic* is that spark which lights up the hearts and minds of everyone in the room at the same time. Magic happens every time something truly creative, spontaneous, and truthful clicks in the group. Suddenly, everyone in the room is on the same wavelength — totally focused, imaginatively involved, and completely immersed in the work going on. The drama space is not just a room anymore — it becomes transformed into a highly charged transitional space in which anything can happen. Time seems to stand still. Students become "potential beings" capable of intense bursts of creativity, cooperation, and appreciation.

You could say that magic is *group flow*. Mihaly Csikszentmihalyi (1990), a psychologist who focuses his study on the positive aspects of life, identifies *flow* as the experience of timelessness and enjoyment one feels when engaged in a structured activity that is intrinsically rewarding and is difficult enough to challenge one to pay full attention and use one's skills to the utmost. When in flow, one stays in the present moment and feels a sense of joy, ease, competence, and autonomy. When magic happens, everyone goes into flow together and is swept away into the realm of the imagination and the possible. You can't force magic or flow to happen, but you can prepare a favorable climate for it through the way you treat your students and through your expectations for how they should treat each other. Magic can only happen when individuals feel respected, feel they can take risks without fear of criticism or attack, and know that even their silly and crazy ideas will be appreciated and accepted.

To successfully teach drama to a student who has a disability, there is one additional key: learn to see the person and not the disability. Avoid the trap of your own and society's prejudices and preconceptions about people with disabilities. Discard stereotypes and stigmas so that you are not blinded to the unique individual who is your student.

This does not mean ignoring the disability or forgetting that the disability is there, but do not let the disability get in the way of developing an authentic relationship with the person who is your student. Look past the outer differences to see the inner sameness that connects us all. We all experience the whole spectrum of human emotions, which need to be appropriately expressed, shared with others, and validated. We all want to be acknowledged, accepted, and appreciated. We all want to be loved. We all have creative ideas, no matter what our level of cognitive or physical functioning.

If you can connect with an individual's feelings, dreams, and innate creativity, you will connect with the person's inner self. If you can value the unique contribution that each person makes to a group, the individual will feel valued as well. If you can begin to see your student in terms of her potential instead of her limitations, in terms of her strengths instead of her weaknesses, you will begin to bypass the trap of confining your vision only to her disability. Believe that each person in your class possesses imaginary wings and can be taught to fly!

Prerequisites to Taking a Drama Class

The first prerequisite for a successful experience in drama is that the student wants to do drama! Drama is not for everyone, just as basketball is not for everyone. A student must be willing to participate in the activities, to play and have fun, to express her feelings and explore those of other people. A good teacher can motivate someone who is shy or confused, jolly a student out of a bad mood, and negotiate a solution to an interpersonal conflict — but is powerless against a closed mind.

The children who have dropped out of drama classes I have taught have done so because they never really wanted to take the class to begin with. Their parents thought it would be a good idea for them to take the class, but never found out beforehand how their child felt about it. Forced into a situation not of their choosing, these students became stubborn and belligerent or withdrew. They refused to participate, refused to make friends, and refused to follow rules. They felt bad, I felt bad, and their parents felt bad. One summer the parents of an adolescent who was recovering from a traumatic brain injury insisted that she be enrolled in the BAPA summer camp, which put on a musical play. This girl had never been interested in drama before her accident; she had been into science. She certainly wasn't interested in something brand new when she felt uncomfortable with a body and brain that was recovering from severe trauma. She particularly had no interest in going on stage when her balance was off and her whole physical being didn't work like it used to. But her parents had been told that being in drama would be very therapeutic and bring her back to herself. Needless to say, this did not happen and she ended up dropping out two weeks into camp after having a miserable time.

The person I felt worst about was a young girl whose parents had died in a car crash and who was living with other family members. She was incredibly shy and did not want to do drama. I tried everything I could think of to help her feel comfortable, get her involved and having a good time, but she did not want to be there. If it had been a group for other kids who were grieving, it might have been different, but I think she felt so different and so isolated that she just was not willing to connect, trust us, or have fun.

The second prerequisite is that a student needs to have achieved a basic ability to connect with and interact appropriately with others. Drama is rarely taught as an isolated, individual activity. A drama class almost always happens in a highly interactive group context. There must be at least minimal willingness on the part of the student to cooperate and work with the teacher and the other students.

Students who have major emotional issues — either hostile, anti-social behavior or severe withdrawal from others — have difficulty succeeding in drama. They might experience more success if they started out in the arts with music or visual art, both of which involve expressing feelings and developing artistic skills, but in a less interactive situation. After their self-confidence has grown and they start liking themselves better, they can begin working on their ability to get along and respect others in a group. Another alternative would be for them to participate in a group that plays social games or non-competitive sports. Competition between individuals or teams reinforces negative social values in that it forces a win-lose dichotomy on most aspects of the experience. What an angry or depressed person needs is win-win experiences so she does not have to face failure yet again. She can focus on participating and enjoying herself with others. Eventually, she may want to try a drama group.

Assigning Students to the Appropriate Drama Class

Activities and assignments in drama, as in any other subject, need to be appropriate to the maturity levels, attention spans, interests, and abilities of the students in the class. If the range in any of these areas is too wide, the class will probably have difficulty working together. For this reason, placement in the appropriate drama class is essential.

Placement by Age

Students in the primary grades are usually enrolled in a creative drama or puppetry class. Students in middle and high school typically take improvisational acting or scene-study classes. Depending on their maturity level and interests, students in grades four to six can opt for whichever type of class most appeals to them. Some children remain interested in fantasy longer than others. Others seriously aspire to perform. If a drama class is being offered recreationally or in a school club, chances are it will not be offered by individual grade level or age.

Classes will cover a range of ages: usually pre-school (ages three to five), early elementary (ages five through nine), upper elementary/middle school (ages nine through 12), teens (ages 12 to 18), and adult (18 and older). Public schools are required by law to offer education services to students with disabilities to the age of 21. If you have young adults between ages 18 and 21, they may want to be part of a teen group instead of an adult group just because of their interests and maturity levels. Usually, it feels more comfortable to relate to a 16-year-old than a 33-year-old if you are 20. However, that should be decided on a case-by-case basis.

I have taught creative drama classes that had a wider age range than those above that worked fine. One of the first classes I taught at Ivymount had children from five to 14 years of age; this was an unusual class in that they were all devoted to drama and knew each other well. The older girls felt very good about mentoring and supporting the younger children and everyone was still heavily into fairy tales and make-believe. There are drawbacks to this wide an age span. First and foremost is the difference in attention spans between a typical five-year-old and a 14-year-old. Older children can usually handle more complex dramatic material and get bored with such stories as "The Three Little Pigs," while younger children cannot stay with a longer, more complex story, such as "Aladdin and His Magic Lamp." Another big issue is subject matter. If one part of the class wants to act out fairy tales and the other part thinks fairy tales are beneath them, you will have a problem finding material that will engage everyone. Carefully differentiate between the creative drama classes and the classes in which more realistic dramatic scenes will be done, and ask students and parents to make a choice about which they would prefer.

Placement by Disability

When I first started the Arts Access Program, I was told in no uncertain terms by several special-needs educators *never* to mix children who have LD with children who have IDD. They said that mixing these two types of students would be like mixing oil and water — they would not get along, the different cognitive needs of each group required a different delivery of information, and to add insult to injury, the children with LD would feel stigmatized. I realized there was a pecking order here and I was not an expert in the field, so I figured I should follow the wisdom of those who were. I was also advised — in equally strong terms — not to mix students who had physical disabilities with students who had cognitive disabilities.

However, the way everyone's availability turned out that first semester, I had to put everybody together or we would not have had *any* classes. I decided that to have some intermixed classes was better than not having any at all. I had students with Down syndrome, cerebral palsy, blindness, Williams syndrome, severe learning disabilities, and mild learning disabilities all in one class together and I discovered that everyone was perfectly capable of understanding what was going on, felt fine about working together, had a great time, and no one felt stigmatized.

The one area where mixing students with different disabilities was an issue involved deaf students. As mentioned in Chapter 3, deaf people do not consider themselves disabled. They are generally of normal intelligence but have been stigmatized by hearing society for hundreds of years as mentally defective. They don't want to put themselves into a situation where they will be associated with anyone who has a disability because they believe the stigma of disability will rub off on them. It was even difficult at first to get deaf students to mix in classes with hearing students because deaf parents were worried that their children would be discriminated against by hearing teachers and students.

My interest was in offering accessible programming for as many people in our community as possible, so I had to figure out how to work around this sticking point. I had done a lot of work with deaf students while I was in undergraduate and graduate school and had seen firsthand how drama empowered deaf students. I felt it was crucial for them to be able to experience theatre arts, especially in a region where there was a large deaf population. A wonderful theatre program existed for teens at the Model Secondary School for the Deaf on the Gallaudet University campus in Washington, DC, but it was only for the students who went to school there. Lots of deaf children and adolescents attended public schools in the Montgomery County, Maryland, area where there were no accessible programs for them.

I ended up recruiting Lisa Agogliati, who at that time was the director of dance and administration, to create a Deaf Access Program. This grew into classes and performing companies, some deaf only, some integrated with hearing, deaf, and KODA (kids of deaf adults) students. Lisa was slowly able to build trust with the Deaf community, hire deaf artist/teachers, and forge relationships that garnered several major grants from the U.S. Department of Education. That story is shared in *Dreams to Sign, which* Lisa and I wrote together in 2002.

As far as segregating students with similar disabilities together in classes to make teaching more streamlined to addressing specific learning needs, I have found that each child in any class has different needs and different styles of processing information. To effectively teach each student, I must adapt my techniques and approach to each one — disabled or not. I think this is true everywhere. Mel Levine (2002) reports in his book *A Mind at a Time* that one of the teachers who had taken his Schools Attuned teacher training program reported back a year later, "…all those spiffy techniques I learned to use for kids with learning problems, I'm now using with every single kid in my class. It's a little weird, but they seem to benefit everyone" (p. 282). Levine goes on:

> So often an intervention technique we deploy to help a struggling class member will indeed help everyone else in that class and at home as well! Many remedial maneuvers may represent nothing more than superb teaching, and who would not benefit from a transfusion of that? Also, kids with a specific dysfunction are invariably jousting with a function that is an issue for everyone in the classroom. It's just a bit more of a problem for the student who is having trouble with it (p. 282).

The three greatest determinants of a child's ability to function successfully in a drama class are her emotional maturity, her group-interaction skill level, and her motivation to do drama. Specifically, a child must have enough impulse control, focus, and flexibility to work out the conflicts that inevitably occur when two or more people are involved in a project together. With a desire to do drama, all things become possible.

Placement by Experience

It can be helpful to offer a beginning or introductory level class and an intermediate or advanced level class for each age group. Beginners often need more structure and more time to learn the rules and develop social interaction skills. Students with a year or so of drama under their belts may become impatient waiting for the newcomers to get up to speed. This will become more of an issue in an integrated setting than in a beginning setting with students who all have disabilities.

On the other hand, students who have some experience can be role models and mentors for beginning students and can help them learn appropriate behavior and new skills more quickly. They already know what to expect and how much fun drama can be. A strong recommendation from a peer will often sell an idea or concept better than any song and dance by the teacher.

Class Size

Overcrowding a drama class causes frustrations for teachers and students. Drama teachers like to give each student high-quality, individual attention. Drama students need to have enough opportunities for participation in each class to grow and learn. Students who sit around too long waiting for a turn get bored and lose interest — and then act out to get attention!

In a rambunctious group of young creative drama students, between eight and 10 students works well, and between 10 and 12 students is an optimum class size for older students. A good upper limit is 15 students, at least until they are able to do a lot of work independently. More than 15 and you are dealing with the law of diminishing returns.

In a class in which only students who have disabilities are enrolled, five to eight students is a good number. In this smaller group situation, everyone can receive a lot of extra individual attention and encouragement. Students who have perceptual difficulties, autism, or attention deficits are not overwhelmed by too much sensory stimulation. Students who have impulse control problems do not have to wait too long before taking a turn. Very shy children will feel less pressured with fewer people to relate to. Less than five is not good because if one or two students are absent, you will not have enough people to play most games or act out certain stories.

When integrating students with disabilities into a "regular" class, you need to evaluate how much time and attention will be needed to make the accommodations required for them. A guideline suggested by one of my Special Needs Steering Committee members who had been the principal of a public school is to count a student with special needs as two "regular" education students because typically a 2:1 ratio is required for teacher time and attention needed to implement accommodations and adaptations. When figuring upper limits for class size and deciding whether to have one, two, or more assistants, he recommended counting each student who needed specific accommodations as two, rather than one. This way the teacher won't be overloaded. In my experience this system has worked well.

Behavior Management

If everyone could always get along, follow directions, and respect themselves and others, teaching would be a breeze. However, every student and teacher has bad days, just as they have good ones. Disagreements happen, personalities clash, and it is easy to bring emotional baggage from earlier in the day along with you to drama class. At its best, behavior management is students taking personal responsibility for their own behavior rather than the teacher controlling the students.

A meta-analysis of 100 studies of classroom management techniques indicated that "teachers who had high-quality relationships with their students had 31 percent fewer discipline problems, rule violations, and related problems over a year's time" (Marzano & Marzano 2003; p. 6). A number of specific teacher behaviors were identified which led to these relationships: appropriate levels of teaching dominance, appropriate levels of cooperation, and being aware of high-needs students. *Teaching dominance* was defined as the teacher's ability to assertively make expectations clear about academic instruction and standards as well as how students were to behave. *Appropriate level of cooperation* referred to setting up the learning environment as a team or community in which all students and the teacher function together in an equitable and fair way. As for dealing with high-needs students, the most effective teachers "did not treat all students the same; they tended to employ different strategies with different types of students" (p. 11). I believe the guidelines I present here reflect these qualities.

Students who have disabilities have to contend with extra frustrations and complications in their lives, which can create disturbances. It can be extremely upsetting for anyone when her body or her brain is not within her conscious control and will not do what she wants it to do. You, as a teacher, will see emotional reactions that may stem directly from frustration over a task that is too difficult or may start if a student is rushed to solve a problem that may be very easy for you but very complicated and challenging for her.

The emotional fallout from years of frustrating experiences and failures can be more handicapping than the initial disabling condition and may color a person's whole attitude and approach to life. Some individuals stop trying and withdraw. Others become timid and helpless. Some may respond with anger while others might become morose and depressed. Rigidity and inflexibility — unwillingness to consider and choose different options — can result from fear of failure.

Creating a Supportive Environment

Some students may enter your classroom expecting to fail because they have failed in academic or social situations so many times before. It is the teacher's responsibility to create an environment that is geared toward success rather than failure. This can be done by focusing on students' efforts and attitudes and on their progress as artists rather than on an end product.

In a supportive classroom no student is labeled "good" or "bad." Labeling a child places a value judgment on her character and assigns her a negative or positive role to play out. Work and behavior should be evaluated rather than character. Appropriate class work and behavior should be rewarded with praise and attention. Inappropriate work and behavior can be pointed out and dealt with in an appropriate, nonjudgmental manner. When students feel accepted for who they are and feel safe from attack and judgment, they are freed from acting out old emotional scripts of failure and can let the most creative, social, and fun-loving parts of themselves out to play and interact with others, without fear of being put on the spot or negatively criticized.

Focus on student strengths rather than weaknesses. We all have both. We get plenty of feedback on our weaknesses from parents, friends, teachers, bosses, and co-workers, but we do not get enough honest appreciation for our strengths. Mel Levine (2002) strongly believes that working with students from a strengths-based perspective is the only way to achieve success. Focusing on deficits brings the deficits to the fore, while focusing on strengths allows both the student and the teacher to access them more readily in order to bypass or to overcome weaknesses. Begin looking for her actual strengths and focusing honestly on them — do not offer false praise.

In planning and running your class, take an approach that is student-centered rather than teacher-centered or parent-centered. What is the difference? What does that mean? It does not mean letting students do whatever they want. A student-centered class starts where the students are, assesses their artistic, emotional, and social needs, and works with their strengths to develop more skills and strengths and to fortify their weaknesses. Whatever growth occurs can then be celebrated.

A teacher-centered class starts where the teacher is and tries to bring the students up to the "teacher's level." Students serve the teacher's vision of achievement and will either measure up or fail to do so. In this situation only a student who hits the teacher's mark has succeeded.

A parent-centered class starts with the product that the teacher or administrator thinks the parents want to see as the end result for the money they have paid for tuition. That end product may not be where the students need to go at this time and may not be where the students want to go in terms of interests. For example, to force every class to end with a performance product may put too much stress on the students, especially beginners or shy students. Pushing toward a product that has nothing to do with where the students are and where they should be going next can make the class process stressful, pressured, and unenjoyable — and when students feel stressed, they act out.

As for behavior management, I am a firm advocate for the proactive rather than the reactive approach. Identify potential problems *before* they occur and arrange the space, the lesson, the materials, and your approach to avoid pitfalls. Then you might not have to use many behavior-management techniques because negative behavior will be less of an issue. Will you be able to head off *all* behavior problems with proactive techniques? No, of course not. But if you take a pro-active approach, chances are that you will be able to spend much more time on teaching than on behavior management!

Reactive behavior management is what happens when you deal with the problem after it occurs. Reactive behavior management is not necessarily bad — it is just not efficient if that is your only approach. Sometimes you will not see a behavior problem coming and it will explode in your face like a land mine. When that happens, there are a number of useful techniques that educators have developed.

Cooperation versus Competition

Competition often creates conflict in a group setting. Keep competition to a minimum, especially in the first sessions of groups and with beginners. Too much of our contemporary American society is based on cutthroat competition. This creates an atmosphere of hostility, aggression, and "every man for himself" — the only way I can succeed is to make you lose.

Play games that stress cooperation, working together, and everyone winning rather than winning and losing. Focus on the fun of playing the game, working together with friends, and coming up with creative solutions to problems as a team. Point out creative, expressive work done by each individual or team as it happens. Students will learn to appreciate the work itself, rather than what the work means in terms of winning or losing. If a game unavoidably involves winning and losing, stress good sportsmanship — I always insist that the winners congratulate the losers for playing a good game.

Setting up the Rules

Be sure the rules of the class are stated clearly at the beginning of the first session and reviewed at the beginning of the next few sessions until everyone is aware of them. Talk about the reasons behind having rules. The purpose of rules is not to impose rigid discipline on students from the outside, but to create a structure in which they can appropriately work with others and control themselves. You, the teacher, want to run an orderly class in which everyone will be safe, have fun, and learn.

Try to have no more than five important rules of behavior. If you have a long list, students will not be able to remember them all. It is often helpful if you create the rules using input from your students in that first class discussion. This takes time away from the drama part of the first session, but it empowers the students to take responsibility for their behavior and could proactively prevent many future difficulties. When people are able to have a say in their social structure, both in what is okay and not okay and what the consequences for not-okay behavior will be, they often feel much more willing to follow the rules and accept the consequences.

Present the rules in the form of positive statements that express what students are expected to do, rather than what they are not supposed to do. Post your rules somewhere in the classroom. If you are developing the rules with the class, this may mean that you make a temporary list the first day and then make a more formalized, readable list by the time of the second class.

Here is an example of a simply, positively worded list of five rules that might work well with a class of elementary school children. This should cover most issues:

- Listen to and look at whoever is talking.
- Keep your hands and feet to yourself.
- Respect the ideas of others.
- Follow directions.
- Do your best.

If you are working in a very distracting space, you might need to also have:

- Respect the space and the things in it.
  or
- Do not touch the things in the room that we are not using.

Emily Neumann, a special education teacher, likes to create a simple word using the first letter of each of the rules (personal communication 2008). For instance, FACE could stand for:

Follow directions.

Always have fun.

Clean up when you are done.

Everyone deserves respect.

Do not expect students to follow a rule that has not been explained. Do not assume students understand what respect, being polite, paying attention, or following directions mean. Remember that having poor social skills does not mean that a student is "bad" — it just means she has poor social skills. Use drama class as a forum in which she can learn better ones.

If you find your rules are not working with the entire class or with specific members, you might need to create a contract with the class or with the specific individual. A contract will formally lay out exactly what behaviors are expected and the consequences for misbehavior. Agree to what needs to be in the contract and write it up. Whoever is involved in the contract, including the teacher and sometimes the parents of the child, needs to sign it to signify that they will abide by the rules and the agreed-upon consequences.

A contract could delineate issues a particular child is having and identify the strategies the student will use to control herself when they come up. For example, if a student who has ADHD needs to take a break from the class when she is overstimulated by an activity, she could agree to take a short break in a specific, quiet, non-distracting part of the room, go down the hall to get a drink of water, or take some other calming, appropriate, agreed-upon action. Consequences, such as losing a turn or having to sit out for the rest of a game, could also be spelled out in a contract to verify that this is the fair outcome of not following rules, not a mean, nasty punishment.

Modeling

Children are natural imitators. They can learn what is appropriate by observing others who are behaving appropriately. Demonstrate positive behavior by modeling it yourself and having your assistant model it. Call attention to students who are modeling positive behavior and praise them — Susie is working so well with Johnny!

Non-Verbal Cues

You naturally use non-verbal cues all the time: eye contact, gestures, looks, facial expressions, and sounds of pleasure and displeasure. Become conscious of how you are using your nonverbal communications and enhance them to positively, proactively reinforce the behavior you want and discourage the behavior you do not want. Smile, nod "yes," and make pleasant sounds when a student is doing good work. Frown, shake your head "no," wrinkle your brow, and hold up your hand in a *stop* gesture as warnings that you want certain behaviors to stop.

Touch

Touch is a loaded subject in many situations. Because of fears of physical and sexual abuse, some places have policies that forbid any kind of touch. If the institution you are working in prohibits touch, you must follow their rules.

Touch tends to be used in drama classes in many games and is necessary in some scenes. Most people enjoy a gentle pat on the shoulder or back when they have done a good job. Be aware of where, when, and how you touch the people that you work with and you should be fine. Link your touch with a word of praise to clarify why you are touching them.

Some people who have been physically, sexually, or emotionally abused do not like to be touched — this should be respected! Also, remember that many people with sensory integration disorders, including those with ASD, ADHD, and TS, are tactilely defensive and will pull away from most kinds of touch. This does not mean that they do not want to be touched; most kinds of touch over-stimulate them and feel uncomfortable. They may respond positively to a firm touch, if you put your hand on their shoulder and press down with a firm, downward pressure. This kind of physical pressure seems to center them and can be used as a technique to calm them down or help them focus when they are about ready to spin out of control. A child who has a sensory integration disorder can sometimes calm herself by pressing down on her head with both hands, pressing up against a wall with both hands, or by doing other types of isometric exercises that create a similar, firm, downward or inward pressure.

Children with DS and WS tend to be very warm and demonstrative about their feelings. They often like to hug or kiss teachers or other students. This can become distracting or inappropriate and is not safe behavior with strangers. Explain to them that other people have personal space and do not always want to be touched. You can say, "We are all friends here, but hugs/kisses are inappropriate/not okay during drama class." If this does not work, you can limit hug-giving to times of greeting and leave-taking. You could only allow hugs from the side. Kisses are never appropriate.

Never touch a student in a private, inappropriate place and do not violate her personal space, even for a hug, without her permission. As the teacher, you have power in the classroom situation and you must be careful not to abuse that power in any way. Think first and avoid actions that could be misinterpreted as physically or sexually abusive or coercive.

Visual Reminders and Positive Reinforcement

Side-coach all the time. Praise good behavior. "Susie, you are doing a wonderful job!" "Sam and Eric, you are both working together so well today!" "I'm really proud of the job you are doing."

Make statements about behavior that you approve of or about skills you see developing. "John is following the rules of the game." "Bill is paying attention very well today."

Head off problems you see brewing by reminding students about rules or directions in a way that states what action you want them to take. "Remember, keep your hands to yourself." "Stay away from the costume rack."

Rewards

Rewards can come in many guises. Praise, positive feedback, and encouragement will make any student thrive but should always be genuine, as people know when they are being patronized. As Thumper's mother said, "If you can't say something nice, it's better not to say anything at all."

If you have students in your class who are having difficulty getting along, you can set up special activities they will be able to do if they cooperate. One creative drama class for students with LD loved to play Duck, Duck, Goose. If everything went well in class, teacher Mandy Hart would let them play it for the last five or ten minutes of every class. Duck, Duck, Goose became their ritual closure activity.

You could provide a snack midway through or at the end of class if students work well together. However, before feeding children, check with their parents and the administration. Sometimes schools have policies about food. Sometimes parents do not want meals to be spoiled with snacks or have a dislike of food being used as a reinforcing tool. Some children have allergies or sensitivities but might eat the forbidden food anyway. Other children might not be able to eat the snack and feel left out of the reward.

Colorful stickers can also be used as rewards. Many special-education classrooms use sticker charts to keep track of the success a student has with academic work or behavior. You can do this, too. All children love getting stickers! They are a visual proof of a job well done and can be shared with parents and friends. If you are rewarding just one behavior, you could make a chart that has a space for one sticker for each class period or for each interval of class time you are measuring. If you are rewarding more than one behavior or each time a behavior is performed, you may want to make a chart with lots of space for each class period. The teacher decides when stickers are given out. Stickers could be given every time the appropriate behavior is performed or all at the end of class. Rewards are more reinforcing if they are given immediately after the appropriate behavior, but you may not want to interrupt the flow of your class to do this.

Freedom to Ask Questions

Tell students that it is always okay for them to ask for help or for more information. Questions might be about anything from how to do an exercise to where to find the bathroom. Students might need assistance doing an art project or dealing with another student who is being offensive, or they may just not understand your directions. If your students feel they have permission to ask questions, they can clarify confusions and misunderstandings before interpersonal problems or frustrations turn into major conflicts.

After you give directions for a task, you might want to ask, "Does anyone have any questions about this?" Then provide some wait time. Even people with normal cognition need from 17 to 20 seconds to formulate a question; people with cognitive issues may need longer.

Look for puzzled facial expressions. If you see any, ask, "Do you have a question?" After I explain something, I will often end with, "Does that make sense?" which allows people to give me feedback about whether I've been clear. Sometimes when you think you are being crystal clear, you are not!

Another way to clarify whether you have been understood is to ask students to repeat what you just said back to you in their own words. If they can paraphrase what you told them, that is a clear indication that they have understood the information. If they have not understood, try to explain again using different words.

Group Discussions

When interpersonal problems occur in a group, never underestimate the value of a group discussion. Whenever students have the opportunity to contribute to solving a problem, they will own the solution and try to make it work. They may be able to give you insights into their difficulties that you had never before considered. They may be able to tell you how they deal with this problem successfully at home or school.

When students talk with each other about how they feel, they form new bonds of friendship and understanding as they recognize how we are all more alike than different. Group discussions can be very helpful in integrated groups. Go around the circle and let each person share what bothers her most or what she feels most insecure about in this situation. Everyone has a special need of some kind and everyone needs the support of others to deal with it.

Pegasus, a performing group for teens with and without disabilities which I directed, had a lot of growing pains in its first few seasons as we worked through interpersonal conflicts. A number of the actors had known each other for years and were entrenched in dealing with their frustrations, disagreements, and miscommunications with each other in very inflexible, impatient, and bull-headed ways. During our first year we had at least one argument at every rehearsal. When a conflict arose, we stopped and talked about it. I insisted that everyone's ideas were valuable and that we needed to give everyone a chance to share. If a number of good ideas were in competition, we tried to work out a compromise in which the best aspects of all the ideas were put to use.

By the second year the Pegasus actors were respecting each other more. We only had major disagreements in the early part of the year. Our third year we had only one argument the whole season and the minute it erupted, both combatants immediately realized they had overstepped their bounds. They separated, cooled off, and then apologized. I was impressed at their growth and maturity.

In a sense, learning to be an artist is the process of learning how to make choices about how to express yourself eloquently, clearly, and truthfully. Teaching your students how to make choices is part of their artistic training as well as part of their socialization. Time spent in discussion is not a waste of class time — think of it as part of their artistic growth!

Sometimes a group discussion goes well, but sometimes it degenerates into a blaming session. This happened during the third session of my very first creative drama class for students with LD. Everyone in the class came in wired from a wild, unusual week at school. The rainy day also seemed to affect everyone's behavior for the worse. A number of exercises we did were successful, but everything broke down while everyone was holding hands in a circle to act out a large hot air balloon. They started pulling on each other's arms, bumping into each other, shoving, and pinching.

I stopped the class and tried to get them to talk about why they were having such a tough time working together. They were so overwrought that they were unable to verbalize any feelings or reasons. They started accusing each other of ruining the class. I explained that no one person was at fault and the best thing would be for everyone to forgive everyone else and start over. That seemed like an excellent solution at first, and everyone started hugging each other and saying, "I'm sorry."

However, Ginger was still very upset. Drama class was extremely important to her and she felt the whole day had been ruined. Instead of hugging Roberto, she went up to him and angrily said, "It's your fault! I hate you, Roberto!" Taking her lead, all the other students suddenly started hitting each other, yelling, "I hate you! I hate you! I hate you!"

For some serendipitous, intuitive reason, my assistant, Marilyn Harwood, who is a musician, and I looked at each other and then simultaneously started singing, "If you're happy and you know it, clap your hands." Immediately, everyone joined in. We had to sing eleven verses of the song before the mood in the room turned upbeat and forgiveness was truly in the air. The twelfth verse we made up was "If you're happy and you know it, hug your friend." They did — and the emotional storm was finally over. The moral of this story: "Sometimes none of the reasonable solutions work and you have to do something spontaneous and filled with joy." Neuroscientist Daniel Levitin says that whenever a group sings together, the neurotransmitter dopamine and the hormone oxytocin are released in the singers (Levitin 2008).

Ignoring Negative Behaviors

When a negative behavior is disrupting class in a major way or creating a safety hazard, it usually must be dealt with the minute it occurs. However, sometimes negative behavior can be extinguished by *not* paying attention to it. Paying attention reinforces a behavior because getting attention is experienced as a good thing. Some people who never get positive attention become addicted to negative attention. Even though negative attention does not feel as good a positive attention, it is better than no attention! When you get no attention, in a sense that means you do not exist!

Whether you pay attention to a behavior or not will be a judgment call you will have to make in the context of the situation. On one hand, if you allow negative behavior to continue, you are allowing the student to model negative behaviors you do not want copied. But if you make a big deal out of something small, the student might repeat it again and again.

Warnings and Directions

If a student is doing an unsafe behavior, such as hitting or tripping someone else, obviously she needs to be stopped immediately and then receive a consequence for breaking the rule. However, if your student is impulsive, it might not be fair to mete out consequences for an infraction, such as talking out of turn, without giving her a second chance. Some teachers like to use an "early warning system." Private code words or phrases worked out in advance can be used to remind a student that her behavior is on the verge of getting out of hand. Or you might speak a short word or phrase that does not interrupt the flow of class to warn everyone that it's time to settle down. To remind students that a serious line was about to be crossed and they needed to settle down and pay attention, Tim Reagan used to say the phone number for emergencies: "911!" Another creative phrase could have the same effect, for example: "Red alert" or "Yellow light" or even the funny name of a prickly animal — "Porcupine!"

Some teachers like to provide students with a series of warnings before they consider a rule broken and move on to give consequences. The first warning is verbal. For the second warning, the student's name is written on the board. The third time the rule is broken, the student must face consequences. How many warnings you give will depend on the situation, the infraction, and the student(s) involved. Whatever you do, make sure that *you* follow the rules and enforce them consistently.

How the teacher addresses the misbehaving student can make a big difference in how the student responds. Be aware of your tone of voice and body language. If you are tense or hot under the collar, chances are that the student will hear only your tone of voice, not the content of your message. This might result in more acting-out behavior rather than less. Try to remain calm, cool, friendly, and firm.

Use proximity to address the problem behavior. Giving a direction is more effective when you are standing right beside the student instead of yelling "Stop fooling around over there!" at the student from the other side of the room. Walk over and say in a firm, quiet voice, "Come over to the circle now. We are ready to start."

When enforcing a rule or giving a direction, make a statement instead of asking a question. "Wouldn't you like to join the group now?" implies a choice. The answer could be, "No, I want to stay over here and play with the puppets." A statement makes clear that no choice is implied and leaves no room for argument: "It's time to join the group now."

Word requests as positive statements that tell students what you want them to do, instead of what you do not want them to do. "You are being silly" or "Don't jump on that chair!" will not give the student a clue about what action you want them to take. What you want them to do may seem like common sense to you, but the action you want is implied, not explicit. If they are not doing what you have told them to stop doing, they may not know what to do instead. "Pay attention to the story" and "Sit on the chair" are very clear, direct, and action-oriented directions.

Use vocabulary that the person understands. Make statements that are clear and concise. "Sit down now" is more to the point than "If you would just follow the directions, we could commence with our activity without further delay, but instead, as always, you continue to gild the lily and procrastinate." It does no good to confuse the situation with long words, elaborate explanations, or justifications. Identify the rule that was broken or the problem that you see, give your direction, and, if necessary, provide the choices that are open. Leave it at that.

Threats can be interpreted as dares or backhanded invitations to continue engaging in the behavior. "If you don't stop, I'll get very angry" might encourage a student to see if she can create some fireworks that would be more dramatic and interesting to her than class has been thus far. At a summer camp for children with emotional difficulties, I watched a camper repeatedly and deliberately "get the goat" of her counselor by always doing what he told her not to do. He was so close to the situation and his feelings were so personally invested in their ongoing conflict that he never saw how she was disobeying him on purpose to get a rise out of him. Invariably, he ended up raising his voice and then a small smile of satisfaction would cross her face. He finally had to be transferred out of that group of children because his ineffectiveness with her had spread to the other campers and he was always on the verge of losing his temper. "If/then" statements will be more effective when they identify the rule that was broken and what consequence will follow if it happens again: "Pinching is not okay. If you do it again, then you will need to take a five-minute time-out."

Using "I" statements can help teachers and students avoid blaming when they discuss behavior issues. Take responsibility for what you feel and encourage your students to do the same. "I feel frustrated when you don't listen to directions. Please sit down and listen." Start out by owning the feeling and then add the action you would like the students to take. For a student speaking to another student about a misunderstanding, "I feel angry when you tease me," is more assertive and effective than "You made me mad! You're so stupid!"

Consequences

Sometimes a rule is broken because of poor communication, a mistake, or lack of awareness/understanding of the rule. When this happens it is best to deal with the situation through a short, rational discussion with the parties involved in order to clarify the confusion. Consequences are not really needed.

Sometimes a conflict happens because of "baggage" — something that happened before class that the student brings in with him that has nothing to do with what is going on in class: the emotion from the previous situation is displaced on someone in the current situation. Clarifying this is also important in sorting out the problem, as is teaching students to leave their "baggage" at the door of the classroom.

One of visual-arts teacher Gail Gorlitz's students entered her classroom so wound up that he jumped through the door, leapt across the table, and knocked over another boy who was standing in the middle of the room minding his own business. This was totally inappropriate and unsafe. She pulled him aside and gave him a lecture about his behavior. In talking with the boy's mother later, Gail discovered that he had recently come to this country from China. The first major cold snap of winter had hit that day, so when he went to school that morning, he wore his winter coat, a pink down jacket he had brought from his homeland. In China, it is culturally acceptable for a boy to wear pink, but not in America! From the moment he arrived at school he was teased by all the boys for wearing a "sissy" jacket. His response when he got home was to ball up the jacket, throw it in a heap on the floor of the closet, and refuse to wear it. Needless to say, he got into trouble with his mother. By the time he entered Gail's classroom in the afternoon, he was ready to explode, and he did! A short talk to find out what was going on and an apology to the boy who was knocked over was all that would have been needed to address the situation

Other times a rule is broken deliberately as a means of getting attention or hurting a perceived "enemy" in the class. When this happens, the poor choices must be pointed out and consequences must be imposed by the teacher or discipline will break down. Other students need to feel safe and they cannot feel safe if they are being bullied or if the teacher is allowing the misbehavior to ruin a game. Consequences might involve removing the student from the group activity until she can work cooperatively with other students.

When warnings are not heeded or if a child loses control, a time-out in another part of the classroom can be an excellent behavior-manage-ment tool. Time-out chairs/booths/corners serve several purposes. A time-out allows for a cooling down period. It removes the child from stimuli that may have been overwhelming. It removes the child from being the center of attention so that the inappropriate behavior is not reinforced by attention. It provides the child with an opportunity to think through and remedy the situation she has created. She gets the distance she needs to identify and make positive choices. If she is unable to identify these choices on her own, she may need guidance from the teacher or an assistant. In addition, a time-out is boring compared with being able to participate in the action of class. A time-out space should be set away from the area where the majority of class activity occurs so negative attention is not reinforced and to cut down on sensory stimulation in case the incident was caused by sensory overload. If time-out will be used as a consequence, make that clear when you first make your classroom rules; do not wait until you need to use a time-out for the first time to explain that timeouts will be used.

Behavior-management specialists suggest having a child sit in time-out for one minute for each year of her age. Ten minutes for a four- or five-year-old is too long. If 10 minutes for a 10-year old seems too long, it would certainly be fine to have an agreed-upon time limit for all time-outs, such as three minutes or five minutes. Put your assistant in charge of keeping track of the time or use a kitchen timer. If you have put an adolescent into time-out, you might offer to let her out when she is able to verbalize what she did to get herself sent to time-out and how she can avoid making the same mistake when she rejoins the group. If disrespect has been involved in the incident, an apology might also be appropriate when rejoining the group.

How to do a time-out: If a student begins misbehaving or showing off during an activity, stop the activity. Give the student a choice to either participate appropriately or take a time-out. Giving people choices highlights that we make decisions and must take responsibilities for the actions we decide to do. She may take this opportunity to turn her behavior around and the activity can continue. If she does not, tell her, "If you can't choose to behave appropriately, then you must take a time-out for [amount of time]." If necessary, have your assistant accompany the student to the time-out area, but try to do it without providing her with additional attention that will reinforce the behavior. If necessary, give her role in the activity to another person, and then continue working with the group.

If the offense needs to be discussed with the student before she rejoins the class, allow her to cool off for a few minutes and then have the assistant chat with her either in the time-out area or out in the hall. Ask the student why she thinks she was unable to participate appropriately in the activity. Then ask what she will change about her behavior so that she can participate again or what she could do differently if in a similar situation. If two students have been involved in an argument, you might need to separate them into different time-out areas and let them cool off before trying to sort out the conflict. When processing a conflict between two students, ask each to report only what her role was in the situation. Have them use "I" statements. In any conflict between people, each plays a part and must own up to her responsibility; otherwise, sorting-out will turn into blaming and nothing will be resolved.

Communication with Parents

Parents can be a great resource in helping you to manage a student's behavior. They can provide you with good ways to get compliance with requests or deal with unpleasant situations. When you have a problem in class, check in with the student's parents. You are not doing this to tattle on the student, embarrass her, or create problems at home for her. You simply need to report the situation. If you have dealt with the behavior in class, there should be no need for additional consequences to be imposed. However, if the behavior is unusual or if the same behavior happens on more than one occasion, you might need more information to learn how to better deal with it, as well as make the parent aware that something is going on.

Approach parents in a calm, reasonable, non-judgmental manner. You can say, "If you have a minute to talk, I would like to tell you about a situation that came up today." State the facts of the situation simply, briefly, and calmly: what the student did or said and what you did or said. Then you can ask, "If this happens again, do you have a suggestion for how I could better handle the situation?" or "Is there any information that you could tell me that would help me understand where that came from?"

If enlisted as a member of the child's team, parents can be your best ally in heading off future problems. On the way to drama class they can remind the child about appropriate behavior. They can provide you with insights as to why this behavior occurred and what you might do to prevent its occurring again.

If the behavior continues and the child must be removed from the class permanently, the removal will not come as a complete surprise. The parents will have been involved in dealing with the situation from the beginning and they will have worked with you on trying to solve it. They will not feel you are making an irrational or hasty decision or scape-goating their child.

It is usually best to check in with the parents immediately after class because this is immediately after the behavior has occurred. Parents want to know at the time something happens, not later. However, there are occasions when you or they do not have time to talk or when it would be inappropriate to discuss the situation in front of the child. If this happens, call the parent at home at a convenient time sometime before the next class time. Use your common sense. Mealtimes and bedtimes are obviously *not* good times for parents to talk.

Some schools or camps send notebooks home every day, containing notes from the teacher that provide a progress report. If a response is needed, the parent can write a note in the notebook. If you are in a situation where there is time to do this, this can be a great communication tool because the lines are open every day, back and forth. Email is also a useful communication tool.

Children with special needs tend to bring home more negative reports than positive ones. Be sure to provide parents with feedback when their child has done a good job, too! Letters providing updates on what the class has been doing and on upcoming events keep parents involved. A quick note or a few comments after class sharing a success their child has had is greatly appreciated. When parents know you are seeing and appreciating the positive aspects of their child, as well as dealing appropriately with the negative ones, they will become your loyal supporters.

Recommended Reading

Csikszentmihalyi, M. (1990). *Flow: The Psychology of Optimal Experience*. New York: Harper & Row.

Horn, S. (1996). *Tongue Fu!* New York: St. Martins Griffin.

Levine, M. (2002). *A Mind at a Time*. New York: Simon & Schuster.

Rosenberg, M. B. (2000). *Nonviolent Communication*. Encinitas, CA: PuddleDancer Press.

Ury, W. L. (1999) *Getting to Peace: Transforming Conflict at Home, at Work, and in the World*. New York: Viking. [published in paperback as *The Third Side*]

6. Creative Drama and Improvisational Acting Classes: Further Adaptations for the Drama Classroom

Creative drama can be done with students of all ages. However, creative drama classes are usually taken by preschool and elementary children, as discussed at the beginning of this chapter.

Students from adolescence through adulthood usually take acting classes that focus on improvisational acting or scene study — these will be discussed later in the chapter. In my experience students who have many cognitive disabilities often retain an interest in fantasy longer than their typically developing age peers. If this is so, they may be happier in a creative drama session.

This chapter looks at leading creative drama and improvisational classes to show more adaptations for students who have disabilities.

Creative Drama

Creative drama is an informal, improvised, extemporaneous dramatic session that may involve the acting out of a story or scene, usually a fairy tale, contemporary children's story, or a story the group has created together. Through the creative dramatic process feelings, attitudes, and ideas about oneself and others are explored and expressed. Basic drama skills are developed.

Presentation of creative drama scenes is informal. It is work done in process or in progress and *by* the group *for* the group. Training students

179

in theatrical skills for the stage or creating a play to be formally performed for an audience is not necessary or even desirable. The content of the dramatic work, the informal process of learning together through group activity, and the development of the imagination are the important aspects of creative drama.

Of course, a scene developed through creative drama can be performed for an audience; however, when this is done, the focus of the work changes from one of learning and process to one of performance and product. After a certain point in the semester the class must stop exploring and start rehearsing. As the performance deadline draws near, energy must be focused onto refining and perfecting the work already created. The students will probably learn more important lessons if they spend time on the creative drama aspects instead of working on performance.

The Dramatic Elements

The elements involved in a dramatic story or scene are similar to those in literature. *Plot, characters*, and *dialogue* create *an idea* or *theme*. However, there are two major differences.

First, in drama all the elements are brought to life by actors instead of by words on a page. The story unfolds in real space and time rather than being an imaginary event that happens purely within the mind of the reader. Second, the descriptive narrative that is found in books is rarely found in drama. Information is largely expressed through the characters' dialogue and actions. It is true that some plays have narrators and that creative drama teachers often serve as the narrator of the story as it is being enacted; however, in both these cases, narration is only the glue that holds the dramatic action together and facilitates progression from one scene to the next. It is never the primary focus of the enactment. From an artistic standpoint, the less narration involved in a play, the stronger its dramatic structure.

The *plot* of the scene or play is structured with a beginning, middle, and end. In creative drama the plot is often based on a fairy tale. It is also possible to create an original story or to change a familiar story to create a new ending. In one class my students decided that they wanted Dorothy to stay in Oz and marry the Tin Woodman instead of going back to Kansas. Another class wanted to explore what might have happened if Goldilocks had apologized for her actions and become friends with the Three Bears.

The plot is fueled by the *characters* that have goals they want to accomplish and problems they need to solve. Improvisation comes into play as the actors create *dialogue* or words that the characters say. Dialogue in a creative drama class is created on the spot by the actors, not memorized beforehand. This gives students a lot of freedom for problem-solving and role-playing as well as for developing their verbalizing abilities and group-interaction skills.

Warm-ups

Depending on the age and attention spans of the students, a creative drama session usually lasts between 45 minutes and an hour. Class begins with a warm-up activity to focus students on the class and prepare them to work together. Warm-ups could be physical exercises, a social game, a movement activity, a sensory exploration, an imagination game, or an art project. Often these serve as skill builders for the work that is going to be done in class that day or an introduction to the story and characters. See Chapter 7 for descriptions of warm-ups.

Telling the Story

Warm-ups are followed by a story that is told by the teacher and then acted out by the class. Stories can be traditional fairy tales, myths, legends, fables, or contemporary children's stories. Often I ask my classes what stories they would like to act out. Invariably they want to work on stories that deal with issues they are working on in their own lives. Bruno Bettelheim's book *The Uses of Enchantment* is an excellent exploration of how the conflicts and themes in fairy tales developmentally parallel those in the lives of children. One of the reasons why "Cinderella" is such a popular story is that it deals with the need to be recognized for all your inner beauty and exceptional qualities. It also provides a healthy outlet for children to evaluate their parent-child conflicts, for example: the Evil Stepmother represents the Bad Mother who punishes them and doesn't let them do what they want while the Fairy Godmother represents the Good Mother who is nurturing and warm (Bettelheim 1977).

Setting up the Story

Before you jump into acting out a story, a few decisions must be made. First, roles must be assigned to students. Then the space must be set up for acting the story. Desks, chairs, and other objects can be arranged to create the "set" or locations needed. Masking tape on the floor can be used to delineate rooms, if you want. Setting up all the locations in a story at the beginning creates smooth scene transitions, especially in a story that moves back and forth between places. Scene changes in the middle of a story take time and you can lose the attention of your audience and actors if you don't keep the action going.

Rehearsing the Story

To ensure safety, rehearse any unusual physical actions, such as acrobatics, or physical combat between the hero and villain. One good technique for safely handling battle scenes is to pantomime all weapons so no one gets hit and to move in slow motion so each actor can remain physically in control. Then the actors don't forget they are acting and turn their staged fight into a real one. A slow-motion battle can become a beautiful ballet. You could even help your actors retain the dance-like quality of their battle by adding music to it or having the audience or other characters provide a rhythmic beat.

Sometimes it is good — especially for beginners — to practice character movements, voices, or important lines before jumping into the story. If a group is very new to drama, I often have everyone act out all the characters together before I allow them to make character choices. If the story is "The Three Billy Goats Gruff," I have the students practice walking and talking like the BIG BILLY GOAT, the Middle Billy Goat, and the little billy goat. Then I would have them all practice being Trolls. Having an experience with all the characters can encourage a wider range of character choices and warm the students up to the idea of using their bodies and voices to create a story.

Acting Out the Story

Once all the preliminaries are in order, the story can be acted out. Have the students who are in the first scene take their places in the acting area. Those not in the first scene can sit to the side where they will make their entrance or they can sit with the audience until it is time to join the scene. Either way, everyone who is not in the story at any given moment should be paying attention to what is going on in the acting area.

Acting as the narrator, the teacher can structure the story and help it unfold. "Once upon a time, long, long ago, in a country far away, was a girl named Cinderella. Her mother was dead and she lived with her Wicked Stepmother and two Ugly Stepsisters. Every day her Stepsisters would make her do all the household chores..." Notice that the narrator quickly moved the story into action the actors could perform.

Beginning creative drama students need more narration to help them through a story than experienced ones. The narrator can cue actions, entrances, and exits. "Suddenly, there was a knock at the door. It was the messenger from the King with an invitation to the ball." If the actors are not sure what to do next, the narrator can remind them, "Cinderella was so upset, she started to cry." He can also cue lines, "So Cinderella said...And the Prince replied..."

If students are non-verbal, they can pantomime the story to the narration. In this situation, the narration must be limited mainly to actable action so the actors are not standing around or sitting around with nothing to do while the narrator blabs on. In any case, if you are narrating a story, do not bulldoze your way through. Leave enough space for your students, verbal and non-verbal, to add lines if they want to. I have been surprised by students who never spoke a word for weeks, suddenly coming out with all the right lines (and more!) when acting out a familiar and beloved story, such as "Goldilocks and the Three Bears."

Children love using colorful costumes and props when acting out stories. For students who have cognitive disabilities, costumes and props can be instrumental in helping their imaginations come alive and giving form and substance to the story. However, you do not need to go overboard about providing physical accoutrements. You can leave some things to the imagination. Actors who have everything given to them are not as challenged to use their bodies and voices expressively or to stretch their imaginations to the fullest.

Replaying the Story

If time permits and interest is high, students may want to act out the story again. Replaying the story with students taking different roles allows them to experience the action through more than one point of view. A child who is playing the little billy goat may have a very different experience from the child who is playing the BIG BILLY GOAT. The little billy goat is afraid of the Troll and escapes by using his wits. The BIG BILLY GOAT is physically capable of standing up to the Troll and knocking him off the bridge. An actor who plays only the little billy goat might remain afraid of the Troll. If he has a chance to play the BIG BILLY GOAT, too, he may no longer fear the Troll, because his character has competently handled the situation and saved his brothers. After this experience, he may even be brave enough to try to act out the Troll himself.

If they are satisfied with once through the story, move on to another dramatic activity. It is always better to plan more activities than might be needed for a class than to not know what to do next with 15 minutes left in the period.

Closure

Class can end with a discussion of the story, a related art activity, or a drama game that provides closure for the session. (See the next chapter for ideas for closure activities.) Sometimes it is nice to take two minutes to go around and let each person say what his favorite activity was that day. Class ends on an upbeat note, the work of the day is reviewed, and the teacher has an idea of what activities made the biggest impression on individuals and the class as a whole.

Structuring a Lesson Plan

When putting a lesson plan for a creative drama class together, alternate between active and passive activities. This allows your students to work off excess energy by using their bodies actively, then resting from their exertions. They will be able to concentrate better because of the variety. If you structure your activities appropriately, you will not need to take a break in the middle of class. The order of the activities will provide all the rest time you need.

If your class begins with a quiet opening warm-up, move on to an active game before having students settle down to listen to a story. After a ten-minute story, they will be ready to get up again and act it out. If you are doing a session of theatre games, move from an active game to a passive one and back to an active one. You might start out with a physical warm-up, sit down for a pass-around pantomime or imagination game, play a rousing movement game, lie down for a guided fantasy relaxation, and end with a series of pantomimes.

Too many active games in a row will run one kind of group ragged and spin another kind out of control. Going directly from one quiet activity to another is a surefire way to turn your students into wiggle-worms. The next chapter suggests good drama games to play.

Pre-Class Activities

If you have a group that tends to straggle in at different times rather than arriving all together, it is a good idea to keep the early-comers constructively occupied. If your students like to draw, this can be a very useful pre-class activity. You could let them draw anything they want or you could ask them to draw a character in the story you will be acting out that day. This will begin to focus them on the work that will be done in class.

Pre-class activities need to be interesting enough to hold attention, but not so interesting that students do not want to leave them to begin class. Everyone rarely finishes a project at the same time. Try to find a stopping point that everyone can agree upon. Projects that are not quite finished can be finished at the end of class or taken home for the final touches.

Beginning Class

Open class in a clear, sure way. Gather everyone together. Sitting in a circle, everyone is grounded and can see everyone else. If students have trouble staying in their own spot in the circle, use colorful carpet squares to help them define their sitting space.

Some groups enjoy a rundown of exactly what is going to happen that day. You might want to list all the activities planned for class in order on the board or on a large sheet of paper. This will keep your students (and you!) organized. Many special-education teachers go over the day's schedule with their students the first thing every morning. They leave the schedule up all day so that if students get confused, they can look up and reorient themselves. This technique will work just as well for you as it does for an academic teacher. In addition, many of your students may already be familiar with the routine.

Other groups like to begin class with the same activity each week, such as a physical warm-up to music, a circle game, or a check-in on how everyone is feeling. The opening becomes a comforting ritual they can count on. One of my creative drama classes insisted that I start with the same welcoming ritual each week. Everyone sat in a row of chairs and I would walk down the row, throw open my arms, and say, "Welcome, Tanya! Welcome, Jason! Welcome, Jeremy!" As I said each person's name, he or she would stand, take a bow, and say, "Thank you!" "That's me!" "Hurray!" or something else appropriate to being welcomed to the group. A number of opening activities can be found in Chapter 7.

Transitions

Make sure the transitions between activities are clear and smooth. Students become anxious and distracted if transitions are confusing or if it takes too long between activities to get started. As much as possible, set up your equipment and supplies before class or have things organized and easily within reach. This way you will be ready to start the next activity as soon as you are finished with the one before.

Giving Directions

Whenever you are explaining how to do something, whether it be playing a game or making an art project, present each step in the sequence separately. If you run through all the directions from start to finish, your students will not be able to follow what you want, due to sequencing and short-term memory problems. Most adults who have normal cognitive functioning cannot follow a whole sequence of verbal directions that are thrown at them all at once.

A way to break down a sequence of directions might be as follows: "I'm dividing you into group one and group two. [Do this.] Group one stand in a line over here. [Do this.] Now I want all of you to stand with your back to the wall. [Do this.] Group two stand in a line right here. [Do this.] Everyone face group one. [Do this.]"

As you present each step, illustrate it through as many different sensory channels as you can. Say, "Sit with your legs crossed." Have your assistant demonstrate sitting this way to provide a visual image. When they sit down and cross their legs, they will understand kinesthetically what sitting with crossed legs means. If they cannot figure out the position by looking at how your assistant is sitting, move their legs into the correct position so they can feel it with their bodies. Or use a visual image: "Sit like a pretzel."

Give clear directions. Use simple, plain words. Allow processing time. State what you want from students rather than what you do not want. It takes the brain more time to process negative statements than positive ones (Hunt 1982). When the negative statement comes in, the brain takes it and removes the negative to find out what the positive action would be. Then it adds the negative back in to cancel out the positive action. I do not have an LD and my brain freezes each time I see traffic signs with a slash through it. I have to stop and consciously reason out if I am supposed to do what the picture shows or if I am not supposed to do it. Students who have information-processing problems can get lost and confused when trying to follow negatively framed directions. A student could pick up on the negative message ("Don't hit Billy"), interpret it as a positive one ("Hit Billy"), and act on it *before* the negative part of the message is processed and understood.

Processing negative commands into their positive messages can leave children at a loss as to what behavior the teacher wants instead. Many times we give a command that has two parts: the spoken message and the implied one. The implied message is often culturally understood as the next action to take. For instance, the implied message of "Don't talk" is "Listen." But a student who has missed picking up cultural constructs because of cultural isolation or because he is very literal, will only know what he *should not* be doing. You need to actively, verbally fill in the missing, unspoken message. Learn to phrase requests in a positive manner. Tell students what you *want* them to do. Instead of saying, "Don't talk while others are talking," say, "Listen while others are talking." Instead of saying, "Don't hit the other students," say, "Keep your hands and feet to yourself."

Rephrasing your communications from negative to positive is easier said than done. Communication style is habitual. If you tend to phrase your directions in a negative manner, for a while you will need to consciously think through directions as you give them. After practice, your communication habits will change and you will not have to consciously think about it as often.

Choosing a Story

Some stories are easier to act out than others. A lot depends on the structure of the plot and whether the characters have clear, actable goals. When working with beginners and students who have cognitive disabilities, it is crucial to choose a story with a strong, clear, dramatic plot structure and easily actable characters.

Some stories have very succinct, simple, and clear plots. They are based on a parallel, *one-two-three* structure, incorporating a lot of repetition. The characters in these stories are usually one-dimensional; that is, they have one main action to play and no major decisions to make. "The Three Little Pigs" is an example of this kind of story. There are three Pigs. Two of them are lazy and one works very hard. One by one, they meet the Salesman and buy materials to build their houses. One by one, they build their houses of straw, sticks, and bricks. The Wolf decides he wants to eat the Pigs, so he blows down the first and second house, but cannot blow down the third house. Hard work wins the day. End of story.

"Goldilocks and the Three Bears" also follows this pattern. Goldilocks is a little girl whose major character trait is curiosity. After she breaks into the Bears' house, she tries out their porridge (too hot, too cold, just right) and she tries out their chairs (too hard, too soft, just right) and their beds (too hard, too soft, just right). When the Bears return home, they check out their belongings in the same order (porridge, chairs, beds), and find Goldilocks in the Baby Bear's bed where she has fallen asleep. She wakes up and runs away. End of story. Other stories that use this pattern include "The Three Billy Goats Gruff," "Little Red Riding Hood," and "The Little Red Hen."

Series in threes are very comforting to children — and adults. Enough tension can be generated from one-two-three that the relief from the resolution is satisfying, there is not *too* much tension, and it does not take *too* long to get to the end. Children who have cognitive disabilities often have trouble sequencing and mentally holding several actions in their minds at once. They can follow the sequencing of these one-two-three story patterns without getting confused or feeling anxious. These stories fit the shorter attention spans of young children and many with cognitive disabilities.

The next level in complexity of plot structure is stories that begin with a one-two-three pattern, but add some complications that postpone the resolution of the plot. "Rumplestiltskin" is an example. The Miller's Daughter is sequentially locked in three rooms to spin straw into gold. A funny little man appears each time and offers to help her, but before he will, she must give him something of value. In the third room she has no jewelry left and must promise to give him her first baby. She marries the King, time passes, and the baby is born. She has three chances to guess the little man's name or he will take the baby. She must send her Messenger throughout the land to collect names so she can figure out the correct name. "Rumplestiltskin" takes a little longer to act out because the plot is more involved. In addition, the characters are more complex — they have more decisions to make.

Another kind of story offers a dramatic plot structure in which the hero must pass through a number of trials, each more difficult than the one before. Sometimes a number of characters try to solve a problem, but cannot. Finally the hero comes along and succeeds. In "The Fisherman and His Wife" the Wife keeps sending her Husband back to the Magic Fish to get bigger and better houses to live in. In "The Stone in the Road" the King blocks the only road into town with a gigantic stone and hides to see if anyone in his kingdom is thoughtful enough to move it. He watches while many characters walk by and ignore it, until finally the Miller's Son pushes it out of the way.

There is more to remember in these stories. More characters are involved. More events happen. Sometimes the events are causally connected, but sometimes they are not. Strong causal connection means that the first event causes the second event which causes the third event, etc. so that the sequence *must* happen in a certain order. The less strong the causal connections in a plot, the more difficult it will be for anyone to remember the sequencing of what comes next. To remedy this, the teacher as narrator needs to focus on the through-line, or main actions, and keep the story moving from scene to scene.

The more complex the plot of a story, the more difficult it will be for beginning creative drama students to comprehend and act out. "Peter Pan" and "The Firebird" are examples of stories that have lots of characters, lots of actions, and many twists and turns in the plot. They are great for advanced students, but confusing for beginners.

Look for stories with lots of actable actions in the plots. Many paragraphs of flowery description by the narrator do not qualify as actable action. Beware of stories that say, "Many years passed and the princess grew in beauty and wisdom." It is very hard to act "growing in beauty and wisdom." "Falling in love at first sight" is also hard to act and not very much fun for boys.

Beware of stories that say, "And many suitors came and each one tried to make the princess laugh, but no matter what he did, each one failed." "Many suitors trying" is too vague to be acted. If you want to do a story of this kind, you, the storyteller must create suitor-characters and invent different specific actions that they take. Without more specifics, when the actors arrive at the suitor scene, all the suitors will walk into the room and just stand there. Of course, it's quite possible to develop the suitors, their personalities, and what they do *after* telling the story and *before* acting it out, but if the students love the story and are anticipating jumping in to bring it to life immediately after the telling, they may not want to stop and develop characters first. You will know the best option once you know your group.

Another plot device that can be problematic when dramatized is repetition. Be careful of choosing stories that repeat identical plot or character actions more than two or three times. "The Elves and the Shoemaker" is a good example. In most versions, the Shoemaker leaves leather out for the Elves to make shoes on four or five different nights. The first night he does not know anything will happen. The second night he leaves the leather out to see if it will happen again. The third night he and his Wife stay up and watch. "And every night the elves would make shoes and he became rich and prosperous." Each time the elves are doing exactly the same thing. This will hold the attention of very young children and children who are into repetition, but it will not hold the attention of intermediate or advanced groups.

Another warning: beware of casting actors as characters who do not have a dramatic purpose in the story. Lords and Ladies-In-Waiting usually do not do anything dramatically important. They are not involved in moving the plot forward. Confidants of the hero or heroine usually do not do much except listen. Passive heroes, such as the Young Master in "Puss in Boots," also pose an acting problem. Student actors who have parts that do not give them anything to do get bored and either wander off or get into trouble.

Stories with strong plot structure that I have successfully used with beginning creative drama students who have disabilities include "The Three Little Pigs," "Little Red Riding Hood," "The Three Billy Goats Gruff," "Goldilocks and the Three Bears," "The Peddler and his Caps," "The Stone in the Road," "The Tortoise and the Hare," "The Lion and the Mouse," "The Magic Toy Shop," "The Little Fir Tree," "Why the Evergreen Trees Keep Their Leaves," "The Frog Prince," "The Giant Peanut Butter and Jam Sandwich," and "The Gingerbread Boy."

Intermediate groups enjoy "Hansel and Gretel," "Cinderella," "Snow White and the Seven Dwarves," "Rapunzel," "Rumplestiltskin," "Jack and the Beanstalk," "The Golden Goose," "The Dragon and His Grandmother," "The Fisherman and his Wife," "The Man and the Tiger," "King Midas and the Golden Touch," "The Brementown Musicians," "Sleeping Beauty," and "The Princess Who Couldn't Cry."

Advanced groups can handle more complex stories, such as "Aladdin and His Magic Lamp," "The Firebird," "The Maids in the Mirror," "Snow White and Rose Red," "Mufaro's Beautiful Daughters," "East of the Sun and West of the Moon," "Persephone," "The Labors of Hercules," "The Wizard of Oz," and "The Six Servants."

Good sources for stories are Winifred Ward's *Stories to Dramatize* and *Grimm's Fairy Tales.* I do not recommend *Anderson's Fairy Tales,* as they are very episodic and do not have a lot of actable action.

Telling a Story versus Reading a Story

Telling a story to a class is much more effective than reading it from a book. Storytelling is more active. A good storyteller makes eye contact with his audience, invests himself emotionally as he describes the plot, and vocally acts out the characters. All of this captures the attentions of the listeners and hooks them into using their imaginations as they follow along. Students become primed for their own enactment of the story because they start to feel that the story is not a past event, but is happening now.

Telling a story gets the drama teacher more involved. When you read a book, you are processing information that was formulated by another person and that is outside of yourself. When you tell a story, you make it your own. You become intimately familiar with the plot, create voices for the characters, develop an emotional relationship with the material, and communicate that familiarity and those emotional connections to your listeners.

A lot of teachers are afraid to tell a story. The first fear I always hear is "What if I forget a part?" You will not forget anything if you prepare yourself properly. "But what if I prepare myself and I forget something anyway?" Even if you do forget, if you know the story well, you will be equipped to mend your mistake. Story listeners who are enjoying themselves are very forgiving of a storyteller who is relaxed and having a good time.

To prepare to tell a story for the first time, read it over a number of times. The first time through, just read for enjoyment, and when you are done, remember the emotional reactions you had. Were there any funny parts? Any exciting parts? Any romantic parts? Where did you feel tension begin to build? (Storytelling pace usually picks up as the tension builds.) Where was the climax, the place where the tension was relieved? What are the strongest images that remain in your memory once the story is over?

photo by Keith Jenkins

Figure 10: A good storyteller uses emotion, facial expression, gesture, and character voices.

As you read through it again, make a list of the characters and how they are related to each other. Outline what happens in the story. Try to see how one event causes the next. If you can find the causal connections in the story, you have found its plot. And if one event causes the next, it will be easier for you to remember as you tell it.

Sometimes you need to adapt a story. It may be too long or the plot may meander around too much. Find a way to cut out the extraneous scenes and make it tighter. Some of the events in the story may not be causally connected. Invent a way to change what happens to make events connect. There may be some violence that you would rather not have students act out. Maybe a character's motives do not make sense. Feel free to make a story stronger for your dramatic purposes. Since prehistoric times storytellers have changed and adapted stories. You will be joining a long and respected tradition!

When you feel you know the story well and can hold the order of events in your mind, practice telling it. As you speak, keep an image of the characters in your mind's eye — what they look like, where they are, what they are doing, and how they feel about it. Your private image communicates itself to your listeners who then begin creating their own images. The images your audience creates will not be identical to the one you have in your head — and they might even be better than your images!

You can start practicing by telling the story to a recording device and playing it back. Or you can tell the story to a friend. As you share different parts, note your listener's reaction. By watching your listener's reactions, you will know when you are being clear, vague, dramatic, or boring. When you are done, ask your listener which moments he remembers most vividly. Those are the moments when you were most connected to the material. Your ultimate goal is to be strongly connected to the story the entire time.

When you feel you can get through the whole story without leaving parts out and when you can retain your emotional connection with what is happening, you are ready to tell it to your class. If you want, write a skeletal outline of the plot and key phrases of dialogue on note cards to keep with you the first few times you tell it. Take a look at the card before you begin, but try not to hold it — if you have it in your hand, you will focus on looking at it rather than on sharing your story to your listeners.

Each time you tell a story, you will make discoveries about it. Each time it will get better. New ideas to improve the structure of the story or enhance a line of dialogue will occur to you. Sometimes you can put those new ideas into practice on the spot. Other times you can file them away for the next time.

Storytelling is truly a magical experience. When a group is captured by a story, all movement in a room stops. All attention and energy becomes focused on the storyteller. Eyes open wide and imaginations start churning. This energizes the storyteller and feeds his imagination. It creates an atmosphere of magic that continues over into the enactment phase of the creative drama class.

========================

How I Became a Storyteller
Mandy Hart, CCC-SLP, RDT

I have always loved reading stories to children, but I have discovered that telling them is much more rewarding. When I first started leading drama classes, I was extremely nervous. I didn't want to tell the stories because I was afraid that I would forget the parts or leave out important characters or confuse the sequence of the story. Instead of telling them, I would read the stories, paraphrasing the difficult vocabulary to insure that the children understood all the words. The children enjoyed the stories, but there was no spontaneous participation and no "magic."

At the time, because my reading was so animated and because I was able to make a great deal of eye contact in between sentences, I felt that it would not make much of a difference if I read or told the story. Now that I tell stories all the time, I realized that it does make an incredible difference!

Gradually, as my confidence grew and I became more familiar with the stories, I became less and less dependent on reading the written text. This provided me with more freedom and allowed me to be "in the moment" as I shared the story. It is great not having to stick to the exact lines written in a book! I felt freer to move around and I really started having fun acting out the different parts. "Magic" began to happen. The children became more involved in the story and began participating spontaneously — bursting out with what was going to happen next. Heads would turn when I pointed down the road to the giant's castle as I told "Jack and the Bean-stalk." I began asking the children questions about the story as I told it. In response, they would act out their answers.

Depending on the children's levels and auditory processing skills, I often begin with stories that are very familiar to them or I use a story that has a significant amount of repetition.

My assistant teacher often tells the story together with me. I narrate and she and I take on different parts, acting out the story as we go along. We agree upon which roles we will do before class, but we do not rehearse what we are going to do or say. We let it happen spontaneously. The children love this. It excites them. They cannot wait for their turn to act out the story.

Many stories have repetitive lines that have rhyme and rhythm. I preserve these. If I need to, I memorize them beforehand to pass them on to the children. Usually, by the end of a session, the children have incidentally learned all the lines and are having fun with them. Making up dialogue once we start acting out the story becomes easier because they have a good start on what each character needs to say. The continuous eye contact I am able to make as a storyteller engages the children and helps them to focus on the story throughout its presentation.

I still usually tell stories with the book open in my hand with the pictures facing the children. Apart from being a good visual aid, especially for children who have attention difficul-ties or auditory processing problems, the book remains my security blanket. But sometimes, when the children are able to focus without a visual aid, I tell a story on the spur of the moment and keep the book on the bookshelf!

I know that it will be scary for you to move from reading the text to making it up, but take it gradually. Practice with friends and children you feel comfortable with. Be confident that you know your stories. I am sure you do — you have probably known most of them since you were about five years old!

Telling stories has made teaching creative drama more enjoyable for me and for the children in my classes.

Telling stories is wonderful — relax and have fun with it!

============================

Assigning Character Roles

When assigning character roles for a story, I ask each student who he would like to play. Sometimes it falls out evenly and everyone wants to play a different character. More often, however, a number of people want to be the same character. When this happens the teacher has several options. The story could be acted out more than once, each time rotating the roles to different children or two or more students could share a role. One student could be Rumple and another could be Stiltskin. They could work together as a team or take turns jumping in the window of the room where the Miller's Daughter is locked. You can make sure each has an equal number of interactions by designating who is speaking or acting through your narration. "Rumple grabbed the ring from the Miller's Daughter while Stiltskin began spinning the straw into gold. They laughed gleefully!"

Sometimes there is a role that nobody wants to play. It might be because the students do not identify with it, do not understand what the character's purpose is in the story, or it may be a very minor part and everyone wants a major part. On occasion no one will volunteer to play the evil character — but many find that playing the bad guy can be the most fun! When I cannot get a volunteer for a role, my assistant or I usually play it.

One of my most memorable moments in creative drama happened while acting out a version of "Cinderella" with five Cinderellas (three girls and two boys) sharing the role. We had two Prince Charmings. My assistant and I played all the other parts. As the Evil Stepsisters, we were so mean! We ordered the Cinderellas around. They had to scrub the floors and wash the windows and beat the rugs and do the washing and iron the clothes and manicure our nails and brush our teeth and wash and dry our hair and mend our clothes. Then we made them get us ready to go to the ball. And we laughed at them because they could not go!

In the next scene, my assistant became the Fairy Godmother while I became the Narrator. Stepping outside the story, I was struck by the beauty of the dramatic moment in progress. I saw five Cinderellas, all in ball gowns (even the boys), sitting in a circle around a big orange pom-pom which served as our pumpkin. They were listening intently and seriously to their Fairy Godmother tell them they had to leave the ball by midnight. There was so much belief in their eyes, so much trust, so much *magic* in the room, I almost started to cry. It did not matter that there were five actors playing the same role. It did not matter that their names were all Cinderella. It did not even matter that two of the Cinderellas were boys. They were having the time of their lives!

Sometimes there are more students than roles and they do not want to double up. Sometimes there are students who would rather watch than participate. When this happens, the students without roles can become audience members during the acting out of the story. Being an audience member is important work, too! And sometimes learning how to be an appropriate member of an audience is difficult to learn and needs to be practiced!

Actor Guidelines

When you are leading a creative drama class, you need to make sure your actors understand the following points:

- The difference between pretend and real.
- Staying in character.
- Listening to each other.
- Respecting each other's work.

The Difference between Pretend and Real

First and foremost, student actors need to understand that they do not become the fictional characters in the story or in drama games. They are only pretending to be them for a short period of time. Some children understand the difference between real and pretend, but some do not. It may seem like a simple concept, but it is not. Often you can teach the concept through action, but if you need an explanation, you can say, "When we act, we are pretending to be somebody else [Cinderella, Prince Charming, the Evil Stepmother]. We act *as if* the situation were real. But it isn't. You are still yourself. I am still myself. We can pretend this room is a palace, but we know that it is really our classroom."

I got into trouble the first time my very first class of students at Ivymount School acted out a story. They did such a good job of pantomiming and playing imagination games during our initial session that I made the mistake of assuming they understood the difference between real and pretend. For the second session I told "The Peddler and his Caps." I brought a big sack full of colorful hats for the Peddler to sell. The minute he saw them, Roberto decided he wanted to be the Peddler. In the first scene he grudgingly let the Townspeople try on his hats in the marketplace. They did not like them and gave them back. So far, so good. But when he got to the forest and fell asleep under the tree, he lay down on top of his hats and would not let any of the Monkeys steal them. As far as Roberto was concerned, he *was* the Peddler. I had given the hats to him personally and he was not going to let anybody take them away from him.

If the Monkeys could not steal the hats, the story could not continue. I tried to explain to Roberto that the Monkeys needed to steal the hats because that is what happens in the story, but he grabbed the hats and held them closer to him sobbing the whole time, "But they're mine! They're mine!" I had to stop the story. We all sat down and talked about the difference between pretend and real. I did not get much of a response from Roberto. He still had the hats clutched tightly to his chest. At this point, it was time for the class to be over — truly a case of being saved by the bell! I do not remember how I got him to leave the hats behind. I think maybe his mother helped me separate him from them.

After thinking about it, I decided the class needed to go back to Square One. The next few sessions we played lots of drama games in which they pretended to be something or someone else. We did a guided imagery exercise each session, which they loved. We worked out a lot of interpersonal problems between group members. After everyone firmly understood the concept of pretend and real, we tried acting out stories again. And we were fine. Ever since that experience, I have tried to introduce the concepts of pretend and real to new students slowly, starting them off with several sessions of games and pantomimes before moving on to stories.

Staying in Character

Actors must learn to *stay in character*. This means that while acting, they must behave consistently like that person. They move like the character would move. They say things the character would say. They can invent new things to say and do, but whatever is invented must be consistent with whom they are portraying. The actors must also stick to the plot of the story unless everyone has agreed ahead of time that the story is going to be changed. Rumplestiltskin cannot grab the baby and run away when the Miller's Daughter (now Queen) guesses his name correctly! The Evil Dragon cannot eat the Prince to stop him from getting into Sleeping Beauty's castle.

Throughout the enactment, actors must stay focused on the pretend situation or the scene or story. In the middle of a scene, it is not okay to turn around and push Billy because you were angry with him before class started. It is not okay to switch from one character to another. It is not okay to decide to quit halfway through and do something else. The other people acting out the story are depending on you to do your part so they can do theirs!

Listening to Each Other

Actors need to listen to each other. Each character in a story must respond appropriately to what the other characters say to him. The only way to do this is to listen to what is being said. If no one is listening to anyone else, the whole scene will break down into total confusion.

Respecting Each Other's Work

Actors must respect each other's contribution to a story. Each actor can decide how he will interpret his character. If someone else has other ideas about how that character should be interpreted, he can share those ideas when he has his chance to act out that character. It will not do for actors to step out of character to argue or criticize each other during the enactment of the story. One of the great things about drama is that each person can have his own interpretation of each role.

Audience Guidelines

Set up your audience area clearly, with chairs or mats for audience members to sit on. Place them on the side of the room where light from the windows will not glare into their eyes or throw the actors' faces into shadow. If your audience members have difficulty staying out of the acting area or your actors tend to wander into the audience space, use masking tape to create a line on the floor between the performance space and the audience space.

Appropriate audience behavior is very important. Audience members are there to share in the work of the actors, so they need to pay attention to what is going on. You might want to review the following rules the first few times your students are audience members for each other:

- Sit quietly in your seat.
- Watch and listen to the actors.
- Respect your fellow audience members' personal space. Keep your hands and feet to yourself.
- If you have a comment or idea, remember it for later on.
- Speaking during the story distracts the actors.
- After the story is over, everyone can talk about how the story went and what they liked or didn't like.
- Respond appropriately to the actors' work.
- Laugh *with* the characters and not *at* the actors.
- Show your appreciation by applauding.
- Booing or saying mean things will hurt the actors' feelings.

If a student in the audience becomes impatient as he is waiting for his turn to act, tell him that as an audience member he is playing an important part, too. His reaction during the story will help keep the actors on track and his comments at the end will help them to become better actors. Remind him that he will get his turn as soon as this version of the story is done. If this does not work, ask him to remember the last time he acted out a part in class. He probably wanted the audience to watch him and enjoy his work. When he acts, he would not like it if audience members paid no attention to him or laughed at him or teased him or made nasty comments. Others will respect him only when he respects them. If he is still being disruptive, have him take a time-out where he cannot disturb the actors and other audience members.

Improvisational Acting

Improvisational acting involves the creation of characters and dramatic situations that are not based on a written script. In many ways improvisational acting is an outgrowth of creative drama because actors are engaged in a very similar informal process in which original scenes are created by the actors on the spot. In addition to creating scenes, students in improvisational acting classes work on developing their acting skills through drama games and exercises.

The appropriate age for students studying improvisation can range from pre-teen through adult. The development of spontaneity, flexibility, and problem-solving skills is highlighted in improvisation. These skills

photo by John Carter

Figure 11: Improvising Washington crossing the Delaware.

are all highly valued tools for living in our modern age. Students with disabilities may have even more reason to develop them in order to survive creatively in a complex and difficult world.

Length of Session

The length of a session can range from one to two hours, depending on the students and the project. Students with strong group skills and long attention spans can handle a longer class. Individuals who process information slowly might need a class of medium length so they can take their time expressing themselves. Students who really love the improvisational process will want to stay in class for as long as they can! If the class is devoted to skill building and the improvisational process, the class can be short or long, but if the creation of an original play is part of the purpose, a longer class may be necessary in order to provide the time necessary for improvisational exploration and rehearsal of the finished piece.

Basic Class Structure

The basic structure for an improvisational acting class follows that of a creative drama class. Begin with a warm-up activity, followed by acting games that teach specific acting skills in an active/passive rotation. The focal point of the session is the creation of scenes or stories through improvisation. Early sessions in a series of classes might consist solely of games to assist students in developing the appropriate improvisational skills in order to create scenes successfully. As sessions continue, more time will be spent on scene work. An improvisational acting session usually ends with some kind of closure activity. See Chapter 7 for examples of drama games and other activities.

Many activities used in an improvisational acting class are similar to those used in creative drama. More complexity is added, as older students have usually achieved a higher level of skills and can handle more complications. More time is usually allotted to each activity since students' concentration abilities are stronger. There are usually more independent group work and team activities, encouraging students to work together on their own.

Setting up an Improvisational Scene

Every scene has a beginning, a middle, and an end. The beginning establishes the characters and introduces the conflict. The middle develops the conflict. In the end, the conflict is resolved.

A good approach for creating scenes is to start with specific choices about the important structural dramatic details: Who, Why, Where, What, When, and How.

Who. The characters are the Who. A scene can have any number of characters. With beginning improvisation students, keep scenes small and simple. Many beginning actors do not yet know how to keep a conflict clear and listen to what the other actors are saying. It is less distracting for them to work on improvisational listening and response skills if fewer actors are involved. In the beginning, work on many short scenes that each have two or three actors in them rather than one long scene involving everyone.

When setting up a scene, include only characters that are absolutely essential to the conflict you have chosen. Each character in a scene needs to have a reason for being there. The characters might be directly involved in one side or the other of the conflict; they might also be involved in complicating the conflict or helping to resolve it. An overpopulated scene tends to lose its forward momentum and can degenerate into confusion as minor characters or extras try to find something to do. The main conflict can get blurred or lost.

Why. Each character must have certain goals or objectives that he will try to accomplish during the course of the scene. To give each character a sense of urgency to accomplish those goals, each must also have strong reasons to justify his goals. These reasons are called the character's motivation or his *Why*. If an actor is unsure of his purpose in a scene, his goal or objective can be clarified by asking, "What do you want?" or "What does your character want?"

What. A scene's What is the conflict or problem created for the characters by the situation they are in or by their crossed purposes. Each character has an objective. Sometimes those objectives lead the characters to work together to solve the problem. For example, two characters lost in the woods have the same conflict and same overall objective: they both want to find a way out. However, they might have different motivations. One might need to get to the nearest hospital because he has broken his leg. The other might be homesick for his family. They could both work together to solve their problem.

More often than not, characters' objectives are at cross purposes and therein lies the conflict of the scene. Taking the example of the characters lost in the woods, despite their common goal, they might not be able to work together. Maybe they do not like each other and end up fighting instead of helping each other. This will make their situation worse.

Usually a character faces some kind of emotional conflict inside at the same time he is facing a conflict on the outside. Before he can solve his outer conflict, he must choose between two different inner goals. The inter-character conflict of a scene might be between a drug dealer who wants to hook a teen on cocaine and the teen who wants to stay clean and sober. The inner character conflict is faced by the teen who wants to stay clean, but also wants to look "cool" to his friends. Once he solves his internal or inner character conflict, he can solve the outer or inter-character conflict. If actors skip over an internal conflict inherent in a scene, stop them and side-coach them through it. Clarifying what each character wants can help the actors understand what the conflict is.

Where. The place or location in which the scene takes place is the Where. Sometimes this is also called the setting. When choosing a place for a scene, be as specific as possible: John's living room, the playground outside school, the loading platform at the train station. If the Where of a scene is clear and specific, many ideas for solving the conflict can come out of the setting.

When. The When is the time, day, season, and year in which a scene happens. Again, be as specific as possible. Does the scene happen this year or last year or one hundred years ago? Is it 4:00 after school on a Wednesday in May or is it 9:00 after a football game on a Saturday night in October?

The When can be used to create a sense of urgency to force the characters to resolve the conflict. If the scene is about cheating in school and the big test is going to begin in five minutes, Bobby will be trying harder to convince Julie to help him cheat and Julie will feel under more pressure to say yes, than if the When is two weeks earlier when the teacher first announced the test and there was still plenty of time to study.

How. The How is the plot of the scene — how the dramatic action unfolds. The plot for an improvisational scene can be developed in two different ways. It can be pre-planned step by step, creating a basic scenario for the actors to follow. The pre-planning can be done by the teacher or by the actors who will be in the scene or by the whole class working together. The actors will follow the scenario as they improvise the dialogue and act out the scene. This is a good method for beginners because they can focus on the creation of their dialogue and character within a given plot structure.

The other method is to set up the characters, conflict, time, and place and let the plot develop spontaneously as the scene unfolds. The actors use ideas for solving their problems as they occur to them and no one knows what exactly will happen. Actors using this method must make sure that all action is motivated and makes sense and that they are really listening to and responding to each other. If actors start ignoring each other, the scene will start dissolving into chaos. Everyone must remain flexible and listen for the unexpected twists and turns that could happen — and follow them to their conclusion. Give your students lots of positive encouragement as they begin acting out scenes. They need to know what is working almost more than what is not working.

Trouble-Shooting

There are some problems that will come up often in impromptu acting. It's a good idea to be prepared in advance with a set of techniques to handle them. In this section we will look at how to troubleshoot some of the more common situations.

Side-Coaching

If actors get lost, stuck or confused during a scene, you do not have to leave them dangling. The teacher has several options for side-coaching to get them back on track.

Freezing. If all that is needed is a word or two, you can tell the actors to momentarily freeze in character. When you say, "Freeze," they stop all

photo by John Carter

Figure 12: Actors freeze while the teacher side-coaches during an improvisation.

talking and movement, as if you had touched the pause button on the DVD player. While they are frozen, you can give them your suggestions. When you say, "Unfreeze" or "Action," they continue with the scene.

Take a Time-Out. Step in like a referee at a sporting event and call "Time-out." This is not the same as a time-out when someone does not behave appropriately; this is for the purpose of refocusing the scene. Stop the scene and discuss the situation or the characters' objectives with the actors. Once the problem seems to be clarified, have them continue the scene from where they left off. Some students feel that the only way they can "erase the mistakes" is to start over. This is not necessary, but if starting over from the beginning would help clear up the confusion, let them begin again.

Simultaneous Side-Coaching. You may want to make minor adjustments to the action or offer an actor encouragement without stopping the scene. Offer comments and suggestions while the students continue to act. Just as when "freezing," actors should stay in character as they listen to your coaching.

This type of scene adjustment requires good concentration skills on the parts of the actors. Students who have cognitive disabilities may have difficulty concentrating on two things at once. They may be unable to process what is happening in a scene and what you are saying simultaneously. If this is the case, it is best to side-coach during a time-out or freeze.

Finding an End to the Scene

Sometimes actors get so involved in their scene that it goes on and on and on. If the scene is interesting and holding the attention of the class, let it go. But if the conflict of the scene gets sidetracked and the class begins to get restless, you may have to step in and help the actors find an end to the scene. This can be done by side-coaching comments like "You need to focus on the problem in the scene," or "You need to solve the original problem which was [briefly state the problem]." If you need to be more direct, you can say, "Now you need to find an end to the scene." If the actors are enjoying being in the limelight and are postponing ending the scene, give them a time limit. "You need to find an end to this scene in two minutes."

Students Who Won't Participate

If you have students who are shy or hesitant to work at first, do not force them to participate. Sometimes new students need to observe for a while before they feel confident enough to risk participation. It may take two or three classes before someone feels safe enough to join in. Do not worry as long as the shy students are attentive to the work that the other students are doing. Keep offering them the opportunity to join in and eventually they will. You may even be surprised by the sensitivity of the work they contribute, once they feel comfortable enough to become active in the group.

One of my students would not join in improvisations until the end of his second semester. He stayed on the sidelines and watched. He said he did not want to act; he only wanted to do the sound effects for our play. I said that was okay because stage technicians are important, too.

During our last class period of the second semester we decided to act out a very exciting situation: a few other students and I were stuck in a burning building and everyone else was going to be on the fire-fighting team. Being a fireman sounded like a lot of fun to him, so out of the blue, he volunteered to take a part. I said, "Great!" But I didn't make a big deal out of it.

It was a very dramatic scene. People were shouting for help and "jumping" from the building into the arms of waiting firefighters "below." Before I could jump, I was "overcome by the smoke" and "passed out." He ran into the building and pulled me out and revived me. From the things he said to the other actors around him, I think he really believed I was hurt. He was very relieved when he found out I was okay. Because of this experience, everything changed for him and suddenly he wanted to act. The next semester he volunteered for scenes all the time and each year his part in the play got bigger and bigger.

I believe part of his hesitation to join in was because of his shyness and part was because of his confusion about what was pretend and what was real. I think he feared if he acted out a character, he would turn into that person and would not be himself anymore. As he participated in the scene, he realized that although he was "fighting a fire," there really were no flames in the room and that even though I was pretending to be unconscious, I was really okay.

Making up Dialogue

If a student has trouble making up dialogue, ask him to think about how his character feels in this situation. Or ask him to think about what he might say if *he* were in this situation. If words do not come, maybe he can express how his character feels or what his character would like to do about the situation through movement or mime. Once again, patience and encouragement will evoke more in the long run than trying to force the issue.

Working Together and Independently

At first, plan scenes with the whole class working together under your direction. This will help them understand how to plan and structure a scene. Then they can divide up and begin to work more independently. You will have groups that will not be able to work independently. That's okay, too.

Advanced students can be divided into smaller groups to work on their own with an assistant. This encourages their independence and creativity, while the assistant is able to monitor their progress and keep them on track. Each group could be assigned the same situation to work on or they could be assigned different ones. After they come up with their scene and practice it, they can share it with the whole class.

A good size for a beginning improvisation sub-group is three or four students. Groups larger than four tend to have trouble coming to consensus. Allow each group 10 to 20 minutes to plan and rehearse their scene. Be flexible. The time needed will depend on the complexity of the scene and how well the group is working together.

Circulate from group to group as they work to check on their progress. Give them lots of encouragement when they are working harmoniously and coming up with creative ideas. Offer constructive suggestions when they seem to be stuck or when they are having difficulty coming to an agreement. Offer them alternatives from which they can choose rather than trying to solve their problems for them. Lower functioning groups and beginners need more help than higher functioning groups or advanced students.

When assigning students to work groups, it helps to know what kind of relationships they have with each other in and outside of class. Sometimes friends work well together because they already have a natural trust and ability to communicate. Other times putting friends together creates friction. Be aware of the cognitive levels and abilities of the members in a group. If your class is integrated, don't segregate students with and without disabilities into separate groups. Divide them so they get to work together and get to know and appreciate each other's creative strengths. If you have highly verbal and low- or non-verbal actors, make sure you have a mixture involved in each group.

Be aware of students' leadership styles. Make sure each group has at least one strong leader. If everyone in a group is passive, nothing will get accomplished. On the other hand, if you have two strong leaders in a group, make sure they are capable of flexibility. Two strong, rigid leaders will have difficulty compromising on ideas.

Working together on group scenes can be very satisfying in the end, but learning to compromise, accept group decisions, and share creative input can be a struggle in the beginning. Whatever conflicts flare up between group members, remind them that they are on the same team and everyone's ideas are valid and important. Everyone deserves a chance to be heard. Everyone's opinion counts.

Discussion

After a scene is acted out, it is helpful to take some time to discuss it with the actors and the class audience. This will help everyone become more aware of good dramatic structure and good acting techniques so that scene work continues to improve. For any given scene there may be a lot to discuss or just a little.

When you are evaluating choices made within scenes, think about two different levels. Choices can work on a content level and they can work on a technical level. Content choices deal with choices that the character made, not the choices that the actors made. There is a distinction. An actor might allow his character to make an unwise choice because it is something his character might legitimately do and the choice furthers the dramatic conflict or creates an interesting obstacle. For instance, a boy might be so angry at the mean man in his neighborhood that he throws stones at the man's house and breaks his windows. While the choice the character made may have not been a socially appropriate one, the actor can be congratulated for creating an interesting, believable character.

To evaluate content choices, ask questions such as:

- What happened in the scene?
- What did the characters say? Did it make sense?
- What did the characters do to find a creative solution to their problem? Did that make sense?
- How else could the characters have solved their conflict?

To evaluate technical choices, ask questions such as:

- Did the actors stay in character?
- Did the actors listen to each other?
- Did the actors stick to the scenario (the plan)? If not, did their new choices improve the scenario or weaken it? Why?
- Did the actors solve the conflict or not?

- Did the actors make their characters' objectives and motivations clear?
- Did one action in the scene logically lead to the next action?
- Did the scene keep moving forward or did it get stuck in one place? If it got stuck, why do you think that happened?
- What are some different choices the actors could have made?

Always focus first on the positive aspects of the scene: what worked or was effective. Only after you have covered what the actors did well or what the character did that was exciting and interesting, should you ask for comments on what was confusing and could have been done more clearly or differently.

There is a distinction between something that did not work and something that could have been done differently. More often that not, an actor's choice is not wrong. It is possible that a different choice would have brought a different ending or outcome to the scene. A good question to ask might be, "Is there something else the character could have done that would have been interesting?" Criticism is better aimed at the choices in the scene made by the character than at the individual actor who made them.

Everyone is learning and everyone can improve on his skills through practice and feedback. If a scene gets off track, it is good to remind students that even professional actors make mistakes. Professionals are always in training and always evaluating their performances to make them better. Constant improvement and study is the mark of a true artist.

Train your students to think positively rather than negatively. Constructive criticism gives an actor food for thought and room for improvement. Destructive criticism and personal attacks only hurt people's feelings and shut them down so they stop trying. Your best tool in guiding your students to learn how to criticize constructively is through your example: how you talk about what has been done and how you phrase your questions will say a lot about what you want from them in terms of giving feedback. Do not be afraid to stop a critical comment that is couched in negative, unhelpful, or vindictive terms.

In discussions of improvisational scenes with beginners, it may be important at first to take time to separate what is real from what is pretend. Do not assume that all adolescent students have worked out that distinction. Stress that the actor is not the same person as the character he plays in the scene. The actor is real. The character is fictional. The character may act as if he is real (that is good acting), but he is not real. When an actor plays a role, he does not change inside, even if he changes on the outside. He is still the same person he always was. He puts on the character the same way he would put on a Halloween costume. He can take off the character when he is done with the scene, just like he would take off a disguise.

If actors get really involved in their characters, you can help them "get out of character" after the scene is over by "shaking off the character" or "stepping out of the character's skin." If you have students who need more literal help delineating themselves from the role that they have just played, you could create a de-roling ritual that is more elaborate, such as pantomiming taking off that character's costume and hanging it up on an imaginary hanger in "the costume shop" or "spraying" the actors all over with an imaginary hose to wash off the character. A clear delineation between the acting area and the audience space can help with this as well. When you step into the acting area, you are portraying a character and when you step out, you are yourself again.

If a character does something "bad" in a scene, such as lying, cheating, stealing, or getting into a fight, the actor might feel a rush of excitement. This can be confusing because while the rush of excitement feels good, the actor knows he has done something wrong. In fact, an actor who comes from a very strict background may even feel guilt or shame after his character had done something illegal. If this happens, you will need to spend some time discussing this to help sort this out.

Relationships between characters in a scene can also cause confusion. Two good friends might refuse to act out a scene in which their characters have an argument for fear it will mean they will not be friends anymore. A boy and a girl might refuse to portray characters who are romantically involved or married because they are afraid that others will think the feelings they express in the scene are real. By the same token, a boy and girl can become so involved in the imaginary situation that they confuse the characters' attraction for each other with a real attraction that may or may not exist between them in real life. (Professional actors even do this sometimes!) The same kind of confusion can happen in scenes of disagreement and dislike. In all of these situations it is important to clarify that the actors are playing a role, that they are different from the characters they are temporarily portraying, and that the other people in the classroom or in the audience also understand that the characters and situations are fictional.

Some scenes will generate long, involved discussions; others will not. If a scene creates a lot of strong feeling and food for thought, it is important to allow students the time to process it before moving on to the next scene or activity. If it is not resolved, students holding on to a strong feeling or confusion generated by a scene will tend to behave inappropriately to get rid of the feeling. Discussion is an important part of the de-roling process.

If a scene does not generate a lot of discussion, just move on to the next one. Discussions do not have to cover all the points listed above. The teacher will usually focus on a few main issues that relate to the scene or on particular acting skills he is currently helping his students develop.

Recommended Reading

Ward, W. (1969). *Stories to Dramatize.* Anchorage, AK: Anchorage Press.

Bettelheim, B. (1977). *The Uses of Enchantment.* New York: Random House.

Gersie, A. & King, N. (1990). *Storymaking in Education and Therapy.* London: Jessica Kingsley Publishers.

Johnstone, K. (1989). *Impro: Improvisation and the Theatre.* London: Methuen.

Kelly, J. Y. (1973). *The Magic If: Stanislavski for Children.* Baltimore: National Educational Press.

Maguire, J. (1985). *Creative Storytelling: Choosing, Inventing, and Sharing Tales for Children.* New York: McGraw-Hill Book Company.

McCaslin, N. (2005). *Creative Drama in the Classroom and Beyond.* White Plains, NY: Longman.

7. Lesson Plans and Activities that Work

As mentioned in Chapter 6, many warm-ups, drama games, and acting exercises are used with all age groups. At different developmental levels, different skills are addressed. The older and more experienced the student, the more complexity can be added to exercises. The longer the student's attention span, the longer each exercise can be sustained with interest. Older, more mature groups can handle activities that include more independence, group interactions, and subtlety.

Choosing Games for Beginners

Concrete Games

With beginners and students who have cognitive disabilities, focus on concrete rather than abstract activities. Concrete games use actual objects rather than imaginary ones, so that students have something real to focus on and manipulate. This means their working memory does not have to hold onto an invisible image while they also are thinking of something related to do with it.

The difference between concrete and abstract can be illustrated by comparing two different versions of the same basic pantomime game.

===

Concrete: The Magic Tube
Material needed: Empty paper-towel cardboard roll.
Group configuration: Everyone sits or stands in a circle.

photo by Alan Honey

Figure 13: With a little imagination the Magic Tube becomes a spyglass.

Purpose: To stimulate the imagination and develop pantomime skills.

Action: Imagine an object that is the same shape as the tube. It could be the same size or bigger or smaller. Show the group what it is by using it as that object. The group guesses what it is. After each turn the tube is passed to the next person in the circle to imagine a different object. Go around the circle once or continue around the circle as long as the group shows interest in the game.

Variations: Use a plastic cup, a Frisbee, an embroidery hoop, a Nerf ball, or a large, colorful scarf — any object with a different shape.

Abstract: Space Objects

Material needed: None.

Group configuration: Everyone sits or stands in a circle.

Purpose: To stimulate the imagination and develop pantomime skills.

Action: Using the shape of your hands, create an invisible object through pantomime. Show the group what you have by acting out how you would use the object if it were really there. The group guesses what it is. Each student takes a turn. Continue the game as long as the group shows interest.

Variation: Space Balls

Create different kinds of balls through pantomime. Differentiate size, shape, and weight by how much space you leave between your hands and how you move. The student who first creates the ball throws it to another student in the circle. This student catches it and changes it to another kind of ball before throwing it on.

=================================

Using the Magic Tube gives students a concrete object that provides enough visual and kinesthetic structure to serve as a mental anchor. The object in hand holds the shape in space and serves as a visual-spatial reminder for the student while she searches back through visual and kinesthetic memory to match it with a similarly shaped object.

I have used the Magic Tube with individuals who had very low IQs and they were as capable of playing this as well as intellectually gifted students, making amazing, creative connections. When I tried the game in the abstract with them — without the object in hand — they had difficulty visualizing the pantomimed object in their mind's eye, remembering it, and focusing on it, as well as imagining a new one.

If you have a source book of acting exercises, go through it to separate the concrete exercises from the abstract ones. Then go back through the abstract ones and think of ways to invent a concrete variation of them.

photo by Lea Ann Rosen

Figure 14: Using concrete props and costume pieces helps students use their imaginations and enter the dramatic space.

Simple Games

Beginners and students who have cognitive disabilities do best with simple games. If you try a game and it does not work, simplify some rules or remove a complication. Then it might work.

Here are several different variations of an animal-pantomime guessing game that will work with different levels of groups:

═══════════════════════════════

Most simple, concrete, and structured: Animal Go-Around

Material needed: Pictures of animals.

Group configuration: Everyone sits in a circle on the floor or in chairs.

Purpose: To develop pantomime skills, physical expressiveness, and the ability to share and appreciate the work of others.

Action: Each student takes a turn looking at the picture of an animal and acting it out for the group.

═══════════════════════════════

Most simple, more abstract, and less structured: Favorite Animal Go-Around

Material needed: None.

Group configuration: Everyone sits in a circle.

Purpose: To develop pantomime skills, physical expressiveness, decision-making, and the ability to share and appreciate the work of others.

Action: Each student, in turn, thinks of and acts out her favorite animal.

═══════════════════════════════

Simple, less structured: Animal Transformations

Material needed: Pictures of animals.

Group configuration: None. Everyone is free to move around the room.

Purpose: To develop pantomime skills, physical expressiveness, respect for personal space, and group cooperation.

Action: Show the entire group a picture of an animal or call out the name of an animal. Act it out together with or without sound.

Comments: Here we have moved into a game where the group is involved in parallel play instead of solitary, individual turn-taking. Students must remain aware of others' personal space and not attack other "animals."

=================================

Medium complexity, concrete: Animal Herds

Material needed: Pictures of different animals.

Group configuration: Two teams on opposite sides of the room.

Purpose: To develop pantomime skills, physical expressiveness, problem-solving, and cooperative abilities.

Action: The teacher shows Team One the picture of an animal. Together they act out the animal without sound for Team Two. Team Two gets three guesses. If they do not guess correctly, after the third try, Team One can add sound. Usually Team Two can guess with sound and movement. Then the teacher shows Team Two a picture to act out for Team One.

Scoring: None. This is not to be played as a competitive game. The point is not to trick the other team, but to do such a good job that they guess on the first try.

Comments: Pictures of animals work better for clarity, secrecy, and large-scale recognition than whispering the name of the animal in a large group. They also present a visual image to young children who may remember the animal upon seeing it, but not upon hearing its name. Pictures also help children who have hearing, auditory processing, or attention difficulties. If children get so excited by the pictures that they have difficulty controlling the impulse to say the name of the animal out loud when they first see it, ask them to cover their mouths with their hands and say the name of the animal to themselves in their head or whisper the name behind their hands so the other team cannot hear or lipread what it is.

If the acting team begins invading the space of the watching team (lions and tigers tend to want to attack and horses like to gallop around), divide the acting area in two by making a line with masking tape in the middle of the playing space. Actors must stay on their own side of the line.

===============================

Medium complexity/abstract: Animal Herds in Consensus
Materials needed: None.

Group configuration: Two teams on opposite sides of the room.

Purpose: To develop pantomime skills, physical expressiveness, problem-solving, and cooperative abilities.

Action: Each team collectively agrees on an animal to jointly act out for the other team. First, Team One pantomimes their animal for Team Two. Team Two gets from one to three guesses and must come to consensus before guessing. If they do not guess correctly, Team One can add the sound. Then Team Two acts out their animal for Team One.

Comments: Coming to consensus is a difficult activity for some groups, but this is a fun way to begin to work on it.

===============================

Most complex: Bird, Beast, and Fish
Material needed: None (to make it more concrete, you can use pictures of animals).

Group configuration: Two to four teams of four to eight actors in different corners of the room. Group leader in the center.

Purpose: To develop pantomime skills, physical expressiveness, problem-solving, cooperative abilities, and good sportsmanship.

Action: Have each team invent a name. Number off team members so each actor has a rotation order. Then each team sends Actor One to the group leader in the center at the same time. The leader whispers (or shows a picture) of the same living creative to all the actors. It could be a bird, mammal, fish, reptile, amphibian, insect, bug, or water creature and it could be currently alive or extinct. The actors run back to their group and begin acting out the creature with no sound! They can act out their creature using all or part of their body. They can show what the animal looks like or what it does; they can show another creature's reaction to it (think *skunk*). As the actors act, the team yells out their guesses. When the actor hears the correct animal, she motions everyone to sit down. The leader asks for the person with the correct answer to share the answer. If it is correct, that team wins a point. For the next round, each team sends Actor Two to the group leader and the game continues until one team has reached the agreed upon score for winning the game.

Scoring: Decide ahead of time what will be the winning score. Remind the teams when you are nearing it and at game point.

Comments: It is helpful to check on the correct answer instead of trusting that the first team to sit down has guessed correctly. In the heat of the game, an overly enthusiastic team can misinterpret an actor's animal gesture to mean "Sit down" or the actor can mishear the guess. Having the team sit down helps the leader figure out which team got the answer first. She can be both listening for the answer and watching for the movement of the team starting to sit down. This makes it easier to decide who has won a close call.

To prevent cheating, you may want the teams to face away from the middle so they cannot read the leader's lips while she is telling the actors which animal to act. This will also mean that they cannot guess the correct answer first by watching a different team's actor, who might be doing a clearer pantomime.

If an actor makes a sound, her team is disqualified from getting the point, even if the team guesses correctly. If you can tell that the other teams heard the sound, no one should get a point. Otherwise, you'll hear "No fair!"

This version of animal pantomimes takes a great deal of impulse control to play. Because so much sound and movement is generated, people who have ADHD, Tourette syndrome, emotional difficulties, sensory integration problems, or autism can become overstimulated. The number of rules and sequences may make it too complex for students who have severe cognitive disabilities.

=============================

When an Activity Bombs

Sometimes a game will work wonderfully with one group and totally fail with another. You may have misjudged the abilities of the students in one of the groups. You may not have explained the game clearly enough one of the times. The failure may have been due to factors outside your control, such as bad weather, humidity, heat, or the emotional states of the class members on the day you play.

If an activity does not work, drop it and go onto the next one on your lesson plan. Do not waste time feeling bad about it or become upset with your students. Take the attitude "what will be, will be." There are hundreds of drama games. If the game teaches a crucial acting skill, you will be able to find another game that teaches the same skill in a manner that your students can handle.

Warm-ups

Warm-ups release physical and emotional tensions that have built up during the day prior to drama class. Once these tensions are released, students will be able to let go of what went on before entering the drama space. They will be able to concentrate better on what is going on in your class in the present moment.

Warm-ups energize students who are weary by getting their blood moving. Revitalizing oxygen is carried to their muscles and brains, while carbon dioxide and other tissue wastes are removed. Students will then be able to focus better mentally and physically.

Warm-ups also serve as relaxation tools. Moving the body and stimulating the senses wakes up parts of the brain and loosens muscles that have been ignored during activities focused on the cognitive, left-brain activities engaged in almost exclusively during the school or work day. Some warm-up activities — in particular those which involve opposite extremities crossing over the midline of the body — enhance the functioning and integration of both sides of the brain with each other. This works because the left side of the body is controlled by the right side of the brain and the right side of the body is controlled by the left side of the brain. When one or both sides cross the midline and touch the opposite side, both brain hemispheres are stimulated simultaneously, enhancing the ability to learn (Hannaford 1995).

For very shy or inhibited groups, warm-ups can help break the ice and loosen up creative thinking. Since they are done with everyone, no one is singled out or put on the spot. Everyone can feel part of the group.

A warm-up usually lasts from five to fifteen minutes, depending on the tension and concentration levels of the students. When the class seems relaxed and engaged, you will sense it. At that point, bring the warm-up to a swift, satisfying conclusion and move on to your next activity.

Group Check-ins

Have everyone sit in a circle. Go around and let each person "check in." Ask each student to share how she is feeling or something exciting that has happened in the past week. It is important in group check-ins that everyone listen to everyone else and not "check out" after having her turn. The purpose of an activity of this kind is to bring the class together and help everyone get to know each other better, as well as to give the leader a sense of where each student and, therefore, the group as a whole, is at.

Keep each student's check-in brief and to the point. If someone begins to monopolize the conversation and the others are not interested, they will get bored and stop paying attention. In a situation like this, you can say, "Thank you for sharing this story with us, but I think it's time to give someone else a turn to speak." If this happens on a regular basis, you could create a time limit for each person or you could put some other kind of limit on the response. For example, you could ask everyone to use only one word to say how she feels or to share the name of one place she went on her vacation.

Name Games

Name games are helpful for learning names in the first session and in reviewing them in succeeding sessions. Usually name learning is an aural and visual process. Name games make it an aural, visual, and kinesthetic process.

Go around the circle and have each person say her name and make a movement or rhythm to go with it. Robert might clap his hands twice. Cindy might hop up and down. Frank might stamp his foot once. Have the group repeat the name and movement after each person introduces herself. Then see if anyone can remember another's name and movement. Robert might say, "Frank" and stamp his foot once. Frank would repeat his name and movement and then might do Cindy's name and movement, passing the game on to her.

Variation: If that version is too abstract for your group, each person can say her name and act out something she likes to do or pantomime something that starts with the same letter as her first name.

Names can be reviewed by saying the name of another person in the circle and tossing her a Nerf ball or a beanbag. Advanced groups can add more balls thrown, bounced, rolled, or passed to add more action and excitement to the game. This is not recommended for a class that has attention deficits or concentration problems, at least at first, because more balls means more movement and vocalizations, which will stress students' focusing abilities.

There are many welcoming songs into which students' names can be inserted. If your group likes to sing, this can be a fun way to review names at the beginning or the end of class. Many social games also involve naming others in the group.

Go-Around Pantomimes

If you are in a check-in circle, it is easy to segue into a go-around pantomime activity. Students can take turns pantomiming something they like to do, their favorite sport, something that they do at school each day, something they do when they go home, something they do on vacation, etc. A go-around can introduce a theme for the day. For instance, if you will be doing a story about Africa, you could ask each person to act out her favorite African animal or if you will be learning about the food pyramid, you could ask each person to act out eating her favorite food.

It is best to keep a go-around moving. If students are shy or need more time to think of something to act out, they can pass for the time being. You can come back to them later when they are ready.

Groups love go-around pantomimes. It is a great way for students to share something about themselves and get to know each other better. It is a quick way to get everyone involved and students can practice being in the spotlight for just a short time.

Shy students will feel safer taking a turn while sitting in an informal circle than when getting up on a stage or standing alone in front of class.

Go-around pantomimes are great transition or rest activities when used later in the session. When students have just finished an active game, a go-around can help calm them down and allow them to catch their breath. Go-arounds can also be used for closure activities at the end of class.

Physical Exercise

Release muscular tension through any combination of the following physical exercises. As students do each movement, ask them to imagine that the tension (or the "tightness" or "soreness" or "hurting" part) in their bodies is loosening up and falling out of them. The purpose of physical exercise in a drama class is to relax muscles, not to build them up. Do the activity gently and carefully, placing emphasis on tension release and muscle warm-up.

Some groups love to do physical warm-ups to jazzy, upbeat music. Find out who their favorite recording artists are and bring in CDs of their music. After a few weeks, students will start bringing in their own favorites for you to use for warm-up. Students take great pride in contributing in this way.

The teacher or assistant can lead the warm-up. Students can also take turns being warm-up leader. Give everyone who wants a turn a few minutes to lead the group.

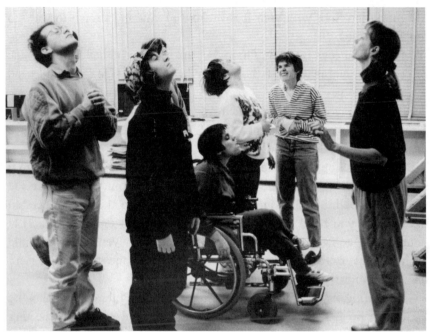

photo by Lea Ann Rosen

Figure 15: Warming up at the beginning of class or rehearsal gets everyone focused.

If you stretch one side of the body, be sure to stretch the other. If you rotate in one direction, always reverse and go the other direction. This balances the work the muscles experience and assures that you have addressed the tension in all body parts. If you have students with physical disabilities who cannot move part of their bodies, warm up the parts they can move.

Shaking. Gently shake each part of your body: your hands, your elbows, your arms, your head, your shoulders, your hips, your knees, your left foot, your left leg, your right foot, your right leg, and then your whole body.

Stretching. Stretch each part of your body. Stretching increases the supply of blood to body parts. Stretch toward the ceiling, toward the floor, toward the right, toward the left, backwards, and toward the person on the opposite side of the circle.

Stretch out your legs one at a time as you lean against a wall or chair.

Sit on the floor with your legs in front of you and stretch forward to touch your toes.

Open your legs into a *V*. Grab your ankle with the hand on that side of your body and reach with the arm on the opposite side over your head toward that foot.

Try some yoga stretches, such as the Cobra, the Bow, or the Cat Stretch, which release the muscles of the back and give the spine a chance to arch in different directions.

Swinging. Loosen your body a little more by swinging it gently from side to side. Bend over and swing your arms in front of you like the clapper in a bell. Stand up and swing your arms from above your head to the floor as you bend at the waist. Swing your legs one at a time. Let your breath go with you as you swing. You can even make a gentle "ahhh" noise or a sigh as you let out the air. Allow the momentum from one swing to carry you into the next.

Swimming. Move your arms as if you were doing the backstroke, the crawl, the breaststroke, the butterfly stroke, the sidestroke, or the dog paddle. As you swim, imagine you are in a cool, blue pool enjoying a perfect summer day.

Rotating. Circle each joint of the body in small and large, fast and slow circles. Rotate in each direction. Rotate your wrists, arms, head (always do this slowly), shoulders, waist (upper body), hips, legs, and ankles (do this last one sitting down).

Bouncing. Bounce or bob gently up and down as if you were a ball. Try to imagine that you are as light as air.

Floating. Imagine that you are filled with helium and, like a hot-air balloon, you can float slowly and gently away.

Guided Imagery Relaxation

There are groups that will not sit still long enough to do guided relaxations and there are groups who thrive on them. Test out your class with a short one and see how they respond.

Begin by having your students lie on the floor on their backs. It helps if they take off their shoes and loosen their belts, but if this seems weird to them, forgo it. If students are in wheelchairs, they can sit in them; if the floor is uninviting or students are wearing skirts, let them sit comfortably in a chair. Relax the whole body progressively from toes to head or from head to toes. Ask students to tense and release each body part: toes, feet, calves, thighs, buttocks, stomach, back, chest, hands, lower arms, upper arms, shoulders, neck, and face. As they tense each part, tell them to be aware of the muscles in that part of the body. As they release each part, tell them to imagine that all the tension is melting out of them or evaporating or draining away.

Another relaxation method is to have students imagine as they breathe that they are breathing warmth and sunlight into their bodies, warming up their muscles and relaxing them. They can start with their toes and fill their entire body up with sunlight or helium or a favorite, relaxing color or energy. Use whichever image seems to work best for them.

Once they are relaxed, you can take them on a guided trip in their imaginations. Start by appealing to their sense memory. Ask them to see what is around them, feel the sun on their face and the wind on their skin, and smell, hear, and touch their imaginary environment. You could lead them on a walk in the woods, a dive to the bottom of the sea, or a space flight to Mars. Structure the imaginary journey so that they have choices to make along the way. This puts them in control of their mental imagery and enhances their imaginative capacity.

Progressive relaxation and guided imagery can be enhanced by recordings of environmental sounds or instrumental music. I like to find interesting music and make up fantasy trips that follow the build in the music. Journeys can be based on a favorite fairy tale or an adventure you know your students would like to have. Time machines, hot air balloons, magic carpets, and mystical ships are excellent guided imagery devices for spiriting your students to a far away time or place. Good sources of guided imagery scripts are Maureen Murdock's *Spinning Inward: Using Guided Imagery with Children for Learning* and Gay Hendricks' two books on centering.

When students come back from their journeys, they can share what happened to them or draw what they saw in their mind's eye. If they are not in a sharing mood or they need to move on to something more active, continue with the next activity in your lesson plan. Guided imagery sessions are useful motivational tools for improvisational projects, especially when you want students to visualize a set of characters or a specific location. They also serve as good rest breaks in the middle of a long class period, giving students a chance to refocus or recharge when they get wound up or tired.

Drama Games

The following collection of drama games is by no means exhaustive. There are thousands of games and game variations. I have included as examples a few games that have worked well for me with different groups of students who have special needs. Please do not limit yourself to the games included here. Look through creative-drama and improvisational-acting books for ideas. Invent your own games and variations. Also see the list of recommended books at the end of this chapter.

Sensory Observation Games

Sensory observation games teach basic awareness skills. They are excellent exercises for students who have cognitive or physical disabilities because they develop sensory and information processing channels that can be used to enhance learning and many other areas of their lives.

Blindfold Walks. Blindfold walks can be done in pairs or by a whole group connected together like a train.

In pairs: One student is blindfolded and the other leads her around the space or outside. The leading partner can guide her by touch or by voice or both. Do this exercise slowly. The leading partner must pay close attention and take care of the blindfolded partner so she does not hurt herself. The leading partner guides her to experience the textures, sounds, smells, and spatial arrangement of the environment in a new way. After five or ten minutes, partners can switch roles.

In a group: A whole group formed into a long line can be blindfolded with only the person at the head of the line able to see. Each person holds the shoulders of the person in front of her. The first person leads the line around. It is helpful to have at least one person free to reconnect students who have lost their handhold on the shoulders in front of them.

Blindfold exercises are good tools for developing trust with other members of a group. It is extremely important that seeing partners do not play tricks on their blindfolded charges. These are good group building exercises, but if your students cannot handle being responsible for the safety of another, wait until they can take responsibility before you do these types of games.

Some people fear being blindfolded. Blindfolds can throw the wearer off balance and disorient her. Be sensitive to this. When a student expresses fear, you will need to make a judgment call on whether you are seeing real panic or just nervousness about trying something new. Encourage the nervous student to try the exercise, but give the truly fearful student an easy out — quietly turn her into an obstacle remover or a door opener so she can participate in the activity in a way that feels safe to her.

Blindfold exercises can also be used to build disability awareness. If you have a blind student in your class, a blindfold exercise will give your sighted students the chance to experience the world from her perspective. It can also serve to initiate a discussion on helping others and being helped: How do you like to be helped? In a manner that encourages and empowers you or in a way in which you feel like a piece of meat being dragged around? Do you prefer specific instructions or general images? Do you want to be touched or not? Do you want rely on your helper at all times or do you want to be allowed to develop more independence?

Airport. A variation of the blindfold walk, this exercise provides practice in listening to and following directions as well as in giving clear verbal commands.

Set up an obstacle course in your room, using objects and students. One student is the Airplane that is coming in for a landing. Another student is the Air Traffic Controller, who must guide the Airplane through the obstacle course using only verbal directions. Speed is not important; accuracy is. The Airplane is supposed to make it all the way through the obstacle course without crashing or "denting a wing." Count the number of times the Airplane touches or bumps into an object or person. Was this because she was not listening to and following directions or because the Air Traffic Controller was not giving clear enough directions?

This game requires strong concentration skills. It is best used with a small group so that most students have a chance to participate either as the Airplane or Air Traffic Controller within a 15 to 20 minute time period. I have had groups that retained an interest in this game for as long as an hour, but that is not typical.

Variation: Have two people involved in giving directions. One, facing the Airplane may only describe where to move through pantomime to the second, facing away from the obstacle course, who must translate the actions into words.

Change Three. Change Three is a visual observation game. It may be done in pairs or with one student standing in front of the whole group. Have the partner or group take a close look at the Changer to see exactly what she is wearing and how she has styled her hair, etc. When they are sure they know what she looks like, the group hides their eyes or turns their backs while the Changer changes three things about her appearance. She might untie one shoe, take out one barrette, and roll up her sleeves. If you cannot trust your group to keep their eyes closed, the Changer can go behind a curtain or out into the hallway to make her changes. When she is done, the group or partner looks her over and tries to see what is different.

Variation: If three changes are too many for a group to remember, change one or two items instead. If a group is very sharp, you can have the Changer change up to five or six things!

Variation: Divide the group into teams. Each team changes three to five things about their appearance and the other team(s) must guess what changed.

Which One Is Missing? This is another visual observation game. Collect a number of small objects and lay them out on the table. Let students look at them until they think they remember all the different objects. Cover the objects with a scarf and remove one, two, or three of them. Lift off the scarf and see who can identify what is missing.

Copy the Shape. One student takes a body position for 10 to 30 seconds and the rest of the class observes and tries to remember the body shape. Then the student relaxes and a volunteer from the group tries to reproduce the position. If you have trouble remembering exactly what the shape is, you can always take a photo of the position with a Polaroid or a digital camera so you can double-check the original shape. This exercise develops visual memory and visual/kinesthetic links in the central nervous system. It will stimulate the mirror neurons of everyone in the group.

Variation: Have the student hold the position while everyone tries to copy it as faithfully as possible.

Back Writing. A variation of the ever popular Telephone or Gossip, back writing focuses on tactile awareness and memory instead of listening skills. Have students sit in a line, one in front of the other. Draw a letter or number slowly on the back of the last person in line. She draws what she felt on the back of the person in front of her, and so on down the line. The person in front draws what she thinks the letter or number is on a piece of paper. If it is not the same as the one you drew, figure out where it changed shape and if it changed only once or several times. This game can be done as a race between two or more teams.

Who's the Leader? This is a very advanced visual observation game, but even children who have difficulty with it love playing it.

Everyone sits in a circle. One person, the Observer, goes out of the room. The teacher picks a Leader by pointing at her. It is important not to say the Leader's name out loud so the Observer doesn't hear it. The Leader starts doing a physical action, such as clapping her hands, snapping her fingers, or nodding her head. Everyone in the circle must copy her exactly. Every time she changes her action, the group changes with her.

The Observer returns to the room and observes the group, trying to figure out who the Leader is. The trick is to look for who is changing the action first. The Observer has three chances to guess who the Leader is. If she guesses correctly, she rejoins the circle and the Leader can go out into the hall to become the Observer for the next round. If the Observer is incorrect, she must return to the hall, the group picks a new Leader, and the Observer must try again.

Group members should not look directly at the Leader all the time or it will be obvious who the Leader is. Yet they must try to remain aware of what the Leader is doing at all times so they know when she changes her action. This in itself can be a real challenge!

Students love being picked to be the Leader and they love going out into the hall, but they can become very frustrated if they do not understand how to identify the Leader or if the group has become very skilled at following the Leader. They may have difficulty if they have poor visual observation skills, a visual impairment, or attention deficits. Your assistant can help by staying with the Observer and pointing out things to look for. Or you could have two Observers who work together.

If students become upset about having to go back into the hall because they guessed wrong (after all, most of us feel badly when we fail), allow the Observer to rejoin the circle whether she gets the answer right or not. The point of playing this game is not to punish a poor Observer; it is to have a good time practicing observation and concentration skills.

Dog and Bone. This is a listening, observation, and body-awareness exercise all rolled into one. One student is the Dog. She is blindfolded and lies down on the floor on her stomach, pretending to be asleep. An object representing her bone is placed in front of her paws (but she may not touch it). The rest of the class stands at an agreed-upon distance. Tape out a starting line on the floor to delineate boundaries. One by one, students sneak up on the dog and try to steal her bone. If the Sneakers are in wheelchairs, the bone could be set on a table in front of the Dog instead of down on the floor so that it is within easy reach.

If the Dog hears any noise or senses any movement, she is supposed to bark and point in the direction of the noise. If caught, a Sneaker must go back to the starting line. If a Sneaker steals the bone, she becomes the Dog for the next round and the old Dog rejoins the group.

Variation: The Queen/King Has A Headache. One student, playing the ruling monarch, sits blindfolded in a chair at one end of the room, wearing a crown. The idea is that everyone must be completely quiet because the Ruler has a splitting headache. Students sneak up to steal the crown or tag the Ruler. If the Ruler hears any noise or senses any movement, she moans dramatically and points to the offender. The Sneaker must go back to the starting line.

Children love these games. They enjoy the challenge and excitement of sneaking up on each other. For some this game is a real challenge because they have difficulty controlling their body movements and vocal sounds. Being Sneakers gives them good practice in becoming more aware of how they move and when they make sounds. They can develop their body control and concentration abilities. Dogs and Rulers get to practice concentration and listening skills as well as their ability to detect sound directionally.

Listening to Sounds. Most students enjoy listening to sound effects on CDs and identifying what is creating the sound. Some groups can do this for five minutes and others stay enthralled for an hour. You can record live sounds or buy a sound-effects CD to play. I sometimes edit together sounds from a number of different CDs to provide a variety of animal, nature, and man-made sounds.

Making Sound Effects. Bring a number of noise-making implements to class and experiment with making different kinds of sounds with them. Make your own class sound-effect tape or CD and listen to it. Does it sound like the real thing?

Sound Symphonies. Divide the class into two or more teams. Have one team make one kind of music, for example, trumpets. Have the other team make another kind of sound, for example, drums or violins. You can choose a song you want them to play on their instruments or they can just improvise as they go along. Signal one group to begin making their sound, then the others. Regulate the volume at which each team is making its noise with the level of your hands: high meaning loud and low meaning soft.

Sound Environments. Create a whole environment through sound. Decide on a place like a city or a forest. Each group or each individual student chooses a different sound that would be found in that place. The teacher or a student serves as conductor and regulates when each sound comes in and goes out and what the volume level is.

Variation: Cast each person as a different character in a specific environment. When the conductor points to that person she must improvise something that character would say in that place.

Sound Stories. A sound story is a story that can be enhanced with sound effects made by the class as you or your assistant tells the story. Many creative drama books have examples of sound stories in them or you can write your own. The Saturday's Rainbow Adventure in the Prologue of this book started out as a sound-story exercise, but became an imagination-pantomime experience as we went along. Sound stories are most fun when they are recorded and played back so students can hear themselves.

Sound stories are excellent beginning exercises to use with young or nonverbal students. Success is built in. Almost everyone can make sounds. If they cannot make vocal sounds, they can usually make sounds with objects. Everyone works together. Everyone listens for her cue to come in and perform. Everyone listens very hard when the recording is played back to hear her voice or sound effect. There is great excitement and pride when a student hears the sounds she has made or those made by a friend. I'm not sure why, but the sound effects recorded for sound stories always sound good when they're played back!

Movement and Pantomime Games

Movement and pantomime games teach body awareness and control.

Freezing. Students move around the room until the leader says, "Freeze!" They must stop and freeze in position. They can move again when the leader says, "Action!" or "Go!" This is a good game for teaching listening skills and body control. Freezing is an excellent technique to use for group control when students get a little wild and need to be calmed down. You can also use it when you need to stop the action to side-coach a story or improvisation. If you like, have students move to music and freeze when the music stops.

Emotion Freezes. Students move around the room and when the leader names an emotion, they freeze into a statue expressing that emotion. *Variation:* The leader names an emotion and students walk around the room in a manner that expresses that emotion. When she says, "Freeze," they freeze into a statue of that emotion. This variation allows students to explore the emotion before committing to its portrayal.

The Magic Box. Place a large, colorful box with a top on it in the center of the circle. The Magic Box can hold any object of any size from any place in the world. Each student must first imagine what is in the box for her. The first student opens the box and takes out what she has imagined, pantomiming it for the rest of the class. The class guesses what it is. Then the next person has a turn. *Variation/Complication:* Before you can take something out of the box, you have to put a gift in it for someone else. *Variation/Complication:* Add an emotion or attitude toward the object you are taking out.

Even though this is an abstract pantomime exercise (the object is invisible) it works for most students who have cognitive disabilities because they have the concrete box out of which the objects come.

Pass the Sound/Pass the Movement. Everyone stands in a circle. One person invents a sound and a movement to go with it, which she passes to the person standing next to her. That person mirrors the sound and movement back to the first person. The second person then invents a new sound and movement to pass on to the third person, who mirrors it and then invents a new one and so on all the way around the circle.

Spontaneity is the name of the game, so do not allow students to stand and think too long about what sound and movement to do next. Rather than stop and lose the momentum, have students repeat the old sound and movement until something new comes to her mind. *Simplification:* Pass the same sound and movement all the way around the circle. After each has gone around, the next student can invent a new sound and movement to pass all the way around. *Simplification:* Pass only a sound or only a movement.

Environmental Walks. Students walk around the room and the leader suggests different environments or situations that would cause them to change the way they are walking. Examples of environments to walk through are mud, sharp rocks, ice, a rainstorm, a desert, a balance beam, the bottom of the ocean, a jungle, a mountain, flypaper, and quicksand.

Variation: Shoe Walks. Students imagine they are wearing different kinds of shoes, which the leader suggests as they walk around. They could be wearing cowboy boots, ballet slippers, ice skates, high heels, flip flops, shoes that are too tight, or clown shoes. How does each different kind of shoe change the way they walk?

Variation: Emotion Walks. Students move around the room and change how they are moving each time the leader calls out a different emotion.

Variation: Speed Walks. Students move around the room at different speeds: fast, regular, slow, and very slow. Try different activities at different speeds. Try talking at different speeds.

Variation: Space Walks. Imagine you are in a bubble of space and you do not want to burst your bubble. Walk around the room without bumping into anyone else. Start at slow speeds and over the course of several weeks work up to very fast speeds. This is a great game for teaching body control and the concept of personal space. If students have difficulty staying in their own spaces, have them begin by holding hula-hoops so they can see where the boundary of the space bubble is.

Transformations. As the leader suggests different plants, animals, and objects, students change their body shape to transform into it. Give students a slow count (three to five) in which to make their transformation so they have time to think about what shape they are about to become and can grow into it. *Variation/Complication:* After students become skilled at this game, have them work together to create the shapes of plants, animals, and objects. *Variation:* Teach the concepts of big and small by alternating between big animals and small animals or big objects, which the students must create together, and small objects, which they must create by themselves. *Variation:* Using this game as a visual-art or geometry introduction to teach different kinds of lines and geometric shapes. For instance, to create a triangle, one student could bend over and put her hands on the floor or she could join hands with two other students or three students could arrange themselves on the floor in a triangular configuration. *Variation:* Use this game to teach the shapes of numbers or letters. *Variation:* Use this game to practice spelling lessons by having students form each of the letters in a word with their bodies.

Making an Entrance. When an actor enters the stage, the audience needs to know how she is feeling before she says a word. This is a good exercise for teaching the nonverbal expression of emotions. The leader and one student go out of the room and decide on an emotion she will act out. The leader comes back in and everyone in class says, "Make your entrance!" The student in the hall enters the room acting out what a person would do and how a person would move if she were feeling that emotion. The class guesses what emotion the student is acting out.

Age Walks. People move in different ways at different ages. A baby crawls awkwardly. A happy six-year-old skips. A pregnant woman waddles. An old man hobbles. The teacher and one student decide on an age she will portray through movement. The class guesses what age she is. *Variation:* Portray an age and emotion at the same time. *Variation:* Portray a profession through movement.

Scarf Dancing. Bring long, colorful scarves made from light, flowing material to class. Let each student choose a scarf she likes. Play soft, flowing music, such as "The Blue Danube Waltz," and let students make their scarves dance in the air as they move to the music.

This exercise easily segues into Scarf Toss, Scarf Juggling, or Magic Scarf in which students try out different ways to use or wear the scarf. To motivate imaginations for Magic Scarf, ask "What could this be?" or "How else could you wear this?" Students will turn the scarves into belts, wedding veils, aprons, dresses, blindfold, ties, capes, towels, and more!

Ghost Guess Game. Students divide into two or more teams. One team goes out of the room or behind a partition. They have a large sheet and choose one member to cover herself with it from head to toe. The Ghost must change the way she moves and the shape of her body to fool the other team. She can try to move like another member of the team or she can try to totally transform her shape and movement. She enters the room, while the rest of her team stays out in the hallway. The other team must guess which member of the first team is underneath the sheet. They have only one guess, so they must come to consensus. A correct guess is worth one point. After each guess, teams switch places.

Using Movement/Pantomime Games with Students who have Orthopedic Disabilities

Start with games that focus on the parts of the body they can move with ease and that engage them on an imaginative level. If they can move their upper bodies, some games, such as the Magic Box, the Magic Scarf, the Magic Tube, or Transformations, would guarantee more success than other games, such as Environmental or Shoe Walks. Once they feel confident and their imaginations are warmed up, you can move on to games that use more movement, such as Making an Entrance or Pass the Sound/Pass the Movement.

Improvisational Games

Improvisational games add the dimensions of plot, dialogue, and character to basic movement games. Often students are paired or divided into small groups to work together to solve the improvisational assignment. This enhances interaction abilities and the ability to compromise.

Statues. Statues can be done in pairs or by a whole group. In pairs, one student is the Sculptor and one is the Clay. The Sculptor creates a statue from her Clay expressing a concept suggested by the teacher — perhaps an emotion or an occupation or an animal or a character from a story. The Clay must remain frozen in the shape that the Sculptor places it in. *Variation:* In groups, one student is the Sculptor and several students are pieces of Clay that are molded into a group statue expressing an emotional situation or a scene from a story. Have the other class members guess who the characters are and what is happening in the scene.

Statues can remain inanimate or they can be brought to life. This is a good technique for introducing the concept of improvising dialogue. Say, "If this statue came to life, what would it say?" The signal to come to life could be a touch on the statue's shoulder or some magic words.

Statues can be a very good game for providing structure for students with ADHD. Before acting out a story, ask each student to create a statue of her character using her own body. This helps everyone have a kinesthetic experience with her own character and discover appropriate physicalization. You can explore statues of the character at different points in the story to discover the character's emotional arc. If a student becomes distracted, you can get her back into character by freezing her into a statue of the character at that moment in the story.

Occupations. Divide students into pairs. Each pair must decide on a job that two people do together or that one person does for another. They act out the job for the class with or without dialogue. The class guesses what occupation it is.

The Hat Game. Collect a number of hats worn by different kinds of people, such as a cowboy hat, a nurse's hat, a chef's hat, and a graduation mortarboard. Give each student a turn to put on a hat and act out the character who would wear it. Students can use pantomime only or make up something to say. Limit this game to about four hats, so students do not get bored. If a group loves this game, it can be played again and again with different kinds of hats each session. *Variation:* Lay out a variety of hats. Let each student pick a different hat. Improvise a scene in which these characters are thrown together. Maybe they all get stuck in an elevator together or maybe they are eating dinner in a fancy restaurant. How does each character walk and talk? How do they get along with each other? What conflicts might develop between them?

Environments. This is an excellent exercise for introducing the elements of an improvised scene. Divide the class into two or more groups of four to seven members. Each group decides on an environment or place they will create together. They can be people, animals, plants, or objects in this environment. They can speak or only pantomime. The environment could be a post office, a desert, a movie theatre, or a schoolroom.

The first group sets up the room as their environment and begins to play their parts. Characters can talk to each other, but try not to say where they are. The others in the class watch until they think they know where the environment is. Instead of guessing verbally, they attempt to enter the environment and become a character in it. If they are correct, the other characters will respond to them. If they are not correct, the other characters will ignore them. When everyone has been integrated into the environment or at a good stopping place, the scene can come to an end and the next group can present their environment. If an interesting scene develops, keep it going, try to resolve the conflict and find a plausible ending.

Interview. Interview is a character development game, a drama version of 20 Questions. It requires students to behave and think as a character who is different from themselves. It forces them to make character decisions. It can be used as an acting exercise or it can be used to enhance character development when rehearsing a play.

One student decides on a character that she will impersonate. It could be a fictional character or an historical character, but it must be someone everyone in the class could know. She must walk, talk, and move like that character during the interview. The character sits in the "Hot Seat" and the class asks her questions. They cannot ask her name, but can ask anything else about her. After they have interviewed her for a while, they can guess who the character is. Then another person has a chance to play. This game can also be played as a TV talk show with one student being the TV host and others coming on as the guests.

Group Storytelling. Group storytelling is a good way to teach story structure, plot development, and listening skills. Sit in a circle. One person begins the story. After setting up the scene with a few sentences, she passes the story on to the next person. That person continues the story for a while and passes it on until the story has gone all the way around the circle. Ideally, the story begins with the first person and ends with the last person in the circle, but it does not have to work out that way.

For a story to make sense and have continuity, everyone must listen to the story as it goes around. Each new storyteller must continue with the same characters and solve or develop the conflict that has been set up so far. To start telling another story before the first story has ended does not fulfill the assignment.

Students must be flexible enough to let the story change. Once the story passes beyond them, they lose their control over what is going to happen. It's okay if someone further on in the circle takes the story in an unforeseen direction.

Beginning storytellers, like beginning improvisers, usually try to solve everything with violence. However, they soon discover that killing the hero off might be exciting for a moment, but it ends the story rather abruptly. Guide students to find more creative solutions to conflicts between characters to keep the story going.

If students get confused about whose turn it is, use a prop to officially designate the storyteller. Students not holding the prop should be listening and not speaking. A toy microphone, a Magic Feather, or a Magic Flower works well because it can easily be passed from hand to hand.

If students have difficulty passing the story on, limits can be placed on the amount of time allotted to each. Set a limit of 30 seconds or one minute. Another method is to allow each student to tell one portion of the story: one sentence, three sentences, or one whole scene.

You can record the story, and then play it back so everyone can hear how it developed. Later, it could be transcribed onto paper to be revised, used as a scenario for further development, or just copied to take home. One class that enjoyed making up stories decided to illustrate them and make a book as their end-of-semester project.

Art Activities

Visual-art activities can be used to motivate and enhance the physical, emotional, and verbal work you are doing in drama class. The arts work best when they are interconnected and integrated with each other.

There are many kinds of visual art. If you have blind students, choose an art activity that involves three dimensions and textures, such as weaving, sculpting, or mask making, rather than a two-dimensional activity, such as drawing or painting.

Drawing. Have students draw their favorite character from a story or the character each as been assigned to play. This will help them visualize their characters more clearly.

Map Making. Many stories involve a journey that the main character takes, having many adventures along with way. Before or after acting out a story like this, students can draw or sculpt maps of the journey. This will help them visualize the events and places the characters experience in the story.

Props and Costumes. If there are important props or costume pieces, students can make them to use before acting out the story. Maybe the king needs a scepter or crown. Maybe the unicorn needs a horn, the rabbits need ears, or the birds need wings.

Think through the props you will be making and come prepared with materials that are easy for your students to manipulate. Know the level of your students' fine motor skills before you attempt a major art project or students may get bored waiting for help with the parts of the task they are not able to do themselves. If necessary, precut and organize materials, leaving your students room for their own personal creative touches to the project. For instance, if you know you will need crowns for 12 dancing princesses, arrive with them already cut out — ready to be decorated and assembled.

An art project can be an outgrowth of a story. After acting out "Beauty and the Beast," students might enjoy learning how to make tissue-paper roses to take home. After "The 500 Hats of Bartholomew Cubbins," students might like to decorate their own hats. After "Hansel and Gretel," your class might like to learn how to make gingerbread houses.

Murals. Work together to make a group mural of the story. Choose a specific scene from the story or have everyone paint in the character she played in a pose that most expresses her personality. This takes planning so no one oversteps anyone else's personal-space boundaries. Flexibility and the ability to compromise are also vital in mural making as students must be willing to let others' visual ideas be in the scene along with their own.

Puppets. Simple puppets can be made out of paper plates, wooden spoons, empty paper-towel rolls, or paper bags. A puppet show version of the story can be done in class or puppets can be made after acting out a story so students can take them home and continue exploring the story dramatically there.

Puppets can be helpful tools for enticing participation from a very shy student or one who is having difficulty improvising dialogue. A puppet can serve as a safe, distancing mechanism when acting with her own body and voice seems too threatening or overwhelming. The puppet is experienced as "not me," so she can project a funny voice and personality onto it without feeling judged or put on the spot. See Chapter 8 for more detailed information about puppetry.

Makeup. A session with makeup can be fun. The easiest, fastest type of makeup to use is a water-based makeup that can be painted on like watercolors. Kryolan makes Aquacolor palettes in natural skin tones and bright colors. Create clown or animal makeup. Design a fantasy makeup for monsters or fairies.

One way to design a makeup is to start with a blank face chart on a piece of paper. The chart can indicate the basic outline of head, ears, nose, mouth, and eyes, but leave all details blank. Create the makeup design by filling in the chart with magic marker or colored pencils. Then go from the page to the face with the actual makeup. If you have young children with short attention spans or poor fine motor skills, the best idea is to paint the makeup designs on them yourself. Older children can paint on each other or look in a mirror and paint on themselves.

Harriet Lesser, an artist-teacher in Washington, DC, has invented another way to design makeup that takes the individual child's face into the design in a more immediate way. It is also a great way to explore makeup with students who have allergies or who don't want to put anything on their faces (for example, tactilely defensive students). Tape a sheet of clear acetate to a mirror. The child sits directly in front of it and looks through it into the mirror. She draws the makeup design directly onto her own facial image (on the acetate on the mirror) with magic marker. Rolls of acetate can be bought at most art supply stores. Make sure you purchase acetate that will hold the marker color rather than bead up and rub off.

Mask Making. Mask making is another way to explore characters and add an interesting art activity to your class. Simple masks can be made from paper plates and attached to the head with elastic or string ties. You might want to cut out the eyes and attach the ties before class. Have students draw on the face or glue on objects (buttons, yarn, ribbon, colorful plastic lids) for three-dimensional features. If your students do not want the mask to touch their face, their masks can be mounted on Popsicle sticks and held in front of their face.

Simple masks can also be made from medium to large paper bags. Cut out eyes so actors can see and half-moons on the shoulders to make the bag fit better. Then have students draw on the face. You can add yarn, fabric, paper strips, or feathers for hair. Both of these types of masks can be made in 10 to 20 minutes.

Some art supply stories sell neutral masks made out of white or clear plastic. These can serve as a simple form to build or paint on. More elaborate masks can be made from papier-mâché molded around a head form or foam rubber. Build up the features by painting or gluing on more foam shapes, feathers, yarn, and other decorative three-dimensional shapes.

If students are older, have patience, and are not tactilely defensive, you can build masks directly on their faces using plaster-of-Paris bandages. The advantage of this type of mask is that it fits the individual's face perfectly. Rolls of gauze covered with plaster of Paris

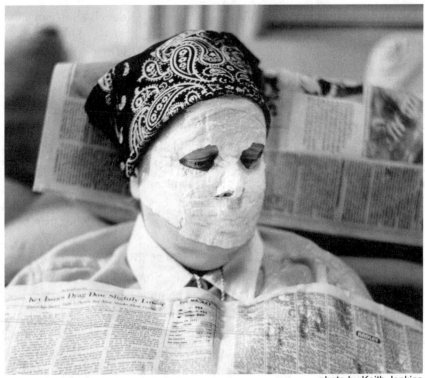

Figure 16: Mask-making student waits while plaster of Paris gauze dries.

can be bought at many art supply and hobby stores. Sometimes they are still carried by medical supply stores or drug stores.

Before class, cut the rolls into small gauze squares. Cover the student's hair completely with a shower cap or bandanna so it does not get caught in the plaster. Cover her face, particularly the eyebrows, eyelashes, and any other areas with facial hair, with a thin layer of petroleum jelly. The ideal position for mask-making is lying on one's back with eyes closed.

The teacher and assistants can make masks on the students or students can take turns making masks on each other. Play relaxing music. This helps make the mask-making experience a pleasant one.

Put warm water in a bowl. Wet the strips of plaster gauze with warm water and work the plaster around a bit to fill in the holes in the gauze.

photo by Keith Jenkins

Figure 17: Painting the mask with acrylic paint.

Place on the face in overlapping layers — at least three layers deep to make the mask thick enough to hold up. Blend the plaster as you go. The student cannot talk while the gauze is placed on her face. Be sure to leave holes around the nostrils so the student can breathe! You can cover the entire face including the eyes and cut the eyeholes out later or you can leave space for the eyes as you work. Ask the student which she would prefer.

You can make a full-face mask or a half-mask. If you will be performing in pantomime a full-face is fine. If your actors need to talk, you will probably want to make half-masks so the mouth is not covered or create a full-face mask with open mouth. You can cover the open mouth on the inside with black mesh fabric if you want the actor's mouth to disappear underneath it.

The plaster will dry in 10 to 15 minutes, depending on the humidity. During that time the student must remain lying quietly on her back. Then the mask can be loosened if the student wiggles her face a little underneath. The mask-maker lifts the mask off from above, gently holding the mask by the sides of the face. The student should keep her eyes closed until the mask is off and she is sitting up so no little stray pieces of plaster get in her eyes.

The mask will need to dry for at least 24 hours and may need several more layers of gauze added to the top to make it strong enough. Character features can be built up with more layers of plaster gauze or with foam rubber. Styrofoam or cardboard shapes can be glued on and covered with gauze. A large feature built up only with gauze will become too heavy and press down on the actor's face. For final finishing, cover the raw edges of the mask with pieces of plaster gauze that flap from front to back of the mask.

After 24 hours of drying, masks can be painted with acrylic paint. This will clean up easily with water when you are done. Do not use tempera paint or watercolors because the water will soak through the mask and it will fall apart. If the mask pushes down in an uncomfortable way on any part of the face, you can use hot-melt glue to place some small pieces of foam inside to cushion the face.

Punch holes in the sides of the mask near by the ears with an awl or ice pick. Measure how much elastic you need to hold the mask on the actor's head plus a little bit more for tying it onto the mask. Then thread the elastic through the holes and tie it off.

This kind of mask project involves several class periods. It might be fun for an advanced creative drama class or a movement/mime class that is preparing a special presentation. I have also used it with classes doing Greek Theatre or animal fables.

Closure Activities

Ending a class on an organized, upbeat note is as important as starting it off well. Good endings are a matter of finding the proper emotional tone and physical balance as one activity concludes and another begins. Students need a chance to calm down from the intensity and excitement of drama class and refocus themselves for whatever is coming next. Closure activities help the leader and students put their experience into perspective before moving on. Many closure activities can be done with any age group.

Running out of time. At first you may find that you plan too much for a class period and then run out of time for a closure activity. If you are playing a game, warn students that you are running out of time and stop the game at the end of the next round. Ending is more difficult if students are in the middle of an exciting improvisational scene or creative drama story. Telling them they can finish next week usually does not offer much consolation. Keep track of time as you move from one activity to another in your lesson plan. Do not start a scene or story unless you know you can move it to a quick ending if you begin to run out of time. After a while you will be able to gauge about how many activities a particular group of students can get through on a typical day.

If you are halfway through acting out a creative drama story and you suddenly realize there are only five minutes of class left, try using your role as narrator to facilitate "jump-cutting" from the climax of one scene to the next. Say, "We're running out of time and we want to finish the story, so I'm going to speed things up a little." Cut the development of each remaining scene to a minimum and let students fill in the important pantomime actions and important moments of climactic dialogue. Finish with the whole class together in an ending tableau as their favorite characters in the story.

For an improvisational scene, warn the actors, "We have five minutes left. You need to find an ending to this scene." If they keep going, warn them again, "Okay, now you have two minutes left. This scene needs an ending." You might need to freeze the actors. "Freeze. I'm sorry. We're out of time. This week at home, see if you can think of a good way to end this scene."

Check-out. In creative drama, acting out the story is usually the main activity. Afterwards, the class can spend a few minutes discussing what they enjoyed most about the story. They might want to share their favorite moments or which character was their favorite to play. In improvisational acting classes students can sit down and review the games they played, what they learned that day, and what they enjoyed doing most.

Songs. Singing always brings people together in a positive way. You might find an "ending" or "goodbye" song that can serve as a closing ritual each week. You might sing a favorite song suggested by a member of the class. The end of class is not a good time to teach a new song, but it is a great time to review a song that was learned earlier.

Art Activities. Art is a good way to tie together dramatic activities that have been done in the period. Have students draw their favorite scene from the story acted out that day. See the section on "Art Activities" earlier in this chapter for more ideas.

Guided Fantasy. A short guided fantasy might serve as a good closing. It can calm students down and provide a safe transition from the end of class to going home or moving on to the next class of the day.

A Favorite Game. Some groups have favorite games that they like to play again and again. The end of class is a good time to replay a game. It provides a feeling of safety and familiarity before going out to face something new.

Passing Games. Gather students into a circle and have each person pass a compliment around the circle to the person next to her. In *Pass the Expression*, pass sad faces or happy faces or funny faces around the circle. Hold hands and pass a squeeze around the circle.

Making a Wish. Pass a "magic object," such as a crystal or a feather, around the circle. Each student makes a wish on that object while it is in her hands. She can either share her wish or keep it secret.

Building Lesson Plans for Creative Drama

A strong creative drama lesson plan uses warm-ups and games as motivational devices and skill-builders for the acting skills that will be needed in that day's story. The following pages offer suggestions for how to lead up to a story through games and acting exercises.

The Tortoise and the Hare

"The Tortoise and the Hare" is a fable that has characters who live life at two different speeds. Each of the speeds has an effect on the personality of the characters. The Tortoise is very slow and deliberate. The Hare is very quick, impatient, and boastful. Prepare your students for this story by focusing your warm-up activities on practice in acting at different speeds.

A lesson plan for this story might look like:

1. Pantomime Go-Around (fast animals/slow animals).
2. Fast/regular/slow actions and voices.
3. Fast/regular/slow freezes.
4. Regular race.
5. Slow-motion race.
6. Tell "The Tortoise and the Hare."
7. Set up the racecourse in the room.
8. Practice character walks and voices.
9. Choose characters for the story.
10. Act out the story.
11. Draw your favorite scene from the story.

Start class with students sitting in a circle. Go around the circle and ask each one to act out a slow animal. Then go around again and act out a fast animal. Talk about different speeds. Together, pantomime a series of actions, such as clapping hands, nodding "yes" and "no," waving, etc., in regular, fast, and slow motion. Try talking at a regular speed, at fast speed like an auctioneer, at slow speed. Stand up and practice moving in slow, regular, and fast motion, freezing students between each speed change.

Organize a sprint across the room. Delineate your starting line and finish line with masking tape on the floor. Then have a slow-motion race. In a slow-motion race the *last* person to cross the finish line wins! It may be hard at first to get across the idea that in order to win this kind of race, you must do the opposite of what you do in a regular race, but once your students catch on, you will be amazed at how slowly they will move! If the slow-motion race is frustrating for them, run another fast sprint across the room to release their tension.

Tell the story. Take a few moments at the end to talk about what the moral means. "Slow and steady wins the race" does not always make sense to young children. The Hare loses because he does not keep on task. He stops to eat, he visits friends, and, eventually, he takes a nap. The Tortoise just keeps moving. The moral means, "If you quit or fool around, you'll never finish the job you started, but no matter how slowly you work, if you keep plugging away, you'll succeed."

Take some time to lay the racecourse out in a very clear way in the room. If you have a carpet, the race could follow its edge all the way around the room. You could tape the racecourse out on the floor. Signs or "landmarks" in the room could show where to go first, second, third, and so on. However it is set up, students need a visual path to follow. If your racecourse is vague ("Just run around the room" or "Run over there and then here and then there.") students will lose their way and the story will fall apart. Decide ahead of time where the Hare will stop to eat, to chat, to fall asleep. Practice running the racecourse with everyone as the Hare and then with everyone as the Tortoise. Choose characters and act out the story. If there is time at the end, draw a picture of your favorite character or your favorite scene from the story.

National/Cultural Themes

Focus on a particular culture or nationality for one or a series of classes. Bring in pictures, maps, and examples of folk art, clothing, or other items indigenous to that culture. Learn a song or folk dance from that culture. Talk about names in the culture and how they are different from names in ours. For instance, in many Asian countries family names are put first instead of last. Native Americans place a great value on names, which are often based on nature or a deed that an individual has done. Depending on the tribe, the individual earns, dreams, or chooses her name. Make food, clothing, or art in the style of that culture. Play games from that culture. If you are focusing on Mexico or the Southwestern U.S., you could teach students how to make God's eyes or how to roll their own tortillas. Tell and act out stories from that culture.

Toy Stories

There are many stories about famous dolls, such as Raggedy Ann, Winnie the Pooh, and Paddington Bear. Begin class with a Go-Around in which each student thinks of her favorite toy. As a group, act out several different toys that will be characters in the story. If you can find music which suggests toys, students will enjoy acting out toys to music. Tell the story. Act it out. End by drawing a picture of favorite characters or toys.

Animal Stories

There are many stories that revolve around animal characters from "The Frog Prince" to "The Musicians of Bremen." Try different kinds of animal pantomime games as lead-in activities to the story. Practice making the animal's sound in different ways to express the different emotions the animal character feels in the story. A frog could "ribbit" sadly, happily, angrily, or hungrily. Create a character voice for an animal based on the qualities of its real animal sound.

If the story involves differences in size, such as in "The Lion and the Mouse," "The Three Billy Goats Gruff," or "Goldilocks and the Three Bears," practice acting out creatures that are large and small. Practice talking in a big voice and a little voice. Practice making big movements and little ones.

Learn a song about one of the animals in the story.

Make a mask to wear while acting out the story.

Building Lesson Plans for Improvisational Acting

Start the semester off with games and activities in which students can get to know each other. Group games, in which everyone participates and works together, are crucial for developing trust and problem-solving skills that will be needed for creating improvisational scenes later. Give students enough opportunities to begin developing verbal and physical expressiveness, but be careful about putting individuals on the spot to perform for the group before they are ready. A nice mixture of group games and individual skill-building activities for a beginning group might look like this:

Session One

Name Game: Say your name and pantomime your favorite animal.

Elbow-to-Elbow.

Transformations: Change your body into different shapes.

The Magic Tube.

The Ghost Guess Game.

Go-Around: Pass the sheet around and each person wears it a different way.

Slowly introduce your actors to solo and partner work:

Session Two

Name Review: Beanbag game.

Emotion walks: Walk around expressing different emotions.

Making an Entrance.

Season Pantomimes: In pairs, act out something you might do in the summer, fall, winter, and spring.

Imagine your favorite food's smell and taste.

Pass a facial expression around the circle.

A later session in the class might look like this:

Session Four

The Magic Box.

The Hat Game, with two or three hats.

Environments: two rounds.

Group storytelling.

By the end of the semester, you may be warming up with a game or two and then opening up the floor for suggestions for scenes that could be created:

Session Eleven

Pass the Sound/Pass the Movement.

Scene Work.

Discussion of Scenes.

Group hand-squeeze.

Sharing with Parents and Friends at the End of the Semester

Formal Presentations

Many schools and organizations like their performing arts classes to make a presentation at the end of each semester or school year for parents and friends. In different places presentations are called by different names: recital, showcase, highlights, sharing, or the class play. There is often a lot of pressure to show parents that they have used their money wisely in enrolling their child in this class. Some of the pressure comes from the administration and some from the parents. Teachers put pressure on themselves because they want to show their students' artistic growth. Students put pressure on themselves because they want to shine in their parents' eyes. However, creative drama and improvisational acting classes are process- rather than product-oriented. Whenever formal presentations must be made, rehearsals begin. Whenever rehearsals begin, class exploration and skill building stop.

There is also the dilemma of the rehearsal schedule. If a presentation is to be put together, at what point in the semester should rehearsals begin? Three class periods before? Five class periods? Eight? The appropriate amount of time for rehearsing a project depends on the students and the complexity of the project being undertaken.

When classes turn into rehearsals, a different dynamic takes over. Class is now about reproducing a result that once was improvised, enhancing it, and improving it so that it is clear and can be shared with others. Stage technique becomes important so that the audience can see and hear the actors. Suddenly the class is in the middle of the creation of a one-act play, which takes on more production values and greater importance the closer the performance time comes. Parents start making costumes, teachers start building sets, and students start getting nervous and upset.

The truth of the matter is that sometimes it is not in the best interest of the student to perform at the end of a semester. The pressure of preparing for a presentation is often too much for beginning students to handle. If they will not feel comfortable in front of an audience, it is far better to devote class time to the development of expression, self-confidence, and improvisation skills. There will be plenty of opportunities to perform in the future. When students are pushed on stage too soon and have a bad experience, they may not want to try it again. I have heard many horror stories from adults who had traumatic experiences in performance situations as children and then never wanted to perform again.

When formal presentations are appropriate, keep them simple and keep them short. Provide lots of structure and lots of rehearsal time so that students are sure of what they are doing. To achieve a polished performance in the professional theatre with trained actors, directors generally like to schedule at least an hour of rehearsal for every minute on stage. Obviously that degree of rehearsal and precision is not required or necessary for a student presentation; however, the guideline is worth bearing in mind when undertaking a project in order to keep it to an appropriate length.

Build in fail-safe techniques to keep students on track during performance:

- Keep dialogue improvised so that it does not have to be exactly the same each time.
- Keep the play moving through the use of a narrator (yourself or your assistant) who can remind students of what comes next and can improvise if something goes wrong.
- Use an assistant as a character in the play who, in character, can remind student actors what comes next.
- Use music cues to remind students of exits and entrances. Different characters can have "character themes" which play each time they come on stage.

If you need to, record dialogue and have the actors pantomime to it. Then they can concentrate on remembering movement alone instead of remembering movement and lines.

Above all, remind your students, tell your parents, and remember yourself that this is a work in progress, not a finished product. If something goes wrong, it is not the end of the world. It's just a taste test, not a full meal.

Alternatives to Formal Presentations

In-Class Sharing. Invite parents and friends to the last class to participate in a typical class. Favorite games and exercises can be taught to the guests by the now-experienced students. Parents can be teamed up against students for games or families can play against other families. In creative drama classes parents can be invited to take on characters in the story and act alongside their children. In improvisational acting classes parents can be included in role-playing and the creation of scenes.

A great time is had by all in this kind of sharing situation. Students forget to be nervous. Parents have the opportunity to see their children in a relaxed, absorbed state. They can see them interact with others. As students work and play alongside their parents, they can see a new side of the adults in their lives — the playful, creative side.

A cautionary note: let parents know ahead of time that they will be expected to participate in the class with their child. If parents sit and watch, the class will turn into a formal presentation — one which has not been rehearsed! Students will feel self-conscious and unprepared and will begin to act out negatively. The whole situation could fall apart.

Videotaped Presentations. A good way to present a story that the group has been working on without the pressure of performance is to videotape work as it is going on in class. A number of different sessions can be edited together for a final class presentation or a special story, scene, or character-development exercise could be staged for the camera. Students and parents can watch the presentation and enjoy it together without the nerves and worry that accompany a formal presentation. You will be sharing your process as a product.

Special Class Projects. If students have done a number of art projects over the course of the semester, have the class spend some time mounting their work and set up an art gallery in the room for the final class. Students can serve as tour guides through the gallery. If students have developed a series of stories, they could be presented in a reading for parents. Similarly, if students have developed a sound recording of which they are particularly proud, the recording or a section of it could be shared.

If you must give a final presentation of some sort, look at your options with an eye to ways you can show off your students to their best advantage. Keep the situation as relaxed and informal as possible. Success should always be the operative word.

Recommended Reading

Aycox, F. (1997). *Games We Should Play in School.* Discovery Bay, CA: Front Row Experience.

Barker, C. (1986). *Theatre Games: A New Approach to Drama Training.* London: Methuen.

Bett, L. & Stockley, R. (1989). *Improvisation Through Theatre-Sports: A Curriculum to Teach Basic Acting Skills and Improvisation.* Singapore: Thespis Productions.

Boal, A. (1992). *Games for Actors and Non-Actors.* London: Routledge.

Delgado, R. 1986). *Acting with Both Sides of Your Brain.* New York: Holt, Rinehard & Winston.

DeMille, R. (1976). *Put Your Mother on the Ceiling: Children's Imagination Games.* New York: Viking Penguin.

Hannaford, C. (1995). *Smart Moves: Why Learning is not all in Your Head.* Marshall, NC: Great Ocean Publishers.

Johnstone, K. (1989). *Impro: Improvisation and the Theatre.* London: Methuen.

King, N. (1981). *A Movement Approach to Acting.* Upper Saddle River, NJ: Prentice-Hall.

Koch, K. (1980). *Wishes, Lies, and Dreams: Teaching Children to Write Poetry.* New York: HarperCollins.

Murdock, M. (1987). *Spinning Inward: Using Guided Imagery with Children for Learning.* Boston: Shambhala.

8. Puppetry

Puppetry is a form of drama that can be very popular and successful with students of all ages. The process of creating a puppet play is enjoyed by puppeteers and the experience of performing for an appreciative audience enhances feelings of self-esteem. Because a puppet play is a highly structured situation in terms of rehearsal and perform-ance, students can be introduced to performing in a situation in which they feel safe. Puppeteers are hidden away behind the puppet stage so the audience does not see them. This can help shy and beginning students deal with performance anxiety and gain confidence in themselves as theatre artists.

Unfortunately, in our contemporary American culture there is not as high an appreciation for puppetry as there is in other parts of the world. Puppet theatre is generally considered appropriate entertainment only for young children. While puppetry is enjoyed by children and can be done by children, it is no more a "childish" art than acting, singing, or dancing. Asian countries, such as Thailand and Japan, have classical puppet traditions reaching back hundreds of years. Their puppet theatres present plays about important cultural and moral struggles and are attended by members of the entire community. Europe also has greatly respected puppet theatres, which perform for large audiences of all ages. Great American puppeteers, such as Peter Schumann, founder of the Bread and Puppet Theater, and the late Jim Henson, inventor of the Muppets, are adult artists who have created puppets and productions for adults as well as children.

Advantages of Puppetry

There are many advantages to working with puppets. In a puppetry class most of what students do is focused toward the final goal of the puppet play. This helps prepare them for being in a performance situation. In a step-by-step, logical, visual, auditory, and kinesthetic progression, the process becomes the product.

Shy or beginning drama students often feel much safer performing with a puppet stage between them and the audience. I have found this true even with college students in my creative drama classes. Puppeteers have an assigned space behind the scenes and usually do not have to move around a lot, but they must make very specific movements within their assigned space. These movements can be carefully choreographed, then the students should be familiarized with them through repetition. This does not mean that your students will not be nervous before performing, but it does mean that they can be prepared and feel comfortable. During the show they are able to focus more on the puppets than on the unseen audience.

Nobody in the audience knows for sure who is playing which character, so the pressure of being seen and judged is off otherwise shy performers. Often, very quiet people become incredible hams when put behind a puppet stage for the first time. They blossom as performers in a way they never could if physically put on stage themselves. In a sense, they are freed to express themselves dramatically for the first time.

Another advantage to puppetry is that students begin working on the puppet play knowing they will have a finished product to take home, something concrete they have made. The puppet becomes a treasured memento they can keep to remember the class and performance. After the class is done, it can also be used at home for continued dramatic play.

An actor uses his own body, but he is inside his body and cannot see himself perform the character. A puppeteer uses his own body, but can see his character from the outside as he manipulates it. As a puppeteer, a performer can have the best of both worlds, as performer and audience at the same time.

Because a puppeteer can see his character as an entity separate from himself while he performs, puppets help an actor understand that the character he is portraying is separate or different from himself. Some beginning actors are afraid if they pretend to be someone else, they will become that other person and lose themselves. With a puppet, a student can project whatever emotions he wants onto the character without worrying that someone in the audience might confuse the character with him — and without being confused himself.

Through puppetry, students can become involved with an in-depth creation of their characters and the play. They make the decisions that determine what their character looks like and how their character moves. Using a physical creation that can be seen and touched, apart from their body, makes inventing dialogue and character reactions easier for some.

Issues to Consider before Choosing Puppetry

While puppetry has many advantages, there are issues to take into consideration. First, do your students have the concentration and interest level to stay with one project over an extended period of time? Young children and children who have very short attention spans or impulse-control problems do better with projects that can be accomplished within one class period, or, in some cases, within ten minutes! They have difficulty delaying gratification from the present to a future moment. If you try to involve them in a long-term project, they may become bored or frustrated.

Second, do your students have the hand-eye coordination and fine motor skills to construct puppets and manipulate them? If your students have physical limitations, pick a type of puppet that will be easy for them to make and manipulate. Rod puppets can be manipulated by anyone who can grasp a stick. Hand puppets require more manual dexterity. Marionettes, manipulated from above, are the most difficult to use.

Because puppeteers' vision of onstage action is limited by their physical placement behind the curtains of most puppet stages, during performances they must rely primarily on sound cues rather than visual cues. This makes participation in puppet plays difficult for deaf or hard-of-hearing students. However, there are some types of puppet stages, particularly those used for marionettes, in which the puppeteers are located above the stage and have a bird's eye view. This would allow deaf students the ability to participate successfully in the puppet show.

Another alternative for deaf students, if you have access to the right technical equipment, might be to provide the puppeteers with a backstage video monitor of the onstage action. A video camera set up in the audience can feed backstage to the puppeteers what the audience is seeing out front. This method was developed by Jim Henson so he and the other Muppeteers could keep track of how the Muppets looked to the TV cameras during taping. Normally, the Muppeteers manipulate their Muppets above their heads while watching the action on monitors below them.

Enough good assistants are crucial in puppetry classes. The more complicated the building process and the art materials and the more fine-motor difficulties students have, the more help they will need. It is better to arrange for a few extra assistants during the building process than to let your students flounder. A student who becomes overly frustrated while trying to construct his puppet may give up on the whole project in despair.

Choosing the right person as an assistant for a puppetry class is as important as having enough of them. Assistants need to be able to understand what the student envisions and help him create the effects he wants by providing the missing manipulative skills or the extra hand needed for holding something in place. The effective assistant shares his expertise and knowledge of the art materials without taking over and doing the project for the student. The teacher and the assistants are there to serve as guides to facilitate the student's creative vision, not their own. If the artistic function is taken from students, they will get the message that their ideas are not valued. They will lose their enthusiasm for the project and stop contributing creatively to the process.

The last thing to take into consideration is to determine if your students believe puppetry is an acceptable undertaking. While I firmly believe that puppetry is appropriate for students of any age, the students involved have to believe this, too. If a class of adolescents or upper-elementary students have bought into the narrow American belief that "puppetry is only for little kids," you could be setting yourself up for an uphill battle. You might get through to them, but chances are, they will not allow themselves to fully experience the creative challenge and joy of puppetry.

You can sometimes get around this mindset by presenting your puppet project as a gift the group will be giving to a child audience. Often older students will then willingly take on a puppet show. I have certainly found this to be true with my college-level creative-drama students. Each semester their final project is to create puppet shows that are presented for pre-schoolers at the public library. The assignment has become the highlight of the semester, to which everyone commits himself 100 percent.

Creating and Developing a Puppet Show

Choosing the Story

Students need to be committed to a puppet project from the outset. The best way to get them to commit is to involve them in the decision-making. Let them choose the story that will be turned into the puppet show. Ask for suggestions of their favorite stories. Write down all the suggestions and talk about the pros and cons of each. Which stories have the most interesting characters? The most exciting plots? The fairest division of roles? Will the dialogue be easy to make up? Will any parts be difficult to stage? Some stories might not have enough characters for everyone to have a part. Some might have too many roles. If there are more characters than students, are a few puppeteers willing to make and manipulate more than one puppet?

Avoid dramatizing favorite television shows or current movies. The characters are familiar to everyone, but the situations usually will not develop into interesting, short plays. Be wary of stories with a weak plot structure or lots of narrative and little action. They may be even harder to dramatize as a puppet play than they would be in a creative drama situation.

While younger students will suggest fairy tales and children's stories, older students may want to dramatize a classic poem, such as "Twas the Night Before Christmas" or "Hiawatha's Childhood." They could base a puppet play on a well-known novel, such as *Oliver Twist,* or contemporary youth fiction, such as *Charlie and the Chocolate Factory*. They could create an original play about a fantasy or a social situation they face. Any material that can be dramatized can be dramatized through puppetry.

After the class has talked about all the ideas and eliminated the ones that everyone agrees will not work well, take a vote on the remaining ideas. There may be a clear favorite, in which case you are on your way. If the group is split, you will need to guide them to a choice that is acceptable to everyone. One way to get a sense of where a general consensus lies is to go through the list of ideas and allow each student to vote for every one he likes, instead of limiting him to one vote for his favorite. Then you will see where the interests fall and what the "hot" ideas are in the group. In a class of ten students, if nine would be willing to work on "Cinderella," seven would be willing to do "Sleeping Beauty," and five would be willing to do "The Valiant Little Tailor," you know you'll have the most interest and commitment if you dramatize "Cinderella."

In the case of an emotional deadlock between two highly contested stories, you could split the class into two different casts and create two puppet plays. Make sure if you do this that you have enough assistants to handle two rehearsals going on at the same time in different rooms. Making one cast wait while another rehearses becomes boring for those waiting and is not a good use of valuable class time.

Casting the Characters

Deciding who will play which role can be difficult, especially if the leading character is an extremely popular one, such as Cinderella. It is rare to find a group who can divide up the roles without struggling with who will play what part. If a class has very mixed abilities, sometimes the teacher needs to step in as the director to cast the roles herself. The larger, more verbal roles go to the students who can handle them better while the smaller, less verbal roles go to the less verbal students. In this way, success can be ensured for every member of the class.

Another option is to cast by lottery. Have each student write his name on a slip of paper and put it into a hat. The teacher starts with the first character on the cast list and pulls a name out of the hat. Whoever's name is on the paper gets the part, unless he declines, then another name can be drawn for that role. The lottery continues until all roles are cast.

Another method is more complicated but takes each student's choices more fully into consideration. Each student writes down his first and second (or first, second, and third) choice of role on a piece of paper. The choice papers go into a hat and the teacher casts each part in the story, pulling out slips of paper from the hat. If Cinderella is the character up for casting, the first slip of paper that is drawn that has the name "Cinderella" on it as a first choice plays that part. When all the first choices have been used up for each role, the choice slips from the remaining uncast students are put back into the hat and the remaining roles are cast from second choices pulled at random from the hat. This method takes longer, but usually ensures that students will get their first or second choice for a role and this makes for a happier group of students.

With the lottery method each student might not get his favorite role. Each role might not go to the actor most suited for it. But students feel that their desires have been taken into consideration. They have had an equal chance to get the part they wanted and the teacher has not played favorites.

Constructing the Puppets

Once the roles have been cast, the construction of the puppets can begin. Making the puppets is a very important component of a puppetry class. To be sure, buying them at the store would be easier, but students would then miss out on the opportunity to make essential character choices and create every aspect of the play.

Working in three dimensions frees many students who normally fail in our language-oriented educational system. In creating their ideas in space rather than in words or in two dimensions, they often demonstrate amazing problem-solving abilities and invent incredibly imaginative designs. I was working with a special-education class on a project that put poetry and puppetry together. They were dramatizing several poems by A.A. Milne, including "The Four Friends," which features Ernest the

Elephant, Leonard the Lion, George the Goat, and James the Snail. Ramona came to me for advice on how to make Ernest's tusks. I looked over the art materials I had brought and did not see a good solution.

"Maybe two straws?" I suggested weakly.

She screwed up her face and shook her head, "No."

I had to agree. "It's not the best idea," I said. "Maybe we can think of something better."

Suddenly Delia was standing next to us with a pair of scissors and an empty masking tape roll in her hand. Delia was about 10 and rarely spoke. She could not read more than a few words. She was making George the Goat who in E.H. Shepard's illustration has very prominent horns. She had looked at the empty masking tape roll and realized that if it were cut into two halves, it would become the shape of goat horns — or elephant tusks! I was so excited that I wanted to jump up and down! She had solved the problem brilliantly — much better than I had — using her visual-spatial intelligence.

Before building your puppets, it is best to explore the characters in the story a bit so students can imagine them visually and kinesthetically. You might want to lead a short improvisation in which each student pantomimes a day in the life of his character. You could take turns saying something each character might say or think of words to describe each character's personality. Have students create a picture of their character. Through this process they can make some initial choices about color and details for their puppet. This drawing can be the visual plan they work from as they make the puppet.

Types of Puppets

There are many sizes and shapes of puppets, but based on manner of manipulation, they fall into five main categories: finger puppets, hand puppets, rod puppets, marionettes, and ventriloquist dummies.

Finger Puppets. Finger puppets fit onto the fingertips. They can be made out of plastic, foam, cardboard tubes, or stiff fabric, such as felt or leather. In order to make finger puppets, students need excellent fine-motor skills because the basic construction and decoration involves small, intricate detail work. Since they are tiny, finger puppets are fine for a puppet show that is going to be videotaped up close, but too small to be seen clearly by an audience. Because of the motor skills needed for construction and their limitations in live performance, I do not recommend finger puppets for most students with special needs.

Hand Puppets. Hand puppets fit over the hand. They can be made out of fabric, socks, empty paper towel rolls, mittens, gloves, paper bags, paper plates, papier-mâché, Styrofoam balls, ceramic clay, or foam rubber.

The simplest form of hand puppet is made with movable arms. The middle finger holds up the head while the thumb and pinky are inserted into the arms of the puppet's body. Another type has a mouth that the puppeteer opens and closes as it talks. The thumb is located in the lower jaw and the four fingers are in the upper jaw.

Rod Puppets. A rod puppet is simply a puppet on a stick. Usually the head is stuck on the rod. If the puppet is a cutout, the center bottom of the whole puppet may be glued to the stick. Some rod puppets have additional rods attached to the puppets' hands so they can be moved independently of the body.

Shadow puppets are a variety of rod puppet. They are cut out of a flat surface (cardboard, heavy paper, or metal) with focus put on their outline. Details can be cut out of the puppet to create the illusion of clothes, hair, facial expressions, or objects in the hand. Sometimes shadow puppets have movable arms and legs that are jointed and manipulated by additional rods. Usually the shadow puppet is placed behind a translucent screen and light is cast from behind to create a shadow on the screen.

Combination Hand-and-Rod Puppets. A puppet with mouth and hands that move is a combination hand-and-rod puppet. In order to create a puppet of this kind, one hand is put into the mouth and one hand controls the rods connected to the puppet's hands. These are manipulated from below either by the puppeteer or by an assistant.

The Muppets are hand-and-rod puppets made from foam rubber and fabric. (Kermit the Frog, the first Muppet, was made out of an old green winter coat that belonged to Jim Henson's mother, two rods from an old umbrella, and a ping-pong ball cut in half for the eyes.) We are not aware

photo by Sally Bailey

Figure 18: Varieties of rod puppets. On the left is a tube puppet. The two puppets on the right have Styrofoam heads and the Witch Doctor is cut out of a plastic lid.

of the rods because they are made invisible through the skill of the Muppeteers and the magic of television.

Hand-and-rod puppets require highly developed fine-motor skills and good hand-eye coordination. Only attempt them with a physically adept, advanced group.

Marionettes. Marionettes are puppets with complete bodies that move by means of strings attached to all their major body joints. The strings are manipulated by the puppeteers from a platform above the puppet stage instead of from below, as with most other types of puppets. Marionettes are difficult to make and operate. Strings can easily become tangled. If marionettes bump into each other during a performance, a major marionette traffic-jam can result. Only attempt marionettes with an advanced, experienced group.

Ventriloquist Dummies. Ventriloquist dummies also have complete bodies. The puppeteer or ventriloquist sits in full view of the audience with the dummy sitting on his lap. He places one hand into the dummy's head from behind and manipulates the head and mouth. The ventriloquist holds a two-way conversation with the dummy. He speaks for himself and he *throws his voice* (speaks without moving his lips) whenever the dummy speaks. Ventriloquist dummies are difficult to construct but, if students want to try, there are ways of working full-sized puppets and human actors creatively into a show together.

How to Construct Simple Puppets

Tools and Materials. Scissors, crayons, felt-tipped markers, paint, sequins, glitter glue, construction paper, buttons, yarn, beads, pipe cleaners, ribbon, seashells, feathers, pillow stuffing, Styrofoam balls and

photo by Sally Bailey

Figure 19: Puppets can be made of many things. The left one is made out of a piece of fur glued into a cylinder. The matador in the middle is an example of a pantyhose puppet. The turtle on the right is made out of an animal slipper

other shapes, and scraps of fabric and foam rubber are very useful materials for puppet making. Save all sizes of colorful plastic bottle tops from shampoo, spices, and other household containers to be used as three-dimensional eyes, noses, ears, and mouths. Old pieces of jewelry and small, lightweight, odd-shaped items can also be recycled into faces and accessories. Paper or plastic egg cartons make great noses, teeth, and eyes. Googly eyes can be bought at hobby stories and really bring a puppet to life. Ping-pong balls and other small, round objects can be made into wonderful eyes, too.

Rubber cement is best used for gluing paper. White glue or tacky glue works well when applying fabric, glitter (if you cannot find glitter glue), and three-dimensional objects, but takes a long time to dry. This can be frustrating as glued-on objects may keep moving around or falling off as the student continues to work on the puppet. Often objects glued on with white glue will come off later, while the puppet is being used in rehearsal or performance.

The best glue to use for three-dimensional objects is hot-melt glue, which will quickly and strongly attach most items onto a puppet without the mess and drying time necessary for white glues. The only problem is that hot melt glue causes burns if it is touched before it cools. If your students are young or have fine-motor problems, the assistant or the teacher should always be in charge of handling the glue gun.

Avoid sewing whenever possible. Sewing by hand or by machine takes time and involves fine-motor skills and patience that most puppetry students do not have. If something must be sewn, use a hand-held, battery-operated sewing machine.

Paper Bag Puppets. Paper bag puppets are simple and inexpensive to make. Collect small brown or white paper bags. Colored additions will show up better on white bags because there is more contrast. The bottom of the folded bag is used as the face. The section under the bottom fold is the inside of the mouth.

Create the puppet's face, clothes, and hair with felt-tipped marker, crayons, or paint. Lightweight items, such as small buttons, sequins, yarn, fabric, feathers, or colored paper, can be added as well. Avoid heavy objects, as the paper of the bag cannot sustain their weight.

To manipulate a paper-bag puppet, place one hand inside the bag with the fingers in the bottom section. Move the fingers up and down slightly to make the mouth move.

Some students have difficulty with paper bag puppets. They cannot "see" the way the mouth works and have difficulty coordinating the small muscles of their fingers and hands. Instead of slipping their fingers into the folded bag, they open it up and hang it on their hands or they ball the whole face up in their fists.

Demonstrate an already finished puppet to your students before they begin making their own. Do not assume they will understand how the puppet works just by watching you work with it. Talk with them about *how* the mouth moves and let them try it on the demonstration model and on a plain paper bag before they start making their own. If they cannot understand the concept of the mouth, have them make a different kind of puppet.

Paper-bag puppets are easy to store but, unfortunately, they are easily wrinkled or destroyed. If your students are hard on puppets, choose a sturdier kind of puppet to make.

Cardboard Tube Puppets. Another very simple and inexpensive hand puppet can be made from cardboard tubes. Collect the rolls left over from paper towels, wrapping paper, mailing tubes, and toilet paper to give students a variety of heights and widths. Heights of tubes can also be adjusted by shortening them with a matt knife. Cover the tubes with white butcher paper (rubber cement works well for this) so they have a surface that can be easily colored with crayon, marker, or paint. The tube becomes the base of the person, which is drawn or painted all the way around to become the puppet character. Fabric, sequins, buttons, feathers, yarn, beads, colored paper, and other media can be glued onto the puppet as well to make hair, hats, clothing, and other character details. White glue or rubber cement works fine for attaching lightweight media, while hot-melt glue is best for heavier, three-dimensional objects.

The interesting design challenge of tube puppets is created by the circular nature of the tube. Students are not working with a separate flat front and back of a piece of paper. They must think three dimensionally and figure out how to continue the character's body and costume all the way around the tube.

Tube puppets can be manipulated by placing them over two or three fingers. Students sometimes find this hand position awkward and the tube may fall off during an action sequence. A more secure method is to use hot-melt glue to place a Popsicle stick, tongue depressor, or dowel rod inside the tube. The puppeteer holds onto the stick.

Paper-Plate Puppets. Paper plates are also simple and inexpensive materials for puppets. The paper plate becomes the puppet's face, which can be decorated with crayons, marker, paint, or lightweight items, such as buttons, yarn, and sequins. A Popsicle stick or tongue depressor is glued to the back of the plate at the "neck" for the puppeteer to hold. Fabric can be glued to the front of the plate from the "neck" down to serve as the puppet's clothing or fur and to hide the puppeteer's hand.

Another variation creates a moveable mouth and head. This works particularly well for animal characters. Fold one paper plate in half so the back of the plate is folded against itself. Cut a second plate in half. Staple or glue the front of each half of the cut plate, rim to rim, against the front of each half of the folded plate. The cut edges of the second plate will end up by the fold of the first plate. The inside of the folded paper plate becomes the inside of the mouth. The outside becomes the snout and face. The puppeteer's fingers fit inside the top fold and the thumb slips inside the bottom fold to make the mouth move. Fabric can be added to the plate to create the "neck" of the puppet and hide the puppeteer's arm. Ears, eyes, nose, and mouth can be drawn or glued on.

Paper Plate and Pantyhose Puppets. Fold a paper plate in half as the inside of the mouth and build up the head around and above it with stuffed pantyhose. Pantyhose puppets make great people heads that have large working mouths and a Muppet look to them. First decide which hand you want to have inside the mouth. Carefully use hot-melt glue to fasten a glove for that hand onto the folded plate with the fingers on top and the thumb below. Hot-melt glue the waist of a pair of pantyhose or the top of a cut-off pantyhose leg all the way around the inside of the folded paper plate. Fill the pantyhose with stuffing — most of it on the top and only a little underneath, as the largest portion of a face is above, not below the mouth. Hand-sewn facial features and/or glued googly eyes, yarn, and objects make eyes, nose, ears, eyebrows, etc.

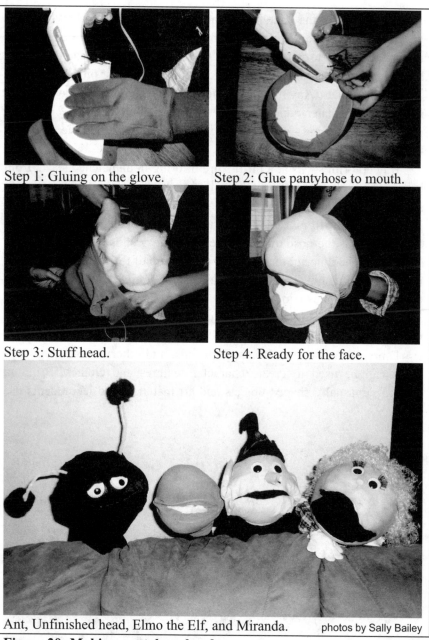

Step 1: Gluing on the glove.   Step 2: Glue pantyhose to mouth.

Step 3: Stuff head.   Step 4: Ready for the face.

Ant, Unfinished head, Elmo the Elf, and Miranda.   photos by Sally Bailey

Figure 20: Making pantyhose head puppets.

Cut the leg of the pantyhose at an appropriate place to let your hand go up into the mouth. Children's clothes or fabric can be glued or sewn under the "neck" to make the body. Cover up the hose inside the mouth by gluing over the inside of the whole mouth with red or pink felt.

Sock Puppets. Anything made out of paper is going to have a short life. Sooner or later paper puppets rip or wrinkle. If they get wet, the paper will disintegrate and the color will run. The most durable of simple hand puppets is the sock puppet.

Buy colorful socks at a thrift store or bring in unmatched socks from home. The socks can be partially stuffed with polyester pillow stuffing to shape heads or snouts. The sock can be held in a number of different positions; each will give the puppet a different look. The toe of the sock can be used as the nose of the puppet with the heel as the forehead. The sock can be held upright making the toe the top of the head with the heel in the front as a chin. The sock toe can also be straight up with the heel in the back to create a long, straight upright shape in front. Cardboard mouths can be cut out and inserted inside the bottom of the foot area to make a mouth that encompasses heel to toe.

Fabric, trim, buttons, beads, yarn, lids, and other three-dimensional items can be used to create character features and clothes. Bring in colorful, unusually shaped objects and art materials and let students use

photo by Sally Bailey

Figure 21: Various ways you can make a puppet out of a sock

their imaginations to flesh out the design of their puppet.

Wooden Spoon Puppets. A very quick and simple stick puppet can be made from a wooden cooking spoon. Either side of the bowl of the spoon can become the face. Paint or glue on facial features. Add yarn, netting, or fabric for hair. Either paint the stick or cover with fabric to create clothing.

Foam Rubber Puppets. Foam rubber puppets are excellent for puppet show performances because their large size and facial features will carry a long distance to an audience. Look for flat sheets of foam rubber between one-half and three-quarters inch thick. This can be purchased from stores that sell foam for mattresses or sofa cushions. Foam rubber carpet padding can also be used.

Cut a rectangle of foam rubber about 12 inches by 18 inches Hot-melt glue the 12-inch ends together and hold until the glue sets. This will create an 18-inch-high foam cylinder. The seam where the two ends come together will be the back of the puppet's head. Foam-rubber-head puppets can be taller or shorter, thinner or fatter, but a 12-inch by 18-inch piece of foam creates a good mid-sized puppet that is easy for any age puppeteer to handle.

Measure up about four inches from the bottom of the cylinder in the front (approximately one quarter of the way up). This is where the mouth will be cut. Make a horizontal cut about one-third of the way around the cylinder.

Using a ruler, measure the distance from one edge of the cut to the other through the middle of the cylinder. This is the diameter of the circle you will need for the inside of the mouth. Halve the diameter to find the radius of the circle. Using a compass opened to the width of the radius measurement, draw a circle on a piece of corrugated cardboard. Cut the circle out and paint one side red. When the paint has dried, fold the circle in half (with the red on the inside of the fold). Use hot-melt glue to fasten the edges of the circle onto the cut foam edge of the mouth. The fold of the cardboard circle will be on the inside, in the middle of the cylinder.

If you are working with young students or students who have fine-motor problems, you may want to precut and pre-glue the cylinders and mouths together. Both beginning steps require holding the foam in place while the hot-melt glue is setting. This requires patience, stamina, and enough manual dexterity to avoid being burned!

Create eyes, noses, ears, eyebrows, and other facial features with pieces of foam, colorful jar lids, seashells, feathers, buttons, pipe cleaners, poker chips, or other interesting objects. Foam-rubber lips can be added to cover up the corrugated cardboard at the mouth. Add hair, hats, and jewelry. Children's clothing or fabric glued around the bottom of the cylinder will hide the puppeteer's arm.

The puppeteer inserts his hand up through the bottom of the puppet and hold onto the cardboard mouth. To help establish a firmer grip and prevent damage to the cardboard from sweating fingers, use hot-melt glue to fasten a mitten or glove onto the mouth. Fingers of the mitten or glove go on the top of the mouth and the thumb goes on the bottom so the mouth opens and closes easily. Before gluing in the glove or mitten, find out if the puppeteer is right- or left-handed!

Flat-Cardboard Rod Puppets. Draw the character on a heavy piece of poster board or corrugated cardboard. Paint it or color it with felt-tipped markers. Cut out the shape and then fasten a dowel or other rod onto the back of the shape with hot-melt glue. Paint the dowel or rod black so it "disappears."

In the Asian theatre tradition, puppeteers dress in black and perform in front of a black curtain, so only the puppet shape is visible in performance. Black gloves will make their hands "disappear." It is not necessary to make the face of the puppeteer disappear, although you can have them wear black hoods with black mesh on the front. However, covering faces is not a good idea if your puppeteers have balance or vision difficulties.

Rod Head Puppets. Puppet heads can be sculpted out of papier-mâché or carved from thick chunks of foam rubber or Styrofoam. Heads can be soft-sculpted from stuffed sections of nylon stocking. Heads molded from Sculpee clay, baked in the oven, and then painted can be very lightweight as well.

Glue a sturdy plastic rod or wooden dowel firmly into the head. Make it thick enough so that it will hold up to a lot of waving around, but not so thick as to be hard for the puppeteer to hold onto. Paint the head. Because many kinds of foam disintegrate if paint or glue is applied directly to the foam, foam rubber and Styrofoam may need to be covered with fabric first. Paint or glue on facial features. Create hair with yarn, fabric strips, feathers, or pieces of fake fur.

One way to create clothing for puppets is to cut two identical bodies from heavy cloth. Lay them on top of each other. Using a single-hole paper punch, make holes along the edges and thread heavy yarn or cord through the holes to hold the two sides together. Turn the outfit inside out. Using hot-melt glue, fasten the neck of the clothing around the base of the puppet's neck.

If you want a free-flowing, shapeless garment, cut a large circle of fabric and make a small hole in the middle. The rod can be inserted through the hole and the fabric hot-glued to the bottom of the head. A small ruffle or paper-towel roll can be glued around the rod under the fabric near the head to create more fullness in the way the fabric hangs down from the head.

Shadow Puppets. A shadow puppet relies solely on its shape to give definition and detail to the character. Have students work out their ideas on paper first. This way they can cut their design out with scissors and test the shadow that it makes. When they have found the shape that creates a shadow they like, use the paper design as a pattern and trace around it on heavy matt board or foam core. If students cannot safely handle a matt knife, assistants will need to cut the puppets out for them.

Moveable arms and legs, mouths that open and close, and body halves that swivel can be created by punching a hole in overlapping joints and joining the sections with a paper fastener or small nut and bolt. Fabric, feathers, and other shapes that stick out over the silhouette and cast a shadow can also be added. For the character of The Fisherman in a shadow puppet version of "The Fisherman and his Wife," one student attached a piece of plastic netting to the Fisherman's hand. On screen it looked like his fishing net. It was large enough for the Magic Fish to "swim into it" in the first scene of the show. Glue the shadow puppets to long dowels or rods and the puppets are ready to go!

Making shadow puppets require a lot of manual dexterity, especially cutting ability, and patience during the construction phase. Students may have to go through several drafts of the initial design to get a shape that projects the shadow they have envisioned. Only attempt this kind of puppet if your students can do the work or if you have a lot of help from assistants.

Scenery

Scenery is often unnecessary for a puppet play. Changing backgrounds and props between each scene can be distracting and difficult during a performance. It is better to leave scenery up to the imagination of the audience than to slow down the pace of a show with a lot of scene changes. Such boring transitions are the times when you will lose your audience.

However, if you choose to include scenery, backdrops can be painted on large sheets of butcher paper, poster board, bed sheets, or unbleached muslin. Backdrops can also be made from large sheets of felt with felt shapes glued on to create the scene. Three-dimensional objects on stage, such as castles or houses, can be constructed from cardboard boxes and tubes, and decorated with paint, construction paper, and interesting shapes. You could also use cardboard or poster-board cutouts reinforced with a triangular brace from behind. A word of warning, however: cutouts tend to fall over during performances as puppets move around behind them. Boxes are studier and more stable.

Performance Issues for a Puppet Play

Puppet plays present a number of performance challenges. Puppeteers have to juggle a lot of different responsibilities simultaneously. Like regular actors, they need to remember their lines and movements. They need to say their lines loudly and clearly enough to project from behind the stage out to the audience. They also need to manipulate their puppets from what is usually a cramped, unnatural position underneath the visible plane of the stage. Sometimes more action is happening behind the scenes of a puppet play with actors jockeying for position than is happening in full view of the audience.

When you add the barrier of a wooden or metal stage between the mouths of the puppeteers and the ears of the audience, it is a wonder the dialogue of a puppet play can be heard at all! Professional puppeteers handle this by wearing body mikes that pick up and amplify their voices as they speak. Student puppeteers rarely have access to this kind of sophisticated equipment.

Recording the dialogue of the puppet play ahead of time is the best way both to cut down on the technical responsibilities of each puppeteer and to insure that the audience can hear the play. Puppeteers will not have to remember what to say or what comes next. They listen to their own voices on the recording and synchronize their puppet's actions to what they hear. This — and not bumping into the other puppeteers — is often more than enough to contend with during a performance.

These suggestions will not help if you are performing a puppet play with deaf students because they will not be able to hear the recording. A possible solution would be to create a carefully choreographed, very visual and physical puppet play and have hearing actors sit on the side in front of the stage to voice the dialogue for the audience. This would base the spoken dialogue on the puppet movement rather than vice versa. Another option might be to create a puppet ballet that is choreographed to music and tells the story with no dialogue. If the deaf puppeteers can see someone who visually cues them to start and keeps the beat of the music for them, they will be able to stay together.

Creating the Script for a Puppet Play

The script for a puppet play can come from many sources. Puppet plays do exist in play collections and can be used for performance in the same way a regular play script is used. If you are dramatizing a poem or short story where it is important to keep the rhythm and rhyme of the original author, such as Dr. Seuss, Shel Silverstein, or A.A. Milne, you might choose to narrate directly from a book The sense of fun and the build-up and release of tension in these poems rely a great deal on word choice, rhymes, and unique rhythm patterns.

Creating original scripts provides students with the opportunity to learn the process of playwriting. The script can be tailored around the strengths and abilities of the puppeteers. The dialogue will be expressed in their own words and manner of speaking instead of that of a professional playwright and will, therefore, sound natural and free. Instead of puppet characters conforming to someone else's vision of the

photo by Sally Bailey

Figure 22: The Gabaa sisters (pantyhose puppets) meet their fans after a show.

story, students can create their own characterizations through dialogue and action. As they add their own creative touches, their version of the story will come to life.

Never underestimate what a group of students can learn from the process of creating an original play. Over the course of one year I saw tremendous growth in a group of students who took three trimesters of puppetry at the Center School, an independent school for children who have learning disabilities. All were between the ages of seven and ten and were quite artistically talented but had no belief in their creative abilities.

The puppetry class was held once a week. During the first trimester, students took little initiative in suggesting ideas for a play. They had faced so much failure in their lives that they were afraid to take a chance on anything. Finally, I read them Shel Silverstein's "The Missing Piece," and they agreed to do it. I wanted puppets that would provide quick, positive feedback, so we made simple flat rod cardboard puppets. The students could not read and would not improvise dialogue, so some friends and I recorded the play. Only a few students were excited about the idea of performing, but once they got in front of an audience, their attitudes completely changed. Suddenly the story and the style of the performance came alive for them. One boy, who a week before had steadfastly refused to participate in rehearsal, turned into the most expressive, excited, focused performer on stage. At curtain call he was lit up like a neon sign! He kept bowing and smiling. Needless to say, the show was very well received and most of the class elected to take puppetry again.

During the second trimester, we tackled two plays: the girls wanted to do "Cinderella" while the boys chose "The Valiant Little Tailor." This time their puppets, made from different-sized paper tubes, became more elaborate. They threw themselves into making scenery and props: castles and ballrooms, pumpkins and carriages, fly swatters and jam sandwiches. A number of students volunteered to work on art projects at home. We worked through many serious differences of opinion as we improvised and recorded the dialogue for "Cinderella." Everyone had strong and divergent ideas about how Cinderella should be portrayed. The performances at the end of the trimester were smashing successes and almost everyone signed on for puppetry again.

By our last trimester, things were really cooking. I felt they were ready for a more challenging artistic project, so we built foam-rubber cylinder puppets. The girls, by now a fully functioning team, decided to make up an original fairy tale entitled "The Magic Kangaroo." I was a little hesitant to give my approval for this after the rather tense recording sessions we had had with "Cinderella," but I was gratified by the way they handled themselves as they developed their play. They listened to each other and respected each other's ideas. When two people had good ideas, they found ways to incorporate both into the story. The boys opted to modernize "Goldilocks and the Three Bears" into "Spike and the Three Bears," the story of a young punk who breaks into houses in the forest. I could not have been prouder of the work these students did and the distance they traveled over the course of nine short months.

The first step in creating an original puppet play is to divide the story you have chosen into scenes. Then make a list of the events that happen within each scene. This scene breakdown is the scenario for the play. It will serve as a guidepost to keep the class on track as the play is fleshed out with dialogue, sound effects, and action.

It is often helpful to have students act out the story on their feet at least once before trying to write it down or record it improvisationally. This makes the characters and the action more concrete. They can better visualize what the characters are doing and how they are feeling after they have actually done it themselves.

If your group does not read well, the best way to devise the script is to improvise the play as you record it. Review the scenario for each scene and briefly practice what each character needs to say and do. Improvise the scene on its feet once and then sit down to improvise it in front of the recorder. If the improvisation goes well, you can move on to the next scene. If someone makes a mistake, no need to get frustrated — just stop and try again. Stay loose and have fun. If you think your students would have difficulty going back and forth, scene by scene, between improvising on their feet and sitting in front of the recorder, improvise the whole story from beginning to end during one session so they have the kinesthetic experience of the story one full time.

If your group can read and write, students can work together to imagine what each character will say and do in the play and then put their ideas into writing. Follow the scenario, scene by scene, as students share their ideas about how to tell the story dramatically. Often there will be many good suggestions for one given moment in the play. Choices must be made and some ideas will need to be adapted or changed. Building a script in this way develops problem-solving skills and the ability to compromise. A student, an assistant, or the teacher can serve as scribe to write down the dialogue as it is made up. The process of creating and writing down the play may take several sessions. When it is completed, the script can be typed up and copied so each puppeteer has his own copy.

Groups that can read, but do not have the patience to sit down and write out their own script word for word, can improvise their dialogue directly onto the tape like non-readers. Then the leader can transcribe the tape to create a typed script, which they can refine and rewrite.

If you are working from a written script, rehearse it a number of times before you record. Work on timing, pacing, cuing, character voices, vocal variety, sound effects, and use of pauses. When the cast is ready, record the script, taking short breaks between each scene to keep the puppeteers' voices fresh and their energy level high. Recording a script can be great fun, if everyone stays flexible. Some students tend to put themselves under great pressure to make the recording perfect the first time. Remind them that if they make a mistake, the scene can be recorded over again.

As the director, you will have more than enough to concentrate on, working the recorder and keeping the cast motivated and working cooperatively together. Do not waste time and energy trying to make this recorded version perfect. You can record several different versions of each scene. Later, you can edit your show from the recordings you made in class. When someone makes a mistake and you need to re-record a scene, you do not need to go back and cover up what you recorded before. Chances are you could go back too far and record over something you wanted to keep. Just keep moving forward; you can edit out the parts you do not want later. After rehearsal, when you are in a quiet place and there is no time pressure, you will be able to make editing decisions methodically and calmly. You can also add special effects then, such as music or sound from a sound-effects tape or CD, if you did not have them available live.

Editing is easier if students leave a moment of silence before and after each "take." That leaves the editor silent space to cue up without picking up sound from the previous "take." Complete quiet in the room where you are recording is also important. Recording devices will pick up every noise in the room. If there are fans and any machines that make "white noise," try to turn them off. Remind students before each take to only talk when it is time for their character to speak.

You might want to test various rooms or areas in your room to find a place that has good acoustics for recording. Some spaces are too echo-y. Voices recorded in those spots will have a tinny, distant quality. Other spaces seem to focus sound and create a very realistic, strong quality.

Listen to your original recording all the way through to make notes of which takes are the ones you want to use: where you need to start and where you need to stop. If certain sections of a scene need to be cut out, time how long the cut should be and what sounds will begin and end the cut. Only then do you edit. When you have your show recording, you are ready to begin staging the puppet show.

Puppet Stages

Sometimes a makeshift stage can be fashioned from furniture in the room. Two long tables placed end to end can be turned into an acceptable puppet stage. Drape a solid-colored cloth over both tables or tape butcher paper to the front to hide the puppeteers from the audience. Students can sit or lie on the floor behind the tables and hold their puppets up over the edge. Scenery can be taped onto the wall behind the table. If any three-dimensional props are used in the show, the tabletop serves as a place to set them.

A short bookcase (between four and five feet high) that has been pulled out from the wall can become a useful puppet stage. Students stand behind the bookcase and have more room to maneuver than if they were sitting on the floor. If the back of the bookcase is facing the audience, the puppeteers can use the bookshelves facing them to store props or puppets when they are offstage. If the bookshelves face the audience, cover the bookcase with a large, solid-colored cloth or tape butcher paper over it to hide the books. The top of the bookcase can be a handy place to set props during the show.

Puppet stages can be designed and built from wood, PVC pipe, or metal frames. If you are making the effort to build a stage, be sure there is plenty of room for puppeteers to stand or sit comfortably and move around backstage. Consider the type of puppets your students will be using: Where is the puppeteer's hand in relation to the puppet? Where is the puppeteer's body in relation to the stage? Hand puppets require puppeteers to be closer to the edge of the stage than rod puppets. Is there a way to position the puppeteer so his hand does not have to stretch way up in the air every time his puppet comes on stage? Will your puppet stage need to be moved around to a number of different places or can it

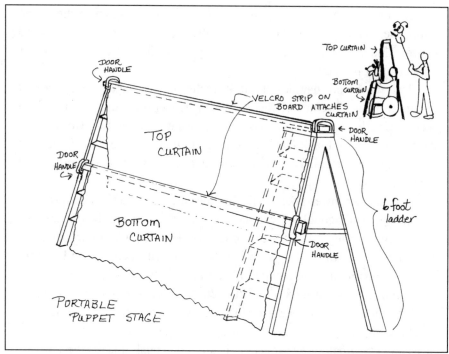

drawing by Sally Bailey

Figure 23: Building a portable puppet stage.

be kept permanently in one spot? If you have students sitting in wheelchairs, can they sit comfortably, make their puppets visible, and still not be seen by the audience?

In trying to devise a puppet stage that addressed some of these issues, specifically portability, adaptability to wheelchairs, and comfortable hand positions for both hand- and rod-puppeteers, I came up with an easy-to-assemble design from items that can be purchased at any hardware store. I started with a base made from two six-foot wooden stepladders. Because they form a triangle when open, stepladders are more balanced and secure than using a single upright pole.

Large screen-door handles turned sideways on the top step of each ladder hold a wooden board in place between them. When purchasing materials, check the handle against the width of the board you are buying to make sure it fits through. A piece of black fabric is fastened to the wood board to mask the top half of the puppeteers sitting behind the stage. The soft half of a long strip of Velcro can be sewn to the fabric while the rough half can be hot-melt glued and stapled onto the wood board. This top board also creates an upper stage that can be used for puppets on long rods.

Two more door handles about 30 inches up from the ground (not 30 inches from the bottom of the ladder, which is on a diagonal), hold a second wooden board in place across the front between the two ladders. A second piece of black fabric is fastened to this board to hide the legs of the sitting puppeteers. This board creates a lower stage that can be used for hand puppets.

Because the lower board is farther forward than the top board (due to the sideways diagonal of the ladder's legs), a space is created for wheelchairs or legs of sitting puppeteers. If there are no wheelchairs backstage, the entire sitting area can be filled with benches end to end, creating maximum sitting space. If you have only a few puppeteers and they need to move around a lot, they could sit on stools with casters on them so they can roll back and forth. In a sitting position, puppeteers' faces are directly behind the top curtain. They hold their puppets in front of it at approximately eye level. This simultaneously places the puppets above the lower curtain of the puppet stage. This arm position is less stressful than holding the puppets up over their heads.

If you build your own stage, paint the entire structure black, so it does not visually distract from the puppets. Use black curtains so they blend into the stage. If your puppets end up being black, you will want to use a different curtain color so the puppets will be easily visible to the audience.

Puppeteers should wear black, if possible. Black is the color of invisibility on stage. Dressed in black, they will blend into the background. If an arm is stuck out a little too far, it will be less distracting if clothed in the same color as the curtain.

Staging and Rehearsing the Puppet Show

If possible, position puppeteers backstage in places they can remain for the majority of the play. Characters who have a number of conversations with each other will probably need to be placed next to each other. Help each puppeteer find a relatively comfortable position to be in when his puppet is on stage and off.

Practice making entrances and exits neatly and efficiently without bumping other puppets or puppeteers. If one or two characters have to move from one side of the stage to the other, try to arrange everyone else to make this possible. For instance, if the tortoise and the hare are racing with each other on the lower stage, the cheering forest folk could be lined up along the upper stage to watch. Puppeteers who have to climb over each other backstage are in an awkward and potentially dangerous situation.

Listen to the recording and have each puppeteer practice synchronizing the lip, arm, or body movements of his puppet with the words his character says and the actions his character takes. Then put it all together with the puppeteers in place behind the stage.

Remind your puppeteers to respect each other's personal space even though they are crowded closely together. They need to put aside personal conflicts for the moment and cooperate with each other for the good of the show. If an accident happens and someone gets elbowed by mistake, prepare puppeteers to apologize, forgive, and forget quickly. Rehearsals and performances are not the time for grudges and hard feelings.

Validate how hard your students are working and, if they are in an uncomfortable position, acknowledge how uncomfortable they feel. Unfortunately, uncomfortable positions are the lot of all puppeteers. Provide lots of encouragement and tell them what a good job they are doing. Praise them when they work hard at getting along.

Sample Puppetry Lesson Plan

Putting together a performance requires many different steps. Here is a sample lesson plan for staging "Bambi."

Week One

Talk about puppets: What kind of puppets are there? What kind have you made before? What do you like about puppets?

Introduction Go-Around: Pass Fred the Frog around to each student, who invents a funny voice for him and lets Fred introduce the student holding him to the other students.

Decide on a story for a puppet show. (In this case, "Bambi" was chosen.)

Tell part of the story of "Bambi."

Decide which character you would like to play.

Draw a picture of your character.

Week Two

Read the story of "Bambi" (a shortened Walt Disney version).

Act out favorite parts of the story.

Week Three

Start making sock puppets.

Week Four

Improvise and record dialogue for three-quarters of the story.

Week Five

Paint the puppet stage.

Listen to the edited version of the work done last week.

Week Six

Make scenery.

Week Seven

Finish improvising and recording dialogue.

Continue working on puppets.

Week Eight

Finish working on puppets and scenery.

Week Nine

Rehearse puppet show.

Week Ten

Rehearse puppet show.

Perform puppet show for parents and friends.

Performing the Show

Keep your puppeteers calm before the show begins. The best way to do this is for the adults in charge to remain calm. Children will model whatever behavior they believe is appropriate to the situation. They will match their emotional state to yours.

Check all puppets to make sure no last-minute repairs are needed. Just in case of emergency, it is a good idea to have a hot-melt glue gun ready backstage. Also handy backstage are extra safety pins and masking tape.

Do a sound check to make sure puppeteers can hear the tape clearly backstage and audience members can hear it clearly out front.

Double-check the position of all puppeteers, puppets, and props before the show begins.

It may be helpful for the teacher or an assistant to remain backstage during the performance to troubleshoot and solve unforeseen physical problems. Eyeballs and hats fall off puppets at the most inopportune moments. Puppets get stuck to clothing and to other puppets. Props fall off the stage just when they are needed in the scene. Moving puppeteers trip and get tangled in each other's arms and legs.

After the show, have the puppets take a bow from the stage. Then have the puppeteers come out from behind the curtain with their puppets in hand to take a bow. They have earned their recognition and they should have the chance to be acknowledged by their audience for their hard work.

Students feel a great sense of accomplishment and pride after performing a puppet show. Part of it comes from knowing they have taken a project from start to finish. Part comes from the acknowledgement and appreciation they receive from the audience, which tells them they have contributed something valuable to their community.

I worked with a special-education class at Meadow Hall Elementary School in Rockville, Maryland, on a puppetry project aimed at motivating reading skills and teaching students how to approach and accomplish a project, step by step. Their teacher wanted to involve her students in a project that engaged every learning channel and that exploited her students' visual and kinesthetic strengths. They made beautiful sock puppets and wrote and recorded their own puppet plays. She shared about her students' reaction to performing their original puppet plays for parents, friends, and schoolmates:

> We were a hit! The classroom was packed to overflowing with parents and relatives of all ages. We did "The Lion and the Mouse" and "Spike and the Three Rad Bears" for the Education Fair Tuesday night. They [the students] set up everything…The next day we performed in the A.M. and P.M. for two classes at a time. We also did the show every other day until the entire school had viewed it (including Head Start and Special Education teachers).

> The kids are so proud of their accomplishments and are working the puppets with more ease and excitement. Classes are impressed, asking many questions as to how they got their ideas and how things were made. We have videotaped each play twice and will make copies for those who want them. The principal enjoyed the show and said it was the "best" he had seen, and one teacher suggested we send it to a children's TV station.

I saw the videotape of the performances. The students *do* grow in confidence and ability with each succeeding performance. Best of all, after the first performance, a large computer-generated thank-you note appeared above the puppet stage. It was sent from one of the regular education classrooms who had seen the plays. It read, "WHAT AN INCREDIBLE PLAY! THANK YOU! WE LOVED IT!" How could you get any better validation than that?

Recommended Reading

Astell-Burt, C. (2001). *I Am the Story: The Art of Puppetry in Education and Therapy*. London: Souvenir Press.

9. Developing Original Scripts for Performance

Why Create Original Plays?

It is essential for novice performers to experience success. A successful experience will encourage them to continue developing their artistic skills, while an embarrassing failure will discourage them from ever getting up on a stage again. A teacher or director can enhance success by carefully choosing dramatic material that is appropriate to the performers' skill levels, limiting material to an appropriate length for the skills and attention spans of the performers, and providing enough rehearsal time for the performers to feel prepared when they step in front of the audience.

Performers who have special needs may need additional support or adaptations in dramatic material in order to achieve success. Most scripts focus on verbal abilities and this may create obstacles for actors who have certain kinds of disabilities. They may be unable to memorize large sections of dialogue from a conventional play. They may not be able to communicate well through words, but may be able to express themselves exceptionally well through movement. They may have short attention spans or difficulty with sequencing or any manner of other physical or cognitive processing problems, all of which make a previously scripted traditional play difficult to prepare and perform successfully.

One way to ensure performance success is to develop original material that is geared to the specific abilities and strengths of your performers. This approach is student-centered, the theatre version of "teaching to a student's strength" or, in social work terms, "starting

photo by Sally Bailey

Figure 24: The actors in the outer space fantasy designed and painted their own costumes.

where the client is." Let your performers do what they do best and help them learn to do it even better.

An approach of this kind will not lead to stagnation and repetition of more of the same. The more skilled and confident actors become, the more challenges they want to take on the next time. The very first play my Pegasus performing company created, *Dreams, Nightmares, and Fantasies*, was extremely simple. Much of the dialogue was recorded so that they would not have to memorize lines. Remembering the blocking, pantomiming to the music and voice-over tapes, and remembering to get the correct props for the next scene was more than enough for the actors to contend with that first year. They performed their play seven times, always to wildly enthusiastic applause, and in the course of performing, found their artistic voices and uncovered a desire to use drama to communicate.

The next year they clamored for a much more complicated script and took on the challenge of memorizing lines. Audience members who saw both seasons' shows were astounded at the major leap the troupe made from artistic and technical standpoints. Yes, I had to push them to get them there, but they chose our artistic goals that second season so they were intrinsically motivated to achieve them.

Work developed through improvisation is a positive choice to make for beginners or performers with disabilities for other reasons as well. It is much easier to understand and to learn something you create yourself. The ideas are yours, the thought processes are yours, the primary mode of expression, be it words, movement, or music, is yours. The dialogue is expressed in your sentence structure and vocabulary.

Most important, improvisationally developed plays put the actors in charge of generating the ideas. They are given an outlet to explore and express the issues that are in their hearts and minds. This is particularly important for adolescents. Teenagers do not think adults ever listen to them — and, sometimes, they are right about this. Much of teenage rebellion originates when teens' ideas are not heard, acknowledged, respected, and validated by the adults in their lives. If adolescents start feeling that their ideas, contributions, and abilities are not wanted or appreciated, their behavior towards the adult world changes from cooperative to passive withdrawal or aggressive hostility.

Individuals of all ages who have disabilities face a similar situation. The community ignores them, discriminates against them, or excludes them. Their voices are not heard or, if heard, are discounted. Playwrights who do not have disabilities often create disabled characters who have little basis in reality and perpetuate negative or untruthful stereotypes. Usually disabled characters are spotless heroes or evil villains — on one end of the spectrum or the other. Unrealistic portrayals of people with disabilities are also perpetrated by casting agents and directors. One blatant example of this is movies in which the deaf character, often played by a hearing actor, speech-reads perfectly, even when the person speaking is not looking directly at her, and then talks to the hearing characters in a perfectly modulated voice using impeccable English sentence construction. No one speech-reads perfectly because so many spoken consonants look alike!

Creating your own play gives voice to the feelings and ideas inside your actors in a constructive way. It provides a forum for evaluating and solving problems. It offers an avenue for appropriately sharing hopes, dreams, and concerns with others, for building bridges of communication instead of blowing them up. Nothing enhances self-esteem more than sharing an important part of yourself with others and having them not only accept you, but applaud you for it.

Teachers and directors often do not consider the option of creating original work because they are operating under false assumptions:

1. Creating an original play is "cheating."
2. An original play is not a "real" play.
3. Creating an original play is too hard.

Creating an original play is not cheating. There is no more reason that a group of actors should perform *The Crucible, Guys and Dolls,* or any other well-known play or musical than a square peg should be forced into a round hole. If your actors' abilities do not fit the needs of a previously written script, it is not cheating to create a play that does fit them.

In fact, molding a play to fit a specific group of actors, as opposed to molding a group of actors to fit a particular play, is a time-honored theatre tradition! Many playwrights originally wrote their plays to display the talents of a specific group of actors. All of William Shakespeare's plays were written to be performed by Richard Burbage, Will Kempe, Augustine Philips, and other members of the Lord Chamberlain's Men, the acting company to which he belonged. He created roles, dialogue, and action that exploited the unique talents and personalities of the actors in the company, showing them off to their best advantage.

Commedia dell'arte troupes, which traveled the European continent during the Renaissance, created plays that showcased the improvisational comedic talents of their members. Each commedia actor specialized in playing one specific type of stock comic character. He or she (commedia troupes were one of the first theatrical groups to hire women to play female characters on stage) would perfect the *lazzi* or comic business for which that character was well known. Each troupe developed a number of scenarios using the stock characters that their actors specialized in. At each performance, the company would choose a scenario and improvise a play on the spot for the audience. If a troupe had a leading actor who specialized in playing Harlequin, the tricky servant, their scenarios would revolve around Harlequin. If they had a leading actor whose specialty was Pantalone, the old, foolish miser, their plays would focus on him.

French actor/playwright Molière (Jean Baptist Poquelin), who provided entertainment for the court of Louis XIV, wrote comic roles for himself and the actors in his troupe. *The School for Wives*, a play about an older man who is in love with a young girl, was written as an acting vehicle for an aging Molière and his pretty, young wife. Even today many contemporary playwrights, such as David Mamet and Mark Medoff, create their plays with specific actors in mind for certain parts.

On to the second false assumption: An original play is not a "real" play. This is absolutely untrue. I feel frustrated when a well-meaning adult walks up to me after the performance of an original script developed by my actors and says in a condescending tone, "That was cute, but why don't you let your students do a *real* play like *Oliver!* or *The Pajama Game?*"

In essence, the message they are giving me is threefold:

1. Young people are incapable of having their own ideas and expressing them in dramatic form.
2. Only a "professional playwright" can write a "real" play.
3. Only a play that has been produced on Broadway can be considered "real."

I cannot disagree with this idea of plays and playwrights too strenuously! Every play that has ever existed started out as an original play. In order for that original play to be a "real" play, it does not need to be published, it does not need to be written by a "professional playwright," and it does not need to be produced first in New York City. It just needs to be performed for an audience somewhere!

False assumption number three: Creating an original play is too hard. It is true that creating an original play can take more time than choosing appropriate material that has been written by someone else. It is true that more time must be spent developing the piece and shaping it before it can begin to be staged and rehearsed. It is also true that creating an original play can be difficult. The actors must be involved in the process. This necessitates cooperation and negotiation on everyone's parts. It also requires flexibility, fairness, and a good sense of dramatic structure. But, however time-consuming and difficult it may be, creating an original play is not too hard. And in some cases, it is easier to direct an original play that has been fit to the performers who will be doing it.

There are many ways to use improvisation to create original plays. Each theatre artist involved in improvisational work develops her own style and approach to solving the dramatic question "What if?" This chapter presents the process that has worked well for me. I have included several sources of other methods for developing original plays at the end of this chapter, which may offer you other useful techniques and ideas.

The situations in which I have created original plays with performing troupes of individuals with and without disabilities have all been under the auspices of non-profit arts and recreation organizations in which the troupe met weekly for one-and-a-half- to two-hour rehearsal periods over six to seven months. From 1988 to 1995 I directed from one to three barrier-free performing companies a year at the Bethesda Academy of Performing Arts. Since 1999 I have directed the Barrier-Free Theatre troupe for the City of Manhattan Parks and Recreation Department in Manhattan, Kansas. I have not had the opportunity to work with a group over a compressed period of time (five days a week for four to eight weeks). So, as you read the description of the development process that follows, keep in mind that timing would be adjusted for a group working within a compressed time frame. The pluses of working over a long period of time are more time for me and for the actors to develop ideas for the play and learn lines between rehearsals. The minuses are the lack of momentum once the play has been written and is being rehearsed. Performance seems a long way off in January; though it is in calendar time, it is not when you consider there will only be 11 to 12 rehearsals, the equivalent of two weeks!

Initiating the Project with the Company

Company Contracts

It is very important to make sure that individuals who get involved in a theatre company understand the commitment that goes with it. Before an actor joins the troupe, I ask her to sign a contract that clearly states responsibilities to the group and to herself during the course of our work, outlining upfront what my expectations are in terms of actor behavior and commitment. This way no one can say, "But I didn't *know* I would need to go to so many rehearsals!" Actors must understand that they have made a promise to see the project through from beginning to end. There can be no, "I have too much homework today, so I'll stay home from rehearsal," or "I'm bored with the show, so I'm going to quit." Disaster would strike if several of the actors decided to quit after a script had been created around them and the play was in rehearsal! Working as an ensemble — supporting each other and sticking together over the long haul — is one of the most important aspects of any theatre company.

Have I ever lost an actor partway through the process? Yes, unfortunately I have. Has it happened often? No. In the few instances this has happened I have made it very clear to these actors that although I like them very much, I cannot have them back in the troupe in the future. They had given me their word that they would stick with the process and since they have not kept it, I cannot trust that they will follow through another time. On a few occasions I have had to remove someone from a performing company because she could not abide by the rules of the group — mainly, respecting others and behaving in a professional and appropriate manner. In these cases, I gave the actor plenty of chances, discussing the situation with her and using an individual behavior contract to specifically identify the behaviors that would not be tolerated. If the actor was not willing or able to abide by the contract, she was asked to leave.

Barrier-Free Theatre Company Contract

Agreement is made for <u>(Actor's Name)</u>   to become an actor/company member of the City of Manhattan Parks and Recreation Department's Barrier-Free Theatre Company for the 2010-2011 theatre season.

    I have talked with Sally Bailey, the director, about the commitment I am making in becoming a member of the Barrier-Free Theatre Company and I understand my responsibilities. I understand the importance of each of the rules listed below and I agree to follow them.

1. I agree to attend every rehearsal and performance.

   Rehearsals are Wednesdays from 5:00-6:30 PM at the Manhattan Arts Center.

   The performances will be Friday, April 7, and Saturday, April 8, at 8:00 PM.

   PLEASE PUT THESE DATES ON YOUR CALENDARS NOW!!!

2. If I am sick or if there is an emergency, I will notify Sally, the director, before rehearsal as soon as possible by leaving a message on her voice mail at xxx-xxxx.

3. I agree to arrive on time for every rehearsal and performance.

4. I agree to behave in an appropriate and professional manner at every rehearsal and performance. This means I promise to respect and work with the other actors.

5. I agree to participate in all rehearsal activities.

6. I agree to learn my lines on time and do any work assigned.

7. I agree to take care of all equipment, supplies, scripts, costumes, props, sets, etc.

_____

Actor

_____

Parent/Group Home Counselor

_____

Sally Bailey, Director

Parents are very appreciative of the use of contracts because it helps them teach the concept of commitment to their children. It serves as a good backup tool for getting reluctant actors to rehearsals on days when it is raining or they are tired and would rather stay home. Inevitably the bad mood goes away once rehearsal starts and they begin interacting with others and having fun.

One first-time performer started suffering from stage fright a week before the first performance. He told his mother he wanted to quit the show because he was too nervous to go on. She was able to say, "Every actor must learn to deal with nerves. You signed a contract that promised you would be at every rehearsal and performance. I can't let you quit." She called me before rehearsal that day and let me know what was happening at home. I was able to address the issue of nerves that afternoon with the whole cast in a discussion about how to get over stage fright and how the actors could jump in and help each other out if anyone forgot her lines. We practiced ways of "saving" each other in different parts of the play. He went on with the show with confidence and in later seasons was a big supporter of others who expressed concerns about stage fright.

To Audition or Not to Audition

I have had the option to audition actors for my performing companies, but I often choose instead to offer orientation sessions where potential new company members can come and find out about the troupe. I find that auditions create an unnatural, stressful situation for most actors. The auditioner feels tense, nervous, strained, and on the spot. She doesn't always behave naturally because she's worried about what kind of impression she is making. She assumes that the auditor is thinking the worst about her and often becomes inhibited and tongue-tied.

At an orientation session I can show a video of some of the work that has been done by the group in the past so they can see other people who are in the group and the type of work we do. I explain the contract I will be asking them to sign. I can let them ask me questions. We can play a few drama games together, so if they have not had a drama class that involved improvisation before, they can get a feel for what they will be doing to create the play and I can get a sense of where their imaginations and group-interaction skill levels are. If I think that they need some more experience before being in a group like this, I may suggest they take an acting class first.

Some people self-select out. They realize quickly after playing a few theatre games that this is not for them. Most people want to give it a try. I have taken beginners into performing companies. The most success has come when people really want to be there as opposed to being signed up for it by someone else (parent, teacher, therapist, or group-home counselor) who thinks it will be "good" for them. Another important component to success is having support from the home environment in terms of getting to rehearsals on time and learning lines!

Rehearsal Space

The creation part of the play development process can be done in an open classroom or on the stage. Being on stage helps remind the actors that they are working toward a performance goal and allows them to become comfortable in the space. However, all too often, stages are shared by many different groups and may not be available immediately. Since the early work is improvisatory in nature and no specific blocking is being done, an open classroom space can work just as well. However, once the play has been written, it is very important to have rehearsals on stage!

Development of the Original Play

The Overall Process

The first three or four sessions are spent building an acting ensemble, developing basic improvisational acting skills, and deciding what the play will be about. Once we have chosen our topic, we improvise characters and situations that relate to it. The improvisation process usually takes between five and seven sessions. Then I take the dramatic material that the actors have generated and structure a written script from it, taking into consideration as many of their ideas and suggestions as possible.

Once the script is complete, the actual rehearsal period takes an absolute minimum of ten sessions — more is better! We read through the written script, block it, and rehearse it until everything flows smoothly. The script serves as a basic guideline or structure for the actors. Lines need to be memorized, but they can be changed and improvised as needed. Things stay loose even after we open the show. Although the same dramatic events happen each time, no two performances have ever had identical dialogue.

Getting Started

For a group to work well together, they need to develop trust, a spirit of camaraderie and acceptance, and the ability to work together as a team. This can be accomplished through introduction games in which the actors share information about themselves and through basic drama games in which they learn about each other through relating physically, verbally, and socially with each other. Basic acting skills that need to be developed by all the members of an acting ensemble include the ability to make eye contact, listen, observe, use their imagination, project, and speak clearly, in addition to basic skills for improvising dialogue and creating characters. When I am continuing with a group I have worked with previously, I focus our beginning sessions on skills that the group had particular difficulty with the previous year. Sometimes I focus on team-building games and improvisations that underline the rules talked about in the contract that they have just signed.

Actor input into the subject matter of the play is crucial. The actors need to be at the center of the creative process so they can own the play. We spend from 10 to 30 minutes during each of the first few sessions brainstorming ideas for the play. Typically, I ask them to think about situations, characters, and ideas that would be exciting to work on and make a play about. I write down every suggestion that is made, no matter how outlandish, on big sheets of butcher paper. This reinforces that their ideas are accepted and valued. If only a few ideas are suggested the first session, I ask them to think about more ideas over the course of the next week and we add to our list the next rehearsal. My experience has been that there is more often a deluge of ideas rather than a dearth of them, especially after the first year a performing company has worked together. Each week between brainstorming session, I organize the ideas into different categories so we can get a sense of the themes that are interesting to the group.

One year my Pegasus performing company developed the following list of ideas:

Halloween

The Night of the Living Dead

Maniac Mansion (making fun of horror movies)

Little Shop of Horrors

Ghostbusters or something where ghosts are haunting a house

School — a student is in trouble

Head of the Class

At the beach

Karate — a spoof on Teenage Mutant Ninja Turtles

Cops/Detectives/Police Officers/Spies

Rescue Squad — a play about safety

A Turtle named Melvin

Family — a comedy about growing up

Where the Wild Things Are

The Hobbit

Something in the army or the military

A TV show

Stories around a campfire

A cabaret with songs and jokes

A play with animal characters

A play about a dentist

A Western

A circus

A kidnapping

Monty Python and the Holy Grail in the Twentieth Century

Running away from home

When I feel we have a list that has enough variety to offer us strong dramatic options, we take a preliminary vote to determine which ideas are the most popular. Everyone can vote for whichever ideas they like. This means everyone can vote more than once. The most popular ideas from the list above were a Western, a kidnapping, cops and robbers, and a family story. From this list, a second and third vote could be taken to narrow down the group's choices even further until one idea appears which appeals to a majority. Usually, however, I stop the voting once we have about five ideas and let the actors discuss them in depth as a group.

I ask for actors who are enthusiastic about the different ideas to stand up and champion their favorite. We go through each idea and people say why everyone should vote for that idea. What would be exciting about it on stage? What would be difficult to do? As we discuss pros and cons some people get excited about ideas they had not considered before and others decide they do not like the idea they previously had been set on. Sometimes we figure out ways to incorporate several interesting ideas into one. In the case of the play I shared examples about, three ideas — a Western, a kidnapping, and cops and robbers — clearly were the favorites. A quick vote confirmed this, with Western getting the most votes. I suggested that we combine all three ideas and create a Western in which there were cops and robbers and a kidnapping. This was greeted with a groundswell of cheers and *Guns Ablazing* was born.

A compromise that includes many different but compatible ideas can get a group past an impasse and keep a majority of actors happy and interested. My very first year directing Pegasus, none of the actors were willing to give up their ideas for what they wanted the play to be about. After many weeks of discussion and debate (and argument and hurt feelings), we finally settled on creating a play about dreams because all of the other ideas: animals, movies, movie stars, feelings, an acting class, space, food, and daydreaming about boys could be incorporated into different dreams. On the other hand, coming to an agreement on an idea can happen very quickly if all the actors are on the same wavelength. In Icarus, one of my adult performing companies, everyone unanimously agreed in our very first rehearsal that they all wanted to do a play about falling in love and sing their favorite love songs.

I point out the pros and cons of ideas that have not been addressed yet by the actors, but I do not make the final decision on what we are going to do. I have taken the position that whatever the group decides — even if I do not like it — is what we will create the play about. At the beginning of Pegasus's second season, the movie *Back to the Future*,

Part II came out and everyone was wild to do a play about time travel. I was very skeptical that they had the skills to take on what I knew would end up being a much more complex project than the dream play they had created the year before. I knew it would be hard to avoid a lot of line memorization and complex sequencing in a script that bounced from one time period to another. I had a very small budget and no technical support. I knew that travel back to several different periods of history would necessitate four or five different changes of costume and set. I had visions of chaos and confusion backstage: panicked actors ripping costumes on and off, long pauses on stage as costume changes delayed entrances, George Washington walking into the middle of King Arthur's Court by mistake. I explained all of this to them and begged them to vote for any other idea instead. They unanimously voted for time travel anyway.

I seriously considered stepping in and saying, "No, I've thought about it and you aren't ready to do this," but I just could not reconcile that action with my philosophy that you can do anything if you imagine it clearly enough and work on it hard enough. So I went to rehearsal the next week and said, "Okay, we're going to do a play about time travel, but it's going to take a lot of hard work. I'm going to have to push you very hard. Once we have the script, you are going to have to spend a lot of time working on it at home. You must come to rehearsal prepared. You must learn your lines by the deadlines I give you. Are you willing to do whatever it takes to make this idea work?"

They all shouted, "YES!"

Improvising *Just in Time* was a lot of fun, but rehearsing it was — as I had predicted — a struggle. There was one rehearsal in the middle of January when everyone was fooling around, no one had memorized their lines, and I had to throw a "director's temper tantrum." In the end, however, we met the challenge and the whole group moved up to a new level of theatrical ability. I truly believe that the reason they were able to succeed was because they had taken on the responsibility for the decision to do the play themselves — and because I did not let them forget it!

Developing the Idea

Once the idea has been chosen, it needs to be developed. The first step is to go back to the brainstorming pad and ask the actors to think of all the different scenes and characters that might be involved in a play based on that idea. For *Just in Time* I asked the actors to think of all the famous people in history they would like to go back to meet if they had the chance. For *Some Enchanted Evening* we started by making a list of all the qualities they would want in "The Perfect Someone." For *Guns Ablazing* our scene list looked like this:

Posse	Country School
Campfire	Gun Fight/Shootout/Showdown
Bank Robbery	Wagon Train
General Store	Hoedown
Kidnapping	Court Room
Stage Coach	Bonfire
Train Robbery	Horse Race
Barroom Brawl	

Characters who might be involved in a Western included:

Cowboys	Stage Coach Driver
Gunfighter harassing a town	Sheriff and Deputies
Indians	Pony Express Rider
Gamblers	Robbers/Cattle Rustlers/Gun
Bank Teller	Runners/Desperados
Judge	Saloon Owner/Dance Hall
School Teacher	Girls/Bartender

With our lists of potential characters and scenes complete we began improvising different situations, giving actors the chance to play different kinds of roles. Almost immediately a gang of desperados named the Wild Rascals were born. They made plans to rob the town bank in one scene, and then did so, shooting at everyone in sight. We replayed the scene with different actors in the roles and instead of shooting everyone, incorporated a kidnapping into the scene.

Following this we improvised a number of scenes in which the sheriff and his deputies investigated the scene of the crime and interviewed the witnesses for clues to the robbers' whereabouts. The actors who had been playing the robbers got tired of waiting around and suddenly showed up at the Sheriff's office with their hostage to discuss the terms of her release. The next week we continued with the basic situation and tried out a number of scenarios for rescuing the kidnap victim. The robbers were finally captured — very unwillingly — and put on trial.

One week we improvised a series of shootouts. All the actors were very excited to challenge someone else to a quick-draw contest. I am opposed to using violence to solve conflict in plays or in life, but I am not averse to spending time in rehearsal exploring *why* it is not a good option. I made sure that anyone who had expressed the slightest interest in a shootout got the chance to experience one so everyone could get it out of their systems. Everyone wanted to shoot at each other, but no one wanted to die. It became very apparent after the first few go-rounds that a shoot-out was a rather short, limited, and boring situation. After about six replays, the group begged to move on to something more interesting. As a result, no one was disappointed when a shootout did not appear in the final version of the play.

Over the next few weeks we developed the wagon train idea, played cards in a saloon, told tall tales around the campfire, invented Indian legends, and explored what school would be like in a one-room schoolhouse on the prairie. As scenes are improvised, notes should be taken on the dramatic choices, character names, and exciting lines of dialogue which are created. A more thorough way to save dialogue and ideas for highly verbal groups is to record improvisations. The recording can be transcribed later and will serve as a rich source of dramatic material. This is time-consuming work, but the time spent is worth it. A transcript of improvised dialogue preserves the way each actor naturally expresses herself — her word choice, sentence structure, thought processes, and grammar. This can be an invaluable aid when devising lines for each actor in the written version of the script. It is much easier to memorize lines that are your own creations or are expressed in your own style of thought and speech than it is to memorize lines in someone else's style.

Sometimes the most amazing and unpredictable things will happen during an improvisation, which provide exciting, unexpected material for the play. While a wagon train was not included in *Guns Ablazing*, one event did occur during our series of wagon train improvisations that contributed enormously to the plot of the play. I set up the wagon train scene by explaining to the actors that in the 1800s when a family left the East to move West, they sold their house and most of their belongings, keeping only the barest necessities. Everything had to fit into a tiny covered wagon. Once people arrived in the West, they usually never went back to visit in the East, never again seeing the friends and family they left behind.

There were three 4' x 8' tables in the room. Positioned end to end they became three wagons in the train. The first belonged to the Wagon Master, the second to the family going West, and the last to the Wagon Scout. First, the family sorted through their belongings, deciding what to pack and what to leave behind. Then they said goodbye to their friends and got into the wagons to leave. They stopped to cook a meal and forded a dangerous river.

When they arrived at the edge of Indian Territory, they stopped. The Wagon Scout went ahead to investigate. He was denied access by a tribe of angry Indians who did not want any white people to cross their lands. The Scout returned to tell the wagon train the bad news. At this point I offered them three options. They could go forward and be massacred by the Indians for trespassing, they could take the Southern route, which would take an additional three months and seriously endanger their food supplies, or they could turn around and go home. I knew they did not want to die (we had already done the shootout session), so I knew they would not choose to be massacred. I figured they would choose the second or third solution. But that is not what happened.

Amelia, an actor with learning disabilities who was playing the mother of the family, came up with a brilliant alternative. She decided to negotiate with the Indians herself. When she made this announcement, all the characters in the wagon train were horrified and begged her not to go because she would surely be killed. But they could not dissuade her. She was determined to save her family and get them to their new home. She set out alone and was met by an Indian scout. He brought her to the village and the chief assembled a council of all the wisest women in the village.

I wish my tape recorder had not been broken that day because the scene which followed was so incredibly poetic and emotionally truthful that anyone who was not there to see it and hear it would not believe that teenaged actors — five who had cognitive disabilities and two who did not — could create such a strong, powerful dramatic scene. Amelia asked the Council of Wise Women for permission for the wagon train to pass through their land. The Wise Women were unimpressed with her request. They listed all the havoc that white people had wreaked on their land in the past: white people killed the buffalo and the beaver, they cut down trees, they hurt little children, they poisoned the water, and they destroyed the crops. Amelia insisted that she was different. She would not do those things. The Council asked why she needed to go across their land. She explained that she had sold her home and had no place for her family to live. She needed to travel across their land to get her family to a new home where they could be safe. The Council carefully weighed her reasons and decided that a mother's love for her children was very important and that everyone needed a home. They allowed the wagon train to cross their land, but said the white people must kill nothing and take nothing on their way through. Amelia agreed to this and went back to the wagon train to announce her success. At that point class was over.

In the final script Amelia became Molly, the owner of the Town Saloon and mother of the kidnap victim. She went with the Sheriff and her Deputies to the Wild Rascals' hideout to arrange for the ransom of her daughter. They took a shortcut to the hideout, forgetting that it was through Indian Territory. The Sheriff wanted to turn back, but Molly insisted on meeting with the Indian Council and negotiating passage through their land so she could save her daughter.

Rehearsal surprises like this can add depth and dimension to a script if you allow them to happen instead of cutting them off. If I had insisted that the group adhere to the three choices I had given them while I was side-coaching the scene, we would never have discovered a more creative way to solve the dramatic situation and I would never have realized Amelia's peace-making talents.

If improvisations get stuck in a rut or go off track, step in and side-coach to focus the actors back onto the dramatic conflict of the scene. If some actors are not listening to the other actors and responding to what is being said, stop working on the play for a session and review basic improvisation skills. Set up situations with very simple, clear conflicts that the characters must resolve through discussion. For instance, a mother could be talking to her daughter about cleaning up her room or a teacher could be talking to a student about the need to study for a test. Both actors in the scene must listen and respond directly to what the other has just said. See the section in Chapter 6 that deals with improvisational acting for more tips on how to teach actors improvisational skills.

If actors have trouble structuring and developing a situation because they have little actual experience with it or with creating interesting dramatic obstacles, cast yourself or your assistant in the scene to keep things on track and to offer suggestions in role. While improvising the courtroom scene when the Wild Rascals were put on trial for kidnapping and bank robbery, my assistant played the prosecuting attorney and I played the defense attorney because we knew the actors had little understanding of courtroom procedure. We were able to guide the development of the scene along an appropriate progression with some sense of court decorum. Witnesses responded to our questions as we examined and cross-examined them and a lot of new material was generated that was used in the scene that ended up in the play.

We used this technique while developing *Death by Grammar*, a murder mystery involving an overbearing college grammar professor named Phil A. Buster. Professor Buster constantly corrected everything the other characters said and wrote until finally they got so fed up, they decided to do away with him for good. The problem in improvising scenes was that no one in the cast had a strong enough grasp of English grammar terms and rules to know when someone else had made a mistake. Our musical director Carol Gulley had to take over the role of Professor Buster during improvisations to help set up our conflict and motivate the other characters' reactions to it.

Art Work

Art work is another good avenue for collecting and developing ideas. It opens up actors' imaginative thinking in visual, spatial, and kinesthetic ways, providing a concrete approach for exploring an idea. Before taking off on any time travel journeys while we were working on *Just in Time*, I asked the Pegasus actors to design their own time machines. They set to work with paper, markers, and crayons and devised the most amazing array of scientific-looking contraptions I have ever seen. I let each present his or her design to the group and explain how it worked and the kind of sound it made. The journeys we took in rehearsal seemed all the more real because they had each concretely conceptualized how they were getting there.

While improvising *Making Connections*, a play about a video dating service done by Icarus, the young adult company, I discovered that no one had any idea how to get to know someone new. Typically when you meet someone for the first time, you talk about yourself and you ask the other person questions about him or herself so you both can find out what you have in common in terms of likes, dislikes, interests, etc. In improvisational scenes where two characters were meeting for the first time, both actors would say hello and just sit there looking at each other. We were not making any headway. So I called on Harriet Lesser to come up with an art activity to help them think of topics of conversation on a first date. As always, Harriet came to the rescue. She brought in magazines with pictures and asked the actors to bring in pictures of favorite people, animals, and things in their personal life. Then each actor spent a rehearsal period creating a personal collage that expressed who he or she was. It was a very simple exercise, but it broke open the creative floodgates. Suddenly, they could talk about themselves because they had a handle on what topics to share about. Not only that, they started making up characters who had interests, jobs, and personality quirks that were unlike themselves. It was amazing!

Double Crossed Bones, a rollicking pirate adventure, developed almost entirely out of a series of treasure maps the actors drew. Each map had an island and a path past many monsters and obstacles to the buried treasure. Each actor presented his or her map to the group and described how to get to the treasure. Then over the course of the next four weeks we improvised a number of treasure-hunting expeditions following the maps.

I recorded the actors' descriptions of their maps as they presented them. Here are a few transcriptions to give you an idea of the complications and conflicts they created for themselves to overcome during their improvisations. Adam and Amelia have learning disabilities; Lisa, Henry, and Jack have Down syndrome; Darryl and Dean are regular education students who have been best friends for years.

Adam's Map: This place is called Adam's Island. Right in the center of here is where the treasure is buried. To get there you have to start at Zebra Point and then you go to Monkey City, Chimpanzee Way, Giraffe City, Duck Avenue, Lion Court, Kitten Boulevard, Flamingo Drive, Swan Alley, Fish Terrace, Bird Park, and this is a lake called Spooky Lake. There are spirits in there. Then there's the buried treasure with stolen jewels. No people live on this island. It's been deserted forever. Only animals live here. You have to get past the animals to get to the treasure. But if you get caught by one, they will eat you up.

Lisa's Map: Here's the buried treasure. And here's the mountain. You have to get past Wendy to steal the treasure. The treasure is on the mountain and Wendy guards it. Wendy stole the treasure and brought it here.

Amelia's Map: This is Amelia Island. There's a purple monster. And if you get to the purple monster, he will shoot you. But if you pass him, you'll come to a sea monster. And here's blood on the ground. And here's a sea castle coming out of the ocean. My treasure is money — gold and silver. If you find it, I'll kill you.

Henry's Map: That's the island. There's the treasure. The treasure is money. That's the ocean.

Jack's Map: This is my clubhouse. This is grass. This is a field. This is the treasure — rings, necklace, pearls, everything. I live on the island. No animals or people. Just me. No visitors. If someone came, I would just talk to them.

Darryl and Dean's Map: We start in our hometown of Xanth. Xanth is all magic. Every person in Xanth has magic of some sort. This is Morag, a treacherous creature in the ocean. And this is Mudah, a monster fish. And this is the Hydra — it has three heads. And they all attack you. So they're very bad and they live in the ocean. Look out for them. They'll attack your boat. They're like termites — they can eat away at your boat. And then you follow the red dots to Hermit's Land and Demon's Dip, which is near Tie-Dyed Island. You go past the Pit of Hell, around Devil's Turn and come down the Strait of Death. And that's guarded by Medusa at Medusa's Manor. And you come out and here is the Lost Forest. It's lost so you have to look very carefully to find it. And once you do, you get lost *in* it. And you come to an *X*, which marks the spot on the map, but in reality there's a big tree like a *Y* (so *Y* really marks the spot). Other sights in our beautiful isle are Patrick's Hippieland, Troll's Town, Goblin's Glen, the Cliffs of Mortality, Dragon's Den, and Spelunker's Hollow. The Dragons, Goblins, and the Trolls guard the treasure. We leave that to your skillful knowledge and intelligence. The treasure is a huge box of golden toothbrushes: hollow chocolate. You have to peel off the tin foil. There's a big commune, a utopian society on Tie-Dyed Island. Patrick's Hippieland is uncharted territory. The Spelunker's Cave is uncharted as well. There are numerous treasures hidden in there — among them the toothpaste that goes with the toothbrushes and mouthwash. And in the mouthwash bottle lives the genie, Listerine. And there really is a great cast-iron compass floating in the water on both of our maps.

The final version of *Double Crossed Bones* had two crews of pirates who were each trying to get to the Island of Lost Causes so they could find the treasure of the Sultan of Xanth. They had to stop off at Tie-Dyed Island to get help from the Old Man of the Sea, the oldest pirate of them all, who lived all alone on the island (and wore tie-dyed clothes). One crew had to face the Three-Headed Hydra in the Sea of Blood and the other had to get past the Mermaids in the Mermaid Sea. Once on the island they had to work together to find the treasure in the Lost Forest and defeat the evil dragon Morag who guarded the treasure. Does any of this sound vaguely familiar?

Music and Dance

Music and dance can add variety and depth to an improvisational show, as well as alternative avenues of expression for the actors. Songs can be incorporated into the fabric of the show to move the plot along at the same time they offer the actors a chance to express themselves by singing a solo or a group number. You do not need to sing all the verses in a song. If one verse gets the point across, and two would be too much to memorize, sing one verse.

In *Guns Ablazing* Renata, a blind actress who loved to sing, played Melly the Saloon Singer. During the bank robbery, Melly was kidnapped by the Wild Rascals. Normally they never took hostages, but they had heard her singing in the Saloon and wanted her to sing them to sleep at night. This led to a scene in the hideout where all the Rascals joined in a rowdy version of "Swing Low, Sweet Chariot," unwittingly providing cover for the good guys to sneak up from behind and capture them.

The Wild Rascals' version of "Swing Low" turned out to be a real crowd pleaser and motivated my normally reticent teenagers to willingly turn *Double Crossed Bones*, the next season's show, into a full-fledged musical filled with sea chanteys and a pirate dance contest. The sea chanteys were excellent devices for climaxing an exciting scene, covering scene transitions, and bringing everyone together on stage at the end of the play. Written for hard-boiled sailors, these songs are easy to sing. They do not require a wide vocal range. They have a strong, clear rhythm and they do not have to be sung perfectly to be effective.

Even students who do not sing "well" enjoy singing. As Carol Gulley, our musical director says, "Music is fundamental." It speaks to the human heart and soul in a direct, immediate, and emotional way. Therefore, the experience of music and participation in it is more important for students than musical accuracy. Accuracy will come in time with practice.

Carol approaches teaching music to the actors by exploring the mood and emotions evoked by the songs. We sing through a song and the actors share what they think the lyrics mean. She also asks them for "feeling" words to describe the sound of the music and the story that the lyrics tell. After singing through "Greensleeves" Carol might ask, "How does the person who is singing this song feel? Who is he speaking to? What has happened between them? What does he want to happen?" If the lyrics suggest a story, students might try acting them out while Carol plays the music. She might suggest that they explore the song further by improvising a dance to it before sitting back down to sing it again. After the actors can identify and express the feelings while singing the song,

photo by Sally Bailey

Figure 25: A pirate conga line from *Double Crossed Bones*.

the musicality of the song naturally begins to develop as the group continues to learn and rehearse the song.

I have found that actors with special needs tend to do better with songs that have simple lyrics and a straightforward, steady beat to serve as an anchor. Slow ballads and rock 'n' roll tunes seem to be their personal favorites for those exact reasons. They find songs which have a familiar, repetitious pattern in lyrics and/or melody easy to remember and enjoyable to sing. They tend to have difficulty with songs that have complicated wording, nonsense words, or a syncopated beat.

Choosing Characters

Before I sit down to pull together all the ideas and create a plot structure for the play, I ask each actor what kind of role he or she would like to play. During improvisation sessions they have had the opportunity to try out as many different kinds of roles as possible. Usually by the time I ask, they have an idea what kind of part they would like to have in the final play. In addition to the type of role, I always ask if they have any suggestions for their character's name and for the title of the play. I try to get a first and second choice of role to give me flexibility in casting and in case several people are interested in exactly the same role.

In *Guns Ablazing* the lines were clearly drawn between those who wanted to be good guys and bad guys. Brian had insisted from day one that he was a renegade Indian named Injun Joe. Darryl and Dean wanted to be Billy Bob Joe and Colt Warren, twin brother bank robbers. They had clearly taken Henry, who wanted to be a bank robber named Robert, under their wing, so he became a Wild Rascal, too. Patrick and Jack, who were best friends, wanted to be the sheriff's deputies, Slim McGillicuty and Charlie Jones. After her experience in the wagon train Amelia was very clear about wanting to be someone's mother and she wanted her name to be Molly. Renata wanted to be the Saloon Singer so she could sing a song. She did not have an idea for a name, so Amelia suggested Melly and the act of providing Renata with a name, gave me the idea to make Molly Melly's mother. Aaron wanted to be the judge. I had several actors who said, "I'll play anything. Put me where you need me. I know you'll give me a good part." With their flexibility, I was able to fill out the cast.

Double Crossed Bones was a little harder to cast. Everyone wanted to be a pirate, with the exception of Betsy, who wanted to be a mermaid, Lisa, who wanted to be pirate *and* a dragon, and Carolyn, who said she would play any part I needed her to play. So I collected information on the type of pirate each wanted to be (Captain, First Mate, Cook, Lookout, Dock Hand, etc.) and pirate name (Erg, Arg, Meriwether, Swerdfager, Dennis, Seagull, etc.) and went from there.

Sometimes actors cast each other in roles. Charlie came up with an idea for the opening of *Some Enchanted Evening* that sent shivers down our spines. He thought that it would be very dramatic if Ellie, who uses a wheelchair, would mournfully wheel herself out onto an empty stage and say, "I'm sad and lonely. Nobody loves me." Then she could sing "Where is Love?" from *Oliver!* a song all about looking for someone special to love. Then, he continued, the Spirits of the Night could appear and offer to help her. Needless to say, everyone thought that was a dynamic beginning. Because the entrance and the dramatic situation were so strong, Ellie became the main character in the play, which followed her experiences as she tried to find the perfect someone to love her.

Of course, sometimes actors do not end up in the role that they want. In *Death by Grammar* several actors wanted to be characters who were in improvisations, but who did not end up in the script. Several other actors asked for one role and got another. After we read through the script, no one was disappointed because everyone loved the play and each actor played an interesting character with lots of fun dialogue and stage business. For years Patrick wanted to play a fireman. He thought he was finally going to have his chance in this play. Instead he ended up as Heywood Jakissime, a Don Johnson-type Hollywood movie star. He told me later that Heywood was his favorite role ever. Or as he put it, "Wow! I really love this part!"

If an actor had been upset about how she had been cast, I would have taken her aside and told her how much I needed her in that particular role, that I had conceived and written the role especially for her, and that nobody else could do the role as well as I knew she could. And because it is an original script, developed *by* the actors and written *for* them, what I said would be absolutely true.

Writing the Original Script

Basic Dramatic Structure

Most well written plays, whatever their length, usually follow a similar dramatic structure. Each has a beginning, a middle, and an end. Most plays begin with *exposition* that sets up the characters, their present situation, and the previous action that has led them to this situation. A skillful playwright builds exposition into the unfolding of the *present action* or *dramatic conflict*, which is best set in motion almost as soon as the play begins. Sometimes the dramatic conflict can begin even before the curtain comes up. An unskilled playwright wastes a lot of time in the beginning of a play if the characters only talk about their past and their relationships without getting the action started.

The middle (and bulk) of the play follows the unfolding of the plot or *dramatic conflict,* developed through a series of causally related incidents which involve *obstacles* and *complications*. As the characters face each obstacle, they must make choices that may help them get beyond it or may make the situation more complicated. Complications often lead to *dramatic crises* in which the action builds, new situations are formed, and further obstacles and complications must be dealt with in turn. The dramatic conflict culminates in one major *crisis* or *turning point*, the most important decision made in relationship to the dramatic conflict. This leads directly to the *climax* of the play where the crisis and the dramatic conflict are resolved to the satisfaction of the characters and audience alike.

After the climax, the loose ends of the play are pulled together in the *denouement* or ending. Unanswered questions are answered, mysteries are solved, and fences are mended. The audience can leave with a sense of completion about the events they have witnessed.

The easiest model for grasping how to construct a scene, act, or play is Fedder's Four, a model created by Norman Fedder, distinguished professor of playwriting at Kansas State University. In every dramatic situation a protagonist *wants* something. *But* there is an obstacle in the way. *However*, the protagonist *wants* that something so much that he will find a way to get around that obstacle. *So* the situation is either resolved or becomes more complicated — which creates the next *but, however, so* until you reach the final *so* which is the denouement at the end of the play. If you look at what you are writing from the structure *I want...but...however...so...*, you cannot go wrong.

As far as written resources go, two excellent books on playwriting are *Playwriting: Formula to Form* by William Missouri Downs and Lou Anne Wright and *Forwards and Backwards* by David Ball. They clearly explain how to craft a well-made play in common-sense, everyday language.

Using the Material Generated in Rehearsal

When you put together a script from the characters and improvisational scenes your actors have created, you will need to think in terms of fitting their work into the structure of a well-made play. Exactly how that play will develop will be different every time because each play presents unique dramatic problems.

Sometimes, you have improvised scenes and characters, but no plot. For *Just in Time* we had improvised about ten scenes from history and everyone had a say about who their favorite characters were. I chose four scenes from the past that seemed to offer the most potential for dramatic staging: the time of the dinosaurs, a scene from King Solomon's Court, the day King Arthur and his Knights created the Round Table, and Columbus asking Queen Isabella and King Ferdinand for money to sail to China. Somehow I had to weave these four scenes together in Time Travel, but we had done very little work on who the Time Traveler was or why he or she needed to go back in time. This character would be crucial to the play as the connecting thread between the different time periods. Without a clear dramatic problem for the Traveler to solve, the journey would become an aimless, meandering travelogue and would ultimately be boring.

I wasted many hours in dead ends and false starts as I tried to solve the problem on my own. Maybe the Time Traveler was going back to each of the different time periods to get an object that was needed in his time in order to save the world? Maybe the Time Traveler had to ask questions of certain people in history to solve a puzzle that was threatening humanity? Maybe the Time Traveler was chasing another time traveler who was trying to make trouble back in history? While these ideas were good, I would have had to create a plot structure that would have been too complex for the memorization and sequencing abilities of my actors at that time.

In frustration I looked back over the list we had made when we were brainstorming ideas for the play (hold onto those — they can be golden). I ran across the words "Small Wonder," the name of a TV situation comedy. All that fall, Brian, who has Down syndrome, had been talking about "Small Wonder" and how he wanted to play Vicky, the girl robot on the show. At first I was puzzled. Why did he want to play a girl? Then I realized that what he liked about Vicky was the fact that she was a robot. She was smart! She knew how to do everything right! He, on the other hand, was going through a stage where he felt very awkward. He kept getting into trouble. He felt like he always did everything wrong.

My solution to the time travel problem was to create Wushin, the Time Machine Robot, and cast Brian in the part. While on display in a science museum Wushin is accidentally turned on by a blind girl (played by Renata) who touches him while her school group is having a tour. As the group moves to the next room, two of the students, who are lingering behind, discover Wushin is functioning. They ask him to take them back in time to meet their favorite characters from history. Since he is a robot, and therefore programmed to follow orders given to him by humans, Wushin takes the three of them off into the fourth dimension in the time machine. Within a day of creating Wushin, the structure of the whole script and the dialogue fell into place.

The lesson to learn from this story: always listen to your students. Their ideas can solve your dramatic problems better than you can. In addition, their solutions will tend to be on the skill level they can handle, while your solutions will tend to be on your skill level. When in doubt, it is always better to go with their skill level than yours.

If you have a group that has low verbal skills, you need to pay attention to which ideas are exciting to the group, what songs and characters capture their imaginations, and what kind of events would appeal to their sense of humor and drama. Then as you write the script, you must put yourself in their shoes, remembering how they process information and choose words, so you can create a play that reflects their personalities, ideas, and abilities. For instance, the actors in the Barrier-Free Theatre in Manhattan, Kansas, are not as articulate as my Pegasus actors were. Several years ago we were working on a Western (a popular theme). I started by teaching them a lot of old cowboy songs. The song that really struck a chord with them was "I've Got Spurs That Jingle Jangle Jingle." The words of the song, sung to different girls, tells the story of a cowpoke who flirts a lot, but does not want to settle down because he likes his free, roaming life. The situation in the song became the opening situation in the play as well as the opening number. The Dance Hall Girls, who are tired of singing and dancing day and night, are so fed up with these Cowpokes who refuse to pop the question that they decide to quit their jobs and start their own ranch. They camouflage themselves as cows to rustle the Cowboys' cattle. The Cowboys go to the Law and form a posse to go after the rustlers (not knowing the Girls are the culprits). They camouflage themselves as cows to steal their cows back, but the Girls have already re-branded them. In the end the Indians have to step in and make peace.

We did lots of improv during the rehearsal period, but because of the verbal abilities of the great majority of the group, a lot of the scenes were primarily movement-based. Recording dialogue and transcribing it would have been a waste of time. However, I got many ideas from scenes we did (especially the solutions we came up with for sharing land between the Indians and the settlers) which I used in the play and the actors got a clear sense of what type of character they wanted to be.

Dealing with Speech and Memory Difficulties

Since I know the strengths and weaknesses of the different actors in my groups, whenever I cast actors in roles and structure the play, I team up different combinations of characters who can look out for each other during the performance. In *Guns Ablazing* two of the Wild Rascals, Injun

photo by Allison Walker

Figure 26: The Wild Rascals plot their bank robbery.

Joe and Robert, had cognitive disabilities and two, Colt and Billy Bob Joe, did not. The Deputies, Slim and Charlie, had cognitive disabilities and the Sheriff, Calamity Kate, did not. In each of these teams of bad guys and good guys there were actors who could handle the bulk of the memorized lines. They could ask questions or give orders that would motivate the other actors' actions and responses. For example:

COLT: Now, behave yourselves. No fighting tonight.

INJUN JOE (disappointed): Awwww! Why not?

BILLY BOB JOE: Because we don't want anyone to notice us.

COLT: Yeah, we don't want to attract any attention so nobody gets suspicious.

MOLLY (taking drink orders): What do you want?

INJUN JOE: Whiskey!

COLT: Beer!

BILLY BOB JOE: Sasparilly.

ROBERT: Yeah!

MOLLY: Coming right up.

BILLY BOB JOE: Okay, I say we knock off the First National Bank tomorrow morning. What do you say? Colt?

COLT: Let's do it!

ROBERT: Yeah!

BILLY BOB JOE: Injun Joe?

INJUN JOE: Okay, Boss!

BILLY BOB JOE: Colt, you be lookout.

COLT: Why do I always have to be lookout?

BILLY BOB JOE: You've got the best eyes. You have to stand lookout. And Robert?

ROBERT: Yeah?

BILLY BOB JOE: You can hold the moneybag.

ROBERT: Okay!

BILLY BOB JOE: Now, Injun Joe, you can break into the vault, can't you?

INJUN JOE: Yeah, I can break into it. I can break into anything!

BILLY BOB JOE: What do you need for this one?

INJUN JOE: I'll break it to pieces!

COLT: You gonna use your bare hands?

INJUN JOE: No, I'll need dynamite. And ear muffs.

COLT: Sounds like it will be really loud.

INJUN JOE: YEAH!

ROBERT: YEAH!

BILLY BOB JOE: YEAH!

Be careful how you structure dialogue of characters who are prompting lines and reactions from characters played by actors who have cognitive disabilities. As discussed in Chapter 6, many people have trouble processing negative commands into positive action. One actor saying, "Don't touch me," as a reminder to another actor who is supposed to touch him, can backfire. The second actor may hear the command and follow it, instead of disobeying it. Try to phrase reminders in a positive manner. Instead of "Don't touch me," the character could say, "If you touch me, I'll scream," or "I'm afraid this bandit is going to touch me!"

In *Guns Ablazing* several actors had speech that was difficult to understand. In the scene where Molly convinced the tribal council to allow the good guys to cross Indian Territory, I created a character who served as translator from English to Sioux and back again to provide enough repetition of lines so the audience could understand what was being said. The scene's dialogue was based almost entirely on the improvisation that came out of the confrontation between the mother of the Wagon Train and the Council of Wise Women.

RED FEATHER (to RUNNING BULL): What does the white woman want?

RUNNING BULL: What white woman want?

MOLLY: Please, my friends and I need to go across your land.

RUNNING BULL: She wants to cross our land.

RED FEATHER: No! She cannot cross our land!

RUNNING BULL: No cross.

MOLLY: Please! It's a matter of life and death!

RUNNING BULL: She says it's a matter of life and death.

RED FEATHER: I'll ask the Council. Council, what do you say? Should we let this white woman and her friends cross our land? I say, "No." The white man does not know how to respect our land. What do you say?

BROWN BEAR: I say, "No." The white man kills the buffalo and the beaver. Soon there will be no wildlife left.

CORN MAIDEN: I say, "No." The white man pollutes the land. Soon nothing will be able to grow.

RED FEATHER (to RUNNING BULL): Tell the white woman, "No, go away."

RUNNING BULL: No. Go away.

MOLLY: But you must help! My daughter is being held captive by some bad men and they will kill her if we can't rescue her! We can only get to her by crossing your land! Please, tell him that.

RUNNING BULL: Okay. Some bad men have her daughter and they are going to kill her. She needs to cross our land to rescue her daughter.

CORN MAIDEN: Ahh! That makes a difference!

BROWN BEAR: Yes, it does!

CORN MAIDEN: I say, "Yes." A mother must help her daughter when in need.

BROWN BEAR: I agree.

RED FEATHER: If you say yes, I will say yes, too. (To RUNNING BULL) Tell her she can cross our land, but touch nothing and kill nothing!

RUNNING BULL: You can cross, but touch nothing and kill nothing. Now, go!

MOLLY: Oh, thank you, thank you!

Even though some of the actors' speech was hard to understand, with the repetition, the physical actions, and the tone of voice used, the dramatic action of the scene was clear to the audience.

The only mistake I made was in my casting. Initially, I cast Roberta, who has cognitive disabilities, as Running Bull, the translator, because I knew that her memorization ability and her speech were limited. I thought the role of the translator would be perfect for her because she would not have to memorize — just repeat the lines said to her by Red Feather and Molly. I also thought she would sound like someone speaking English as a foreign language because in real life she speaks in a halting manner.

Unfortunately, my brilliant idea was not so brilliant after all. Roberta had short-term memory problems, which meant she could not listen to a sentence and immediately echo it. She became very confused and frustrated. And so did I. I wanted to scream, "It's so easy! It's the easiest part in the play!" But I didn't scream. Instead, I sat down, thought, and realized that her brain did not process information the way I had assumed. Instead of making it easy, I had asked her to do something that was very, very difficult for her.

Once I had established the problem, my next step was to figure out how to remedy it so that everyone felt comfortable. I asked Roberta if it would be okay to switch roles in the scene with Towanda who was playing Brown Bear. She was immediately agreeable to the suggestion, as was Towanda. So Roberta played Brown Bear and Towanda played Running Bull. Roberta was very relieved to be off the hook and Towanda felt like she had been promoted to a very important part with many more lines! The moral of the story: There are many more kinds of information processing difficulties than you might at first suspect. Make sure you know what your actors' specific strengths and weaknesses are. You might think you are doing them a favor, but instead do them a disservice.

Dealing with Physical Limitations

I also take actors' physical limitations into consideration as I structure the responsibilities in the play. During the rehearsal period for *Guns Ablazing* Aaron was recovering from an operation on his legs. His energy was limited and so was his ability to move. As the judge, he was able to sit on stage in his wheelchair, listening sagely to the court case and banging his gavel for order.

In our updated version of the Cinderella story, *Once upon Today*, a play composed of three updated fairy tales, one of our actors used a motorized wheelchair. This became the taxi that took Cindy to the big corporate party. A little cart was hooked onto the back of his chair so that our Taxi Driver could drive on stage. Cindy could climb on behind him and be whisked away in style. He enjoyed turning his chair into a different kind of vehicle than it was designed for and she enjoyed the ride. Wheelchairs have also been used as movable thrones for Kings and Queens in numerous plays, making the monarchs' entry and exit from stage even more regal.

Renata, who was blind, was led around during *Guns Ablazing* by the Wild Rascals because Melly, her character, was the kidnapped saloon singer. They blindfolded Melly so she could not see where they were taking her. This freed her from worrying about how to get gracefully from here to there on the stage where the scenery was constantly changing from one scene to the next.

Scripts for Non-Integrated Groups

What can you do when, for whatever reason, the majority of your actors have difficulty remembering lines and plot sequences? When you do not have anyone who has enough stage experience to keep the play moving forward if others get lost? The more inexperienced your actors, the more tightly you must structure the play.

Narrators. By the standards of good playwriting, a narrator is a weak structural device. However, for the purposes of keeping beginning actors on track, a narrator is one of the most reliable and useful devices at your disposal. Structure the play so that the teacher, an assistant, or a really strong reader in the cast can serve as an omniscient narrator who moves the play along from scene to scene. Just like the narrator of a creative-drama story, the narrator of the play can remind actors of entrances, lines of dialogue, or bits of business. The narration can be written out, but the narrator should also be able to jump in and improvise when things go wrong. One musical revue, *The WBAP Love Hour*, had no plot. The only way to keep the sequence straight was for the "deejays" to introduce each song and dance. They sat at a big counter on stage with scripts on clipboards. Just like TV newscasters, they could look down at their script to see what the next number was.

Teachers in role. The teacher or assistant can take on a character in the play whose role is that of an authority figure or helper. In this way they can serve the same function as a narrator, but from inside the play. One spring my improvisational acting class for teens decided to put on their version of *The Wizard of Oz* for their end-of-semester project. The script did not need to be written down because everyone knew the story and what the characters should say in each scene by heart. However, most of my actors had never performed in front of a live audience before and I was very nervous about how they would react. To give them a little extra support I cast my assistant as Glinda the Good Witch of the North and had Glinda serve as the guide for Dorothy's entire journey through Oz.

The afternoon of the performance, I was so glad I had had the foresight to include an adult in role in the play. The curtains opened. We heard the winds of the twister blowing. Dorothy Gale blew onstage. She took one look at the audience and blew right off again. She was scared to death.

I thought to myself, "The show's over. There's no way we can get her back on."

Just then Glinda floated on and called out, "Are you a good witch or a bad witch?"

Immediately, Dorothy ran back on stage and responded, "I'm Dorothy Gale. From Kansas." Having another character to relate to took her focus off her nervousness and the audience. She was fine from then on. Throughout the performance Glinda was able to ask pertinent questions, gently reminding characters that it was time to move on or motivate actions through subtle suggestions, such as "Maybe the Wizard could help him, too."

Music. Music can be very helpful in providing transition cues to actors. Just as in a classical melodrama, every time a character enters or leaves a scene he or she can have signature music. The teacher, an assistant, or a student volunteer can run the CD player when the music is not created live.

Since I wanted to avoid reproducing the MGM movie version, each character in the above-mentioned production of *The Wizard of Oz* had an appropriate signature tune recorded from the actor's favorite rock artist. For example, the actor who played the Wizard loved MC Hammer, so his theme song became "U Can't Touch This." The actress who played the Wicked Witch of the West loved Michael Jackson, so her theme song was "I'm Bad." Every time they heard their music, they knew it was time to come on or go off.

Sections of a play might be danced or mimed to music. Many students who have difficulty remembering lines of dialogue can remember movement patterns. If they have difficulty sequencing exact patterns, they can usually follow the beat of the music and rhythmically pantomime their character's actions.

Recorded Dialogue. Another way to introduce or narrate sections of a play that keeps actors involved is to record the narration or dialogue in their own voices and have them pantomime to it for the show. *Dreams, Nightmares, and Fantasies* used this technique to good effect. Each dream was introduced by an actor's recorded voice:

PATRICK: Dream Number One — The Circus Dream. I had a dream about me being a clown.

Sometimes the narration was followed by music, sometimes by songs, sometimes by an improvised scene or more recorded narration. The actors were free to improvise dialogue as they felt appropriate, but the structure of the play was preserved for them through the sound cues. The script for Dream Number Seven looked like this:

MANDY (recorded): Dream Number Seven — The Haunted House!

(On the recording wolves howl and there are scary noises while the actors get into place to act out the dream.)

AARON (recorded): I was driving a big truck down the highway.

(ESTHER pushes AARON's chair across the stage.)

AARON (recorded): I parked the truck outside this big old house.

(ESTHER stops the chair by a box and helps AARON out of the chair. He walks up to the house.)

AARON (recorded): I walked up to the house and onto the porch. I opened the front door and someone said, "Come in."
ALL ACTORS (live): COME IN!

(AARON pantomimes opening the door and stepping inside.)

AARON (recorded): I walked in and the door shut behind me.

(Sound of a door slamming. AARON turns and tries to open the door to get out.)

AARON (recorded): It was locked! Everything grew dark and scary!

(Evil laughter on recording. ACTORS, bending very low, are led around by MANDY until they are in front of AARON in a semi-circle.)

AARON (recorded): A trap door underneath me opened and I fell into the basement!

(Sound of trap door. ACTORS stand up and raise their arms on the word *basement* to create the effect of AARON falling. Then the group splits in the middle in front and lets AARON out to look around.)

AARON (recorded): There were some silver and gold pieces on the floor. I was in a treasure house and this was the robbers' gold! Just then I turned around and saw some monsters.

(ACTORS turn into MONSTERS and start making scary sounds.)

AARON (recorded): They were coming after me!

(MONSTERS chase AARON around the boxes stage right and across to the box stage left. AARON sits on the box, out of breath. The MONSTERS surround him.)

AARON (recorded): I ran into a corner! I was trapped! I couldn't get away! They got closer and closer and then...[alarm clock rings on recording]

MOTHER (recorded): Aaron! Time to get up! It's morning!

AARON (live): Saved by the alarm clock!

===================================

Taking the Playwriting Plunge
By Patti Woolsey

My involvement with special-needs populations happened by chance, and consequently, so did my career as a director and playwright. After majoring in drama in college, my focus was primarily on acting. Although I was working, it was not enough to pay my bills. I met a woman while waitressing at a local restaurant in DC who taught ED/LD students at a high school and asked if I would be interested in applying as an assistant teacher, so I did. I got the job and found that I loved it. This job did not pay enough, so I left after one year, but my interest in special education was piqued.

The next year I traveled, worked in retail, and was professionally very unsatisfied. I did not know what my next step was to be. Then one night, at an ungodly late hour, I was watching a local news show and saw a report on Sally Bailey's integrated teen acting company Pegasus. It hit me so hard: this is what I wanted to do! It was such a powerful "Aha!" moment, but unfortunately the only information I had was the name Pegasus. I did not know the director's name, the theatre it was associated with, nothing.

However, synchronicity was looking out for me. One week later at a dinner party I met a woman who worked at the school where the Pegasus Company performed! She connected me with Sally. I interviewed and was hired as the stage manager and choreographer for the group. I also began teaching drama and movement classes for younger children with special needs.

I did this for a few years and was quite content until Sally said the dreaded words, "Now it's time for you to direct your own company." My immediate response was, "I can't do it. I'm not ready," but Sally was persistent.

Although my background was in theatre, I had absolutely no formal training in directing or playwriting. What I learned about myself in this process is that I am a very careful observer and had actually absorbed much from the years of experience as an actor, stage manager, props person and other theatre jobs I had done. I needed the push. Otherwise, I would never have taken the plunge into directing or playwriting. It changed the direction (no pun intended) of my career. I love facilitating the ideas of the actors and designers into a cohesive whole.

My greatest trepidation was writing the play. I was not sure how to structure a plot or create interesting, yet accessible characters. I expressed this to Sally and she suggested that I present several stories that already existed to the actors — stories I felt could be adapted for the number, strengths, and abilities of actors in the troupe. After several weeks of telling and acting out different stories, the company would vote on their favorite and we would develop it through improvisation. This was a wonderful compromise. Adapting an already existing story made the daunting task seem more manageable because the plot structure and characters were already there.

The first year I told "The Wild Swans," "Pinocchio," "Peter Pan," and "Aladdin." I chose these stories because they had many characters and I had 14 actors in my troupe. They chose "The Wild Swans." One of the things I love most about working with folk tales is that there are unlimited variants of each story. The basic plot structure provides the who, what, where, and when, but the whys are not always provided. There is usually no background from which to understand the actions of the characters — they just do what they do. This provides a rich tapestry of possibilities from which to draw.

One of the surprising things that happened during the development of this first play of mine was that one of the more secondary characters, the evil stepmother, ended up becoming a main role. This happened organically because the actions of this character were the least motivated in the story. Why did she act the way she did? Are the evil stepmother's actions always unjustified? Doesn't she have a story as well? What happened to make her so angry and vengeful? It became apparent that this character needed a strong voice to share her point of view. Playing with the balance of good and evil in folk tales is one of the most rewarding and fun parts of the process. It is my experience that no character is totally good or totally evil. They share the flaws of human nature.

Writing is a birthing process that is always hard. The most difficult parts are sitting down to do it, doing it, and then handing it over to someone else to read for the first time. To my surprise there are always unexpected insights about the characters and their actions that pop up as you are writing. I have written seven plays so far for barrier-free troupes and one for a small professional children's theatre; each one has been a revelation.

For two years I stuck to my original system of basing the work on an already existing story. As my confidence grew, I opened the floor up to general ideas that the actors would develop in the rehearsal process. By the time I sit down to write, I have been working with these ideas for months. Some plays flow easier than others. Last year, I wrote the play in two hours, which I had never done before. It was all there in my head and I could not type fast enough. This year the play was excruciating to write. I could only squeeze out a little bit at a time.

One image about writing that expresses the process well is to pretend that you are a frog, just trying to get across the pond from one lily pad to the next (one idea at a time) until eventually, you are at the other side of the pond (in play-writing terms, the end of the play).

I am now in the role of mentor, helping to assuage the fears of the newest director/playwright working for my new non-profit, ArtStream, which provides arts experiences to underserved populations in the Washington, DC, metropolitan area. The new director/playwright is filled with doubt and insecurity, but I know she is ready for the challenge and I will happily support her through the process. My advice is always to push yourself. In creating your own works in collaboration with others, you will learn so much more about theatre than you would in any other arena. I am very grateful for my playwriting experiences and feel it prepared me for professional theatre work more than any other experience I have ever had. I continue to learn from the actors and from myself during the process. It is empowering to know that you can do it.

Go on — take the plunge, then just hop from lily pad to lily pad until you get to the shore on the other side.

=================================

Length of the Script

Keep your script short. A good length for a one-act play is 20 to 30 minutes. You do not want to create a script that is longer than you have time to rehearse, especially if you only meet once or twice a week.

There are no exact formulas for computing how a given number of pages of script will equal a certain amount of stage time. This is because there are several different styles of formatting a script and different ones put different amounts of material onto a page. In addition, a page that has long speeches on it will take more time to perform than a page with short speeches. Also, a stage description of blocking may take much more time to perform than it takes to read or vice versa. The only reliable way to gauge how long a script will take to perform is to read it out loud (with good readers), pantomiming any extended physical actions as you go. That said, you can often guess that one page of relatively short speeches will take about a minute of stage time.

When deciding the length a script should be, first consider the basic needs of the story you are telling. What is the essential action that must happen in order for the story to make sense? The audience must understand what is going on.

Second, consider the needs of your actors. Do not overburden them with too much material to memorize, whether words, songs, or movement. Take into consideration the actors' ages, attention spans, sequencing and memorization abilities, verbal abilities, dramatic skill level, and commitment to the production.

Third — and most important — keep in mind how much time you have to rehearse the piece. It is much better to do a short play that is well rehearsed and shows the actors off to their best advantage than to bite off more than you can chew and arrive at opening night unprepared.

Memorization versus Improvisation

Allow the play to remain basically improvisational in nature as the actors rehearse and perform it. If your play has been developed through improvisation, it is the creation of the actors in the company. There is no reason to require that each word in the written script be adhered to religiously. After all, the actors helped create it! It is their script! If they want to change something as they go along, they have the right to, as long as their changes make sense and make the play better.

An improvisational approach to lines allows the actors to adjust what they are saying to what they are capable of comfortably remembering. Usually lines taken directly from the actual words spoken by an actor or expressed in her style of speaking are easier to remember. However, this is not always the case. Even though it is based on what was once spoken, the written dialogue can turn out to be too difficult to memorize. The lines might be too long or too complex to commit to memory. If so, they can be simplified in writing the script and during the rehearsal process.

I have come to view the rehearsal process as the time when the extra fat I have written into the script is rendered out as the actors pare the play down to the essential meat and bones of the creature we have created together. If I have done a good job of capturing their voices and editing what they said, very little will change. If I have done a good job of capturing my own voice, a lot will be modified as we go.

When the script is approached as a tool to create structure for the improvisationally created play, the actors are free to devise strategies for helping each other if someone forgets what to do or say. If actors listen to what the other characters are saying to them, they can probably figure out an appropriate way to respond. I also suggest that if an actor looks lost, someone else who knows what is supposed to happen next can add a line or change a line or ask a question that can provide the lost actor with the missing information and move the scene forward. In this way the actors are all on stage looking out for each other, putting the best interests of the play first. This creates strong ensemble work and develops problem-solving abilities.

This approach also eases actors' fears about missing lines or making a mistake. They know they are not up on stage alone. They feel support from their fellow cast members. When a mistake is made (which is inevitable, even in the best of professional productions), rather than pointing the finger of blame at each other, the actors jump in to solve the problem and cover up the mistake before the audience realizes anything went wrong.

With that said, the actors should still work very hard to learn their lines. The lines hold the sequence of actions and events that happen in each scene. They provide a lot of important information that the audience has to know if they are to follow the story. The word choice and syntax of specific lines also serve as characterization devices and jokes — certain characters speak in certain ways. For example, a very proper, straight-laced character will talk differently from a very relaxed, informal one. Chapter 10 contains more information on how to help actors learn lines.

Recommended Reading

Ball, D. (1983). *Forwards and Backwards*. Carbondale, IL: Southern Illinois University Press.

Boal, A. (1985). *Theatre of the Oppressed*. New York: Theatre Communications Group.

Boal, A. (2002). *Games for Actors and Non-Actors, 2nd Ed*. London: Routledge.

Clifford, S. & Hermann, A. (1999). *Making a Leap: Theatre of Empowerment: A Practical Handbook for Creative Drama Work with Young People*. London: Jessica Kingsley Publishers.

Downs, W. M. & Wright, L. A. (1998). *Playwriting: Formula to Form: A Guide to Writing a Play*. Fort Worth, TX: Harcourt Brace College Publishers.

Gray, R. & Sinding, C. (2002). *Standing Ovation: Performing Social Science Research about Cancer*. Lanham, MD; Altamira Press.

Rohd, M. (1998). *Hope is Vital: Theatre for Community, Conflict, and Dialogue*. Portsmouth, NH: Heinemann.

Salas, J. (1993). *Improvising Real Life: Personal Story in Playback Theatre*. Dubuque, IA: Kendall Hunt Publishing.

Telander, M., Quinlan, F. & Verson, K. (1982). *Acting Up! An Innovative Approach to Creative Drama for Older Adults*. Toronto, ON: Coach House Books.

Wiegler, W. (2001). *Strategies for Playbuilding*. Portsmouth, NH: Heinemann.

10. The Rehearsal Process

Scheduling Rehearsals

How much rehearsal does a particular script need? Generally, an hour of rehearsal time is necessary to properly prepare for each minute of performance time in a show. I have prepared a 25 to 35 minute play in as little as 20 hours of rehearsal, but I have felt *very* pressured and desperately wished for more time. It is always better to overestimate the amount of rehearsal you will need because events will inevitably happen to put you behind schedule. Blocking often takes longer than expected. Cast members get sick and miss rehearsals. Snow days happen. Sometimes actors do not learn their lines on time. There is always a fly in the ointment.

Work out your rehearsal schedule on paper. The cast will need to start with a read-through of the script. The next task is blocking the movements that the actors make on stage. Then each scene needs to be worked through several times from moment to moment so the actors begin to understand what they are doing and develop an ease to their delivery of lines and actions. Once the play has been carefully rehearsed in small pieces, it is time to put it together and run through the whole play from beginning to end without stopping. This creates a sense of sequencing and flow. The last stage is the technical and dress rehearsals, which add the final ingredients of costumes, props, makeup, sound, sets, and lights to the production.

Type up and distribute to the cast and crew the rehearsal schedule, listing all rehearsal and performance dates and times and identifying all important deadlines. Indicate when the actors need to have their lines memorized for each scene. It is better to wait until after a scene has been blocked before requiring it to be memorized.

Do not require the entire play to be memorized on the same day. It is easier to memorize small chunks over a long period of time than one large chunk all at once. Spread out the memorization assignments. I usually require a scene to be memorized on the day we will be working it through moment-to-moment. Since we will be starting and stopping anyway, it is okay if the actors are struggling with line recall.

The sooner lines are due to be memorized in the rehearsal process, the better. This gives the actors lots of time to practice remembering them, lots of time for forgetting and making mistakes. Do not under any circumstances let actors slip through an entire rehearsal process without getting off book! Actors who wait until the last minute to memorize lines will inevitably forget them the first time they get in front of an audience.

Give the actors a copy of the rehearsal schedule with each scene's line memorization deadline *clearly marked!* If the actors are living at home, make sure parents get a copy of the schedule with a written request to assist their child in learning his lines. The same request can be made of support staff in group homes or supported living environments. Parental or other support (roommate, friend, or group-home staff) for this issue will make all the difference in the world. Impress on your actors that it is okay to ask for help. More suggestions on how to make line memorization effective will be provided through the description of each stage of rehearsal.

Be efficient in your use of rehearsal time. Schedule everybody in the cast on those days you are working large group scenes. Schedule scenes that have just a few characters in them for separate rehearsals with only the actors needed. Young actors who sit around at rehearsals with nothing to do tend to lose interest in the play or to get into trouble while your back is turned.

Think about ways to get the most work done in each rehearsal session. Keep your actors as busy as you can. If you have scenes that involve different groups of actors, assign your assistant to rehearse one scene while you are working on another. If you do not have an assistant, ask a responsible cast member to work with one group of actors while you work with another. At the very least they can go over their lines together. If you are working on a musical, the musical director can work on songs or the choreographer can work on dances with one group while you work on dramatic scenes with a different group. If one or two actors are not on stage for a while, the assistant or stage manager can take them aside and help them work on lines.

As the date of the first performance nears, think of ways to build momentum. If you only rehearse once a week, scheduling two or more rehearsals a week during the last weeks will provide the actors with more frequent repetition and generate excitement. Keep the actors clearly focused on what they still need to accomplish and how long they have to do it. Try to do this in a calm, organized manner without creating a sense of impending doom, even if you are feeling that way. You want to push your actors but not panic them. Make them believe they can do it. Even though rehearsing a show can become stressful, especially as opening night looms before you, it is crucial to keep the process fun and exciting. The director must build the cast's confidence and enthusiasm at the same time she is pushing them to give their best, most polished, and professional performance ever.

Types of Rehearsals

Read-Through. The first step in the rehearsal process is the read-through. This is when everyone sits down together and reads through the play from beginning to end. Usually when this is done, the actors read their parts and the stage manager or director reads the stage directions out loud. If you have actors who have reading problems, pair them with actors or assistants who are good readers to help them follow along in the script and pronounce the hard words.

Take time during the read-through to stop and explain things that do not make sense or to act out physical actions that are only described in the stage directions. It is important for the actors to visualize what is going on in the play so they can understand it. It is also important for them to understand what is going on, and why different characters do what they do. Answer questions as you go instead of waiting until the end.

photo by Keith Jenkins

Figure 27: The first read through of the script provides exciting discoveries.

The script should be printed in a typeface that is easy to read, both in terms of style and point size. Make margins big enough so there is enough white space that the words do not look crowded. At least an inch margin on each side should suffice. Copies of the script should be clear and clean, and only on one side of the page. Bind the scripts in notebooks or paper folders with three-hole fasteners so the pages do not fall out and get lost.

Attach a pencil on a string to the script so the actor has it to write down blocking and notes in his script. This idea, invented by Brian's ingenious mother, saves lots of time. When the actor needs a pencil, he does not need to go far to find one; it is already there.

Make sure the actor's name, address, and phone number are on the script so if it is left at rehearsal or gets misplaced, it can be returned to its owner. An actor cannot learn lines without a script! And, just in case a script gets lost or destroyed, make a couple of extra copies.

In each script, highlight that actor's lines and stage directions with a yellow highlighter before the read-through. This way each knows exactly what he says and where it is in the script. When it is time to memorize, he will be able to find all the sections he needs to work on.

If my actors are good enough readers, I make an audio recording of the read-through, edit out the stops and starts, and make copies for each member of the cast. Listening to a recording of the dialogue over and over familiarizes the actors with the action of the play and the sequence of events. Auditory learners often find this is a helpful method for line memorization. If the first read-through has too many starts and stops and explanations, I schedule a second read-through and make my cast recording from that. The time spent on the second read-through is a worthwhile investment if it helps expedite line memorization.

When I am not able to get a decent recording of the script from read-throughs, I ask friends to help me read through and record the script. If you do this, make sure each person reads only one character. Actors will listen for the sound of a specific voice to learn those lines and if a reader is doing multiple parts, the actor might memorize lines are not his.

If the play has songs, I make each cast member a recording of the songs including words and music and, if I can, just the music. The actors can listen to the songs in order to learn the words and music and can practice singing the songs at home between rehearsals using the version without the words. I also edit the songs with words and music into the recording of the whole show.

Blocking Rehearsals. Blocking is the theatre term for the movements an actor makes during a play. Blocking includes moving from one part of the stage to another; specific body positions such as sitting, standing, or kneeling; specific hand, arm, or head gestures; actor focus (where an actor is looking); and use of props. Blocking rehearsals get the actors physically expressing the actions of the play. The director tells the actors where to move and what to do at each moment of the play. As the director gives blocking, anything that is not already written down in the script should be added by the actor next to the appropriate line of dialogue. Actors can suggest blocking, too, but it must be approved by the director. All blocking should be noted in pencil in case it has to be changed later.

Blocking is important in the memorization process because knowing where and when you move during the play makes the lines and the actions more concrete and physical. When an actor can visualize himself in space while going over lines or actually walk through his actions, it is often easier to learn the lines. Helga and Tony Noice, a psychologist and theatre director, respectively, have shown that actors engaged in movement from place to place on stage were better able to recall lines than when they sat in one location and tried to remember them (Noice, Noice, & Kennedy 2000; Noice & Noice 2001). This was true even if the lines did not literally refer to the actions being done.

photo by Lee Ann Rosen

Figure 28: Rehearsing a dance is a great way to express yourself and have fun.

If you are not able to rehearse on the stage you will be performing on, it is important to block the show in a space that is as large as your stage will be. Tape the edges of the "stage" on the floor of your rehearsal space with masking tape. The actors will then be able to see and experience the physical limits of the performing area and begin to develop a sense of the relationship of stage to audience. If there are curtains, wall, set pieces, or furniture that you do not have for rehearsals, tape them on the floor, too. Try to rehearse in the same place each time so the actors do not become confused about the spatial relationships.

Blocking rehearsals usually feel long, boring, and frustrating to actors and directors alike. It takes an extra effort to pay attention, but it is important to do so. Most actors find it easier to memorize lines if they know what their body is doing at the same time the line is being said. They can reinforce the line with the visual image by imagining themselves in the stage space doing the action, or they can actually do the actions as they learn the lines, reinforcing the lines with a kinesthetic experience.

It is helpful to stop blocking early enough in a rehearsal session to run through everything that was blocked that day at least once. The director can see during a blocking run-through if traffic patterns on stage flow easily or if any part of the action looks confusing. The actors can pinpoint what they forgot to write down or where they are confused. The immediate repetition of movement helps cement the blocking in their memory.

When possible, block the play in chronological order from beginning to end. This will make more sense to the actors. Sometimes for reasons of scheduling efficiency, it is necessary to jump from scene to scene. If you do this, try to jump in chronological order so there is some semblance of the play's order for the actors.

Work-Through Rehearsals. Once the play has been completely blocked, it is time to work through the play from moment to moment. Work-throughs are important for clarifying the dramatic action and helping each actor understand his character's motivations and reactions. Work-throughs mean starting and stopping the action. They involve making mistakes, talking through motivation, struggling with newly memorized lines, practicing lines and movements until they flow naturally, and making any necessary changes.

Usually a play that has been improvisationally developed by the group has been explored thoroughly in the development process before the script was written down. However, sometimes more character development is necessary. Additional acting exercises or improvisations might be done as part of a work-through rehearsal.

Work-throughs are a key time in the memorization process of the script. Helga and Tony Noice have discovered how professional actors memorize their many lines in full-length plays and precisely retrieve them night after night. Professional actors do not learn their lines by rote. Instead they use a learning principle the Noices' term "active experiencing" (Noice & Noice 2004). As he rehearses, an actor searches for multiple, very specific meanings on emotional, social, cognitive, and physical levels for the character in each beat (short section of the script) in order to understand what the character is experiencing at that moment. Then at every subsequent rehearsal and performance, an actor tries to actively, genuinely experience those levels with the other actors in the play moment-by-moment. Many professionals report that immersing themselves this fully in the meaning of each moment for their character and connecting their words and performed actions at the deep goal-level (What does the character want to achieve?) makes line memorization happen almost without effort (Noice 1996; Noice & Noice 2007). What does this mean in terms of your actors? It means the more clearly they understand what they are doing on an emotional, cognitive, and physiological level in each moment in the play, the easier it will be for them to remember their lines.

At the end of each work-though, save enough time to run through the scene that you have worked on at least once from beginning to end without stopping. Often things looked at in isolation do not make sense to an actor, but will make sense when put together with what comes before and after.

Run-Through. Once you have worked through the entire play moment to moment, it is time for the first run-through. In a run-through the actors start at the beginning of the play and go all the way through to the end. Run-throughs develop pacing and sequencing in a play.

Normally the first run-through is done off book (all lines memorized). The first run-through tends to be extremely long. The very first time through a play that is supposed to run about 30 minutes can last anywhere from one to two hours, depending on how many things go wrong, how many different set changes have to be choreographed, and how many actors do not know their lines. This time differential can be very disconcerting to the director.

It is difficult to know exactly how much time will be cut off the running time once the actors have found the correct pace and once all the scene transitions are moving smoothly. If the play seems to be horrendously long and there does not seem to be enough time left before opening night to properly rehearse all of it, you may need to start looking for places to make cuts in the script.

The first run-through can also be agonizingly painful for the director to watch because most of the work that the actors have done in the previous moment-to-moment work goes out the window. Do not panic. Do not give up. Do not tear your hair out by the roots. Do not lose your temper. Take a deep breath and keep working — it *will* get better.

Take notes during the run-through. Afterwards, have the cast sit down with their scripts and pencils. Go through your notes with them in order from the beginning of the play to the end of the play. Present your comments in an upbeat, encouraging manner, but point out honestly the areas that still need work. Use humor to make your points, but not sarcasm. Demonstrate blocking changes and other notes rather than just talk about them. Get the actors up and work through sections that you want to change or correct.

Stress the work that needs to be done by each cast member. Be specific: "Speak loudly and clearly. Say each word. Memorize those lines in Scene Four." Saying, "You've got to work harder" is not specific. Present your notes in a manner that leads cast members to believe they can accomplish each task with just a little more commitment and hard work.

It is just as important to tell actors specifically what they are doing well as it is to tell them what they are doing wrong. They need to know not to change something that is working! They need encouragement. "Scene One was excellent! Everyone came in at just the right time.

Everyone is talking at the right speed. Everyone is listening to each other and looking at whoever is speaking. Good job!"

In addition, knowing what is working, what is up to an appropriate level of pacing and energy, provides actors with a concrete model to compare with the not-so-good sections. They know how the scene that is working well feels and they know how the scene that is not working feels. It is much easier to make a change when you know how that change will feel when you get it right.

It is helpful for actors to write down, in their scripts, the director's comments that apply to them so they can review them later. If actors cannot write down their own notes, you can type up your notes after rehearsal and email them or hand them out to be put into script folders before the next rehearsal. Some directors like to give notes immediately after a run-through so that whatever happened in rehearsal is clearly in the minds of all. Other directors find that giving notes before the next rehearsal refreshes the actors' memories on what they need to work on this time.

One technique that works well is to ask each actor before a run-through starts to think of one or two things he will concentrate on improving during that rehearsal. Allowing the actor to decide which of his notes to focus on helps him think critically and objectively about his performance. It also helps him invest himself actively in the improvement of his performance.

After the first run-through, decide if you need to revise your rehearsal schedule or continue with your original plan. You might need to go back and work through certain scenes again or you might feel that more run-throughs would help pull the show together. The last few rehearsals before the dress rehearsal should be run-throughs.

Technical Rehearsals. Technical rehearsals provide the technical crew (light, sound, prop, costume, and set crews under the direction of the stage manager) with a chance to practice what they will be doing during the show. The show should be as together as possible from the acting standpoint *before* the technical rehearsal so the technical crew can get their sight and sound cues clearly from the actors. Patience is the order of the day. Actors should be prepared to stop and start and to run though certain moments of the show several times. Up until this point the actors have had many weeks of rehearsal to get ready. The technical rehearsal is the technicians' first opportunity to rehearse.

Sometimes, if a show is very technically complicated, the technical rehearsal may be done as a cue-to-cue rehearsal. This means the actors do not run through the entire show from beginning to end; they jump from one technical cue to right before the next. A cue-to-cue rehearsal can be very confusing to a cast because the continuity they have become so accustomed to is suddenly gone. I advise against cue-to-cue rehearsals with casts who have special needs unless there is no other way to work out all the cues in the amount of time allotted for technical rehearsal.

A good alternative to a cue-to-cue is a *dry tech*, which is a technical rehearsal that jumps from cue to cue with no actors, only technicians. One drawback of a dry tech is that if a number of cues are visual (based on actions done by the actors) rather than verbal (based on lines spoken from the script), the technicians might not be sure when to enact their cue. Another drawback with improvisational shows is that the lines may change from performance to performance. Technicians will often need to rely on the sense of the scene rather than on literal lines written in their script.

Dress Rehearsals. Dress rehearsals give the actors and technicians a chance to work with all the physical aspects of the show before getting in front of an audience for the first time. Try to run the play from beginning to end without stopping in order to simulate a real performance. If you are brave, invite a few friends or parents to preview the show in order to provide the actors with the experience of having someone out there watching and reacting to their performance.

In theatre there are no guarantees. Do not believe the old saw about a bad dress rehearsal meaning a good opening night or vice versa. I have had good dress rehearsals that led to good opening nights and bad dress rehearsals that scared the cast so much they dug in and pulled together for a good opening night. However, I have also had bad dress rehearsals that led to bad, embarrassing, dreadful, painful, mortifying opening nights. The only thing that inevitably makes a show come together is hard work and commitment from the very first day of the rehearsal by everyone involved. The Theatre Elves will *not* show up at the eleventh hour to throw some fairy dust around and fix your show for you.

Technical Aspects of a Show

Try to keep your show as technically simple as possible. I cannot emphasize that statement enough. Leave as much as you can up to the imagination of the audience. There is great beauty in simplicity — and great theatricality. Ultimately, great theatre happens in the hearts and minds of the audience, not in the trappings on stage.

If the script and the acting are not good, superfluous set dressing, costume changes, and props will not enhance the play. The extra window-dressing will only add more items for the actors to remember or, as will be more likely the case, to forget. Mechanical error goes hand in hand with human error. The fewer technical cues or scene changes in a show, the fewer opportunities there will be for technical disasters.

It is crucial to get as many of the props and set pieces into the hands of the actors as soon as possible in the rehearsal process. All actors — particularly beginners and actors who have cognitive disabilities — have difficulty imagining props and set pieces. They need to work with the real thing. If you cannot get the item that will actually be used in the show, get a reasonable facsimile to use in rehearsal until the real one is bought or made.

Make props, costumes, and set pieces as sturdy and unbreakable as possible. Choose plastic or wooden props over glass or ceramic. One of the immutable laws of the theatre is that if there is a way for an actor to break something during a show, he will. For this reason, always think in terms of safety and worst-case scenarios.

When you have quick costume changes in a show or actors who have limited mobility, arrange for costumes to be built with Velcro fastenings rather than buttons, laces, or zippers. Avoid costumes that will get caught in actors' wheelchairs or other mechanical devices. Make sure long skirts are not so long that they will be tripped over.

If it is possible to have more than one technical or dress rehearsal, do it. Bring the stage technicians in to see a run-through before the technical rehearsal. If they cannot come, videotape a run-through for them. The more knowledgeable they are about your show, the more prepared they will be and the more support they can offer you and your cast.

photo by Lee Ann Rosen

Figure 29: Building and painting scenery, props, and costumes is a way some students enjoy contributing to a production.

Technicians might be other students with or without disabilities who have an interest in being part of the show, they might be teachers or other professionals working for your organization, or they might be parents or volunteers who want to lend a hand. If they have never done this technical job before, provide them with lists of their responsibilities, rules for backstage conduct, directions for turning on and using their equipment, what to do in case of emergency, what to wear during shows, and rehearsal and performance dates and times. If they will be running complicated equipment for the first time, such as a sound deck, lighting board, or followspot, arrange for a time when you, the stage manager, or the technical director can give them an orientation or training session.

Arrange for plenty of backstage help. It is better to have too many stagehands than too few. Stagehands should be given clear assignments during the running of the show. All assignments should be written out and posted on the walls backstage and/or given to the stage manager and stagehands to carry around with them on a clipboard.

Make sure there is a place where the actors can quietly sit when they are not onstage. Assign a stage manager or stagehand to keep an eye on the actors to make sure they do not wander off. Warn actors five minutes before it is time for them to go on, if possible, and then get them to their place of entrance ahead of time.

If actors need to make a costume change, take care of it in a timely fashion. Do not wait until the last minute. Invariably a zipper will get stuck or a hook will get caught and delay the actor's entrance.

Some actors may need a little reminder when to enter at the appropriate moment from the stage manager or backstage assistant. The actor might hesitate because of nerves or get so involved in watching what is going on out on stage that he forgets it is his turn to enter. Some actors need to be reminded what the beginning of their first line is before they are sent out.

Do not ask an actor to try anything new at the last minute — especially anything unusual as far as sets, costumes, and props go. Every actor needs time to rehearse and adjust to changes in the show. It is better to wait and work the change in before the next performance than to throw an actor's performance off by changing an entrance or adding an unexpected responsibility.

The First Performance

Opening Night is a time of great anxiety and excitement. How the director handles the cast prior to the opening curtain can determine how successful the performance is. Stay calm and focused. Actors will mirror the director's mood because the director is the leader. This means the person(s) in charge must be very aware of their verbal and non-verbal emotional messages. If the director is harried, upset, or nervous, the actors will assume they are supposed to feel the same way and mass hysteria will result. If something goes wrong, minimize the size of the problem to the cast. Calmly and efficiently invent a quick and easy solution. After all, the show must go on.

Opening night nerves — stage fright — is a common problem for actors. I know professional actors who have worked in theatre for 30 years who still get so scared before opening night that they throw up. Sir

Laurence Olivier, one of the greatest actors who ever lived, went through a period of stage fright in the middle of his career. While he was playing Shylock in Shakespeare's *The Merchant of Venice* he could barely force himself to go on stage each night. Some performances he was so frightened that he could not look any of the other actors in the eyes; he just focused on the floor.

Stage fright can be dealt with if actors understand what causes it. Whenever a person feels stressed or fearful, his adrenal glands, which are located on top of the kidneys, secrete a hormone called adrenaline. Adrenaline is used by the body to create extra energy for two purposes: attacking a problem or running away from it — the proverbial fight-or-flight mechanism that living creatures experience when faced with danger.

Facing a performance in front of a large audience of family, friends, and strangers is a very stressful situation, so great amounts of adrenaline are released into the bloodstream, creating all those strange feelings of panic, those butterflies in the stomach. If an actor allows his flight pattern to kick in, he will forget his lines and freeze up on stage. If he concentrates and channels his energy, he can tap into his fight response and use it to enhance his performance.

The key to channeling adrenaline-based energy is getting enough oxygen. When a person feels nervous or tense, breathing becomes shallow. This cuts down the supply of oxygen to the body. The muscles in the body tense up, because the toxins created by stress are not being cleaned away by the oxygen in the blood. As less oxygen gets to the brain, thinking becomes confused.

To stay calm and use energy wisely, an actor needs to continue to breathe slowly and deeply. With his oxygen supply restored, his muscles will relax and he will start thinking clearly again. His energy will become focused, his body will become centered, his emotions will feel balanced, and his mind will become alert. He then has at his disposal all of his most powerful inner resources. Mind, body, and emotions will be connected and ready to do his bidding.

I explain as much of this process as a group is able to understand. Since one of the symptoms of stage fright is the inability to focus on what is going on around you, I usually go over the information with the cast at the dress rehearsal *before* they start feeling nervous. Then I go over it again on opening night in my pre-show speech.

An explanation might be as simple as: If you feel nervous or scared during the show, just take a few slow breaths and let yourself relax. Then you won't feel as scared. Try not to think about being scared. Try to focus on what you are doing on stage.

When suggesting to actors to breathe, caution against breathing too quickly. If they start to hyperventilate, they could pass out. This will make matters worse.

If the actors are not wearing a lot of complicated makeup, call them to arrive at the theatre about 30 minutes before curtain time. This is usually enough time to get everyone in costume and ready to go on. Nervous actors waiting around backstage with nothing constructive to focus on will only become more nervous.

About five or ten minutes before curtain time, call all the actors together. This is the time for everyone to collect themselves and make last-minute attitude preparations for the performance. You might choose to run a short warm-up or give them a motivational speech. Different directors have different rituals they like to perform with their casts before the opening night of a show.

I try to boil my notes down to three things I want everyone to remember while they are performing. One year I told them, "Speak loudly, clearly, and slowly. Don't think about how nervous you are; think about how much fun you are having." Another year I told them, "Remember the three Ls: Listen (to the other actors), Look (at whoever is talking), and Loud!" I remind them to relax and keep breathing. Most importantly, I try to build up their confidence by telling them what a great job they are doing. Actors need to feel that their director thinks the world of them.

BAPA had a nice opening-night tradition: Everyone held hands and passed a squeeze around the circle. Once the squeeze had made it all the way around, everyone said in unison, "One for all and all for one. Have a good show!"

Expectations

In my theatre training, the highest compliment that could be paid to a student actor was that he or she performed as a professional or at a professional level. I hold my actors to the same standard. I insist that they approach the rehearsal process and performance experience with as professional an attitude as possible. And I insist that we have fun at the same time.

The amazing thing about audiences is that they can tell if the actors are miserable or if they are having a good time. They can tell if the experience of putting on the show has been a positive or a negative one. An audience's enjoyment of a performance is ultimately tied to their perception of the actors' enjoyment and engagement with the work.

If the performance is not perfect, that is okay. There is no such thing as a perfect performance. Mistakes happen even in the professional theatre. What is important are the goals you set for yourself and how you handle yourself as you go about striving for those goals. The distance traveled from the beginning of the process to the end is what determines the success or failure of a project, not the final product.

When I was working at a summer arts camp, a student in my musical-comedy class was so shy and quiet that I could barely hear her speak when I was standing next to her. I did not know her background, so I do not know what caused her lack of self-confidence, but she was so afraid to express herself that in conversation she spoke in a monotone. She rarely gestured or showed any kind of emotion. In that class I had the good fortune to be working with an incredible team of co-teachers who really knew how to encourage and train young students in acting, music, and dance. By the time we presented our original musical revue at the end of camp, she had developed enough self-confidence and stage presence that I could hear every single word that she said clearly from my seat at the back of the house. She danced, she sang, and she had expression in her voice. I was so proud of her for facing her fears and working so hard!

After the performance another counselor who had no connection with the project made a remark to me about how mediocre this camper's performance had been in comparison with the other campers in the show.

He was judging her solely on her final product. He did not know the progress she had made and how incredibly far she had come in four short weeks. But the girl knew how far she had come, and so did the other cast members and the staff members involved with the show.

As a result of her experience, this young woman became less timid. Her self-confidence grew. Most important, she learned how to take a risk. In truth, she probably learned more and grew more as a performer than anyone else in the cast. Out of all the students I taught, out of all the performances I coached, *she* is the one I consider my biggest success story of the summer.

In looking at the success or failure of a performance, your evaluation cannot be based solely on the final product, but also on the journey that was taken to get there. What skills were learned along the way? How many friendships were formed? How much fun did you all have together? These are the signposts of success.

So go out and do your best, and have a great time doing it.

What Being Involved in Theatre Means to Me
by Claudia Bocock

In 1995 I wrote a play about my life entitled "How Can I Keep from Singing?" At the time I was a part-time student in Boston University's Theatre Arts Division. Eve Muson, my theatre professor and director, gave me the option of writing and performing a play about my life in the spring semester. I did so much writing day after day, independently answering Eve's questions. Then Eve would help me edit the details of my past life and my future dreams into a play. I learn better with one-on-one instruction anyway, therefore, I was so diligent with all my writing and talking to Eve. I trusted her idea, that my speaking out and sharing honest feelings and realistic facts would be worth all the effort. Other selected actors helped me present my life on stage, helped me know more of myself. I learned how to work around whatever situations were in my life the right way and look at how I wanted to change it. My play was presented in our School of Fine Arts and in the Vermont Festival. Although I was glad to have done that, some scenes were so uncomfortable with painful memories. However, all the thinking, writing, and acting was therapeutic to me and worth all the effort. Enough that I want to do the same kind of work writing details of my life after 1995 and have someone re-edit all my writing into a play with some new positive flavors.

To me, theatre is about all kinds of different stories being acted out. Anyone who allows him or herself the freedom of imagining what his/her character's objective is can clearly present the flavors, colors, textures, and tones of his/her character. Theatre is partly for actors' enjoyments and partly for the sake of expressing their many feelings and thoughts that they can otherwise not completely do in the real world off stage. It is certainly therapeutic to me, helping me feel that I am being heard. I also understand that theatre presentations are done for the sake of the audience member to learn by watching the characters' journeys. So to me, theatre is for fun and education whether I act and sing on stages or watch as an audience member.

Through musical performances like listening to the Boston Symphony Orchestra or singing in a church choir or the Boston University chorus I can feed my heart, soul, and mind, enabling me to leave at the end feeling I have had a good experience with a smile to last me awhile. My listening to lovely music sung by choir members often brightens my spirit. And just as much my own singing of hymns, songs, and tunes in concerts and musical performances is such a good comfort. I believe that the audience *hears* me and my voice. I feel the same way whether I'm singing a solo or not.

There are many ways theatre has been important to me. Many times my concentration of acting in clear characters with some big expressions coming out of me was and will always be therapeutic, partly because I feel that I am being heard and much more listened to than I am in the real world. While I have been doing more and more stories on stage, I have been learning bit by bit to project better in the best

possible way for the audience's sake as well as for my
character's sake. I also enjoy it because relationships on stage
seem more definite to me than the discomfort of my not
knowing the truth of some relationships I have with others in
the real world. That is why I am more poised on stage than in
the real world. Since scripts can't be changed, I'm more
secure and comfortable knowing what to expect through each
journey.

Acting has most certainly helped me believe more in
myself. It still helps me find more of what I want to be in life.
Acting and singing are "self-searching life batteries" to keep
my life running well. I feel so normal on stage, despite my
disabilities.

=========================

Being an Actor
J. P. Illaramendi

In high school I went to an acting program and I was
excited to have the opportunity of learning how to act and
how to become an actor. I love learning new things. I am so
excited to be able to perform in many plays. I love to create
characters that are associated with myself or characters that
are very different from myself.

First of all, when I receive a script, I have to memorize all
the lines of this character. I read it very, very carefully and use
my emotions to know what the character is saying underneath
his lines. Let's say that the character is classy and there's a
line in the script that is classy, I would perform it that way. Or
if the character is selfish — I would have to learn how to be
selfish and I would say the line in a selfish way. Finding the
character is in the moods of the character, it's the behavior of
the character, the attitude of the character. It's all underneath
the lines.

When I am acting, it's as if I am that character because my
name is no longer JP. I become that character. The character
is using my emotions, he is using a part of me to portray his
emotions, but these emotions are the character's emotions,

and JP is private — outside of the acting. I know that I'm not the character. I really use my own emotions — my outside world — while I am acting, but I am no longer JP, but I am also still myself.

Being in theatre affected my personal life because I got to be part of the outside world and pretend. Being able to pretend you can do something wrong and learn the big difference so you don't do it in real life. It is better to pretend and not do some things for real. Acting is based on real life. We must portray things realistically, but we cannot have the audience think that this is really happening — it's just part of the play, it's just part of the show, although at the same time it is part of your self.

I have made a lot of good relationships with others that were in the same plays as me and I've learned how to get along with my cast members and my director. We support one another, we work hard in rehearsals, and we give our best to make a good performance. Sometimes you help out others. You need to worry about your part, but at the same time support the other person. It's a give and take. If someone messes up a line during the show, I would help him myself. As my character I would say something that would help him remember his line. I did that during *Godspell* with the actor who played Judas.

I decided I wanted to be a professional actor when I was in *Lyle the Crocodile* and I signed autographs and got paid for it. I thought, "Hmmm I can do this with other shows." So I've done it with another called *Perfectly Persephone*. I recently did a documentary film about people with disabilities finding jobs called *Imagine Working*.

Off stage I work as an usher at the Kennedy Center. When I am ushering, I am making sure that all the patrons are feeling okay and are able to go on and see the show. I sit them down in their seats and pass out play programs if they have forgotten to get one earlier and I flash my flashlight for those that come late because it is so dark in the theatre. When they ask for directions to go somewhere, I tell them. If it's a question I can't answer, I get someone else who can tell them better than me. I see the shows that other actors do and I sometimes can think of myself as being up there on stage without actually doing it.

I just want to be like everybody else: to be a professional actor, to get paid like everybody else. I just have this dream like being like others who have Down syndrome like me. Like Chris Burke. My goal is to take the example of this guy. I really want to go out there and expand my artistic abilities as an actor in theatre. Right now my goal is to keep doing it — to be a real actor, whether it is being a fictional character or portraying a real live person. I can be anybody I am asked to portray — real or pretend. I'm ready to go out there and do other performances with other theatres. That is a new goal for me. I can audition for professional plays and if I do get accepted, then I am ready to act for the performance. I just love acting. Keep on calling me and I'll audition because I am happy to keep expanding my ability as an actor.

======================

What My Drama Experience Means to Me
Mary Ann McNally

As a disabled American, I have been faced many times with having to prove myself to others, but I was welcomed freely into the drama program at BAPA while I was a teenager and accepted just as I was. Over the course of three years, I participated in Pegasus, the Senior Shakespeare Company, and several acting classes: one in scene study, one in musical theatre, and one in ancient Greek theatre.

With the help of my classmates and my teacher Sally Bailey, two things happened for me. First, I proved to the people who came to the plays that a person with a disability can do anything a person without a disability can. Second, I had an absolute BLAST in the process. Because I had never been included in theatre productions at my high school, I never knew how exciting acting could be. I even won an acting award at the Folger Shakespeare Festival High School Competition, playing the role of Phebe, the Shepherdess, in a scene from *As You Like It*.

In 1995 Sally was contacted by the Kennedy Center for the Performing Arts. They were looking for a teenaged actor who used a wheelchair. She thought I would be interested in being in a professional production and I was! I went to the audition and they cast me in *Fiesta!*, a children's play that was having its premiere. It was an exciting experience and I felt like a real professional actor!

These things combined taught me what acting truly means to me. When I am on stage, it is as if a light has been turned on inside me — a light that shines brilliantly from my head to my toes. A feeling of freedom fills my heart and soul like a wave crashing down on me. It is at that pivotal moment that this feeling takes the form of a voice in my head saying, "Let go — you're free! Free to forget all your problems, all your concerns, all your worries, and for one glimmering moment, be someone else." It is as if suddenly I have become my character and my character has become me.

I will never forget my drama experience as long as I live.

====================================

A Parent's Experience
Joyce Glenner

Sarah's introduction to public speaking was in high school when she was invited to join MELS (Montgomery Exceptional Leaders), a group of high school students with disabilities who met with elementary school students to tell them about their disability and their hopes and dreams in order to increase disability awareness. Sarah prepared her talk, but on the day she was to speak, she panicked and fled from the classroom.

I was delighted a short time later to receive a call from Sally Bailey asking me if I knew any young people who might be interested in taking a drama class and being part of a special needs program at the Bethesda Academy of Performing

Arts. Sarah was her first student and from the first class, she has had a successful and gratifying experience with drama.

After several years taking classes and performing in a show every year, Sarah began joining other companies. With the Paradigm Players, a community theatre of actors with and without disabilities, she performed as a chorus member in *Godspell* and *Working*, and played the role of Rebecca in *Our Town*. She has also danced with Seize the Day Mixed Abilities Dance Company. Sarah enjoys attending the theatre and has many friends in theatre companies in the area.

Through discussion, improvisation, character development, and acting, Sarah has learned important life and job skills. In her acting career she has developed listening skills, respect for others and their opinions, how to follow directions and to focus on the task. At her job she has become more flexible and learned how to behave in difficult situations. Personally, she is more self-assured and confident and takes pride in her accomplishments.

As a parent I have watched and wondered at the growth in my daughter and anticipate her continuing to enjoy acting. On a visit to London she was introduced to Dame Judi Dench, one of England's greatest actors. Sarah said, "I'm happy to meet you. I'm an actor, too!"

=====================================

A Parent's View
Karen Martel

I cannot put into words how wonderful this drama experience has been for my daughter. It has helped her find her identity and has expanded her pool of friends and her style of socializing. She has been exposed to a wider range of kids that she gets in her class at school.

I have seen the child we knew was inside, but which we rarely saw at home, come out on stage. In real life my daughter is very shy and quiet in social settings, but during the plays she is not afraid of the audience. On stage she is at her most confident, most assertive, her most centered self. Being in the plays gives her something entirely her own. With Pegasus she decides for herself: she chooses to participate, she helps write the play, she decides what role she's going to play. She doesn't have to prove anything. It is something all her own.

It is very hard for kids with special needs to have a large group of friends. They tend to be very isolated. I see her involvement in drama class as a great social experience. In class the staff model appropriate and respectful behavior for the children and they pick it up and model it back. They treat the children as young adults and listen to their ideas. The students learn by their actions how to treat others with respect.

The very first year our daughter was in Pegasus, she said, (and I will never forget this), "Sally makes us get up on stage and shout out our lines." She said this with so much pride and excitement. Most of the time adults tell our children to be quiet. They do not want to hear what they have to say. But in drama what they have to say matters.

By the end of the year she has had not only a great theatrical experience, but she has learned how to stick to a task, how to be responsible and show up for rehearsal, she has created and maintained many social relationships, and she has a sweet taste in her mouth, looking forward to next year.

The Arts Access Program has given us the chance to see our daughter shining. In our family life she is usually not the shining one. But on stage she can do it better than anyone else in the family. There is a ripple effect into how all of this affects the lives of the immediate and extended family of the child who has a disability. It is extremely hard for these families to find something that the whole family can participate in and enjoy together and it is almost impossible to find something in which the family can celebrate that child — celebrate something that the child can do that no one else can do better. Our family and friends and neighbors can come to see our daughter in the performances and celebrate her success. After they see her in a play, they begin to see her in a whole new light.

========================

One Grateful Brother
Ken Moore

Six days before Mother's Day 1993, liver cancer stole my mother from my sister and me. The month before my sister had performed in *The WBAP Love Hour*, a musical performed by an arts access troupe for people with and without disabilities. I have watched my sister Leslie Ellen perform for more than 13 years, but her troupe's performance in 1993 will always be the one I most remember. It will always be the one that best demonstrates the power and importance that theatre and drama have on my sister's life.

In the last production my mother saw Leslie perform, my sister sang "Wind Beneath My Wings." Although the song was incorporated into the musical that her troupe performed, the message was clear. Leslie pointed to our mom, sang to our mom, and smiled to our Mom, hiding the tears for backstage where we gathered after the show.

Leslie's director, Sally Bailey, knew the severity of my mother's illness and gave Leslie the gift she needed to help her cope and grieve my mother's illness and soon-to-be death. Singing "Wind Beneath My Wings" gave Leslie the opportunity to say goodbye. For my mother, the song — and show — gave her final hope that Leslie would always have a circle of friends that would support her.

Leslie has performed with her troupe ever since. Although no year has been as emotional, the power of her inclusion in drama is certainly still poignant. Drama gives Leslie access to express her voice and her musical talent. On stage, Leslie is not a woman in a wheelchair — a woman with disabilities. Leslie is a performer who moves audiences with her dance, smile, and song.

Theatre has been a blessing to Leslie and our family. I cannot imagine my sister's life without her having the opportunity to act, sing, and perform. As well as giving her the chance to shine in something she enjoys, drama has given Leslie the chance to grow.

Through the years, I also saw how others grew from their involvement in Leslie's company.

For years, I worked as a professional in the disability field, assisting students with disabilities transition from school to work. I saw the importance drama programs had on students in their preparation for careers and work endeavors. By performing in an intense, yearlong experience, actors learned a wealth of skills that they took with them to their jobs. Drama helped students in development of important social and professional skills. Because cast members were given specific roles and expected to perform to professional standards, they learned the same type of expectations inherent in any work atmosphere.

Performing in an acting troupe also allowed students the opportunity to develop essential communications skills to be able to present themselves professionally and confidently to employers. Most importantly, actors learned commitment and a work ethic: commitment to a work schedule, commitment to co-workers (the acting troupe), and commitment to following a task from its beginning to end.

But drama programs do not only impact the actors and actresses with disabilities who are involved, it inspires advocacy, awareness, and change in the audiences and in the cast members without disabilities. While watching a show, audiences are not only entertained, they also watch inclusion at its finest — where everyone works together, where everyone has a role.

===========================

The Paradigm Players
Jade Ann Gingerich, Director of Employment Policy, Maryland Department of Disabilities

In 1996, as a part of my graduate work for a Masters of Science in Special Education with a specialization in Transition from The Johns Hopkins University, I founded The Paradigm Players, a community theatre company for individuals with and without disabilities. This volunteer-run 501(3)(c) company had as its motto "celebrating differences, challenging perceptions" and was designed to offer a high quality, integrated performing arts experience for all performers.

Funded by the Maryland Developmental Disabilities Council, the members of the Paradigm Players represent the broad spectrum of disabilities including individuals with visual impairments, mobility impairments, and developmental disabilities, such as autism and Down syndrome as well as individuals without disabilities. Having a core of individuals with developmental disabilities, who, through the Arts Access Program at the Bethesda Academy of Performing Arts had received excellent training and were ready to participate in an integrated experience, aided in the success of this company.

Individuals without disabilities who participated in The Paradigm Players productions were drawn by the quality of the work, which is of utmost importance for integrated opportunities to be effective and meaningful. Setting high expectations, while providing appropriate supports, allowed all the participants, particularly those with disabilities, to achieve above and beyond their previous abilities. Performances were directed and designed for disability to be secondary to artistry. As a result of the success of The Paradigm Players, the number of performing opportunities for individuals with disabilities in the Washington, DC, area has increased dramatically, although the need still exists for high quality training for individuals with disabilities and integrated performing opportunities.

Linking Performing Arts to Employment

While the arts are often viewed only as fun, well-designed arts training can be a critical aid in increasing the employability of individuals with disabilities. Employment is an achievable outcome for individuals with disabilities if they possess the necessary skills, including: job-specific, job-seeking, and so-called *soft* skills, such as the ability to get along with others, follow through with work assignments, arrive at work on time, dress appropriately, etc. While soft skills are frequently cited as the most critical to obtaining and sustaining employment outcomes, this area of skill development receives the least amount of formal training. The performing arts can serve to develop these less tangible, but equally important skills. Many skills required for success in the workplace can be obtained through the rehearsal and performance process.

Understanding Employer Expectations Related to Daily Work Behaviors

Being able to participate as part of a team, showing up on time, arriving ready to work, knowing how to provide and receive constructive criticism have all been cited by employers as critical skills. These are all skills that can be acquired and refined through the performing arts.

In addition to these skills, participation in the performing arts allows individuals with disabilities to learn to take risks, try something new, manage nervousness, and be more flexible and adaptable, all of which can improve their job performance. Developing their acting skills enables individuals with disabilities to learning how to appropriately select and express emotions based on the context or setting. Finally, taking direction and listening, being held accountable, and developing an understanding of how individual contributions contribute to the success of the whole, are all skills that can be learned and refined through engaging in the performing arts.

Appropriate Interviewing Skills

Learning how to make eye contact, building and being able to exude self-confidence, and "selling" oneself on stage leads to improved interviewing skills that, again, improve employment outcomes. Even choosing an appropriate interview outfit can be developed through learning how to select appropriate costumes.

Reading, Memorization, and Related Necessary Educational Skills

In some cases, linking the arts to a necessary educational outcome can be very beneficial. In one instance, an individual with Down syndrome, who loved to act and wanted to take an acting class at a local community college, was required to pass a remedial-reading course in order to enroll. When he saw the link between the remedial reading course, something he had struggled with, and the acting class, something he greatly desired, he was able to successfully pass the reading course.

Developing a Personal Network

Personal networks are valuable both for social interactions as well as job networking. The majority of jobs result from personal networks. Too frequently the individual with disability's networks are small and consist mainly of other individuals with disabilities. Engaging individuals with and without disabilities in arts experiences can lead to valuable personal networks that, in turn, can result in job opportunities. This experience also provides long-term friendships, personal satisfaction with life, and more meaningful daily lives.

For those who have jobs, having arts experience can serve as a personal interest that an individual with disabilities can share with co-workers. Common personal interests with work colleagues, be it the arts or sports or other areas, are critical to building effective working relationships. Having something in common helps to divert focus from the ways in which people are different and allows them to bond over the ways in which they are alike. Positive social relationships can be critical to the success of individuals with disabilities in the work place.

Handling Disappointment and Getting Along with Colleagues.

The nature of the performing arts is such that not every individual has a chance to play the role that they want. Learning to deal with disappointment, particularly when it comes to casting decisions and working at doing a good job with whatever role is assigned on stage or off, regardless of its perceived importance to the overall production, can be a very valuable skill. Life is not fair, but we do not have the luxury, either in theatre or at work, to do only what we want, lash out at others, or to walk away, when we do not get what we want.

Types of Arts Experiences

While the performing arts can be a means to acquire skills that correlate with employment success, there are several types of arts-based experiences for individuals with disabilities. In the design, implementation, and marketing of performances that include or feature individuals with disabilities, it is important that the type of arts-based experience be reflected accurately. The various types of arts based experiences include:

- Therapeutic (process-based and focused on individuals using the arts to express their feelings).
- Recreational (based on fun and camaraderie and less on quality).
- Educational (for the purpose of acquiring specific skills or abilities to be used either for enjoyment or for mastery of specific process-based or outcome-based skills).
- A combination of the three types.

Process versus Outcome-based Arts Experiences

When engaging in outreach and marketing, it is important to accurately reflect the intent of the arts-based experience. Misrepresenting the type of experience can sometimes lead to negative stereotypes of the artistic abilities of individuals with disabilities, particularly when process-based therapeutic, recreational, or educational programs are presented as being professional arts products.

Because of their enjoyment of the process focus of therapeutic, recreational, and many educational arts experiences, individuals with disabilities may decide to seek a career in the arts. If this happens, they need to be prepared for the realities and challenges of professional training. That is not to say that individuals with disabilities are not able to meet the demands or expectations of training for a career in the arts, but they must be prepared and understand how the expectations and demands will differ from the process-based experiences they have enjoyed participating in.

Increasing Opportunities for Individuals with Disabilities in the Arts

Increasing opportunities of any type for individuals with disabilities to engage in the arts is important. Equally critical is for individuals who are interested in careers in the arts to be equipped with the necessary skills and encouraged to pursue professional level training. Having more professional artists with disabilities is essential to ensuring that disability, as a natural part of the human experience, is accurately reflected on stage, on television, on screen, and in print. As a result of legislation, such as the Americans with Disabilities Act, individuals with disabilities are now visible in every aspect of society and it is important that all aspects of the arts reflect our contemporary, diverse communities.

=================================

Open Circle Theatre: A Professional Barrier-Free Theatre
Suzanne Richard

Open Circle Theatre (OCT) is Washington, DC's, only professional theatre dedicated to producing professional productions that integrate the considerable talents of artists with disabilities. DC has a vibrant and varied theatre scene, supporting roughly 70 professional theatre companies that focus on anything from theatre and dance fusion to promoting the work of different cultural and religious groups. I heard Bill Ivey, the former Chair of the National Endowment for the Arts, speak one afternoon. He promoted the idea that the way people with disabilities should begin achieving equality in our society was to start with the arts: putting the role models on stage and screen and getting involved in other areas to begin to shape their own image. As an actress with a disability myself, it occurred to me that what the Nation's Capitol lacked was a place where artists with disabilities could be showcased and mentored.

In 2003, at the urging of the local community, we set out to present Christopher Durang's comedy *Laughing Wild* as the first Open Circle Theatre production in a local theatre pub's back room. As I had a physical disability myself and would be performing as well as co-directing the play, I suggested to the group that we advertise ourselves as a company interested in showcasing artists and arts administrators with disabilities in order to see if we had any interest from the public.

To our delight, the response was overwhelming and many of our current staff and board members are people with and without disabilities who responded to our new mission statement and came to not only support, but to get involved. We had clearly identified and tapped into a community within the DC theatre scene which had been feeling underrepresented and without a voice. They helped us to create a solid board and to begin the process of raising the level of programming to that of a small, non-profit theatre company. We decided that our second project would be more ambitions: Andrew Lloyd Webber & Tim Rice's rock-opera *Jesus Christ Superstar*.

After holding open auditions, we had a cast of 27 people including six with identified disabilities, a production staff of 10 including four with identified disabilities and set off on an odyssey of growth and creativity. Artists with and without disabilities pushed the boundaries of their own perceived limitations. We were able to integrate ASL or real-time captioning throughout the production using the screen also used for multi-media design, shadow interpreters with fully realized characters, and, in one case, a Deaf actress cast as a Priest and another character playing her actual interpreter. Dances were choreographed for people with and without wheelchairs, vision, and hearing.

In the end, we were able to stay true to the Open Circle ideal that disability can enhance a performance, not be an obstacle. When Jesus told the sick from his wheelchair to heal themselves, the impact could be felt in the room. All of the hard work produced a show the *Washington Post* called "creative and refreshing" and received four Helen Hayes Nominations (DC's equivalent to the Tony Awards), including Outstanding Resident Musical.

A favorite anecdote I like to tell, an example of how we were able to meet another Open Circle ideal of showcasing artists with and without disabilities by showing themselves and others skills they may not have realized they possessed, involves an actor who is blind. He had been a singer with the same band for twenty years and had trouble getting evenings off from that band to do the show. They were not interested in having him "moonlight" in a field that they saw as having no correlation to their own work. In fact, they had refused to give him a Saturday night off that fell on our closing night. Reluctantly, we had searched around and found a wonderful understudy for the final show. Although the actor had invited his band members often to come see the show, they had not been able to make it until the weekend before the show ended. After seeing our artist sing, dance, and act, they were amazed. They not only gave him the next Saturday off, they began to incorporate him into the dance moves they had been doing for the last twenty years that they had assumed, due to his lack of sight, he would not be able to do. He is now an even more vital member of the band.

As we looked to continue our work, we all agreed that disability does not limit the range of works that can be produced on stage because, when it comes down to it, we all have disabilities of one sort or another. With this in mind, we set out to produce Bertolt Brecht's moving and politically charged show *The Caucasian Chalk Circle*. This cast of 15 had five actors with disabilities and the production staff included five people with disabilities including one of the co-directors. The show focused more on communication, with all actors learning to sign most of their lines and also creating a gestural language, as well as including two audio describers in the company so that every show could be accessible to patrons who were blind or had low vision.

Our fourth production was a return to our small-cast beginnings, looking to explore women's self-image as influenced by our society's preoccupation with pornography and fantasy. By casting Clare McIntyre's classic of modern feminism *Low Level Panic* with two women without identified disabilities and one woman with a disability, we hope to engage the community in a healthy discussion about the sexuality of people with disabilities, which is often marginalized.

As we seek to expand, we are heartened by our history of growth. The artists and designers that we have worked with have come to be very adamant about describing people with disabilities as having "identified disabilities." They discovered, through working together, that everyone has strengths and weaknesses and, in a sense, their own disabilities. And our artists with disabilities have gotten work in other theatres in the community as this attitude has spread into the mainstream of DC theatre. We are inspired by our ability to show the community at large that people with disabilities can do and be anything in the roles they play on stage and the functions they fulfill off stage. Open Circle Theatre faces the future with great hope.

Recommended Reading

Hodge, F. (1971). *Play Directing: Analysis, Communication, and Style*. Upper Saddle River, NJ: Prentice-Hall.

11. Drama as a Classroom Teaching Tool

Learning Styles

Each person has an individual learning style, a unique way of taking in and understanding the world. Learning style depends on sensory channel preference, strengths and weaknesses in various areas of intelligence, motivation to learn, emotional orientation toward the subject and the specific learning environment (teacher, school, classroom), thinking-style preference (for example, global versus analytic-specific), the presence or absence of a cognitive disability, as well as various other health, social, and emotional issues.

A teacher who understands the basic learning style of each student will be more successful in communicating with and teaching all her students. A teacher who understands her own basic learning style knows her personal bias for presenting information to others and can compensate for her natural proclivities by consciously presenting material in other ways. This will make her teaching methods accessible to all her students instead of just the ones who have a style similar to hers.

Our current educational system is structured to present most information in a manner that favors individuals who have an auditory learning channel preference. Lectures, followed by individual reading assignments and worksheets, are the primary teaching strategies. Students are treated as passive receptacles into which education is poured by wise teachers. Despite many years of attempts at educational reforms to make schools more active and interactive, most classroom environments remain static, stationary, and regimented. Each student is assigned a desk in an orderly row for the majority of the school day. That small, rectangular workspace must suffice for all learning activities. This arrangement can create order and structure for students, by helping to organize and focus them and providing enough physical and mental discipline to free them to grapple with the academic material in the curriculum. But for some students, those who need to move and use their bodies to learn or who need a variety of visual models and demonstrations to understand, this type of classroom structure can be stifling. For students who learn best through social interaction, this isolated type of learning can feel like being exiled or imprisoned. After all, by the time they start formal schooling, developmentally students have progressed from solitary through parallel and associative to cooperative abilities in relating with others.

Whether they have a cognitive disability or not, many students will not do well in our current educational system if they do not process information best in the style in which it is primarily presented. Teachers can reach more students if they center their teaching approach on students' learning needs and intelligence strengths. At first glance, this sounds very complex, mysterious, and difficult to undertake. Teachers feel intimidated and say that it is hard enough to cover all the content they are required to cover without getting fancy in their delivery of information. To provide a number of additional approaches individualized to students or to add any additional areas to the curriculum seems like an overwhelming burden, an impossible, exhausting task.

The truth is, however, that the more sensory channels, intelligences, and abilities that are addressed in the learning process, the more *all* students learn and the more they retain. Curriculum material that is retained does not need to be repeated year after year after year. Students can go on to new and more advanced areas of study, applying their new knowledge to previously acquired information and skills. As a bonus, students who are engaged in learning are not creating trouble or tuning out.

In practice, teaching to students' learning styles is exciting, challenging, and fun. This approach brings out the creativity and joy of education in teacher and student alike. Suddenly, students' educational needs are being addressed and they look forward to coming to school. Instead of sitting sullenly and passively at their desks, they *want* to participate in class. They begin to actively seek out knowledge on their own, teach themselves, and become life-long learners.

This chapter offers a number of suggestions for using drama and other arts as tools to enhance teaching in regular and special education classrooms. Before focusing on specific exercises or looking at different curriculum areas, a closer look will be taken at sensory channel preferences, socio-emotional learning, and Howard Gardner's theory of multiple intelligences (M.I. theory). A teacher who can incorporate these three philosophies along with the arts when looking at, thinking about, and experiencing their students' learning styles has an eye-opening and unbeatable combination on her side. Please keep in mind that all of these theories are constructs to help frame thinking about delivery of teaching. They are windows into alternate processes of generating learning different from the traditional chalk-and-talk methods.

Sensory Channel Preference

We experience the world around us first and foremost through our senses. Therefore, our senses are our main avenues for learning — our primary tools for bringing information into our brains and making contact with the curriculum. To fully exploit and enhance the senses for learning purposes, every teacher must understand how these learning tools work.

There is some discussion among experts about how many senses the human body actually has. The five senses — vision, hearing, smell, taste, and touch — bring information from the outside in. In addition, the human body evaluates its experience from the inside using deep senses — balance, proprioception, deep pressure, hunger, thirst, pain, cold, and heat. Each sense, interior or exterior, carries a different kind of information through the nervous system to the brain for interpretation, evaluation, and, usually, for some type of action.

Vision or sight provides information about color, line, shape, depth, movement, and distance of objects from the self in the outside environment. The eye is the organ of sight. Light enters the pupil of the eye and strikes photoreceptor cells (rods and cones, so called because of their shape) located in the retina at the back of the eyeball. These cells convert the light into electrical impulses that are carried by the optic nerve to the visual cortex located at the rear of the brain. There the impulses are translated into information that we recognize as visual.

Humans consciously rely on their sense of sight more than any other. The human eye provides more information, especially in regard to color and depth perception, than the eyes of many other creatures. This is because human retinas have cones which are sensitive to the color wavelengths of light and because the shape of our heads and placement of our eyes on the face makes stereoptical sight (seeing an object with both eyes at the same time) possible. The importance of vision to the human being is indicated by the fact that ten percent of the brain is devoted to the visual cortex, a larger percentage of brain area than that given over to any other sense. Between 80 and 90 percent of information taken in by our brains is visual (Jensen 2000). The visual cortex is very specialized: vertical lines are processed by one type of brain cell, horizontal lines by another, diagonal lines by yet another, and so on.

The brain is biased to notice color, light, darkness, motion, form, and depth; therefore, when varied and contrasted, these aspects of vision will be memorable for learners. Experiments have shown that pairing information with color can strengthen memory recall for that information (Vuontela et al. In: Jensen 2000). Color, in particular, has a strong effect on learners because it can affect how we feel. Some colors promote alertness while others promote relaxation. The optimal colors for learning seem to be yellow, light orange, beige, or off-white because they stimulate positive, alert feelings (Jensen 2000).

Hearing processes sound waves or vibration, providing information about the presence or absence of sound, tone (sometimes called timbre), volume, pitch, harmony or dissonance, rhythm, distance, and direction of the vibration's source. The ear is one of the most complex sense organs. The outer ear, or auricle, gathers sound waves and channels them into the ear canal, which leads to the eardrum. The eardrum vibrates and these vibrations are enlarged and passed on by the ossicles in the middle ear: three small bones called the malleus (hammer), the incus (anvil), and the stapes (stirrup), respectively. The ossicles pass vibrations on to the inner ear or cochlea. The cochlea looks like a snail shell and is filled with fluid. The enhanced vibrations create waves in the cochlea, which then vibrate its basilar membrane, and the hair cells attached to it. This sets off nerve impulses that are sent by the auditory nerve to the auditory cortex in the center of the brain. These impulses are translated into information we "hear."

The ear itself does not differentiate among the sound waves coming into it. It just collects and passes along all vibrations in the vicinity. It is the job of the auditory cortex and frontal lobes to sort through the incoming stimuli and decide which information to pay attention to. At any given moment there may be 10 different sounds going on around you, but you may be aware of only one or two at a time. What you are hearing is called foreground noise. The rest of the sounds your attention places in the background so they can be temporarily ignored or blocked from consciousness. With a quick refocusing of attention, these background sounds can be brought to awareness in the foreground.

Smell provides information about chemical substances in the air. Tiny molecules floating in the air are breathed into the nose and pass over the olfactory epithelium located on the roof of the nasal cavity just below the level of each eye. Millions of tiny smell receptors there interact with the molecules. Some scientists believe that odor is based on the shape of the molecule, which fits into a particular smell receptor the same way a key fits into a lock, but alternate theories suggest that smell could be based on the vibration or electrical charge of the molecule instead of its shape (Burr 2003). The jury is still out on this, but in any case, nerve impulses are sent via the olfactory nerves to the olfactory bulb to the thalamus and on to the olfactory cortex where the information is processed and recognized as different odors. Smell impulses also go to other parts of the limbic system.

The human brain is capable of detecting as many as 10,000 different odors. This sounds like a lot, and it is, but it does not come close to the number of odors that other mammals and insects are capable of identifying. Dogs, for example, have more olfactory receptors and are capable of identifying many more smells than we can.

Smell is used for detecting approaching danger. The first indication of a fire is usually the smell of smoke, not the sight of flames or the sound of a fire alarm going off. Animals use smell to mark their territory and to attract mates. Humans do this, too, as evidenced by the millions of dollars spent each year on perfumes, potpourri, sachet, deodorant, and other scented products that change or enhance the odors on our bodies and in rooms.

The most interesting aspect of smell in relation to education is its emotional aspect. Because olfactory impulses are relayed through the limbic system, smells are deeply laden with emotional associations. Particular smells will bring up strong visual, aural, emotional, and kinesthetic images of moments from the past. The recall experience is often so vivid that, for a few seconds, the smeller actually feels transported back to that remembered time and place.

In a series of experiments, children had better recall when a word list was paired with olfactory cues than when it was memorized without any cues (Ackerman 1990). Certain odors, such as peppermint, basil, lemon, cinnamon, rosemary, and jasmine — provided they do not have negative connotations to individuals — have been found to increase mental alertness while others, such as lavender, chamomile, orange, vanilla, citronella, and rose, evoke calmness and relaxation (Doheny 2001; Jensen 2000; Watson 2000). Alan Hirsh of the Smell and Taste Treatment and Research Foundation in Chicago discovered that a floral smell helped improve people's ability to solve a maze-like puzzle (Weiss 1995). Researchers at Yale University Psychophysiology Center have studied the intermittent use of certain pleasant, invigorating smells to heighten alertness, wake up the metabolism, reduce stress, and enhance positive attitudes, while studies at the University of Cincinnati have shown that certain fragrances injected into the atmosphere at intervals can increase productivity and efficiency in the workplace (Ackerman 1990). The idea of teaching by pairing odors with information could offer interesting educational enhancement for students in general and alternatives for students whose ability to pair information with visual images or auditory stimuli are weak. Scents used while learning could then be worn or sniffed during tests, helping to retrieve the information from long-term memory.

By the same token, unpleasant smells might create learning situations in which it is difficult to concentrate or in which behavior problems erupt. Researchers at Brown University (2005) discovered that when students associated an unfamiliar scent with a frustrating experience, all further educational activities taking place while exposed to the same smell evoked feelings of frustration and led to lack of motivation in solving problems presented. Hirsh found that when the unpleasant odors from a nearby mulching site were strongest, students at a school in Chicago had the most behavioral incidents (Doheny 2001).

Taste provides information about chemical substances (mostly those in food and drink) which come in contact with the taste buds on the tongue. Each taste bud has about fifty receptor cells that send a different chemical transmitter via the taste nerve to the gustatory cortex in the brain. Tastes fall into five categories: sweet, bitter, salty, sour, and savory.

Taste and smell are closely linked. The subtle and distinctive flavors of different foods are created when the brain combines the messages it receives from the olfactory nerves, the taste nerves, and other temperature and pressure receptors in the mouth. In fact, the whole sensory experience of eating depends on the interaction of all the senses. Food seems to taste better if it looks pleasing. Auditory experience can enhance dining; this is why many restaurants pipe in soothing music. Part of the delight of crispy foods is their crunch and texture, just as part of the soothing quality of creamy foods is their silence and smoothness.

Touch provides information about the texture and temperature of objects that come in contact with the skin. The skin also alerts us to painful stimuli. There is argument among sensory scientists whether each type of sensor in the skin (hot, cold, pain, pressure) should be considered a separate sense or part of one. In any case, various nerve endings just below the surface of the skin pick up stimuli that are sent via electrical and chemical impulses through the nerves, the spinal cord, and the thalamus to the somatosensory cortex in the brain, where the information is deciphered and interpreted. Certain areas of the body are more sensitive than others because they have more sensory nerve endings per square inch and more neurons devoted to processing them in the brain. Examples of high-density areas of skin are the fingertips, the feet, the lips, and other areas of the face.

Balance is located in the vestibular system in the inner ears. Three loops, the semicircular canals, provide the brain with information about the exact position of the head in relation to the rest of the body and the direction in which it is moving. Crystals in the fluid inside the canals respond to gravity, creating nerve impulses that travel along the vestibular nerve to communicate the position of the head in relation to the ground. Tiny hairs attached to the sides of the canals respond to the movement of the fluid. Whenever the hairs bend, impulses are sent along the vestibular nerve to the brain to indicate which way is up.

Proprioception provides the brain with its understanding of the body's position in space. The muscles, tendons, and joints have kinesthetic receptors that pass on movement commands from the brain and communicate back about current body position. Proprioception is the sense that lets you know you are sitting up, lying down, or standing, even if your eyes are closed and you cannot see your body position. Most people are strongly aware of proprioception only when they are in the process of learning a new physical skill, such as riding a bike, driving a car, or typing. Once the movements of muscles, bones, and joints become familiar, awareness of proprioception fades and the activity can be performed with a minimum of conscious concentration.

Without proprioception a person would have no inner connection or control. In fact, individuals who have lost their sense of proprioception say they feel disembodied (Sacks 1985). Although they are not paralyzed and can move, they feel no connection with their muscles and are, indeed, missing the necessary interior feedback to unconsciously manipulate various body parts. It takes a great deal of conscious effort and the use of vision and hearing to substitute for the missing information contributed by their proprioceptors.

Deep pressure, internal sensitivities to heat and cold, hunger, thirst, and internal pain, such as headaches, toothaches, and cramps, are sometimes considered part of proprioception and sometimes considered to be senses on their own. In any case, all respond to stimuli from the inside of the body rather than from outside. Because they are located deep within the body, they are harder to study than the eyes, ears, nose, or tongue. For the most part, they are "invisible" senses of which most people remain unconscious and unaware unless they signal discomfort. The deep senses are usually lumped together as part of the sense of touch and referred to as our *kinesthetic senses*.

Sensory Learning Channel Preference

We depend on three major sensory systems when taking in information: hearing, vision, and kinesthesia. Smell and taste are very minor learning channels in formal education settings, although crucial in terms of survival. Each person — with or without disabilities — typically relies primarily on one or two sensory channels for learning, although some well-rounded individuals rely equally on all three (Markova 1991).

Auditory learners are people who understand best through hearing information. The current academic system in the United States is geared toward auditory learning. If you give verbal directions to an auditory learner, she will be able to remember and follow them easily. If you lecture, she will be able to sit and listen for long stretches of time and will probably remember a great deal of the information without taking copious notes. Auditory learners tend to express themselves most fluently and easily through spoken language. They have good auditory recall and tend to imagine conversations or sounds rather than visual images. Auditory learners usually join the debate team and love to answer questions in class. They will be the first to volunteer for panel discussions and oral presentations because this puts them in the medium they feel most comfortable with: the spoken word (Markova 1991).

Visual learners understand best through seeing and visualizing information. A visual learner tends to understand information better if it is presented through a visual form: pictures, diagrams, charts, or printed words. Visual learners tend to express themselves better through visual media rather than through the spoken word. They would rather draw, diagram, sculpt, or write their contributions than speak them. Their imaginations are primarily visual and they use words with an emphasis on the images they create rather than on the logic or sound of the words. The use of PowerPoint presentations makes lectures more accessible to visual learners.

I am a visual learner. I have discovered that focusing on visual activity is the only way I can capture the invisible words of a speaker. Whenever I am at a lecture or meeting, I can follow what is going on only by taking constant notes, thereby making the auditory stimuli visual, or by doodling. For me and other doodlers, doodling is a way of paying attention to what is being said, not blocking it out (Markova 1991). If I stop doodling, I cannot pay attention and I begin to daydream.

Kinesthetic learners understand best by using proprioception, touch, taste, smell, balance, or some combination thereof. Kinesthetic learners must funnel the learning experience directly through their muscles and tactile senses in order to understand information best. They often succeed in subjects where information is experienced primarily through physically doing something: manipulating with their hands, touching, tasting, and smelling. They may excel on the playing field, design and sew beautiful clothes in home economics, or create exquisite furniture in woodshop, but may get lost in a class, such as math or history, that does not involve hands-on learning methods. They are fully capable of abstract thinking, but not through auditory or visual learning channels. They need to use physical, concrete means to learn.

Kinesthetic learners may be able to memorize lines by writing them out again and again or by typing them, rather than saying them out loud or looking at them. They may study best for a test while pacing, dancing, or walking rather than sitting at a desk. They may need to act out the material in order to retain it, while an auditory learner would prefer to listen to it or a visual learner to read it. They would do well in classes in which there were laboratory experiments. The Montessori system, which involves a lot of hands-on manipulation, works extremely well from a kinesthetic perspective. Many so-called learning-disabled students may be kinesthetic learners in an educational system that refuses to teach them through their preferred learning channel.

Sensory Channel Configurations

Rarely is a person only an auditory, visual, or kinesthetic learner. Usually students are capable of learning through all their sensory channels but, for a wide variety of reasons, everyone tends to favor one or two. It could be that one sensory channel is highly sensitized or that another is partially blocked. A student who has a heightened sensitivity to color might become a visual learner. Another who has difficulty recognizing visual patterns might be able to hear or sense them through rhythm (auditory learner). One channel may appeal more to an individual because of emotional makeup. Someone who feels he must test out ideas, rather than take them on the word of the teacher, might be a kinesthetic learner by temperament.

How do people discover what their learning-channel preference is? Learning-channel preference tests ask a variety of questions that can help pinpoint learning style. The Swassing-Barbe Learning Channel Preference List identifies strengths in the three areas and you can check to see which column reflects how you learn. Excellent books on the subject of learning channel preference are Dawna Markova's *The Way of the Possible: A Compassionate Approach to Understanding the Way People Think, Learn & Communicate* (1991) and her follow-up volume *The Open Mind* (1996).

The best way to discover your learning channel preference is to become aware of how you respond to being presented with different types of information. How do you best take in information, process it, and put it back out? Do you like to listen to lectures and tapes or do you prefer reading a book? Can you understand a concept better through looking at images or do you have to physically make something to really understand it? How do you attend to a guided fantasy? Some people have very clear visual imaginations. Others have vivid auditory imaginations and see few pictures in their heads. Still others feel the adventure in their bodies rather than visualize or hear it. Do you like to talk about ideas or would you rather write them down or draw them out or make a model of them?

How do you talk about understanding? A visual learner will tend to say things like, "I *see* what you mean," or "I get the *picture*." An auditory learner might say, "I *hear* you," or "That *sounds* good." A kinesthetic learner might say, "This *feels* right," or "Let me *try* this on for size."

What are the situations in which information just goes over your head? Do you get lost during lectures? If you do, you are probably not a strong auditory learner. Do you get confused by maps and charts? If so, you are probably not a strong visual learner. If you are a complete klutz and hate performing experiments or building things with your hands, you are probably not a strong kinesthetic learner.

When faced with a project that must be done, how do you like to receive your directions? Listening to another person who has done it before talk you through it? Looking at a picture or diagram? Written directions? Watching someone else do it first? Jumping in and figuring it out through trial and error?

What are your hobbies and recreational activities? When left to your own devices would you rather read, talk to friends, listen to music, write in a journal, draw pictures, listen to a storyteller, dance, play sports, or build something in your workshop? When you communicate with others, do you prefer to talk, write, draw, or act things out to illustrate your point?

I did not realize I was a visual learner until in my mid-30s when I took a learning channel preference quiz in a workshop. If I had known that I processed information best through visual means when I was a child, my life in school might have been a lot easier. I would have paid attention to lectures and directions in a different way. I felt humiliated quite a few times in elementary school when I did not process verbal directions given for an assignment correctly. I can still remember my second grade teacher saying, "That's what you get for sleeping in class!" as she handed me back a paper with a big red zero on it. I was truly shocked! I had been listening carefully in the morning when she said the directions, but obviously I missed some crucial auditory information.

By chance I developed a number of strategies that helped me succeed in secondary school and college. In sixth grade I learned how to take notes and write things down. I never got confused about the requirements for assignments after that. In high school where teachers started spending most of the class period lecturing, I started doodling. Doodling felt right, so I kept taking notes and doodling all through college and graduate school.

Once you figure out your learning style, it is easier to pinpoint that of others. Again, listen to the way they talk about ideas and experiences. Find out how they spend their free time. Try a guided fantasy and listen to the ways they describe what they imagined. Do they report mostly visual details, sounds, smells, feelings, or actions? When you present material to students, be aware of the kinds of sensory information they pick up on easily and those they do not pick up on as quickly.

The safest and wisest teaching approach is to present information to all students using all sensory channels. Instead of relying only on lectures and reading assignments to communicate an idea or teach a skill, explain verbally how to do something *and* demonstrate it *and* show pictures or videos of it *and* have your students get up and act it out *and* create projects or experiments for them to explore it. The more senses that become involved in the learning process, the more the information will make sense in a meaningful way. Additionally, because the information is coming in through a number of channels, it can be grasped in more than one way. Information is repeated and rehearsed, but it is not received in a boring, repetitive fashion. Each reinforcing encounter is perceived by the student as fresh and exciting.

The arts are the most comprehensive sensory teaching tool at any teacher's disposal. The arts involve *all* the senses in a two-way process of communication. For example, a student who looks at Picasso's *Guernica* comes to understand the concept of war and man's inhumanity to man through the visual sense and, if he has a gut reaction (through his mirror neurons) to the graphic visual images in the painting, also through the kinesthetic senses. A student who uses the act of painting or drawing to create an expression of his own response to war uses his visual, kinesthetic, and proprioceptive responses to express his ideas and communicate them visually and viscerally to another.

Not only do the arts involve the senses, they integrate them, making cross-sensory connections and cementing the information into long-term memory through experience, narrative, feeling, and rehearsal. Drawing, painting, and sculpting involve both visual and kinesthetic learning channels. Music creates auditory experiences through sound and kinesthetic channels use rhythm and the physical activity of making music. Dance simultaneously engages the auditory and kinesthetic channels. Acting combines all three.

Emotions and Learning

In the 17th century, when French philosopher Rene Descartes said, "I think, therefore, I am," he led Western philosophers and educators to conceptualize thinking as reasoning devoid of emotion. The body was judged to be "lower" than the mind; feelings were impure and not to be trusted, while reason was pure and reliable. However, in late 20th and early 21st centuries, brain scientists have discovered that emotion is part and parcel of thought. Neuroscientist Antonio Damasio (1994; 1999) has explored in depth how reason and emotion work together to help us develop judgment and critical thinking skills, create an internal moral compass of what feels "right" and "wrong," and ultimately support us in making decisions. Feelings, thoughts, the body, and the senses must all interact for a person to truly assess all aspects of a situation and understand it.

Learning in a state of stress, fear, threat, or other negative emotion shuts down concentration and memory abilities. Information can be better retained if the learning environment stimulates enjoyment, trust, and positive feelings. As Eric Jensen (2000) says, "Our emotions help us to focus our reason and logic. Our logical side may help us, for example, set a goal, but it is our emotional side that provides the passion to persevere through trying times" (p. 199). He goes on to say:

> Our thinking is not "contaminated" by emotions: Rather, our emotions are an integral aspect of our neural operating system. Emotions speed our thinking by providing an immediate physical response to circumstances. When a result makes us feel good, naturally we're going to select it over a result that makes us feel badly. And when we value something strongly, whether it be a principle or a person, or a thing, that relationship becomes "emotionally charged" (p. 201).

Damasio (1994) reports on patients with brain damage who find it difficult, if not impossible, to access their emotions while thinking. They could only "think rationally" and this led to either an inability to make *any* decision when faced with a choice or the tendency to make very poor decisions. These people were, in essence, paralyzed — their ability to think impaired by their inability to feel.

Other research on learning indicates that positive emotions may improve learning experiences through generating situations in which students can organize cognitive material better, think creatively, and solve problems. When in a state of positive affect, students can be simultaneously relaxed and alert. They feel empowered to "think outside of the box" which enables them to relate and integrate divergent material, form new associations, and reorganize old knowledge into new concepts (Greene & Noice 1988).

The arts can be key components in integrating emotion with reason in learning. In his book *The Arts and the Creation of Mind* Elliot Eisner (2002) talks about lessons that the arts provide to students:

> Judgment depends on feel, and feel depends on a kind of somatic knowledge that enables one to determine if the form at hand has what Nelson Goodman once called "rightness of fit." The body is engaged, the source of information is visceral, the sensibilities are employed to secure experience that makes it possible to render a judgment and to act upon it. What would such considerations mean in writing up a scientific experiment, in organizing a project for a civics class, in creating a short story or writing an essay? I believe that such a consideration is fundamental to good work on any of these tasks (p. 201).

Eric Jenson (2000) concurs, repeatedly connecting music, drama, art, dance, and writing to learning styles, emotion and learning, and memory and recall throughout his book *Brain-Based Learning.*

Cognitive neuroscientists from seven universities across the United States were funded by the Dana Foundation on the Brain to study why arts training has been associated with higher academic performances. A number of interesting discoveries were made, including that interest in a performing art (music, dance, or drama) led to a high state of motivation. This positive state produced the sustained attention required to do the art activity and this enhanced attention training was able to be generalized to other areas of academic study (Gazzaniga 2008). Training in acting was shown to lead to memory improvement and increased abilities in divergent thinking. Correlations were found between music training and reading acquisition because of the skills in phonological awareness used by both processes. Links were found between training in music and visual arts and specific aspects of mathematics, in particular geometry and spatial reasoning. Training in dance was shown to improve observation skills. More research on these and other areas is planned in future neuroscientific studies.

Teaching to All the Intelligences

As a scientifically measurable entity, intelligence is a young concept in education and psychology. The first intelligence test was developed in 1904 by psychologist Alfred Binet to help French educators identify at-risk children who needed remedial instruction in order to succeed academically. The test was adopted by the U.S. Army as a way to evaluate new recruits for appropriate job placement and by the U.S. public school system for placement in tracked classes. By the mid-1920s intelligence testing was entrenched in the American way of evaluating academic ability and potential educational achievement (Gardner 1999). Binet's intelligence tests focused on verbal and mathematical intelligences because those were easily measured with pen and paper and related to the language and calculation skills involved in the major academic subjects. The scores from the tests were combined to create a numerical score: the *intelligence quotient*, or *IQ*. Because it was factored down to one number, intelligence began to be perceived as a singular intellectual faculty.

In 1983 Howard Gardner, an educational psychologist with a background in developmental psychology and neuropsychology, proposed his theory of multiple intelligences (M.I. theory) as a clearly defined challenge to Binet's concept of intelligence. The brain is now seen by neuroscientists, not as a monolithic information processing unit, but as an overall modular system with many separate, interconnecting systems that process and share information (Gardner 1999; Mithen 1996; Ornstein 1991; Pinker 1997). Each system contributes to the functioning of one or more domains of knowledge used by humans: linguistic, mathematical, musical, social, natural, etc. This is the basic construct of how brains function, from which Gardner's theories stem.

Gardner defines intelligence as "a biopsychological potential to process information that can be activated in a cultural setting to solve problems or create products that are of value in a culture" (Gardner 1999,

p. 33-34). For one of these potentials to be considered intelligence, it must meet eight criteria:

- An intelligence must originate in a particular area or areas in the brain.
- An intelligence must have an evolutionary history. In other words, evidence of its use can be shown to exist throughout human culture from pre-history to today.
- An intelligence must have an identifiable core operation or set of operations. For example, linguistic intelligence uses phonemic discriminations, syntax, grammar, and word meanings; visual-spatial intelligence uses two- and three-dimensional space.
- An intelligence can be encoded in a symbol system. For linguistic intelligence, this would be the alphabet or ideograms; for mathematical intelligence, this would be numerals; for musical intelligence, this would be notes, for visual-spatial intelligence, this would be diagrams or holograms.
- An intelligence has a distinct developmental history. In most people, it arises at a similar age, develops through a similar progression, and typically peaks at a specific time in life.
- There exist savants, prodigies, experts, geniuses, and other exceptional people who exhibit this intelligence.
- Its existence can be supported by experimental psychological tasks.
- Its existence can be supported by psychometric tests, although testing does not have to be accomplished through paper-and-pencil means.

An intelligence can be activated in an individual, depending on genetic inheritance, health, the values and opportunities in her culture, opportunities specifically available to her, and the personal decisions made by her and/or her family, teachers, and other significant people. In other words, intelligences arise from a combination of a person's genetic heritage and life conditions within a given culture and era. All human beings free of cognitive damage possess all of the intellectual potentials, but each human has a unique profile. Besides having the means and opportunity for a potential to develop, a person also usually has a *crystallizing* or *positive experience* in early childhood with a particular domain or discipline that uses that intelligence. This motivates her to develop her potential in this area. Conversely, a person might neglect developing an intelligence because of neurological damage, lack of encouragement, lack of means or opportunity, or because she had a *paralyzing* or *negative experience* which turned her off from pursing this particular domain.

Verbal-linguistic intelligence involves the ability to use spoken and written language, the ability to learn languages, and sensitivity to the different functions of language. Someone with this intelligence has sensitivity to the meaning of words, word order, sounds, rhythms, and inflections of words. People who have high verbal-linguistic intelligence might become writers, poets, journalists, salespeople, lawyers, storytellers, motivational speakers, or speech pathologists.

Logical-mathematical intelligence involves the capacity to analyze problems logically, carry out mathematical operations, and investigate issues sequentially and scientifically. Individuals with high logical-mathematical intelligence might become mathematicians, logicians, chemists, computer analysts, accountants, economists, statisticians, astronomers, or physicists.

Musical intelligence leads to skills in the performance, composition, and appreciation of musical patterns, the ability to recognize tonal patterns, and sensitivity to rhythm and beats. Musicians, singers, and composers have high musical intelligence.

Visual-spatial intelligence allows a person to perceive the physical world accurately, to recognize and manipulate the patterns of wide space (as in cartography and navigation) as well as the patterns of confined area (as in sculpting, painting, or chess), and the ability to recreate one's visual and spatial understanding. Painters, sculptors, architects, navigators, pilots, chess masters, surgeons, choreographers, designers, and cartographers need visual-spatial intelligence.

Bodily-kinesthetic intelligence provides a person with the ability to use her body to solve problems or make products and to manipulate objects skillfully. Dancers, athletes, farmers, surgeons, musicians, weavers, sculptors, actors, mechanics, carpenters, and other crafts persons require this kind of intelligence.

Interpersonal intelligence has to do with the capacity to notice and understand others' moods, temperaments, desires, motivations, needs, intentions, and, consequently, to motivate and work effectively with others. Interpersonal intelligence is crucial for teachers, therapists, counselors, coaches, salespeople, politicians, managers, actors, diplomats, mediators, and any kind of leader in business, religion, or politics.

Intrapersonal intelligence deals with the capacity to understand oneself, to create an effective working internal model of one's own psychology: fears, desires, motivations, attitudes, emotions, and capacities. A person with intrapersonal intelligence is able to use that self-knowledge to regulate her life effectively and achieve self-insight and mental health. Many introspective people have high intrapersonal intelligence.

Naturalist intelligence relates to the ability to recognize and classify species and patterns in nature, both organic and inorganic. A person with high naturalist intelligence usually enjoys spending time outside and has a talent for caring for, taming, or interacting subtly with living creatures. Farmers, biologists, botanists, gardeners, cooks, hunters, fishermen, veterinarians, environmentalists, archeologists, geologists, paleontologists, and ecologists would have naturalist intelligence.

Finally, existential intelligence is used by religious leaders, mystics, prophets, and philosophers to allow them to appreciate the greater existential questions of the human condition, such as the significance of life, the purpose of suffering, and the meaning of life and death.

M.I. theory is a more complex and inclusive way of looking at how the human brain processes information. It acknowledges many more of the unique abilities, skills, and talents that humans possess than the IQ approach, which focuses mainly on verbal and mathematical abilities. According to Gardner, each individual possesses a combination of strengths and weaknesses in each of the intelligences. Rarely is an individual strong only in one area: it is more common to have a number of strong areas, a number of medium areas, and a few weak ones.

When taken as an educational philosophy, M.I. theory offers opportunity for students to exercise and develop all the strengths and talents they have in order to become truly well rounded human beings. Many students who have failed in conventional educational institutions that stress achievement only in the verbal-linguistic and logical-mathematical intelligences find that they can learn when their areas of intellectual strength are addressed and incorporated into the classroom. Not only can they learn, they can use their strengths to grasp concepts in domains in which they may be weaker. For instance, mathematics is usually taught through abstract reasoning methods, but it can also be taught through word problems (verbal-linguistic), physical manipulation of objects (visual-spatial and bodily-kinesthetic), rhythm and song (musical and bodily-kinesthetic) and dance or games (interpersonal and bodily-kinesthetic).

Thomas Armstrong has written several excellent books on applying M.I. theory to the classroom. Highly recommended are *Seven Kinds of Smart* and *Multiple Intelligences in the Classroom*. Harvard University's Project Zero, where Gardner worked for many years, has many publications about how M.I. theory has been incorporated into schools around the country, including *Multiple Intelligences: Best Ideas from Research and Practice* by Mindy Kornhaber, Edward Fierros, and Shirley Veenema.

The theory of multiple intelligences dovetails very nicely with the concept of sensory learning channels and can lead to identifying very specific learning profiles for each student. However, a word of caution: do not confuse similar terms used in both systems as identical concepts. Sensory learning channel preference deals with the taking in and processing of information while M.I. theory deals with areas of knowledge and skill. Just because one is a visual learner does not necessarily mean one will have high visual-spatial intelligence. A visual learner could have high intelligence in any intelligence. A person who is blind, who cannot learn by visual means, could have very high visual-spatial intelligence and be a sculptor or designer, able to create skillfully in two and three dimensions.

Just as the arts can be used to integrate and express the senses, they can integrate and express the intelligences. A social studies project in which students learn about a Native American culture by learning music, dances, arts, and legends, and then creating a presentation complete with authentically designed costumes, sets, and props will require the exercise of skills from each area of intelligence in order to achieve the final product. Naturalist intelligence was part and parcel of how Native American cultures functioned, so this intelligence will be crucial in understanding how all aspects of the chosen culture fit together. Native cultures' arts and interactions with nature were connected to their spiritual beliefs; therefore, existential intelligence will be drawn upon to understand this unit. Verbal-linguistic intelligence is involved in the creation and performance of the script. Visual-spatial intelligence is involved in the design of the sets, costumes, and lights. Logical-mathematical intelligence is involved in building the sets and costumes and in execution of the lights. Musical intelligence and bodily kinesthetic intelligence will be incorporated into the creation of the music and dances. Interpersonal intelligence will be utilized in all the interactions involved in the creation, rehearsal, and performance of the production: how to compromise and reach consensus, when to follow and when to lead, how to share ideas in a way that others can understand. Intrapersonal intelligence will be called upon by each student as she manages her feelings and ideas throughout the process.

Using the Arts to Enhance Learning

The knowledge gained through an arts process is not limited to memorizing isolated details; it is holistic, interconnected, and systemic. An arts process incorporates more complex knowledge as students gain personal, hands-on experience with social customs, belief systems, and values of the people being studied. They come to understand the place of the individual within that society and how that particular social system fits into the greater scheme of the cultures that surround it.

There is strength in the accumulation and banding together of many small strengths. A bundle of sticks is harder to break than a single stick alone. Students' abilities to learn can be thought of in the same way. When many intellectual strengths are engaged in the learning process, more learning and retention will occur.

Approaching the curriculum through the arts may sound over-whelming, as if lesson planning will take a great deal more energy and time. It will take time to get into the habit of thinking in terms of interactive, sensory approaches if you have never done it before. However, as with any unaccustomed approach, the more you do it, the easier it gets. After a while, creating lesson plans that teach through the senses and involve the arts and multiple intelligences will start to feel natural. In any case, the investment of time and energy pays off in enhanced learning and motivation to learn on the parts of the students.

The first step is to evaluate the problem that needs to be addressed; in this case, begin by taking a look at each area of your curriculum. Some subjects naturally lend themselves to drama, music, or art. Literature, science, and social studies are easy to open up through the arts. Try projects with them first. When you experience success in these areas, you will feel on firmer ground. As you begin to feel more confident, you can branch out into teaching math, spelling, penmanship, and other subjects through the arts.

Language Arts

Storytelling: The Teacher as Storyteller

Storytelling is a dynamic way to involve students in any subject. Instead of talking *about* a story that your class is going to read, introduce them to it by *telling* it to them. Instead of lecturing *about* science, math or history, *tell a story* about how Alexander Fleming discovered penicillin or how Pythagoras developed his ideas about plane geometry or how Sojourner Truth led slaves to freedom on the Underground Railroad. A different energy is involved in storytelling. A personal, direct, intimate connection is made between the storyteller and the listener that is not present when a lecturer is talking at an audience. The listener feels personally included and willingly gives attention to the teller of the tale. Facts can be interwoven with images and feelings, which then, together, are more easily remembered through the process of chunking and indexing.

> For communication, memory, and learning purposes, stories are likely to be richer, more compelling, and more memorable (Schank & Abelson 1995, p. 7) than the abstracted points we ultimately intend to convey…this is because [stories] have more

indexes than abstract points. The more indexes, the more likely we will be reminded of something through which we will understand the new example (Schank & Berman 2002, p. 293-294).

Our memory structures are based on experiences or stories. When we learn, we modify or update our memory structures. In order to do this, first we have to be reminded of the stories we have stored. The right time for a story is whenever listeners want to learn and can use the new information to accomplish something immediate and important to them. Priming students for stories with a strong introduction or attention grabbing start is also important. Then the new story must enable the listener to fill in gaps or explain confusing or inaccurate information in the old story. This can be done through interesting details that clarify or add to the details of the old story.

The strongest stories are those in which listeners can see themselves in the role of the hero. The closer we can come to relating to the hero, the more personally relevant the story becomes and the more likely we are to learn from it. That means that if the storyteller can get us to really sympathize with the hero, it also implies that we can imagine being in the same circumstances, and we begin to think about what we might do, or how we might feel if we were in the hero's shoes. Adding to a story rich details that touch on reference the broader public understands assists this effect (Schank & Berman 2002, p. 308).

Even though a story is shared aurally, it engages more than just auditory learners because it calls upon students' imaginations. A good storyteller appeals to all the senses of her audience, creating visual, aural, olfactory, gustatory, tactile, and emotional images for the listeners. Visual learners will start making pictures in their minds when listening to a story. Kinesthetic learners will start experiencing the story in their bodies. Once these images are associated with the information being taught, the factual details will be recalled along with the recall of the images. Or, in Schank and Berman's terms, the story's images become new indexes that will be filed away to later help access the new facts learned.

As part of a unit on self-esteem and getting along with others for a group of special-education students at the upper elementary level, I decided to tell the story of "The Little Fir Tree." In this story, a Fir Tree is very dissatisfied with how she looks. She hates her green needles and wishes for green leaves so she can look like the other trees in the forest. The West Wind blows by and gives the tree her wish. But the goats in the meadow eat the Little Fir Tree's new leaves. Then the Little Tree wishes for golden leaves, so she will look pretty and no one will be able to eat her leaves. But when the West Wind provides her with gold leaves, thieves come into the meadow and steal them. Then the fir tree wishes for glass leaves, which will look pretty, but not be edible or valuable to anyone. The West Wind provides her with beautiful leaves of glass, but the North Wind blows roughly through the meadow and breaks them to pieces. Finally, the Fir Tree decides she wants her needles back, realizing that she can be happy and satisfied with herself just the way she is.

The students in this class had moderate to severe learning disabilities; a few had intellectual and developmental disabilities. The classroom teacher warned me that they might not be able to sit still long enough to listen to a story because of their short attention spans. But the moment I started telling the story, the room became so quiet, you could have heard a pin drop. All eyes were on me from the moment I said, "Once there was a little Fir Tree and she lived all alone in the middle of a meadow…" until 20 minutes later when I finished with "…and she is still standing in the meadow and is still very happy being a fir tree with green needles."

Their teacher was astounded at how long and completely they had concentrated on the story. At the time, I was amazed, too. But since then I have realized that the success of the session was not due solely to my storytelling technique or to the students' joy at being freed from their regular classroom routine; it was due to the ancient contract that has been wordlessly struck between every storyteller and every story listener since prehistoric times. The process of telling and listening to a story moves all parties into the transitional space where everything is possible, where everything has a high emotional and relational charge, and where old information is effortlessly called up and new information is integrated with it. This is the place where meaning is made and learning happens.

Johnny Moses, a Native American storyteller, says that in the language of his people there is no word for "myth" or "legend." The word his people use for the tales they tell their children translates into English as "the teachings" (Moses 1992). Story was the original medium of the teacher; the method our ancestors used before the invention of writing developed to pass important information on from one generation to the next. The information can be remembered because it is woven into the fabric of a narrative that has personal, emotional, and sensory connections inside the individual who is listening. Recalling the narrative retrieves all the information embedded in it. By neglecting this ancient and primary teaching tool, modern educators are missing one of the strongest, most powerful, brain-based tools in their arsenal. See Chapter 6 for more information on storytelling and a story by Mandy Hart on how to tell stories.

Storytelling: The Student as Storyteller

Storytelling can be used to motivate the development of language and oral communication skills. Start off by listening to a few professional storytellers on video or CD, so students can be pulled into the web of a skilled teller. Discuss what they liked about the story and about the storyteller. Talk about the ingredients that make stories interesting: exciting details that create pictures in listeners' minds, interesting dialogue that fits the characters, speaking in the characters' voices and acting out their actions, pacing, building suspense, making eye contact with the listeners, and caring about communicating your message to others.

A good way to start storytelling is to tell jokes. Jokes are really very short, humorous stories. To avoid off-color jokes or jokes that are too sophisticated for the students' age level and understanding, look for ideas in a book of children's jokes available in most libraries and bookstores. Have students choose a joke they like and take turns telling them.

Then let your students begin telling their own personal stories. Offer a list of true life events that could have happened to them, such as cooking dinner for the first time, an adventure on a dark and scary night, the best or worse night of babysitting, my favorite Halloween costume, staying up late while my parents were out, or even my most exciting summer vacation. Have them choose a topic and tell a short story about the event and why it was memorable.

As they gain confidence speaking in front of others, provide students with simple scenarios to tell their classmates. Base the scenarios on simple, familiar fairy tales or fables or make up simple scenarios of your own. Make sure the characters and the actions in the story are clear and sequenced in an orderly, logical progression so they make sense to the teller.

Let students practice their jokes, personal stories, or simple fairy tales and share them again. Are the stories more interesting the second time? Do they create stronger pictures? Are they more expressive vocally and facially? Do they feel more comfortable speaking in front of their audience? Do they feel a connection beginning to develop between themselves and their listeners?

When your student storytellers begin to feel more confident, move on to more complex stories or have students write their own. Arrange for them to tell stories they have practiced and polished to younger classmates at school. Hold a story-telling festival to which parents and friends can be invited.

Acting Games to Improve Verbal Skills

There are many acting games which can help students improve their ability to give directions or express their ideas clearly with words.

Clues is a game that can motivate verbal expression. One child goes out of the room and everyone remaining agrees on where in the room to hide an object. Together think of a number of clues to describe where the object is. The student returns to the room and is told the first clue. If she can't figure out where the object is, she is told the second clue, then the third, and so on until the object is found.

A teddy bear might be hidden in the supply closet. Three clues might be:

Teddy says, "It's dark in here!"
Teddy says, "I'm sitting on a shelf."
You must open a door to find him.

Assemble a Design is a game of verbal description played with a partner. Cut out various shapes from colored paper. Make duplicates of each colored shape so there are at least two sets of each. On one piece of paper glue an arrangement of shapes. Give this design to one partner. She will be the Describer. Give the other partner the loose duplicate shapes, a blank piece of paper, and tape or glue. This person will be the Arranger. The Describer tells the Arranger how to arrange the shapes on the paper so they are identical to the glued-down one. The Describer cannot show her paper or point to where the shapes can go. She can only use words.

Airport and Group Storytelling, described in Chapter 7, are good games to teach verbal description to students.

Improvisation with Puppets can be a wonderful way to practice language skills. Children who have difficulty using language or initiating conversations with people will sometimes be willing to talk to a puppet. If a child has a tendency to be overwhelmed with aural or visual stimuli, the puppet can be less threatening or less stimulating than a live human being. A puppet can also act as a distancing device onto which a child may project her emotions and words. Because it is inanimate, a puppet can be controlled by the child and will make no unexpected demands.

One year I had a pleasant young man who functioned on a very high verbal and social level join one of my adult performing companies. I was not told his "diagnosis" so I assumed he had learning disabilities. He quickly proved himself to be a highly creative, sensitive, hardworking, and delightful addition to the group. I was astounded several months later when his mother informed me that until he was ten years old, he had never initiated a conversation with anyone. All he could do was repeat what others said to him. This condition called echolalia is often found in people who have intellectual and developmental disabilities or autism. Then one day he saw a marionette in a store at the mall and started to talk to it. His mother realized immediately that something magical had happened and bought him a number of marionettes and puppets. Through talking with these inanimate theatrical beings, he learned how to initiate speech and then began to talk to people.

Use improvisational scenes with puppets to teach basic communication skills and appropriate ways to respond in different social situations. Practice conversation skills by having children talk to a puppet operated by the teacher or by pairing children who each have a puppet to role-play a situation for the class. Make or buy puppets that can "teach" specific skills. For example, a doctor puppet can teach children about health and hygiene issues; a fireman puppet can teach fire safety or fire drill rules; a dentist puppet or a tooth puppet can teach about oral hygiene; a dog puppet can teach about how to take care of pets. After the puppet (with teacher as puppeteer) presents the information, the students can rehearse it by becoming puppeteers and presenting the information themselves or by answering questions which the teacher and other students ask the puppet to review for them.

Students can use these puppets to create improvised puppet shows for each other on material that has been presented. For example, a student puppet could go to the dentist puppet for a check-up and the dentist puppet could examine his teeth and tell him what he needs to do to avoid having cavities. Depending on the abilities of the students, the teacher can either set up the scenario of the puppet play or allow the students to create their own from the information they learned in class.

Puppets can often elicit information from children about how they are feeling or why a behavior problem exists when other methods fail. The distancing function of the puppet comes into play, allowing the child to express his feelings and motives in a way he might be afraid to when confronted by an authority figure, even if the authority figure is the puppeteer. The puppet is seen as a friend and confidant who will not judge or reject the child. If you are the puppeteer, please remember this and allow the puppet to stay within its confidant role so it can remain a tool in emotionally difficult times. By the same token, a puppet on a child's hand often can verbally or physically express for her what she cannot express as herself.

Acting Games to Improve Verbal Expressiveness

Students who are having trouble reading out loud with expression can practice vocal expressiveness through tone-of-voice games. Take a few innocent sentences:

I am going to the store.

Red is my favorite color.

John is going to be a fireman.

Have each student say the sentence with a different emotional meaning. Try each sentence with anger, sorrow, joy, excitement, confusion, unhappiness. Then have students say each sentence as a statement, a question, a command. Try to read each sentence as a different character might: as a cowboy, as Dracula, as a robot, as a ghost, as a farmer, as an old man, as a baby, as a really cool teenager, as a mother, as a minister.

If your students have difficulty reading simple sentences, tone of voice and emotional expressiveness can be taught through sounds. Ask your students to roar like a lion who is happy, sad, hungry, sleepy, angry, embarrassed, sloppy, etc. Repeat the exercise with the sounds made by other animals (*ribbit* like a frog, *moo* like a cow, *meow* like a cat). Allow students to use their bodies to express the emotions their voice is creating. The body and voice are intimately connected and often if the body cannot move, the voice becomes "disembodied" and expressionless.

Open Scenes. Open scenes are short dialogues which can be interpreted in a variety of ways depending on the tone of voice used. They are used in acting classes to teach subtext and can be useful and fun for practicing vocal expressiveness.

Here is one open scene:

A: Give me the ball.

B: No, I want it.

A: Give it to me.

B: No, I won't.

A: Yes.

B: No.

A: Yes.

B: No.

A: Yes.

Assign each student a specific character role with an emotional outlook on the situation. Character A could be a bully and Character B could be intimidated by the bully. Character A could be a bully and Character B could refuse to be intimidated. Character A could be a parent wanting a child (Character B) to come in and go to bed. Both characters could be three-year-olds who do not know how to play together.

You can write your own short dialogues appropriate to your students' reading abilities and interests. After reading through them, let students get up and act them out. You might be surprised at the natural acting abilities you uncover through this game.

Whole scenes can be created through the use of two simple words, such as "yes" and "no" or "red" and "blue." Give each student a specific objective. Maybe Student A (using the word "Yes") wants Student B to go to the store with him and Student B (using the word "No") does not want to go. Maybe Student A (using the word "Red") wants to paint the room red and Student B (using the word "Blue") thinks blue would be a better choice. One student must try to convince the other to accept his point of view using only his one word. The scene finally ends when one agrees with the other by saying the other's word.

Acting Out a Story. Acting out a story before or after reading it gives students the opportunity to verbalize and physically express the plot, characters, and meaning of the story themselves. Standing in the shoes of one of the characters and looking at the situation through her eyes makes an abstract character from the page of a book feel very real and concrete. If a student has had difficulty understanding the conflict of the story, acting it out can often make the conflict clear. Switching roles and playing another character who is on a different side of the conflict, opens a student's eyes to differences of opinion and divergent points of view, which all good literature tries to provide the reader.

Poetry and Other Forms of Creative Writing

There are many ways to generate writing projects that excite instead of intimidate students.

Guided Imagery. Take students on a guided-imagery journey to a place where they have an adventure or meet a famous person. When they come back from the "trip," have them write about what they saw, heard, smelled, tasted, touched, and felt. See Chapter 7 for more about guided-imagery journeys.

Sensory Exploration. Any of the sensory learning games described in Chapter 7 are good jumping-off points for writing. Students can describe how it felt to be blindfolded, to smell different smells without seeing them, or to identify objects only through touch.

Music-Generated Writing. Play different kinds of music that evoke strong emotions or situations and ask students to listen with their imaginations, then write about a scene they saw or a story they made up as they listened to the music.

Art-Generated Writing. Have students draw pictures of a special place or a special person and then write a story or poem about what is in the picture.

Bring in a reproduction of a painting or photograph which suggests a story or has interesting people or animals in it. Have students write a story about what is going on in the image.

Have students draw as they listen to music and then create a story or poem out of the drawing.

Storytelling. Begin telling a simple story to the class. Introduce the characters and their conflict, but stop the story just before the climax and point of resolution. Let the students write about how the characters feel or come up with an ending for the story.

Use group storytelling (described in Chapter 7) to create an original story idea with everyone in the class. Then have everyone write their own version of how they would like the story to develop and end.

Creative Drama. Physically being involved in a story will engage students on a deeper imaginative and emotional level than storytelling alone. Set up a situation for the students to dramatize. Instead of acting out the ending, have them write out their version.

Dramatize a familiar story and ask students to write about what they think happened after the end of the story or ask them to invent a new ending. If a story is typically told from the point of view of one particular character, have students write the story from the perspective of a different character, after acting it out and interviewing each character from his/her unique point of view.

Radio Plays. A radio play can be an exciting project to motivate reading and writing skills as well as a way to enhance group interaction skills. Radio plays also introduce the concept that the spoken word and the written word are interconnected and related. Whenever I have created radio plays or puppet plays with students, I have seen "light bulbs" go on inside their heads when they suddenly realized that their spoken words were being written down and "saved" on paper so they could be spoken again later on.

Since students live in a television-oriented society, they may never have heard a radio play before. Play a CD of a classic or current radio play to your class to introduce them to the concept of radio drama. Radio dramas communicate everything about the story through dialogue and sounds instead of through verbal descriptions and visual images. Talk about how the play you listened to did this.

Divide students up into groups of three to six and let them choose a familiar story to dramatize (see Chapters 8 and 9 for methods of developing a script). Type up the scripts they create and practice reading them out loud, adding sound effects to enhance the story whenever possible. Record the stories. You have created your own radio show!

Puppet Plays. Puppet plays can also be great motivators of reading and writing. They have the added benefit of involving a physical and visual product, which can help make the characters and the play created seem much more real to visual and kinesthetic learners. See Chapter 8 for more on creating puppet plays.

Science

Since science is about the physical world around us, it makes sense to teach it in a physical way. Dramatizing concepts, systems, processes, or cycles can be very illuminating for students because their bodies become part of a system that interrelates and connects. What initially might have looked to a student like a random jumble of parts actually is connected in a cause-and-effect pattern. Once the student can experience the pattern in a personal way, the whole system begins to make sense.

For example, the circulatory system can be set up in the classroom with students playing the different chambers of the heart, the lungs, the blood, and cells of the body. One chamber of the heart will send the blood to another chamber and then out to the lungs where the blood can pick up oxygen (red-colored cards, perhaps?), flow back to the heart and get pumped out to the cells in the body where oxygen is delivered and carbon dioxide is picked up (blue-colored cards?). An enactment like this can be very simply staged or can become a very elaborate class project complete with costume and props.

Students can become water molecules and take part in the evaporation cycle. They can act out different planets in the solar system and revolve around the sun. They could even become the atoms on the periodic chart of elements and combine in different ways to create simple chemical compounds. Drama and science are natural companions in the classroom!

One of the most exciting teaching experiences I have had was a series of ten drama sessions that I led for an upper elementary class of students with learning disabilities who were studying insects, specifically ants and butterflies. As I read several books on the subject, I found the rigid social organization of ants to be fascinating. I was also intrigued by the differences in sensory perception between humans and insects. Ants' compound eyes see only light and dark. Living underground most of the time, they do not have a need for eyes that focus on images as we do. They rely primarily on their senses of touch, taste, and smell. Butterflies have compound eyes that register movement and color, but do not really focus. They also rely quite a bit on their senses of taste and touch, located on their feet and antennae, respectively. I decided the best way to approach insects was to begin with exercises which let the children experience the world the way insects do.

We set up a maze in the room using desks and chairs. Students were blindfolded and had to find their way through it using their sense of touch, smell, or sound. After everyone had a chance to try it at least once, we sat down and talked about what was easy or hard about using the different senses to get around.

Since anthills with tunnels leading in, out, and around to different underground chambers are like mazes, we practiced solving mazes on paper. Then we learned how to draw mazes ourselves.

In one session we created two "anthills" in the room using desks and chairs. Everyone was assigned to one of the ant societies by scent. I fastened one of two different types of incense cones to each student's shoulder. The cones looked similar but smelled different. Just as an ant tells whether another ant is part of its anthill by how it smells, each time two students met they had to sniff the other's shoulder to find out who was a friend and who was a stranger.

Once the ant societies had separated into opposite anthills, their jobs in the society were assigned by taste. I passed out small pieces of wrapped candy to everyone. If they had a lemon taste in their mouths, they were the queens (since each ant society only has one queen, I had only one lemon flavored candy for each group). The queens had to go to their laying chambers in the center of their anthill and for the duration of the enactment could only "lay eggs." This task involved taking Styrofoam peanuts out of a bag one by one and carefully arranging them on the floor.

If their candy had a strawberry taste, they were nursery workers and were to take eggs one at a time from the laying chamber to the nursery. If I said, "It's getting hot outside," the nursery workers had to move the eggs to a chamber closer to the surface of the anthill. If I said, "It's getting cooler," the nursery workers had to move the eggs to a chamber farther in toward the center of the anthill.

Students who had orange-tasting candy were worker ants and had to go out of the anthill and gather food (small paper tubes and wooden blocks) and carry them back to the anthill's food-storage chambers. Worker ants could not carry more than one piece of food at a time and had to use both hands to do it. Each time they came out of the anthill and went in search of food, they had to follow the same trail.

There were a few more rules. No one was allowed to talk. No one was allowed to do anything but his or her assigned job. Each time two ants met outside the anthill they had to smell each other to see if they were friend or foe. If they were from the same anthill, they could help each other. If they were from the other anthill, they had to quickly move away from each other.

If ants got hungry, they were allowed to stop and eat. Nursery ants and queens had to get food from a worker ant (but they could not ask for food; they had to get the worker ant's attention by tapping on his head and motioning to their mouths). The anthill had to remain neat and clean at all times.

After about 20 minutes of quiet, industrious activity, we stopped and talked about the experience of being an ant. Everyone had lots of ideas and feelings to share. Someone said it was hard not being able to communicate through talking. Another agreed and said it was sometimes confusing to only be able to gesture or to get someone's attention by tapping them. So many things seemed to take more time. Their teacher and I talked more about life in an anthill and the students began making connections between the facts we shared and the experiences they just had. Everyone agreed that being able to do only one job your whole life would be boring and decided unanimously that it was wonderful that as human beings we were able to learn new things and have variety and change in our lives.

That whole week during recess a new excitement for learning gripped the students. They began watching ants on the sidewalk. Their teacher overheard long discussions about what kind of ant this was (herder, food gatherer, queen, or nursery worker), how old it was, and if it was a member of the same society as the ants on the other side of the playground. Hours were spent in front of the ant farm in the classroom discussing the fine points of ant etiquette and social structure.

They would have been happy to re-create their ant societies and explore them further the next week, but we moved on to act out the life cycle of the butterfly. Our last few sessions were devoted to writing and illustrating poems about the insects we had studied. Students who had never willingly put pen to paper joyfully jumped in to express what it had felt like to be a caterpillar, butterfly, or ant.

I put the poems and illustrations together into a book and made copies for each student. When the books were completed, we had a poetry reading. Everyone actually wanted to stand in front of the room and read her poems to the rest of the class. But the best part of all was when everyone passed their science test. For once, no one had any doubts about the correct answers!

Here are some of the wonderful poems that came out of their first-hand experiences with insects:

ANT

Hi.

I'm an ant.

I will tell you how it would be

If you were an ant.

If you were an ant,

The queen ant would never give you a rest.

You would have to work until you die.

You could not see

And it's hard to talk.

It's painful to crawl

And you have to watch for predators.

I have three body parts

And I could smell and touch and taste.

RED ANTS

I am a red ant.

Red ants sting

And they bite.

I was walking one day

And I saw a man.

He stepped on me.

But I was still alive.

I was mad!

He broke my antenna.

He leaned down and tried to pick me up,

But I bit him.

And he said, "Ow!"

So he left.

So remember this is what will happen to you

When the powers of the red ant comes for you!

THE QUEEN

I am a queen ant.

I lay eggs.

But when I leave my eggs,

My sitters watch my pretty eggs
While I am in the room where I get dressed.
Today I have a meeting with two worker ants
Because I need my house to get bigger.
Because I will soon get more eggs.

THE SOLDIER ANT
I am black and big.
I am a soldier ant.
I am not a nice ant.
I spray formic acid
If you touch my house.
If you touch my house,
I will spray formic acid on you.
So whatcha gonna do
When I come for you?
That's the way I am.
The soldier ant is back!

FEELING LIKE A BUTTERFLY
I am a caterpillar.
I shed my skin five times.
Boy, it was hard.
I had to push —
Like having a baby.
Oh, my gosh!
I turned into a pupae stage.
I came out on 11/2/1981.
It felt good.
But when I came out,
I fell down on the ground —
My head first.
I said, "Ouch!"
Then I went walking to a flower.
It was a rose.
I jumped up.
Then I started to fly.
I met another butterfly.
Her name was Amy.
She became my girlfriend.
An elephant was going to step on Amy!
I was a super butterfly.
I picked up the elephant
And I took him back to Africa.
When I came back,
I asked Amy, "Are you okay?"
She said, "Yes."
Then we kiss with love.

Social Studies

History, geography, and the study of human societies across the globe can be enhanced by actively employing the arts as a teaching tool.

Time Machines. Create a "Time Machine" in your classroom to enable you and your students to travel back in history. Once you have arrived at your destination in the past, students can act out important scenes from the lives of historical characters or everyday life experiences. If you journey back to medieval times, each student could create his own family coat of arms or join a guild and learn how leather was made or shoes were cobbled. If you go back to the 1800s, your class could join a wagon train's westward journey or pan for gold in the California gold rush.

Costumes, Props, and Sets. If involving students through active role-playing seems too intimidating at first, involve them in roles through the use of costumes, sets, and props during lessons. Dressing up as someone else is always appealing. One of my fondest memories from fourth grade was geography class. Mrs. West, our teacher, always got us physically connected with the place and people we were studying. I will never forget making a burnoose and wearing it each class period we studied

photo by Lea Ann Rosen

Figure 30: Student creates a medieval coat of arms by using a stencil.

Saudi Arabia. When we learned about Polynesia, we circled our chairs around a "palm tree" in the back of the room and munched on real coconut. I remember virtually nothing about geography class in any subsequent years, but the information from fourth grade is still vivid to me.

Explore a Culture Through its Arts and Crafts, its Food, and its Festivals. Through an experience with folk customs and arts, the people and culture of another society will come alive for your students. Learn the songs, dances, and games that are integrated into daily life or special holiday traditions. Cook and eat authentic food. Create folk art in the style of the culture. Hold a holiday festival where everyone can share and celebrate their adopted cultural heritage. Facts will no longer be dry, meaningless minutiae, but will become living information.

Bringing Historical Characters to Life. History comes alive when figures from history become real human beings for students. After studying an historical period, have each student choose a famous person in that period who interests her. After doing some research, lead a guided fantasy where students meet their historical character at an important moment in her life. Have them imagine they become their character at an important moment and experience the world from her point of view. When the students return from their journey, have them write a short monologue (a speech in the first person) in which their historical character talks about something important she saw, did, or felt. The monologues could be memorized and performed in costume to create a presentation on this period in history, and could be videotaped.

A less formal way to meet historical characters is to invite them to class and interview them in person. Have students choose a character to play and provide time to research their lives. During an interview session, run your class as if it were a TV talk show. Each student in role answers questions about her life. The teacher could be the interviewer, one student could be assigned as the TV host, or the whole class could ask questions in role as their character.

Mathematics

Drama provides a method of grasping abstract concepts through concrete means. Here are a few simple drama games that can be used to teach basic math and geometry.

Grouping by Number. Students walk around the room until the teacher calls out a number. Students must find the right number of other students to join in order to form a group of that number. Leftover students can group together in one area as the "remainder." For instance, if the teacher calls out, "Three!" all students must assemble in groups of three. Once everyone is in a group with the correct number, the round is over and the game starts again.

Addition. Once students understand how to play Grouping by Number, a variation of the game can be played which demonstrates what happens during addition. Just as in Grouping by Number, students walk slowly around the room until the teacher calls out a number. They assemble in a group of that number. Then the teacher adds to that number and students must reform their groups. For instance, if the students are in groups of three, the teacher might call out, "Add two!" or "Plus two!" When each group has added two to its number, the teacher asks the students to count and see how many three plus two is. As the game is played, students begin to recognize addition patterns. Every time two is added to three, there are five students in each group.

Subtraction. This is another variation of Grouping by Number. In this version, once students are in a number group, the teacher calls out a number to subtract from the group and the class evaluates the sizes of the groups that are left. For instance, if students are in groups of three, the teacher might call out "Subtract one!" or "Minus one!" One student must leave each group. The original groups will have two students left in them.

Geometry. The teacher calls out different kinds of lines (straight, zigzag, curve, long, short, etc.) and different kinds of simple shapes (circle, square, rectangle, triangle). Students create these lines and shapes with their bodies. Once students understand how to play this game alone, they can learn to play it with other students, creating more complex shapes (polygon, pentagon, rhombus) or lines by using more people.

Students who have created shapes and lines with their bodies have an easier time drawing them or cutting them out.

Story Problems. When introducing story problems in math class, have students actually act the problems out so they have the opportunity to see and physically experience the situation instead of just imagining it. A simple story problem like, "If Joan gave Bill three apples and then had four apples left, how many apples did she have in the first place?" could be worked through using real or plastic apples.

Working through story problems in this manner not only makes them more concrete and real, but more human. Students with interpersonal intelligence strengths will become more motivated to learn math if they can relate it to actual people and real life situations. Problem-solving skills develop along with social-interaction skills.

Once students have learned to solve story problems through action, have them create their own story problems for the class to solve.

Developing Emotional Intelligence

Students with or without disabilities can have difficulty getting along, difficulty respecting the differences or special needs of others, difficulty communicating effectively with each other, or difficulty accepting certain aspects of themselves. Many of the basic drama games described in this book, particularly in Chapter 7, can help teach skills in all of these areas. When teaching the unit on self-esteem and getting along with others mentioned earlier, I used a combination of drama and social games, art activities, role-playing, relaxation techniques, storytelling, and creative drama to develop students' abilities to observe others, become aware of their own feelings, and develop positive strategies to work together.

In the first session we played the social game Come Along, a variation of musical chairs. Everyone sat in a circle in chairs except for one leader who stood in the center. When I started the music, the leader went up to someone sitting in the circle, held out her hand, and said, "Come along." That person grabbed onto the leader's hand and followed her around the circle, moving in time with the music. The second person asked a third person to "Come along," the third person asked a fourth, and so on until I stopped the music. Then everyone ran for a chair. The person left without a seat was the leader for the next round. This is a game children are excited about playing because it involves receiving positive attention by being chosen to come along with someone else. Positive attention is continued throughout the game — everyone who is "coming along" is being watched by the members of the group who are sitting. Even the person who ends up without a chair in the rush for seats at the end of the round is not a loser because she becomes the leader (a positive role) for the next round. No one is eliminated or punished for not making it to a chair. Everyone continues to play and have fun together. The group can continue playing the game as long as they are having fun.

After Come Along, we played an animal pantomime game and The Magic Tube. These games gave the student opportunities to use their bodies, voices, and imaginations expressively. I was able to evaluate where they were in terms of expressive, social, and imaginative abilities.

I started the second session by asking each child to draw how she felt that day. I passed out sheets of paper that had outlines of heads with noses and blank eyes on them. The children filled in the rest of the facial features. I asked each child to show the face she had drawn and say how she felt. Everyone drew a happy face, but not everyone said she felt happy. It was obvious there was some confusion with identifying emotions. We talked about why each face looked happy.

Then we listed different kinds of emotions a person might feel. I divided them up into two categories: comfortable and uncomfortable. Comfortable emotions included happy, surprised, excited, and joyful. Uncomfortable emotions included angry/mad, sick, sad, grouchy, worried, and scared/afraid. We took turns acting out the different emotions we had listed with our bodies and our faces. As each person acted out an emotion, I pointed out what parts of the body changed to express it. As we went along, I asked them to help me identify the changes.

Next we moved on to sculpting emotions. I did not think they would be able to sculpt each other because they did not know how to touch each other appropriately, so I sculpted each student into a statue of a different emotion. The others guessed which one it represented. They did very well with this.

Then we looked at pictures of people's faces and identified how they were feeling from their facial expressions. There was a little confusion about some of the more subtle expressions, but on the whole the class did well. To review, we talked about how we could tell how other people are feeling when we look at them: through the expressions on parts of the face (eyes, mouth, cheeks, eyebrows), through the person's body position, and through the kinds of movements they make. Then we closed the session by breathing together for relaxation. I found that if we slowly raised our arms together as we breathed in and lowered our arms as we breathed out, the students were able to stay together, breathe slowly, and remain serious about what they were doing.

We started the third session by reviewing our list of comfortable and uncomfortable emotions. Then I asked everyone to draw a sad face on their face outlines. We shared the faces we drew. Some faces looked sad and some didn't. We talked about why they looked sad or not.

Then we looked at more pictures of people's faces and identified how they were feeling. Students were much better with this exercise the second time around. Each time someone identified a feeling, they had to say what they saw that told them it was that particular feeling.

As soon as interest in the pictures waned, we moved on to play a rousing game of Making an Entrance, followed by Come-Go-Stay, and a few simple tone-of-voice exercises. To introduce the tone-of-voice concept, I said each student's name with different emotions in my voice. They had to identify how I felt about them. This was fun and easy for them. Then I had them practice saying hello to each other with different tones of voice and asked the others what the person who was speaking felt. We ended the session with some breathing relaxation.

The fourth session began the same way the third had. We listed our comfortable and uncomfortable emotions on the board. Then I asked them to draw an angry face. Almost everyone was able to do this. We shared our pictures and talked about why they looked angry.

I showed them more pictures of people's faces and asked them to make a sound that person might make which expressed what she was feeling. Then we role-played a number of situations in which they might find themselves during the day in the classroom. The situations included several that their teacher had identified as causes of emotional upsets earlier in the year. The upsets, in fact, were the reason she had asked me to work with the class, hoping that I would teach some pro-social behaviors. The scenarios we acted out included: someone pushes in front of you in line, someone walks by and takes your pencil off your desk, you feel sick and want to be left alone but someone keeps talking to you and gets right in your face, a friend has hurt your feelings and comes to apologize to you, the person next to you starts to copy off your paper during a test. After each role-play we talked about how each character in the scene felt, what the actors did, and what else they could have done.

The classroom teacher and I were both quite surprised when the students always opted to play out the positive behavior choices in every role-play situation. I tried to get them to be "bad," but they insisted on being polite and helpful in every scene. Afterward the teacher said, "This tells me that they really do know the appropriate way to behave, even if they don't always make that choice." We ended that session, as we had the others, by breathing slowly together.

The last three sessions I decided to teach positive behavior choices through three different stories which focused on accepting oneself, awareness of others' feelings and needs, and getting along with others. The fifth class we acted out "The Little Fir Tree," the sixth class we acted out "Miss Nelson is Missing," and the last class we did "The Stone in the Road." We had time to act out each story at least twice, so students could try out different roles and see how it felt to play a different character. Everyone was on their best behavior and cooperated well together. The classroom teacher said that she observed a positive change in behavior and awareness of feelings in class at other times during the seven weeks we worked together.

Developing Life Skills

Some special-education classes focus on teaching life skills, such as how to shop for food at the grocery store, how to travel by public transportation, how to cook, how to order in a restaurant, and how to do laundry. Role-playing real-life situations before actually doing them provides students with the opportunity to rehearse actions and words.

Real-life situations do not seem as overwhelming if they first have been practiced in the safe environment of the classroom.

In addition to practicing what is supposed to happen in a real life situation, students can learn to deal with situations that do not go according to plan. Individuals with special needs can sometimes be taken advantage of by others. They can become confused when something unexpected happens. If they have not previously developed coping strategies, they can be at a loss for how to handle themselves in these situations. Role-play situations can be set up in which something goes wrong and students must figure out how to solve the problem or correct the situation. What if you are riding the bus, fall asleep, and miss your stop? What do you do? How do you get home? What if you buy something at a store and the cashier shortchanges you? What do you say? How can you prove you did not get the right amount of money back? Students can try several different strategies for dealing with each situation and evaluate which seem to be most effective for solving the problem. For more information on role-playing for educational purposes, see *Sociodrama: Who's in your Shoes?* by Patricia Sternberg and Antonina Garcia.

Dealing with Test Anxiety

Many times students do poorly in test situations, not because they do not know the material, but because they are so anxious and worried about failure that they freeze up. Remind your students that the purpose of taking a test is not to prove what they *do not* know, but to provide them with the opportunity to show off how much they *do* know. Tests let the teacher know what material she has done a good job of teaching.

Take time each day to teach and practice physical relaxation and breathing skills as part of your regular classroom routine. Some of the basic warm-up activities suggested in Chapter 7 will work quite well to loosen up students' muscles, oxygenate their blood, and clear their minds for concentration. There are many good suggestions for teaching relaxation skills to students in *Spinning Inward: Using Guided Imagery with Children* by Maureen Murdock, *Why Zebras Don't Get Ulcers* by

Robert Sappolsky, *Fighting Invisible Tigers* by Earl Hipp, and *Smart Moves: Why Learning is Not All In Your Head* by Carla Hannaford.

Positive mental images about learning and taking tests can be suggested in short guided-imagery sessions. When creating a guided-imagery journey, use positive images that put the student in control. The images could be as literal as students imagining taking a math text in a relaxed state, effortlessly writing down all the correct answers, and receiving the test paper back with an *A* on it. Images could be symbolic of success. Ask students to imagine they are flying through the air, effortlessly climbing to the top of a mountain and looking around at the surrounding countryside, sailing across the surface of the ocean and seeing deep into the sea beneath them, or jumping hurdles on a horse.

Some students find that spending a few minutes engaged in a right-brain activity they enjoy, such as drawing, singing, or dancing, is a good pre-test relaxation technique. This works because it engages parts of the brain not involved in analytic tasks, giving them a short break. The student comes back to academic work refreshed and better able to concentrate.

Providing students with a short period of relaxation or guided imagery before each test is very important. It gives them the chance to put their relaxation skills into practice in a real-world situation. Teaching relaxation techniques and then not making time for them in your schedule undercuts your message that you want them to do well on their tests and that relaxation is a powerful and important skill. Actions speak louder than words!

=============================

Drama for Transition from School to Work
By Cindy Bowen

I started using drama when I was a support counselor at Ivymount School, an independent school for students with disabilities in Rockville, Maryland. A lot of students would express themselves through negative behavior. My job was to help students express what they felt in an appropriate way with people within the classroom and outside in the community. My first task was to get them to cool down. Then I would go through a process of talking about what the problem was and how they reacted to it and then talking about alternative ways to react to it. Before they went back to the classroom, we would role-play the appropriate behavior. I would be the person that they needed to communicate with better or I would role-reverse and be them and they would play the other person. Then we would go back to the classroom and the teacher would come out and practice the new behavior with them as well.

When I moved into the transition specialist position, I noticed that there was a lot of talk, a lot of things to look at, and things to read about. But most of our kids didn't read. They had a lot of verbal communication problems and had a hard time retaining the skills we were trying to teach them to do in the community: job skills, how to order in a restaurant, how to take the bus, and so on. In the Transition Class I would do drama with them. For the first week of a unit, say, how to dress at work, we would talk about the skill and watch videos that showed the right way to do it and the wrong way. Then I'd have students do concrete activities. They might cut pictures out of magazines of appropriate clothing for work or school or recreation, followed by a fashion show where some of the students would model different kinds of clothes while the rest of the class identified what kind of clothes they were wearing and where these people were going. So I would put the information in the unit into a concept they could look at concretely and remember.

For the job interview unit we videotaped the students practicing interviews. I would portray a boss who was looking to hire an employee and I would talk about the job that I had available. I'd interview one student at a time and then have them go back to the group and describe what kind of boss I was and what kind of job I was hiring for. They would need to look at my verbal behavior and my nonverbal behavior to assess that and draw conclusions. This was important because being able to read people was very difficult for them.

I developed a questionnaire about "What Do You Want Your Future to Look Like?" I sent it to the parents and I had the students do one as well. I would practice with the students before their IEP (Individual Education Plan) meetings, so they were able to talk about what they wanted for their future and advocate for themselves. I'd say "Self-advocacy is one area. Where do you see you need help in that area?" So they might say, "I want to be able to vote." Or it could be as simple as, "I want to be able to tell my parents what I want," or "I want to make my own choices about what I wear." When we got to the career, we'd role-play it. We'd have students in the classroom play the other parts. For living arrangements, they might say, "I want to live in an apartment" or "I want to live in a house with other people." So we would play it out. And then we'd practice how they'd tell their parents what they wanted. I also would meet with the parents and have them do the same thing, "This is what I want for my child." This was a lot of work for both the parents and the students, but it was worth it.

One area of difficulty that drama helped with was many of the kids had "pie in the sky dreams" about what they wanted to be. I'd tell them that I had wanted to be an opera singer, but I'm not because I don't have the voice for it. But I still like to sing and can sing in the church choir. A lot of kids wanted to be professional basketball players. I would have them research the job and asked them what they liked about it. Then I'd ask them to think of other jobs available around here that might include some of the things they liked about that job that they could do. Sometimes it would turn out to be the uniform that they liked and sometimes it would be the basketball. I'd say, "Well, you can play basketball now."

I would have parents role-play with me how to respond when their child came home and said, "I want to be a professional basketball player." Instead of saying, "That's ridiculous! You can't do that!" I'd have them practice asking their child questions to get to what the real goal in having a job is and what the needs are that he has wrapped around that particular choice. Also, we would work on how to convey that their child needed to have a backup plan, because not everyone can become a basketball player

I also ran a group with the social workers called "Express Yourself." We would deal with some aspect of relationship communication — either parents with kids, kids with kids, or kids with bosses. We would brainstorm all the different scenarios that could happen. It might be something that actually happened to them or it might be something they heard about or worried about happening to them. We'd practice these scenarios and then the group would act them out for another classroom. We'd stop in the middle of the scene and have the students in the classroom react to what they thought was going on: was it a positive way to handle the situation or was it a negative way? That was really effective. Again, material that was usually covered in a theoretical way was turned into something concrete. I know this was effective because when I went to a job site, I would have students ask me, "Did I handle this like so-and-so handled it in the play?" I could say, "Yes, I think that's a really good way to handle it." They were able to pick up on appropriate behaviors and generalize them better. They got words from the role-plays which they could use, because for some of our kids coming up with the words was often the hardest part

Performing for another group was like being the teacher for the day and improved their self-esteem. When these older students got to perform for the younger ones, mentoring relationships developed. I would facilitate sessions in which the teens would tell the younger students what it was like to work in the real world so that the students would think, "Hey, I can do this because there are older kids at this special school who are doing this. He's working, so I could work, too!" Many of these children had never been exposed to the idea that they could grow up and have a job in the community.

In parent groups I worked on skills for dealing with adolescents. I would role-play their teen doing something and the parent showed how they typically handled the situation. I often found that the teens were being treated like they were much younger than they actually were, so I'd say, "Okay, this is the way you used to do it when your child was young. How could you do it now that your child is a transitioning adolescent?" Then we'd practice new ways that were more age appropriate.

Now Ivymount has students with more language difficulties that require adaptive apparatuses, such as speech talkers and text support that enhance their ability to communicate. These students can't generalize well. That makes drama even more necessary. Role-play helps them figure out how to communicate and solve problems on the spot. Then when they get into a situation on the job, they aren't so scared and they don't freeze up.

The Transition team also has had business consortium meetings with job development staff. The community businesses were very nervous about having our students in their workplace, so we felt they needed to have a group where they could support each other. Either we go out into the community or they come to us and, as a group, we talk about the different disabilities that they may come across if they have one of our students, how to handle medical emergencies, and how to deal with behavior. We role-play with them because behavior management is generally not part of their job. This can facilitate the employers giving directions directly to our students instead of our job coaches always having to correct them. Ultimately, we want our students to not need a job coach and become more independent.

========================

Recommended Reading

Armstrong, T. (1993). *Seven Kinds of Smart.* New York: Penguin Books.

Armstrong, T. (2000). *Multiple Intelligences in the Classroom.* Alexandria, VA: Association for Supervision and Curriculum Development.

Asbury, C. & Rich, B. [Eds.] (2008). *Learning, Arts, and the Brain: The Dana Consortium Report on Arts and Cognition.* Washington, DC: Dana Press. Available from www.dana.org.

Blakemore, S. J. & Frith, U. (2005). *The Learning Brain: Lessons for Education. Boston:* Blackwell Publishing.

Eisner, E. (2002). *The Arts and the Creation of Mind.* New Haven, CT: Yale University Press.

Gardner, H. (1993). *Multiple Intelligences: The Theory in Practice.* New York: Bantam Books.

Gardner, H. (1999). *Intelligence Reframed: Multiple Intelligences for the 21st Century.* New York: Basic Books.

Hannaford, C. (1995). *Smart Moves: Why Learning Is Not All in Your Head.* Marshall, NC: Great Ocean Publishers.

Jensen, E. (2000). *Brain-based Learning: The New Science of Teaching & Training.* San Diego, CA: The Brain Store.

Markova, D. (1991). *The Art of the Possible: A Compassionate Approach to Understanding the Way People Think, Learn, and Communicate.* Newburyport, MA: Conari Press.

Markova, D. (1996). *The Open Mind: Exploring the 6 Patterns of Natural Intelligence.* Newburyport, MA: Conari Press.

Murdock, M. (1987). *Spinning Inward: Using Guided Imagery with Children.* Boston: Shambhala.

Sternberg, P. & Garcia, A. (2000). *Sociodrama: Who's In Your Shoes?* Santa Barbara, CA: Prager.

12. Inclusion

Inclusion is a very important issue and can be an emotionally volatile one. Years ago students with disabilities were removed from regular education situations and segregated into classrooms or schools which were adapted to their needs, but which kept them away from the rest of the school population. Because in many ways they were hidden away, they became stigmatized. Students in regular education classes rarely met students who had disabilities. They rarely had an opportunity to develop friendships with each other and to discover that disability or no disability people are all very much the same.

Today the push in education is for students to be placed in the least restrictive environment. Opportunities for inclusion are looked for as much as possible. The Americans with Disabilities Act (ADA), passed in 1990, prohibits discrimination against people with disabilities in terms of employment, public accommodations, services provided by state and local governments, public and private transportation, and telecommunication relay services. Schools, recreational programs, and theatres fall under the public accommodation category.

There has been confusion about what the ADA requires. It asks for "reasonable accommodations for individuals with disabilities in order to integrate them into the program to the extent feasible, given each individual's abilities" (Child Care Law Center, 2002). The key issues are reasonableness of accommodation, individuality, and integration.

Reasonableness of Accommodation. An organization needs to make an honest effort to provide accommodations by acquiring adaptive equipment, removing barriers to access, and modifying programming so people who have disabilities can participate. A reasonable accommodation in physical access would be to provide a ramp so people in wheelchairs could get into a building that could only be entered by steps or to relocate a meeting to the first floor if there was no elevator. In terms of program access, a reasonable accommodation would be providing a TTY so deaf customers could call for information, allowing a therapy/assistance dog to accompany a client into a building, or making any of the changes suggested in this book to help a student participate in a drama class or theatre production. However, the operative word is reasonable. If a specific accommodation is unreasonable — too expensive or will fundamentally alter the nature of the program — the organization is not required to make it. Some structural changes are outside of the financial abilities of an organization. Most programmatic changes are doable. One exception to this would be if an individual's condition would pose a significant threat to the health or safety of other children or staff in the program and there are no reasonable means of removing the threat, for example, a student who went into uncontrollable rages, hitting others or destroying property. It is not reasonable to accommodate someone who is going to injure others.

Individuality. Each person is going to have differing abilities and needs. Accommodations will vary from person to person. What one person with LD needs will be different from what another person with LD needs. People who are blind have differing amounts and kinds of vision. One may need a script in enlarged print, another may need a Braille script, and still another may need to have the script on tape or CD.

Integration means that individuals with disabilities need to be included with others without disabilities in programming. If the appropriate accommodations are made, the playing field can be leveled and everyone can participate together. "When Are You Required to Admit a Child with a Disability?" is a helpful chart that the Child Care Law Center publishes on their website (www.childcarelaw.org). (See the chart and corresponding ADA information that were in effect when this book was published on pages 426-427. The client provides a clear rubric for assessing whether inclusion is appropriate or not for an individual. When laws change, the CCLC revises this chart and its other documents to keep them current.

I am a firm believer in inclusion. I think it works in most situations. However, in order to succeed and have a positive experience in a drama classroom, students need to have reached certain levels of social skills and artistic confidence. Equally important, teachers, directors, staff, and administrators need to have the knowledge, skills, and appropriate attitude to make the accommodations needed by the included students. If a person is not made welcome in a group, his experience will not be a positive one.

Drama involves interactive, cooperative, symbolic play. Students who are still in solitary, parallel, or associative play stages are not developmentally ready to fully join in drama activities. They may shut down, go off by themselves, suffer painful shyness, or get into conflicts with other students. A student who is not socially and emotionally prepared to be included will not have a successful experience. Faced with yet another situation of failure, he will turn off to the arts.

How can you tell if someone is ready? One way is to do an assessment to see if drama is appropriate and, if so, what type of drama class would be best. Set up a session where you can play a few drama games, such as The Magic Tube, Transformations, or Animal Pantomimes, and act out a short story together. You will quickly be able to tell if he can follow directions and how long his attention span lasts. You will also be able to tell if he is able to interact with you or if he prefers to play alone. You can explain what happens in a drama class.

Ask him if he likes pretending to be other people or animals and if he enjoys acting out stories. Ask if he would like to be in a class where he can do those things with others. It is important to discover whether or not a potential student wants to take a drama class. No matter how highly developed his social and emotional skills are, if he does not want to do it, he is not going to have fun! There is a young man in Manhattan, Kansas, whom I would love to have in my Barrier-Free troupe, but he is just not interested in theatre. His love is sports, so he prefers to participate in Special Olympics.

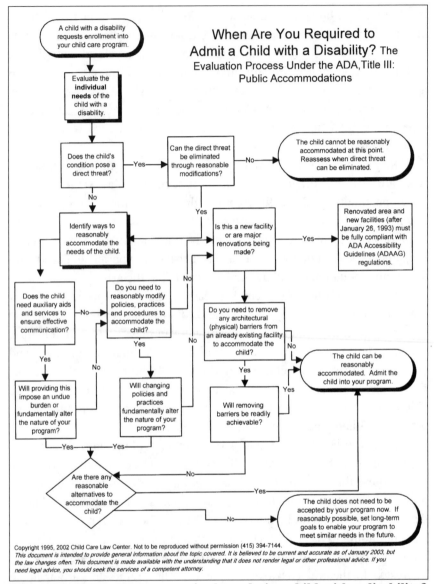

Figure 31: When are you required to admit a child with a disability? Part 1. From the Child Care Law Center. Used with permission.

THE AMERICANS WITH DISABILITIES ACT (ADA)
A NEW WAY OF THINKING: TITLE III

ADA GOAL:

> To *make reasonable accomodations for* individuals with disabilities in order to *integrate* them into the program to the extent feasible, given *each individual's* abilities.

ADA PRINCIPLES:

- INDIVIDUALITY
  the abilities and needs of *each* individual;

- REASONABLENESS
  of the modification to the *program* and to the *individual;*

- INTEGRATION
  of the individual *with others* in the program.

TYPES OF MODIFICATIONS:

- AUXILIARY AIDS AND SERVICES
  special equipment and services to ensure effective communication;

- CHANGES IN POLICIES, PRACTICES AND PROCEDURES;

- REMOVAL OF BARRIERS
  architectural, arrangement of furniture and equipment, vehicular.

REASONS TO DENY CARE:

- ACCOMMODATION IS UNREASONABLE, and there are no reasonable alternatives.

  - For **auxiliary aids and services**, if accommodations pose an *UNDUE BURDEN* (will result in a significant difficulty or expense to the program) or will fundamentally alter the nature of the program;
  - For **auxiliary aids and services**, or **changes in policies, practices or procedures**, if accommodations *FUNDAMENTALLY ALTER* the nature of the program;
  - For **removal of barriers for existing facilities**, if accommodations are *NOT READILY ACHIEVABLE* (cannot be done without much difficulty or expense to the program). Child care facilities built after January 26, 1993 must comply with ADA Accessibility Guidelines (ADAAG)

- DIRECT THREAT
  The individual's condition will pose or does pose a significant threat to the health or safety of other children or staff in the program, and there are no reasonable means of removing the threat.

This document is intended to provide general information about the topic covered. It is believed to be current and accurate as of Januray 2003, but the law changes often. This document is made available with the understanding that it does not render legal or other professional advice. If you need legal advice, you should seek the services of a competent attorney.

Figure 32: When are you required to admit a child with a disability? Part 2. From the Child Care Law Center. Used with permission.

In determining what kinds of accommodations might be necessary, you can gather a great deal of information from observing a child in his school environment. Speak with the teacher about the student's strengths and weaknesses. Knowing a child's abilities is particularly important because they can be used to provide opportunities for him to shine. Ask what the teacher is working on academically with him at this point. He might need to develop some skills, such as listening, following directions, or initiating action, which you can work on through your class. If a teacher says something like, "Well, I don't know how he'll do in your class, he's always daydreaming (or playing with action figures or making up stories)," that could be a very good sign in terms of drama!

Talk with the potential student's parents. Ask if he does dramatic play at home. Does he play with puppets or dolls? Does he act out animals or characters he sees on TV or from stories his parents read? Ask about other drama experiences he might have had at school, at camp, or at day care. Find out if he has had other inclusive experiences and how they went. You can avert mistakes by finding out what went wrong in a different situation. You can utilize what succeeded without having to go through trial and error yourself. Find out what the parents feel his strengths and weaknesses are — this may be very different from what his teachers think. Ask them why they think a drama class would be good for him. Find out if they have explained to him what drama class is all about and if they have asked him how he feels about taking one.

While parents usually know their child better than anyone else, avoid relying entirely on a parent's assessment of the child's ability without also meeting the child. Parents sometimes overestimate or underestimate their child's ability. Julia was one student who could have been included in regular drama classes from the outset. She had learning disabilities and went to a private, special-education school, so her mother assumed that her daughter would need a segregated learning experience in the arts and signed her up for my special-needs creative drama class. Very quickly I realized that Julia had excellent group skills, wonderful balance and coordination, and, although English was her second language, she expressed herself well verbally. If I had known in time, I would have put her into a regular class with her age peers her first semester, but by the time I discovered her many strengths, classes were already underway.

The next semester she joined a regular dance class and fit in extremely well with the other students, making friends who she invited home to play.

On the other hand, one mother told me over the phone that her son's major difficulty was a language delay. This, I told her, would be something that could be accommodated in a regular class. However, she neglected to tell me about his extreme attention deficits and spinning behaviors because she did not realize they would be a problem for the other children and the teacher. They were, and the teacher and I had to work very hard to come up with ways to address his needs along with those of the other children who were distracted by his constant movement!

In another situation, a well-meaning family signed up their teen-aged daughter, who was recovering from a traumatic brain injury, for summer camp, having been told that theatre would be therapeutic for her. She had never been interested in drama before her accident and she was even less so now. She was not given any choice in the matter because they were determined to do whatever it took to help her rehabilitation. Needless to say, she was miserable and so was the girl assigned to be her companion. Fortunately for everyone involved, her family found another summer program that focused on math and science, which they decided would be more therapeutic for her, and pulled her out of camp after a few weeks.

Dealing with Teachers and Administrators

Making programmatic accommodations requires providing support and education for teachers and other professionals who will be interacting with students who have disabilities. As Arts Access Director I made sure that all teachers were aware whenever students with special needs registered for their class. I provided copies of written information about the disabilities involved and written ideas for how to help the student adapt. I talked them through their fears and answered questions either on the phone or in person. If the student had been in another teacher's class, I would connect the new teacher up with the old one who, having already succeeded with the child, could serve as a consultant. This really empowered the teachers because they now saw themselves as experts on inclusion along with me. A number of them have written the teacher essays in this book. I would visit a classroom if the teacher wanted feedback on her interactions with the class. I also offered workshops at least once a year on disability awareness, behavior management, learning styles, or accommodation.

Did all of the teachers and administrators jump on the bandwagon and become experts on inclusion? Alas, no. There were a few holdouts who saw students with disabilities as a burden added to their class. They saw the disability, not the child. One camp director did not feel she needed me to do a pre-camp workshop for her staff and did not pass out any of the written information I had copied on the disabilities her staff would need to know about. I found the stack of copies months later stuffed in a cupboard and immediately understood why I had had to be called in repeatedly for emergency consultations during the camp — no one had been provided with the basic information the staff needed to proactively provide accommodations from day one.

If your staff does not buy into inclusion, it will not work. Students take their cue on how to relate to each other from the adult in charge. If the teacher feels uncomfortable working with a student who has been included, the other students will intuitively sense that and feel uncomfortable, too. On the other hand, if a teacher takes an active lead in including and accepting the differences and needs of all students, everyone in the class will have the same opportunities.

Dealing with Typically Developing Students

Making accommodations for students with disabilities also means making sure typically developing students are ready to welcome them into class. This is less a problem today than 20 years ago because more inclusion has been done in public schools; however, awareness and education on disabilities is still lacking and this lack causes people who are "different" to be stigmatized by those who "aren't."

Typically developing students in the age range of five to nine years are often accepting of others who are different from them. They may be very curious at first, but if the "differentness" is openly and immediately addressed, they usually forget about it. However, children in this age

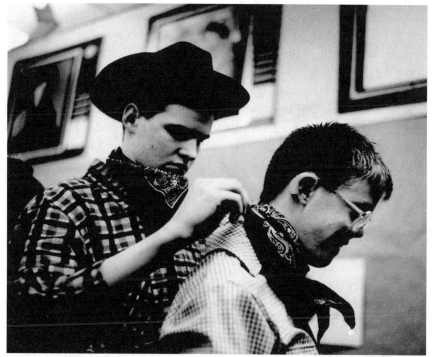

photo by Keith Jenkins

Figure 33: Inclusive experiences in the arts build friendships.

range are *also* in the process of learning very basic group-interaction skills. They have not always developed the social skills or emotional maturity to be able to help and encourage another student who is struggling to participate in the group.

By the time they reach their pre-teen and adolescent years, typically developing students have usually developed better group skills, but they may have become judgmental and unaccepting of others who are "different." One of the major socio-emotional themes of adolescence is finding a way to fit in — and the best way to do this is to be as similar to everyone else as is possible! Teens often feel insecure and, once they make up their minds about how they feel about someone, can be very stubborn and cruel.

If a disability is an obvious one, such as cerebral palsy, deafness, Down syndrome, or use of a wheelchair, be open and honest with all the class members about it from the beginning. The other students will see the disability and be curious about it. If the disability and their curiosity are not acknowledged and processed at the outset, the proverbial elephant will stand in the middle of the room and students will continue to see the disability and not the person.

The concept of working as an ensemble is an important one in theatre. It is important to introduce it early to young actors. Stress that everyone is here to help each other and to have a good time together. Actors must learn to work with each other, respect each other, and support each other in order to excel individually and as a group. In an introductory session, let each person share how the others can help him do his best. Each student and the teacher can be given an opportunity to share his own special needs and sensitivities with the class — for each of us has them. One teacher shared the following story about an introductory session with her class:

> I started the circle by saying that as the teacher, I had a special need that they all listen to me when I was talking, because if they didn't listen, we wouldn't be successful in our class. As we went around the circle, I was amazed by what I heard. One child said that he was very short and he needed people not to make fun of him because of this. Another child said that she got embarrassed easily and needed people not to laugh at her. When we got to Cheryl [a girl with cerebral palsy], she was very upfront and honest, explaining that often others were scared of her or didn't want to be near her because of her leg brace, etc. She asked that everyone just relax around her and treat her normally (*Wings to Fly* 1993, p. 347).

Caleen Sinnette Jennings also addresses how to open a discussion about students' needs in her essay later on in this chapter. If the disability is an "invisible" one like a learning disability or ADHD and the student does not choose to share it during the introductions, the teacher does not need to point it out or make an issue of it. She can quietly make adaptations in the class structure to help the student.

Particularly in the first few weeks, and throughout the semester, make sure students are partnered and grouped in a variety of ways in order to mix everybody together. This allows everyone to get to know each other and discourages the formation of cliques. It also allows students to see each other's strengths up close.

Be ready to stop and confront conflicts between students if they arise. Your class rules should require students to respect others and their ideas. You might be able to nip teasing in the bud with non-verbal cues or verbal reminders. You might need to pull an individual who is behaving insensitively aside and talk to him. You might need to stop class for a group discussion. Maybe some role-playing or a few disability-awareness exercises would be appropriate to help the typically developing students understand the situation of the student who has special needs. Drama is about resolving conflicts and coming to understand other human beings better by putting yourself in their shoes for a short time. A class that covers less material, but learns something about the human condition and how to relate sensitively to others, has had a more successful semester than a class that produces a slick end product, but has only generated competition and animosity among the participants.

Use students to support each other. If a student has dysgraphia or an auditory processing problem, another student can help by writing down homework assignments or the director's notes. If a written in-class assignment, such as a character biography or a script analysis, is given, the teacher or assistant could serve as a scribe and take dictation from the included student. An even better strategy for this situation could be to turn the assignment from an individual project into a partner or group project. A number of students could work together to brainstorm ideas while one writes them down for the group. If a student has a reading problem and a script is being read out loud by the class, pair him with a friend who reads well. Both will benefit from this interaction.

When handled correctly, inclusion offers as many growth experiences for the typically developing students as for the included students. Experiencing diversity early in life helps children learn to accept and appreciate others for their inner, creative being. It teaches children not to stereotype individuals based on physical appearances or first impressions. It enhances their ability to communicate with many different kinds of people and encourages them to see people as wonders to be discovered rather than as problems to solve. One mother of a typically developing student wrote this about her daughter's experience in the Pegasus performing company:

> This was a worthwhile experience for Jane, who learned about handicaps [sic] and disabilities and how people can still have satisfying and fulfilling lives in spite of them. The Pegasus experience enlarged Jane's world and further sensitized her to people. Furthermore, it enhanced her perspective, which has been, due to limited worldly experiences, somewhat confined. I feel very positive about the Pegasus experience for Jane and feel it might even affect her future choice of career.

Assistants and Companions

If the child being included has concentration problems or is easily distracted, an assistant can help keep him on task. If the student has problems with fine-motor skills and the class will be doing a lot of artwork, an assistant can offer an extra hand so that the teacher can keep circulating among all the students. If the child has problems with gross-motor skills and the class will be doing a lot of movement, the assistant can help him keep up with the rest of the students so he does not feel left behind.

Providing a companion for a student who requires a lot of assistance is an alternative or an additional option to hiring a class assistant. Companions can offer more one-on-one, continuous attention than an assistant who must be shared with the whole class. If a companion is close to the age of the student — maybe a young person in high school or college who is interested in working in the areas of special needs — he can then become a "buddy" as well as an assistant to the student and help him through stressful or confusing situations. Sometimes you can get companions to volunteer; sometimes you need to offer a stipend. The cost of the companion could be covered by the parents or by the organization.

Classroom Adaptations

Most of the adaptations mentioned in Chapters 3 through 11 can be used in an inclusive drama classroom and will serve to make a teacher's lesson plans and class structure stronger. Everyone — hearing and deaf — needs to have good lighting in order to see to speech-read and, therefore, hear the teacher well. Everyone — blind and sighted — can be confused and distracted by background noise. Everyone — regardless of level of cognitive processing abilities — can benefit from a clearly presented, carefully sequenced lesson.

Avoid using exercises in your lesson plan in which an included student would not be able to participate. Use your common sense. A game of leapfrog would not be appropriate if one of your students uses a wheelchair. However, do not automatically throw out an exercise until you have thought it through creatively for ways to adapt it. For example, to adapt a circle game for wheelchair users, everyone could move to a different X on the floor rather than exchanging chairs. If you have non-readers in the class, pictures can be substituted for words on flash cards used for acting games.

Be aware of sensitivities students may have. For instance, children with auditory processing problems, Asperger's syndrome, emotional issues, or certain kinds of hearing impairments may have sensitivity to loud noises. Usually the only way to find out about this is by asking. Students will sometimes, but not always, let you know in advance.

Adapt teaching pace to the processing abilities of the students. Students with language- or auditory-processing difficulties may need a slower pace of delivery and more time to respond. It is possible to slow down the pace of a class by talking just a little bit slower and/or spending just a little more time on each activity in order to allow the included child time to catch on, while simultaneously keeping other students engaged. The key is to focus students on developing concentration skills, seriousness of intent, and intensity of purpose. You will know as soon as boredom sets in; your students will become restless and distracted. If this happens, switch to a new activity or add a level of complexity to the exercise for students who are ready for it.

Class pace may need to be speeded up a bit to keep students with attention deficits or impulsive behavior engaged. If the rest of the students have normal to above-average cognitive processing, the pace of the class can probably be accelerated just a bit without anyone suffering. Provide a wider variety of exercises in each lesson plan. Instead of staying with one exercise for 15 minutes, spend five or 10 minutes on it, then move to the next. Review and repeat exercises or do variations on them from week to week. In this way, over the course of the semester, certain skills can be introduced and more solidly developed through repetition and rehearsal.

Casting Scenes and Plays

Casting can be approached in a number of different ways. In a professional situation the best actor is cast in the role in order to achieve the best artistic product. The ultimate goal is to have an artistic and critical success and earn lots of money. In educational theatre the purpose of a performance to help students grow as actors. A teacher or director needs to balance personal artistic desires and the need to present a successful overall product to parents with the need for individual students to achieve success while they are learning new artistic skills. In other words, the best actor might not get the role; it might go to the actor who is most willing to work, stretch, and grow or to the actor who has not had a chance to be on stage before and deserves the opportunity. Does this always happen? No. Sometimes in educational theatre, as in professional theatre, the best actors or the same actors get the roles.

Many teachers and directors like to play it safe and *typecast* actors in roles that they have played well before or that are similar to their real life personality or physical type. In a situation like this, an outgoing student would be cast as a social, confident character while a quiet, shy student would be cast as the "wallflower" in the play. An athletic-looking young man would play the jock or the love interest while a thin, sensitive-looking boy with glasses would end up as the nerd or the second fiddle.

Applied to students who have disabilities, typecasting means that a student who is deaf could only play a deaf character: Belinda in *Johnny Belinda*, Helen Keller in *The Miracle Worker*, or Sarah Norman in

Children of a Lesser God. A student who uses a wheelchair might be cast as Brick (whose leg is broken) in *Cat on a Hot Tin Roof* or as Franklin Delano Roosevelt in *Sunrise at Campobello.* This might be done whether the actor was appropriate for the personal qualities of the character or not.

Teachers and directors who typecast often justify it by saying that typecasting is done in professional theatres, so students should get used to it. While playing a character close to oneself is not necessarily easy, playing only one kind of character again and again does not stretch the physical, emotional, or imaginative range of any acting student. Giving a student different types of roles sends the young person a message of "you can be anything you want to be" instead of "you can't be..." This message is easily generalized from the classroom to everyday life.

The opposite of typecasting is *casting against type,* which allows students to be challenged with roles that are unlike themselves. This can generate artistic growth if the character is not too far away from the student in age and experience and the teacher/director offers plenty of coaching support. However, it will only generate frustration and confusion if the character is too complex or too far away from the student's current abilities and experience. Asking a fifth grader to perform King Lear will probably be too big a stretch; asking him to play Demetrius, the young lover, in *A Midsummer Night's Dream* will probably be an excellent challenge. The teacher/director must be able to judge when a student is ready to be stretched and what kinds of challenges are currently needed to stimulate his growth.

It is important in professional theatre to allow actors with disabilities to play disabled roles instead of casting able-bodied actors in them. Mark Medoff has stipulated that all professional productions of *Children of a Lesser God* use deaf and hard-of-hearing actors for the deaf and hard-of-hearing roles. This makes sense because it provides employment opportunities for disabled actors; however, to only offer disabled roles to actors who have disabilities is unfair and limiting.

When casting students with disabilities, I like to use *blind* or *nontra-ditional casting.* This type of approach casts the actor in terms of acting ability and emotional rightness for a character rather than physical similarity to it. For example, an actor in a wheelchair who has a strong voice and stage presence might be very appropriate to cast as John Proctor in *The Crucible* or Jesus Christ in *Godspell*. Director Peter Sellars used this nontraditional casting approach when he cast Howie Seago, a virile actor of great physical presence who is deaf, as the mighty Greek hero Ajax in his production of Aeschylus' *Ajax*.

Casting should take the actor's strengths and weaknesses into consideration. An actor with a good sense of timing and verbal dexterity can do a lot with a character from a farce by word masters, such as Oscar Wilde or Tom Stoppard. An actor with good physical control and an ability to exaggerate will enjoy the challenge of bringing stock characters from the commedia dell'arte to life.

If you know a student has difficulty memorizing lines, you can cast him in roles where most of his lines are motivated by answering questions of other characters or responding to physical actions done to his character by others. This way the majority of his responses are directly initiated by another character in the play. If he listens closely and reacts, there's a good chance he'll be able to figure out what to do most of the time.

A student who has a poor sense of himself in space can be cast as a member of a group of characters who enter and exit together. He can stick with the other members of the group and take his movement cues from them. If he begins to wander, they can get him back with the group.

Instead of just ignoring them, assistive devices can be creatively incorporated into a play. A wheelchair can become a moveable throne, a boat, or a royal carriage, turning it from an image of impairment into an image of strength and authority. A crutch can become a sword. A loop-style hearing aid could be incorporated into a robot costume or used as an espionage device for a spy.

A brilliant example of creatively employing assistive devices for conscious artistic purposes was used in the Goodman Theatre's production of *She Always Said, Pablo*. The play portrays Gertrude Stein's turbulent relationship with Pablo Picasso by juxtaposing Stein's words with dramatized images of Picasso's paintings. Director Frank Galati cast Susan Nussbaum, an actress who uses a motorized wheelchair, as Gertrude Stein. Nussbaum's chair became part of the design and blocking strategy of the play, integrating Picasso's famous image of Stein in her armchair into every onstage portrayal. Nussbaum as Stein elegantly glided in and out of life-sized Picasso images, weaving the play together with words and movement.

Helping Students with Script Memorization

Sooner or later in most acting classes, students begin working with scripted material. Monologues and scenes must be committed to memory before they can be performed. As my high school acting teacher used to say, "Acting doesn't really begin until the lines are memorized. You can't act with a script in your hand."

Memorization of lines can cause problems for many students, particularly for students who have cognitive disabilities. No matter how you slice it, memorization takes time and commitment. Very few individuals have photographic memories or are what theatre people call "quick studies." However, there are ways to make memorization, if not pain-free, then at least a little easier. The following suggestions can be used for actors with and without disabilities.

First, make sure the actors understand what they are saying. If the lines don't make sense, they will be harder to memorize. Memorization is done primarily through a cognitive device called *chunking*. Bits of information are associated with other bits and slowly built into easily recognized units or patterns that are stored in the brain (Hunt 1982; Schacter 1996). If the information does not make sense, it cannot be chunked to anything else and then it will be difficult to recall. Compare the task of memorizing an unrelated list of items, such as a shopping list, with a poem that has a rhythm, images, idea or story, and a rhyme scheme to hold it together. Unless the items on the shopping list are associated with emotional and sensory images or are all the parts of one recipe, they will be difficult to associate and remember. On the other hand, a poem can be remembered for years without rehearsal. I have found again and again that lines that students cannot remember are lines they do not quite understand. One actor could not remember a joke because he did not understand what was funny about it. Once I pointed out the play on words, which had been obvious to me but had escaped him, he was able to remember the joke perfectly.

The best method for memorization is different for each person, depending on his dominant or preferred learning channel. Most people who have auditory processing strengths will read their lines out loud from the script over and over again. This repetition of saying the lines and listening to them serves to anchor them and their sequence in long-term memory.

Actors who have reading problems and auditory strengths can record a scene or speech and play the recording over and over again. This is how most of us learn popular songs. We hear them 40 times on the radio and suddenly discover that we're singing along. If actors can read, following along with the script while listening to the lines can help reinforce the lines visually and aurally at the same time. If an actor's reading is poor and he cannot read his lines smoothly enough to sound natural on a recording, the teacher or a parent can make the recording. Whenever I have the first read-through of a script with one of my barrier-free performing companies, I tape it and edit out the mistakes and side comments. Then I make copies and give them to all the cast members. Even the cast members who do not have disabilities like to learn their scripts by listening to the recorded version.

Students with kinesthetic strengths sometimes memorize better when they are moving. Several of my actors always read through their scripts or listen to their tapes while riding in the car. Somehow the motion of the car helps them focus and learn the lines. Other actors pace the room, rock in a rocking chair, or swing in a swing while they memorize. Some perform their blocking as they say their lines aloud.

For visual learners, lines and blocking could be videotaped. This worked well when I was teaching sign language to a group of hearing actors or choreography to a variety of actors. If the play involves a journey, visual learners might be able to hold onto sequencing and lines by drawing a map of where their character goes scene by scene. If no journey is involved in the story, a diagram of where the actor is on stage when she says each line might help associate the line with a place and action.

A long monologue could be broken down into a mind map, a diagram of all the important ideas and associations involved in the unit. This might help a visual learner or a global learner connect the ideas and phrases in a monologue in a non-linear, but meaningful way. (For more information about mind maps, see books on creativity and thinking by Tony Buzan.)

Lisa, one of my Pegasus actors who has Down syndrome, found that typing out her lines on the computer and then reading them back to her father helped her learn her lines. Other students find the same benefit from writing out lines by hand. The kinesthetic and visual repetitions help cement the words into long-term memory.

If an actor does not know his dominant learning style and you have not guessed it from observing which kinds of teaching examples he responds to most quickly, ask him to try several of these methods until he finds one that works well.

It is crucial to enlist the help of parents, siblings, and friends in practicing lines. Most lines are in the form of dialogue and each line is a response to what another actor has said. Knowing one's cues is as important as knowing one's lines. Without cues, the actor doesn't know when to come in with his line! Running lines with a friend or family member can become a fun social ritual. Many parents have commented to me that they enjoy their time working together with their child on memorizing their script. It is much easier to work on a project with someone else than to do it alone. Sometimes unexpected bonuses come out of it, too. Lisa's father had this to say about her line-learning experience:

> She was delighted [typing out her lines on the computer and reading them back] and it helped her learn her lines. It also led to a computer letter to her sister describing her role. Eventually she learned her lines very well and could recite the lines of many others as well.

Running lines with another person is one of the best ways to review and maintain lines once the initial memorization is done.

Another aspect of memory that needs to be taken into consideration is emotion. It is easier to remember something if it is associated with an emotion. This is because our brain links emotion to information in our brain's limbic system, one of the areas responsible for creating long-term memory (Hannaford 1995; Jensen 2000; LeDoux 1998). Our brains are built to pay attention to information that is emotionally charged in some way because, if the information is arousing, there is a good chance our survival is connected with it. Understanding what the character is feeling when saying a line and allowing oneself to feel that emotion while working on memorization and rehearsal will help plant the line in memory. This is not hard to do since most lines are meant to be said with emotion and meaning. This fits with what Helga and Tony Noice have discovered about the active experiencing principle discussed in Chapter 10. Actors connect all the emotional, cognitive, and physiological information they know about their character and join that with their lines to help them truthfully re-enact each moment of the play in every performance (Noice 1996; Noice, Noice, & Kennedy 2000, 2001; Noice & Noice 2007).

Above all, learn lines in short practice sessions. Trying to cram a whole script into one's head at one time only creates frustration, exhaustion, and memory blocks. There is too much information to put it into long-term memory all at once. Learn a bit, then stop and rest or do something else. Research shows that we do a lot of our consolidation of what we learn when sleeping, so a good night's sleep helps in creating new memories (Jensen 2000; Schacter 1997). When you go back to learn lines the next time, review the bit you learned before, then move on to a new section. Eric Jensen (2000) suggests: "repeat new learning 24 to 48 hours following an initial encounter, then daily, and every other day subsequently" (p. 157).

Words of Experience from Colleagues and Students

A series of essays on inclusion follows. I asked colleagues to explain what they have learned about teaching drama to integrated groups and I asked students with and without disabilities to share their experiences of being integrated in the arts. I think their testimony is more effective than my voice alone to support the value of inclusion.

==

Experiences with Inclusion
Elizabeth van den Berg

I have been fortunate to have had several students with disabilities included in my drama classes. I say "fortunate" because these students have taught me more about teaching than any others and have helped make me a better teacher.

I had many concerns the first time I was told I would have a student with special needs in an acting class. My first concern was crucial: would I know how to help this child have a successful experience and not turn her off to theatre and the arts? My second concern was about the other children: how would they react, how would they treat her, would they work with her in the ensemble style of my class? What would I do if there were problems?

I was given information about Stacy and her disability. She had hydrocephalus, which had caused learning disabilities and attention deficits. She also had some difficulties with speech and movement. Even though she had never taken an acting class before, the arts access director had met her and felt she would do very well included in a regular acting class for her first experience.

At first I thought my worst fears were being realized when the group noticed that Stacy was different and began to ostracize her. I made use of her lateness to class one day to have a talk with the rest of the students about her uniqueness and asked the other students for suggestions on how to best help her and make her part of the class.

As it turned out, Stacy was a wonderful addition to the group. She could not remember her blocking, so I enlisted other class members as her helpers. I always paired her with a responsible child who was making an entrance or exit at the same time and who would make sure Stacy got to the right spot on stage

I helped Stacy draw diagrams of the groundplan [the arrangement of furniture on the set] and trace her blocking pattern. She had trouble with line memorization, so I always gave her mother an extra copy of the script. At home they made a cassette tape of Stacy's portion of the dialogue so she could review her lines through listening to them as well as through looking at them in the script.

Stacy's mom was a dream. She was very open and always in communication with me about how class was going and how Stacy was doing. As a result, Stacy had a successful experience and came back to take many more drama classes at BAPA. It took a lot of give and take, patience, and keeping the lines of communication open with everyone to make it work.

Peter had auditory processing problems. His mother told me that he had recently gone through the Tomatis ear training method and was now able to make better sense of sounds. However, she did not make it clear to me that because of this, Peter would be extremely sensitive to loud sounds.

I had planned one class around balloons — jumping over, with, and around them, and then becoming a balloon. During the first exercise, one balloon popped. I had prepped the class that this might occur, and they all seemed to feel it was okay, except for Peter, who put his hands over both ears and would not take them away. I recognized the problem and changed my lesson plan immediately so as not to have any more popping balloons. However, the damage was done. It was only after class when he left the room and went into the hallway that Peter finally removed his hands from his ears. His mom then explained his sensitivity. From then on, I avoided loud sounds and we had no more difficulty.

To me, the most important issue in inclusion of students who have disabilities is keeping all lines of communication open. This means being upfront about problems with parents, students, their fellow classmates, and the administration. Having an arts access director as a liaison has been invaluable and very important in helping me get the information I need about each student. In addition, I have learned not to be afraid to ask students what they need in order to learn.

Positive Experiences with Inclusion
Caleen Sinnette Jennings

I believe that theatre has the power to heal. I have seen the power of theatre to build self-esteem and confidence and because of this, I have always prided myself on managing the classroom experience so that each child feels respected and valued. The stakes for me were raised significantly when I learned I would have a student with Tourette syndrome included in my acting class. I was, quite frankly, intimidated.

The wonderful thing about teaching is that you are forced to live by your own dictates. Often I tell my students, "When you're feeling scared and nervous, and the stakes are at their highest, that's the greatest opportunity for learning. To risk is everything!" Now it was my time to risk.

The first thing I did was to read several articles on Tourette syndrome, including a chapter from Oliver Sack's book *The Man Who Mistook His Wife for a Hat*, entitled "Wiccy, Ticcy Ray." I was fascinated by this mysterious condition, especially by the fact that it often manifests itself so perniciously in such highly intelligent and creative people.

"Okay," I thought, "it would be terrific if Gerald and I were able to work one-on-one, but I will have at least 19 other kids in the classroom, kids who are bright, creative, demanding, and somewhat pampered. Now what am I to do?" My biggest concern was that either I or one of his classmates would say something to hurt his feelings or, worse, to physically endanger him.

I knew that the only way I could honestly deal with the situation was to confront it outright. I decided to speak with Gerald and ask him openly about his condition, his past experiences in acting, and his concerns about interacting with his classmates. Gerald was a bright, articulate, and compassionate young boy. We spoke briefly and he answered my questions candidly and with unusual maturity.

One of my standard first-day exercises has always been mirroring. I have students stand opposite each other and mirror each other's body movements and voices. Clearly this would not do in this situation. So I went back to my acting texts and devised some other icebreakers. Gerald's presence in the class had already forced me to discard some old teaching habits in a positive way.

The first thing I did on the first day of class was to assemble everyone in a big circle. I told them about myself and outlined the way in which we would build the script for our final class presentation together. I told them the importance of working in an ensemble and how they had to trust and respect each other. I then called on them to introduce themselves to the group and tell us what was important to know about them. I made sure that Gerald was towards the middle of the process so that he was not immediately put on the spot.

When it came around to him, Gerald talked about himself, briefly mentioning his condition at the end of the introduction. I asked him if he would mind fielding some questions. He said that would be okay. I asked him:

What is important for us to know about Tourette syndrome?

How do the symptoms manifest themselves?

What did he need us to do when he had one of his episodes?

He explained that he knew the sounds he made were strange and disturbing to others and that he did not make them voluntarily. He also knew that many of his classmates would be tempted to imitate the sounds he made. But he told us that this was the worst thing we could do because that would intensify the symptoms. He said that during an episode, he would stay off to the side and asked that the group just ignore him.

I asked the group if they would commit themselves to the ensemble by respecting Gerald's wishes. They agreed unanimously. There were a few more questions from students, then I thanked Gerald heartily for his candor and moved on to the rest of the introductions.

In the middle of an exercise that day, Gerald had an episode. He made uncontrollable clicking and whooping sounds, tapped with a pencil, and kicked his foot against the chair. The sudden explosion of noise, quite naturally, attracted our attention. But because Gerald had prepared us, we watched for only a few seconds, as if to confirm the information that he told us, and then refocused on our work.

I wish I could say that the students rallied around him and he instantly became an accepted member of the group. But why should ten-year-olds be any different from adults? Most of the students shied away from him.

However, I only had one instance of a student making fun of him. When I noticed Matt clicking along with Gerald during an episode, I stopped the class. I said in a firm voice, "Matt, do you remember the ensemble commitment we talked about in the first class? Do you remember Gerald's request that we not imitate him?"

"Yes," Matt answered sheepishly.

"Well, I want all of us to stick to those commitments we made. Now let's get back to work."

There were no more incidents.

I paired Gerald with lots of students in different games and exercises throughout the beginning classes. As I got to know the rest of the students, I began to get a sense of who would make good scene-partner combinations. I eventually put Gerald in a scene with two other boys and a girl who had shown maturity and compassion throughout the semester. They developed a wonderful rapport working on the scene and this carried through into performance.

As the semester went on, Gerald had many episodes of varying intensity. The astonishing thing was that they never occurred during his scene work. He was an excellent actor. He loved the theatre, could sing any one of a thousand show tunes, and always had his lines memorized before anyone else.

Our show went up and Gerald did a splendid job. I got positive feedback from his parents, but the best feedback was Gerald's smile during the curtain call.

I used some of the same techniques the next year when a young deaf woman joined my summer camp acting class. Kim Smith was accompanied by Lisa Agogliati, the camp counselor for the group, who served as an interpreter. The first day of camp we did similar introductions. I was able to ask Kim and Lisa how they worked together and what we could do to ensure good communication. I asked for information that I genuinely wanted to know, in addition to information her classmates might want to know but be too shy to ask:

When we talk to you, should we look at you or your interpreter?

Where do you want us to stand when we are talking to you?

Will you let me know if I am speaking too quickly?

Do you prefer to sign without speaking or to speak as you sign?

In this case, my students were fairly mature adolescents and there was less risk of imitation or mockery. My greatest challenges were remembering to speak slowly and not to speak with my back turned away from her. I made it a point that the class learn simple signs to communicate with Kim.

Kim's acting was powerful and she soon had the respect of her classmates. Her biggest obstacle, as one might expect, was using her entire body and allowing her voice full volume for maximum expression. I felt that encouraging her to release her voice would free her physically and mentally. Just as with the other students, I gave her acting notes in front of the class. Everyone shared in each other's growth and development. I knew that once Kim knew we would not be shaken by the sounds she made, she would be freer to commit her body and her mind to the monologue at hand. I wrote her a special monologue entitled "SHHHH." The piece dealt with the frustrations of being told to shut up and not talk so loudly.

Kim performed the piece with an anger and intensity that were riveting.

I now teach at the university level and my prior experiences with inclusion have been invaluable. I am encountering more and more students who have forms of dyslexia and other learning challenges. I had a young deaf woman in one of my improvisational acting classes. Figuring out the logistics for her interpreter during the improvisational scenes took considerable thought and planning, but we created some fabulous improvs! I also taught this same student a semester-long independent study in playwriting during which she created a script about her coming of age. We worked without an interpreter in this instance.

I still find what makes me most nervous, but what ensures the greatest success, is to openly acknowledge the special circumstances involved in the interaction and to have each student clearly articulate his/her wishes to me and the group. We can then move forward with awareness and a beginning measure of trust.

It has been helpful to learn from, share resources with, and get support from colleagues who also work with the learning disabled and physically challenged. And, of course, the smiles and hugs I get from my students are the nicest part of the whole experience!

Including a Child Who Uses a Wheelchair
Jeanie Hayes Hatch

Daniel was a student who had osteogenesis imperfecta, a condition commonly known as brittle bone disease. He took my Story Theatre class for 8- to 12-year-olds at a two-week summer drama camp. In each class we played drama games and acted out a story from Greek mythology, fairy tales, or folk tales. The last few classes were focused on creating our own improvised stories.

Daniel used a wheelchair, but had complete use of his hands, head, and upper body. Accordingly, I chose warm-up exercises at the beginning of each class that could be played sitting down so that Daniel could be involved. One game we played was "Thumper." It involves using your hands to describe your favorite hobby. For example, if a student liked to read, he would put his two hands together, flat out, like an open book. After everyone in the circle had pantomimed their hobbies, students would pass them back and forth to each other without speaking.

In another game we passed around a scarf. It was up to each actor to make the scarf into something different from what it actually was. For example, it could be rolled up and worn as a belt or hung around the neck as a necklace or folded up into a sandwich.

After warm-ups we would play a drama game that stressed verbal skills. For example, I might ask each child to describe his favorite play space and show us using the drama space. With the help of an assistant, Daniel was able to describe and show us where he liked to play.

If I used exercises that involved only physical movement, I made Daniel my assistant or the game caller. Here he could be involved and feel important as he monitored the game. At the end of every class we played "On the Bank/In the River." In this game a line of masking tape on the floor creates the "river bank." When the actors are on one side of the tape, they are "on the bank." When they are on the other side, they are "in the river." A caller tells them to jump "on the bank" or "in the river." When they hear the command, they must immediately hop over the tape to the correct side. Commands are quickly alternated or repeated and if an actor gets confused and lands in the wrong spot, he is "out." Daniel was always the caller and whenever he spoke, the other students jumped. It was one of his favorite games to play.

The last class was an informal presentation for the parents. We played Typewriter, an improvisational game in which one actor "writes" the story on the spot and the others have to enact the story as it is being created. Daniel was the Author who "typed up" the story, improvising it as he went along.

Daniel was involved in every aspect of the class. He appeared to be having fun and found no obstacles to his participation in any exercises. The other students enjoyed the class as well. They accepted Daniel and responded to his directions with respect when he was serving as the caller for games like On the Bank/In the River.

The most important factor in the success of the class was Daniel's enthusiasm and intense desire to do drama. He is an excellent actor. Channeling his emotions into drama activities is one of his true delights. I think he could probably never have enough of it. He would be happy doing drama all day long.

Osteogenesis imperfecta is a very frustrating condition for an active and intelligent ten-year-old boy, but Daniel never gave up trying. He was always ready to participate and he always wanted to learn more. Because of his creative spirit and his indomitable courage, he has been a teacher to me.

==============================

Including Children with Special Needs
Tim Reagan, RDT

My first experience with a child with disabilities was when I was in high school, working as an assistant swim teacher for the American Red Cross's Learn to Swim Program in Camillus, New York. One energetic eight-year-old had Down syndrome. She had been placed with a group of children two to three years younger and she functioned extremely well in the class. Her love for the water was a positive influence on the other children. They realized that they were all in the same boat — either you learned to swim or you sank to the bottom! I was given no training in terms of special needs, so in my naiveté, I made an intuitive choice to treat her like the other kids. I believe that because I set up no psychological barriers through my approach and because she had no physical disabilities to hinder her learning to swim, she was accepted by the other children. Her disability did not stop her from meshing with the other children or keep her from "diving" in.

Just after finishing graduate school, I was teaching drama classes at the Bethesda Academy of Performing Arts. Brian, a child with Down syndrome, was included in my creative drama class. As rewarding as this experience was, my biggest frustration was when Brian had to wait his turn with an activity, such as taking on the role of an audience member or critic while observing the work of his peers, typical children without disabilities. Brian had difficulty maintaining personal self-management skills and regularly became distracted. Fortunately, the pace of the class served as an encouraging challenge to him. I discovered that he thoroughly enjoyed himself in the two semesters of my creative drama class. He really appreciated being treated like a "regular kid." Brian continued studying drama by participating in many other class and performance opportunities.

Brian and I have stayed in contact over the years. In fact, we have worked on various theatre projects together, including a production of *Bless Cricket, Crest Toothpaste, and Tommy Tune* by Linda Daugherty at Sidwell Friends Middle School, where I now teach. The story captures the struggle of a teenage girl named Cricket as she comes to terms with her older brother Tom who has Down syndrome. I invited Brian to perform the role of Tom as a guest artist. His mere presence at rehearsals demystified the stigma of someone with a disability. My students learned more about someone with Down syndrome from Brian. And, not only did my students help Brian throughout the rehearsal and production process, Brian helped them eliminate the stereotype about people with Down syndrome. Brian's many years of theatre in summer camp, classes, and performing companies made him able to come in as a performer and an educator. He was able to feel comfortable about discussion groups, etc. because he had been on stage so many times. I could not imagine him being able to do something like that when he was a teen!

Today, Brian is 30 years old and lives in an apartment with his wife Emily, who also has Down syndrome. They had a formal commitment ceremony in September of 2004. He and Emily live in a typical apartment under the supervision of a counselor. Brian works during the week at a local restaurant bussing tables and washing dishes. He is active in his local parish church as an usher and regularly makes visits to the home of his parents on weekends. Brian takes public transportation and participates in a number of social groups, including a Playback Theatre company which I now direct. We are entering our next phase working as artists. I look forward to what the future brings.

When I worked at BAPA, I was coordinating an integrated arts program for a children's center in the same facility. That is where I met Anita. She joined the center's Kindergarten Complementary Program because she was not having a positive experience with her previous child-care provider. Anita was blind in one eye and had partial sight in the other. She wore thick glasses and had a tendency to bump into or trip over objects that her peripheral vision did not pick up.

I did not know how severe Anita's impairment was, so I conducted my creative drama class the way I always did. Anita immediately caught on and began to flourish. The arts opened a door for her. She found something she could do and enjoy as well. Anita became wonderful at using her imagination. She began to use full sentences, express her thoughts and ideas clearly, and communicate very effectively to the other children. Because of her experiences in this class, and with the others she took later on, Anita generated a strong sense of self-esteem and came out of her shell. It's now more than 15 years after I first met Anita and, just the other day, I received an email from her. She sought me out after doing some research on drama therapy. Anita was very involved with theatre throughout high school and is now a sophomore in college with a minor in theatre.

I find it truly amazing to hear about the lasting effects theatre/drama has had on the lives of the children I have taught and directed. As a drama therapist and theatre educator, this is one of the greatest rewards of the profession.

========================

Integrating Students who are Deaf
Lisa Agogliati

My background is dance and theatre — in that order. I am a movement person first and foremost. It is no wonder that my career in the arts ultimately found its niche with a language that "moves" as much as I do!

My first experience with inclusion was life-changing. In 1989 I worked as a counselor for a musical theatre camp for middle-school students at the Bethesda Academy of Performing Arts. In my group of 18 students, I had Kim, a 14-year-old girl who was deaf. She had always been interested in the arts, but the camp would be her first intensive experience working with dance, acting, and music classes in addition to performing in a full-scale musical.

My main concern with making this experience a successful one was communication. I had met with Kim and her mother a month and a half before camp started and learned that Kim had been included in her school through the Cued Speech program, a manual system of communication that involves the use of handshapes placed around the face which represent all the different consonants and vowel sounds of any spoken language. I immediately jumped right in and took a crash course.

Cued speech combined with occasional fingerspelling worked very successfully. Although sign language was not Kim's primary mode of communication, we did incorporate sign into several songs in the production, which provided her with a feature role in the show and the entire cast with a new learning experience. The summer proved to be a turning point in both our lives. I became particularly fascinated with sign for the stage, because of its incredible ability to fuse so naturally with theatre and movement. This was not an experience I wanted to keep to myself. Over the course of the next year both Kim and I started learning sign language, which ultimately led me to create a unique opportunity at BAPA for deaf and hearing teens to work together and learn about one another through theatre.

In 1990, with the support of Sally Bailey and the Board of Trustees, we formally established the Deaf Access program to offer performing arts programming for deaf and hard-of-hearing students, including a specialized teen company designed to bring together deaf and hearing teens through theatre. Fifteen years later, the program is now led by a deaf and hearing team of directors (myself and deaf artist/educator Donna Salamoff) and operates out of a new state-of-the-art facility in Bethesda, Maryland. Deaf Access is among only four deaf theatre programs in the country to receive three consecutive three-year grants from the U.S. Department of Education, along with several national honors for our program's innovative work. We have published two books: *Dreams to Sign* (with Sally Bailey) in 2001, a resource for hearing and deaf educators; and *The Garden Wall* (with award-winning author/illustrator Phyllis Tildes) in 2005, a children's book about the friendship between a hearing boy and a deaf girl.

Our current programming has come a long way from just one student to now over 150 each year and includes:

The Senior Deaf Access Company, comprised of deaf, hard-of-hearing, and hearing high school students, presents a unique style of children's theatre that blends sign language and voice, along with music, mime, and dance. Their innovative, highly visual productions are designed with multicultural themes and feature renowned deaf and hearing guest artists who conduct workshops on the selected culture. The Company works under the guidance of a professional production staff of deaf and hearing artists, playwrights, choreographers, composers, and designers.

Hand In Hand, an adult company of professional deaf and hearing actors who perform for school field trips and general audiences. Presented in sign language and spoken voice, the productions are fully accessible to both deaf and hearing audiences and are designed to increase public awareness of the culture of the Deaf.

Junior Deaf Access Company was created to serve as a training program for the Senior Deaf Access Company. Deaf, hard of hearing, and hearing middle school students can practice the theatrical techniques needed for combining sign language and English on stage and prepare for auditioning in the future. Hearing students can become more fluent with ASL; deaf students can learn to sign more expressively and theatrically.

Creative dramatics classes are offered on Saturday mornings for Deaf and KODA (Kids of Deaf Adults) children. These focus on teaching expressive communication, working together as a group, and learning how to tell stories through words, body, facial expression, and action.

In-school drama residencies of eight to 10 weeks duration are offered in Montgomery County Public Schools which have programs for students who are Deaf and hard of hearing at the elementary, middle school, and high school levels. This program has been very successful with integrating the arts into the curriculum for deaf and hard-of-hearing students. The use of informal drama provides a process-oriented experience for students and its connection to their areas of study gives the opportunity to enhance themes, units, and literature while they create an active learning environment. The main goals for the students during the residency are to sharpen the use of imagination, to develop collaborative learning skills, to encourage expressive use of the body and voice, and to experience active learning through informal drama.

Sign Theatre workshops are a part of our summer programming for middle-school musical theatre camps, and at least one song in sign language is incorporated into the final production. The goal of the workshops is to use drama games, acting techniques, and sign language together, training students to use their bodies more expressively while learning basic sign-language skills.

In addition, Donna Salamoff offers ASL classes for BAPA staff members so they can learn to communicate on a basic level with deaf parents, board members, staff, and theatre patrons.

Over the years I have been asked what the best part about my job is. Each time, I find myself coming back to the same answer: having the opportunity not once, not twice, but so many times — year after year — to see a dream come true. The incredible students and staff who are a part of our program are the reason such a dream lives on and hopefully will continue for many more years to come.

The most interesting thing to me about where Kim is right now is not that she is a teacher, but that she wound up teaching in an environment that reaches out to both deaf and hearing young people. She is witnessing again the bringing-together of two different worlds, only this time she is the leader, not the participant! It is her goal to be in a position to use the arts to educate, enrich, and entertain — to use the power of the arts to make a difference in young people's lives, just as they did in her own.

===================================

A Glimpse of American Sign Language through Theatre
Kim Smith

Being an educator for the past five years, teaching American Sign Language (ASL) along with teaching theatre to elementary and high school students, has made me realize the beauty and significance of the language to bridge the communication between Deaf and hearing. I have witnessed this kind of bridge many times in the past five years, especially when theatre opportunities are included. There are many examples that I could tell you about, but I will discuss two main ones that I feel obviously point out how ASL and theatre used together make a connection between Deaf and hearing.

Chime Charter Elementary School has an inclusive program; therefore, having Deaf and hearing communicate is important because it supports their philosophy. When ASL was being taught, I would see the "light bulbs" go on for the children of both worlds as they realized how ASL can help them communicate, especially to play together at recess time or in after-school programs. Having an ASL instructor come to classes is crucial, as signs are taught to show concepts of words or sentences in order for the children to understand lessons better. However, from my previous experiences, I thought theatre activities would enhance learning and fluency, using the signs that they learn every week in another context. I realized that I had to do something in order to support that theory, so I got in touch with an ASL/theatre coordinator from Deaf West Theatre who taught at in-school workshops. She was absolutely ecstatic that I recommended Chime, as I explained to her the unique philosophy of the inclusive program there.

All the deaf students there and some hearing classes that were specifically invited to the workshops truly enjoyed ten weeks together participating in highly stimulating activities, simple games, and stories using ASL. I was glad to be a witness and observe how growth and confidence naturally rise when deaf and hearing students learn to sign and are completely included together. That is when I knew for sure that having ASL taught through theatre works efficiently.

I left Chime to work as an ASL high school teacher at Granada Hills Charter High School and, once again, I have seen how ASL and theatre create an impact. I teach ASL to all levels of high school students, following the standards of Foreign Language Framework for California Public Schools. I do not use "voice" or an interpreter to communicate with my students. I use only finger-spelling, signs, and gestures. At first, students get confused or frustrated because they are not used to the world of silence when learning a second language. However, every year around in December we have a holiday show in ASL in which we require our students to be involved. The holiday show is a mixture of holiday songs and skits in which all students sign. Some students learn to be "voicers" by watching students sign on the stage. This part of the ASL curriculum is just amazing because, from late August when school starts to early December when school is just ending for winter break and when rehearsals for the holiday show are starting, students reach a plateau of learning vocabulary, sentences, and paragraphs. But right after the holiday show finishes, the plateau quickly changes and students begin to pick up ASL more quickly.

In conclusion, there are many ways for Deaf and hearing to learn to communicate with each other; there is not one right answer for the communication bridge to connect both worlds, but teaching ASL through theatre enables Deaf and hearing to be able to communicate with each other by sharing and teaching each other. Simply by being in each other's presence while learning ASL and expressing themselves through theatre, they experience each other's world by being open-minded about how communication works.

=======================

Challenging College Students
Elizabeth van den Berg

One of the biggest lessons I have learned over the years in working with challenging students is that their learning process is enhanced through a partnership with the educator. Even if both parties are willing to listen to one another and discuss openly ways to accomplish learning, a positive result will only be achieved if both parties uphold their ends of the agreement. The educator must be willing to extend a hand, but the student must also take it! Of course, this begins with disclosure. The teacher cannot even hold out the hand if they do not know how it should be offered.

On the McDaniel College campus we have excellent Student Academic Support Services (SASS). It is the student's responsibility to take their documentation to the center and discuss their individual accommodations with the counselors. The counselors provide each student with a "blue sheet" listing their various accommodations, such as extended test time, use of computers for exams, etc. It is then the student's responsibility to bring the blue sheet to each of their individual professors.

I have been most successful in helping these students accomplish their educational goals when I have been handed the bluesheet on the first day of the semester. I am then made aware well in advance of their requirements and, if I perceive any difficulties in meeting those requirements, I feel free to discuss them with the student and SASS. We work in partnership to meet those accommodations, sometimes conferencing throughout the semester whenever issues arise.

When SASS revealed before the start of the semester that I would have Matt, a student who has Asperger syndrome, in my beginning acting class, they also sent along an information sheet that stated (in part):

"Characteristics:

...characterized by a qualitative impairment in social interactions. These individuals may be keen to relate to others but do not have the social skills...

...communication problems include standing too close, staring, abnormal body posture, and failure to understand gestures and facial expressions..."

I was terrified. This is a course all about social interactions revealed by characters on the stage through body posture, gesture, and facial expression. Matt's mom had made disclosure but asked for discretion — which meant I would have to be extremely careful about public critique, a technique which is commonly used in courses such as this. The class peer mentor was also made aware of the situation and we talked about strategies before the course began. I knew we would both have to work closely with Matt to help him understand the craft of acting.

There were excessive requests for assistance with homework in the beginning — but the peer mentor was made aware of need for clearly defined boundaries and she learned to tell him exactly when to call her, and when to stop. When he was paired with a scene partner, there were initial difficulties as this freshman student (the partner) had a hard time defining specific boundaries. She was used to being overly "polite" and did not wish to appear bossy. Eventually, with help, they worked out a specified schedule and the scene was successful.

I did not want to assign a class member for the final scene, as each student has specific areas to work in, and I did not want their scene to be coupled with other problems. Luckily, the peer mentor is often involved in the scenes for class, so this solution worked the best. Matt passed the course with flying colors: a positive final result. He is not majoring in theatre, so I only see him for advising once a semester now. Although he did not make any close friends in the course, students said later that they missed having him in the department.

=================

Inclusion in the Arts
Molly Work, MSW

I have a mild case of cerebral palsy. My parents made the smart decision to insist that I be included in regular education classes in the Washington, DC, Public Schools from the very beginning. I went to Stoddert Elementary and then to Hardy Middle School, both of which had their arts classes once a week at Fillmore Arts Center.

When I was in elementary school my favorite classes were dance, drama, and music. Looking back on it now, I realize that the reason I was drawn to these classes was because they required me to be physical and practice my speech in a fun way. I was already working on these things through private physical therapy and speech therapy sessions. When I was in elementary school, I had this attitude that I could do anything if I tried. I also had this belief that if I worked hard enough, the cerebral palsy would disappear. I truly did not recognize some of the physical differences between myself and other children. If a classmate asked me about my differences, for example, "Why do you talk or walk that way?" My reply would be simple, "Because I have cerebral palsy." I answered the question in a matter-of-fact way.

In Ms. Meenahan's class I remember being part a group and trying to perfect a dance. At that point I was not self-conscious about my body. I strove to dance as well as the others and did not feel excluded by the children or the teacher. Ms. Meenahan always made me feel safe in her class. One of my issues during childhood was drooling. I remember that when I was really concentrating on the dance moves, sometimes I drooled on the floor during class and I would get a little embarrassed, but Ms. Meenahan never made me feel bad or ashamed about it; she would discreetly wipe up my saliva from the floor. I remember thinking she was so kind not to draw attention to it in front of my classmates.

I loved drama, particularly improvisation. Mr. Marvin would give us a situation to act out. Most of the time I felt comfortable putting in my ideas and other times I would go along with what the others were planning, depending on how I was feeling physically that day. There were days when my body tone was down and on those days it was harder to speak as clearly as I could. I remember having to repeat myself on those days and I hated that. As an actress it made me feel self-conscious. When I was nervous, I would giggle when I was onstage. This would also happen in other classes in school as well as in drama. I had the sense that Mr. Marvin knew that I was not trying to disrupt class but, at the same time, I would get embarrassed. In fifth grade Mr. Marvin gave my group an assignment to create a funeral scene and I got nervous about giggling at the wrong time in the scene. The group decided that a beloved teacher at the school passed away. I decided that my character, a student, did not like this teacher, so when the preacher said something nice about the teacher, I would giggle because I did not agree. I remember the audience really thought it was funny because they caught on to what I was trying to portray.

In middle school I started not wanting to take drama or dance. At this point in my life I began to realize how different I was from my classmates and Mr. Marvin taught Shakespeare. In terms of dance, the teachers changed and, without Ms. Meenahan, I did not feel comfortable taking a movement class. I knew my classmates cared more about appearance and would care if I screwed up a line or giggled or fell on the dance floor during a routine. I began to actually dread Fillmore in some ways because I just did not want to go there and do things that required me to perform. I switched to creative writing and sometimes I did art. I think, as I got older, I was expressive of myself and that was true not only in the arts, but also in class as well. I didn't have many friends and it was a very lonely time for me.

In high school I went to Thornton Friends School, a private school in Maryland with only 54 kids. I took a drama class my first year and Irma, the teacher, was wonderful. She encouraged me to do a long monologue from *Glimpses.* I did it and it made me feel great. Another project in that class was an improvisational play. I played a character named Mildred who was always studying, never wanted to play, and always took things very seriously. I could relate to Mildred's character because she always tried to do everything right and she was a very isolated person. Irma was a really great teacher in terms of inclusion — really supportive, making me feel like I belonged there and could actually contribute something artistic.

Unfortunately the next year another teacher came and I withdrew from the class because I just did not feel included. I got the sense from this instructor that she did not want me there and I just did not want to feel that way. In my senior year of high school there was yet another drama teacher so I signed up for the drama class again. The class decided to do the female version of *The Odd Couple*. I was told to work behind the scenes and I felt really excluded. In the second semester we did scenes from William Shakespeare, but my scene was from *The Glass Menagerie* and I portrayed Laura who has a disability. I realized at the time that in separating me and the typically developing students, he was trying to create something "special" for me. That did not feel good at all. At the time I did not know how to voice it.

I was a counselor at BAPA summer camp for two years and worked with kids who were seven to nine years old when I was 15 to 17. Campers with and without disabilities were integrated and I had some with physical disabilities in my group. I remember trying to be supportive of them but, despite all of Sally's attempts at educating the staff on how to work with kids with disabilities, I felt the adults running the program were not really tuned in to the students' differences. It seemed to me that the director of the play was more interested in a good performance than in enhancing everyone's drama abilities. She would often look at me in a condescending manner. I used to dread working with this director, but I had to put up a front for the kids. The attitude toward people with disabilities was not really positive and it made it very hard to work there.

I had a more positive experience working with an Arts Access performing group called Phoenix. I was doing my senior volunteer project and I was asked to be the assistant to Mandy Hart, the director of the troupe that year. Mandy and I worked very hard to come up with a way to incorporate everyone else's ideas in the play. It was a play about wishes and we wanted to enhance the belief that the characters and the actors who played them could be whoever they wanted to be. Everybody had a part. One student was not very verbal and was in a body cast but we tried very hard to include him. I even got to act in the play.

Drama, music, and dance are really important parts of education. They stimulate the mind and help physical and mental growth. I think it is very important that all kids have the opportunity to do drama, music, and dance, no matter what their limitations are because it is just a part of living. Drama, especially, is very fundamental to growth because people act all the time. Even as adults, we have to go out and act differently in different situations. Interviews are exactly like being on stage. You have to know the lines, you have to know the answers, and you have to sell yourself. To limit children in terms of their ability to express themselves in a theatre role, to discourage them from pretending, is damaging to their development and self-esteem.

When working with children with disabilities in an integrated setting, I think the worst situation is when an instructor gives out the message that the child with the disability is different and has to be treated differently. The other kids in the class will take the lead of the teacher. I always knew who accepted and welcomed my differences and I really appreciated it. The teachers who did not accept my differences made me feel really inadequate and as a result I just wanted to isolate myself. I strongly believe that teachers have an obligation, a duty, to enhance the self-esteem of children, no matter what their difference is. One of the things I like about the philosophy of social work is that everyone deserves to be treated with dignity and respect. I am just a real firm believer in that. I have had experiences in drama where I felt accepted, I felt encouraged, and it was those experiences that helped me later in life to stand up for myself and "play the part" I needed to play to succeed.

It is interesting, these days I feel like I play a part every time I walk out the door. For someone with disabilities it is hard to be out in the real world. I think I have somewhat mastered the ability to adapt in the world. If you act like you belong, then you belong; if you do not act like you belong, you stick out like a sore thumb. I have seen it happen to people without disabilities, too. When they feel insecure, it shows. I have seen other folks with disabilities that do not feel the least bit insecure — that shows, too. I think it all comes down to being secure with oneself. And that is really hard to do for anybody.

========================

A Look Back on Inclusion
David Fogel

When I started performing in Pegasus with peers who had disabilities, I had many reservations as to whether or not it would be a worthwhile pursuit. Fifteen years later, I can say that it was a worthwhile pursuit and that those experiences and lessons played an intrinsic role in shaping me as an individual, artist, and professional. My friends in the early days of Pegasus, people who I still consider friends today, educated me in the fundamental life principles of patience, compassion, understanding, and the various lenses that we view life through.

The lessons learned during those years that I spent with the Pegasus Company ring true today as I work with people from all different backgrounds in the field of urban planning and community development. They ring true for me as an individual by helping me solidify and better my relationships with the people around me. They ring true for me as an artist as I utilize the improvisational skills refined in the classroom and during every performance as I gauge the audience and adjust to their feedback.

Many of the people I worked with 15 years ago are still a part of my life today. They are teachers to all who come into contact with them, opening minds and providing new perspectives. All one has to do is be open oneself and willing to listen.

Epilogue

When Jacob started out in my Ivymount creative drama class, he did not have any friends. Why he did not soon became very clear. He was an instigator. He loved to set up fights between other people and watch them go at it. He was a real master at this. He would sit back and observe the others to see where their emotional weaknesses were that particular day. Then he would start feeding one unsuspecting student ammunition to use against another: ammunition that was too juicy to ignore.

"Roberto's hair looks stupid today," he would whisper to Sharon.

"Sharon has a button missing from her blouse," he'd whisper to Roberto.

Soon Roberto and Sharon were busy insulting each other and, if I did not intervene quickly enough, they would come to blows.

Each week when we turned off the lights and lay down to go on our guided fantasy, Jacob would position himself right in the middle of everyone else and kick an arm here, nudge a leg there, bump an elbow, tickle a side, blow on the top of a head.

I'd hear:

"Stop it!"

"Hey, stop it!"

"Don't touch me!"

And the disturbance was always originated by Jacob.

Finally one day while we were on an underwater treasure hunt, I could not stand it anymore. I silently signaled Marilyn Harwood, my assistant. She swooped down, picked up Jacob, and bodily carried him out of the center of the group into the hall.

"What's the problem with you?" she asked. "Why do you always pick fights with other people?"

"Because no one is my friend," he replied.

"How can they like you if you pick on them all the time?"

"I don't know. People just don't like me."

"Well, I like you."

Their conversation about making friends and wanting to be liked went on for about 20 minutes. Finally they returned to the classroom and Jacob was much calmer and more focused.

Slowly, over the course of a year, Jacob stopped being an instigator and became a class leader. He loved acting out animals, particularly large birds. We started having a great time together. In drama class he had found a place where he was accepted for who he was and his creativity was given an appropriate outlet.

With his acceptance came another change. He started to want to have a friend. He picked Willard, another boy about his age, who was also extremely creative and active. They worked together in class and got along well, but since they lived at opposite ends of the metropolitan area, their relationship ended each week when class was over and their mothers took them home.

One day in late November, Jacob decided he wanted to stay after class and play on the swings outside with his new friend — extending his friendship to a new level. Only he could not ask. Asking meant facing rejection. His internalized personal history told him nobody ever really wanted to be his friend.

Jacob's mother arrived before Willard's mother did. Jacob whispered what he wanted to do in his mother's ear. "Well, ask him," she said.

"I can't," was his reply and he wandered aimlessly around the classroom for a while.

Back to his mother a few minutes later, he whispered in her ear again.

"*You* have to ask him," said his mother.

"I can't!" He sighed in frustration and wandered away.

It took five whole minute to summon up the courage to ask, but finally, he did. He went over to Willard and said, "Willard, would you run up the hill with me?"

Willard's face lit up, "Sure!"

And off they went, racing up the hill to the swing set together.

Jacob's mother got tears in her eyes and turned to me. "I can't believe he did that. It's so hard for him to make friends. That was wonderful to see."

Connecting with others is the real reason we are all here. But to connect with another human being means taking risks. The risk of rejection. The risk of failure.

When I am afraid of taking a leap into the unknown, I think of Jacob summoning up the courage to say, "Willard, would you run up the hill with me?"

And I know if he could do it, I can do it.

You can, too!

Appendix: Checklist for Building Accessibility

Getting in the Front Door

Outside pathways from parking lot to front door

Are they smooth, solid traveling surfaces?
Are there any steps or abrupt changes in level (more than ¼ inch)?
Are pathways wide enough for a wheelchair?

Accessible parking

Is the space large enough?
Is it close to the accessible entrance?
Is it correctly marked?
Is the way to the closest accessible entrance marked?

Curb-cuts

Is there one by the accessible parking space?
Are any along the path to the accessible entrance?
Is there one at the main accessible entry drop off?

Entryway

Are there steps?
If so, do the steps have handrails?
Do you need a ramp or a lift?
Is the door wide enough?
Is the door revolving?
Does the door have a double vestibule?

If so, does it need to be automated?
Is the entry floor slip-resistant?
If not, do you need to add mats?

Restrooms

Doors

Are the doors wide enough for a wheelchair?
Are the doors too heavy to open easily?
Does the door have a double vestibule?
If so, can the inside door be propped open?

Flow of space inside room

Can wheelchairs maneuver around freely?

Toilet stalls

Is the door wide enough for a wheelchair?
Is the stall wide enough?
Are there grab bars in the right places?
Are they hung at the right height?
Is the toilet paper within reach?
Is the toilet easy to flush?

Sinks

Is there clearance under the sink for a wheelchair?
Can the faucets be reached?
Can the soap dispenser be reached?
Is it easy to use the faucets and soap dispenser?

Other items

Can the towels be reached?
Can vending machines be reached?
Is the mirror low enough?
Is the floor surface not too slick/not too rough?
Is there enough lighting?

Getting Around Inside the Building

Floor surfaces

Are they slip-resistant?
Are they too rough?
Are they carpeted?
If so, are the carpet edges tacked down?
Do you need an alternative surface for wheelchairs to roll on?

Changing levels

Are all floors accessible to wheelchair users?
Which places in the building are not accessible?
Do all stairs have handrails?
Do all ramps with more than a six-foot rise have handrails?
Are buttons in elevators within reach of someone sitting in a wheelchair?
Are buttons in elevators clearly marked? In Braille? Raised numbers?

Doorways

Are they wide enough for a wheelchair?
Do they have raised door sills that might impede movement?
Are doors too heavy to open easily?
Do they need to be automated?
Are the door handles easy to use?

Lighting

Is it bright enough?
Is it even enough?
Is it easy on the eyes?
Are light switches within reach and easy to operate?
Are important places, potentially hazardous areas, and signs highlighted
    by lighting?

Hallways and aisles

Are they wide enough?
Are they well-lit?

Is the traffic flow good?

Are there obstacles protruding from the wall which a patron using a cane might run into?

Office equipment

Do tables and desks have wheelchair clearance?

Is the flow of movement good within offices?

Can a wheelchair maneuver around in the space?

Communications

Do you have a TTY?

Can you amplify the sound on at least one phone?

Do you have an amplified pay phone?

Is the pay phone mounted correctly on the wall?

Is the pay phone designed with clearance for/reachable from a wheelchair?

Are the phones easy to dial?

Signs

Are all rooms and areas clearly marked?

Are all accessible areas and adaptive devices clearly marked?

Are signs clearly lit?

Do you use international pictographs and accessibility symbols?

Are signs easy to read?

Clear and large lettering?

Color-contrasted?

Are there raised lettering, shapes, or Braille?

Are signs at eye level?

Water fountains

Is at least one accessible to wheelchair users?

If not, do you have paper cup dispensers by at least one?

Emergency devices

Do the fire alarms flash in addition to making sound?

Are all fire exits clearly marked?

Are the routes to the fire exits wheelchair accessible?

Accessibility in your Theatre Space

Stage and backstage areas

Can all actors get onto the stage?

Can all actors get around backstage and through all backstage passageways?

Are dressing rooms accessible?

Can wheelchairs get around inside the dressing rooms?

Do makeup tables have enough clearance for wheelchairs?

Are costumes accessible?

Is there a comfortable changing bench for actors who can't stand on their own to use?

Is the lighting/sound/stage management booth accessible?

Auditorium

Are the aisles wide enough for a wheelchair?

Are the aisle surfaces smooth and without obstacles?

Are the aisles clearly lighted?

Are there strips of glow tape on steps and other potential hazards for patrons moving around in the dark?

Are spaces left for wheelchairs in the seating areas?

Do these spaces have clear sightlines to the stage?

Are seats reserved for deaf patrons in a spot with good sightlines to sign-interpreters and the stage?

Are seats reserved for blind and low-vision patrons in areas where they can see and hear well?

Do seats have a space for patrons with seeing-eye dogs to lie at their owners' feet during the performance? If not, arrange for an empty seat next to the patron so the dog can lie in front of it.

Box office

Do staff know how to accommodate the needs of different patrons?

Is there a TTY so deaf patrons can order tickets?

Is there a writing surface for patrons in wheelchairs?

Is there a low window for patrons in wheelchairs? If not, staff will need to come out of the box office to take care of ticket transactions.

Have you posted notice of all accommodations available to disabled patrons?

Programs and brochures

Have you used appropriate language and correct terms when referring to disabilities and the individuals who have them?

Do you publicize all accommodations available to disabled patrons?

Do you have large-print versions of publications for patrons with low vision?

Do you have versions available on cassette tape or CD for patrons who can't see or read?

Do you have versions in Braille?

Do you have volunteers who could read material to patrons who can't see or read?

Translation and amplification systems for performance

Do you have an auxiliary listening system for hard-of-hearing patrons?

Do you offer audio descriptions of performances for patrons with low vision?

Do you offer sign-interpreted performances for deaf and hard-of-hearing patrons?

Do you caption the dialogue in performances for deaf and hard-of-hearing patrons?

Do you use another kind of assistive captioning, interpreting service, or interpretive device?

References

Ackerman, D. (1990). *A natural history of the senses*. New York: Random House.

Armstrong, T. (1993). *Seven kinds of smart*. New York: Penguin Books.

Armstrong, T. (2000). *Multiple intelligences in the classroom, 2nd edition*. Alexandria, VA: Association for Supervision and Curriculum Development.

Asbury, C. & Rich, B. (2008). *Learning, arts, and the brain: The Dana consortium report on arts and cognition*. New York: Dana Press.

Attwood, T. (1998). *Asperger's syndrome: A guide for parents and professionals*. London: Jessica Kingsley Publishers.

Bettelheim, B. (1977). *The uses of enchantment*. New York: Random House.

Blum, D. (1998). Face it! *Psychology Today, 32*(5), 34, 36-39, 66-67.

Bowman, S. (2002, August 27). Dressing with purpose: Fashion designers use artistic abilities to help community. *Kansas State Collegian*, 7.

Blakemore, S. J. & Frith, U. (2005). *The learning brain: Lessons for education*. Malden, MA: Blackwell Publishing.

Brown University (2005, January 6). Scents and emotions linked by learning, Brown study shows. *ScienceDaily*. Retrieved January 2, 2010, from www.science daily.com/releases/2005/01/050106105622.htm

Brown, V. J. (2003). Reaching for chemical safety. *Environmental Health Perspectives, 111*(14), A766-A769. Retrieved January 2, 2010, from www.ncbi.nlm.nih.gov/pmc/articles/PMC1241736/pdf/ehp0111-a00766.pdf

Burd, L. (1992). Educational needs of children with Tourette syndrome. In: Haerle, T. (ed.). *Children with Tourette syndrome: A parent's guide*. Bethesda, MD: Woodbine House.

Burr, C. (2002). *The emperor of scent: A story of perfume, obsession, and the last mystery of the senses*. New York: Random House.

Callo, K. (1987, November 26). Drugs can halt spread of leprosy in body. *The Washington Post*, A.2.

Cozolino, L. (2002). *The Neuroscience of psychotherapy: Building and rebuilding the human brain*. New York: W.W. Norton & Company.

Crain, W. C. (1985). *Theories of development: Concepts and applications, 2nd ed.* Upper Saddle River, NJ: Prentice-Hall, Inc.

Csikszentmihalyi, M. (1990). *Flow: The psychology of optimal experience*. New York: Harper & Row.

Damasio, A. R. (1994). *Descartes' error: Emotion, reason, and the human brain*. New York: Avon Books.

Damasio, A. R. (1999). *The feeling of what happens: Body and emotion in the making of consciousness*. San Diego: Harcourt, Inc.

Dealing with dyslexia, language is a factor. (2001, March 16). Kansas City Star, A.4.

Diamond, A., Barnett, W. S., Thomas, J., & Munro, S. Preschool program improves cognitive control. *Science, 317*(5855), 1387-1388.

Dixon-Krauss, L. (1996). *Vygotsky in the classroom: Mediated literacy instruction and assessment*. White Plains, NY: Longman Publishers.

Doheny, K. (2001, November 4). The nose knows stress. *Kansas City Star Magazine*.

Dykins, E. M., Rosner, B. A., Ly, T. & Sagun, J. (2005). Music and anxiety in Williams syndrome: A harmonious or discordant relationship? *American Journal on Mental Retardation, 110*(5), 346-358.

Edelson, S. (1996, February 1). Interview with Dr. Temple Grandin. *Center for the Study of Autism*. Retrieved on January 2, 2010 from www.autism.org/interviews/temp_ int.htm

Eisner, E. W. (2002). *The arts and the creation of mind*. New Haven: Yale University Press.

Ekman, P. (2003). *Emotions revealed: Recognizing faces and feelings to improve communication and emotional life*. New York: Henry Holt & Company.

Eyman, S. (1987, March 3). Leprosy, the ancient disease, still hits millions. *The Washington Post Health*. 11.

Fisher, B. E. (1998). Scents & sensitivity. *Environmental Health Perspectives, 106*(12), A594-A599. Retrieved January 2, 2010, from www.ehp.niehs.nih.gov/docs/1998/106-12/focus-abs.html

Flavel, J. H. (1963). *The developmental psychology of Jean Piaget*. New York: D. Van Nostrand Company.

Frith, U. (2003). *Autism: Explaining the enigma, second edition*. Malden, MA: Blackwell Publishing.

Gardner, H. (1973). *The arts and human development*. New York: Basic Books.

Gardner, H. (1991). *The unschooled mind: How children think and how schools should teach*. New York: Basic Books.

Gardner, H. (1993). *Multiple intelligences: The theory in practice*. New York: Bantam Books.

Gardner, H. (1999). *Intelligence reframed: Multiple intelligences for the 21st century*. New York: Basic Books.

Garvey, C. (1990). *Play*. Cambridge, MA: Harvard University Press.

General information about traumatic brain injury: Fact sheet number 4 (FS4). (1997). Retrieved on January 2, 2010, from www.kidsource.com/NICHCY/brain.html.

Gibson, W. (1960). *The miracle worker*. New York: Samuel French.

Ginsburg, H., & Opper, S. (1969). *Piaget's theory of intellectual development: An introduction*. Upper Saddle River, NJ: Prentice-Hall, Inc.

Goffman, E. (1963). *Stigma: Notes on the management of spoiled identity*. New York: Simon & Schuster.

Goleman, D. (1995). *Emotional intelligence: Why it can matter more than IQ*. New York: Bantam.

Graesser, A. C., Olde, B., & Klettke, B. (2002). How does the mind construct and represent stories? In: Green, M. C., Strange, J. J. & Brock, T. C. (Eds.). *Narrative impact: Social and cognitive foundations*. (pp. 229-262). Mahway, NJ: Lawrence Erlbaum Associates, Publishers.

Grandin, T. (1995). Thinking in pictures and other reports from my life with autism. New York: Random House.

Grandin, T. (2002, May 6). Myself. *Time Magazine.* Retrieved on January 2, 2010, from www.time.com/time/magazine/article/0,9171,1002370,00.html

Grandin, T. (2002). Teaching tips for children and adults with autism. *Center for the Study of Autism.* Retrieved on January 2, 2010, from www.autism.com/families/therapy/teaching_tips.htm

Grandin, T. & Barron, S. (2005). *The unwritten rules of social relationships: Decoding social mysteries through the unique perspectives of autism.* Arlington, TX: Future Horizons.

Grandin, T. & Scariano, M. M. (1986). *Emergence: Labeled autistic.* New York: Warner Books.

Greene, T. R. & Noice, H. (1988). Influence of positive affect upon creative thinking and problem solving in children. *Psychological Reports, 63,* 895-898.

Hallowell, E. M. & Rately, J. J. (1994). *Driven to distraction: Recognizing and coping with attention deficit disorder from childhood to adulthood.* New York: Simon & Schuster.

Hannaford, C. (1995). *Smart moves: Why learning is not all in your head.* Marshall, NC: Great Ocean Publishers.

Hansberry, L. (1987). *A raisin in the sun.* New York: New American Library.

Harrison, J. E. (1917). *Ancient art and ritual.* Bradford-on-Avon: Moonraker Press.

Hathaway, W. (2005, March 15). A window to the brain: Imaging studies suggest a physiological basis for attention deficit/hyperactivity disorder. Hartford Courant. D.4.

Heath Resource Center. Online clearinghouse on postsecondary education for individuals with disabilities. Retrieved on January 2, 2010, from www.heath-resource-center.org

Hipp, E. (1995). *Fighting invisible tigers, revised and updated.* Minneapolis, MN: Free Spirit Publishing.

Hodge, F. (1971). *Play directing: Analysis, communication, and style.* Upper Saddle River, NJ: Prentice-Hall.

Hughes, L. (1951). Harlem. In: *The panther & the lash.* New York: Alfred A. Knopf, Inc.

Huizinga, J. (1950). Homo ludens: *A study of the play-element in culture.* Boston: Beacon Press.

Hunt, M. (1982). *The universe within: A new science explores the human mind.* New York: Simon & Schuster.

Iacoboni, M. (2008). *Mirroring people: The new science of how we connect with others.* New York: Farrar, Straus & Giroux.

Jensen, E. (2000). *Brain-based learning: The new science of teaching & training, revised ed.* San Diego: The Brain Store.

Johnstone, K. (1989). *Impro: Improvisation and the theatre.* London: Methuen.

Jones, J. E. (2005, June 20). Finding my voice. *Time Bonus Section, 165*(25), F.14.

Knez, I. (2005, May). Non-visible flicker from fluorescent lighting: Psychological impact. [Electronic version]. Right Light 6, retrieved August 1, 2005 at ID011. www.rightlight6.org/english/proceedings/.

Kornhaber, M., Fierros, E., & Veenema, S. (2004). *Multiple intelligences: Best ideas from research and practice.* Boston: Pearson Education.

Laike, R. K. T. (1998). [Abstract.]The impact of flicker from fluorescent lighting on well-being, performance and physiological arousal. *Ergonomics, 41*(4), 433-447.

Retrieved on January 2, 2010 from www.informaworld.com/smpp/427974937-81205297/content~content=a713808103&db=all

LeDoux, J. (1998). *The emotional brain: The mysterious underpinnings of emotional life.* London: Weidenfeld & Nicolson.

Lessac, A. (1967). *The use and training of the human voice: A practical approach to speech and voice dynamics.* New York: Drama Book Specialists.

Levine, M. (2002). *A mind at a time.* New York: Simon & Schuster.

Levitin, D. J. (2008). *The world in six songs: How the musical brain created human nature.* New York: Dutton.

Lewis-Williams, D. (2002). *The mind in the cave.* London: Thames & Hudson.

Lichtenberg, P., van Beusekom, J., & Gibbons, D. (1997). *Encountering bigotry: Befriending projecting persons in everyday life.* Lanham, MD: Jason Aronson.

Lollar, D. J. (2001). SBAA fact sheet: Learning among children with spina bifida.. *Spina Bifida Association of America.* Retrieved August 3, 2005, from www.spinabifida association.org/site/c.liKWL7PLLrF/b.2700281/k.E95C/Learning_Among_Children_with_Spina_Bifida.htm

Lyon, G. R., Shaywitz, S. E., & Shaywitz, B. A. (2003). A definition of dyslexia. *Annals of Dyslexia, 53*(1), 1-14.

MacDonald, A. (2003). Imaging studies bring ADHD into sharper focus. *BrainWork: The Neuroscience Newsletter, 13*(2), 1-3.

MacDonald, A. (2003). I feel your pain (and joy): New theories about empathy. *BrainWork: The Neuroscience Newsletter, 13*(4), 1-3.

Markova, D. (1991). *The art of the possible: A compassionate approach to understanding the way people think, learn, and communicate.* Emeryville, CA: Conari Press.

Markova, D. (1996). *The open mind: Exploring the six patterns of natural intelligence.* Berkeley, CA: Conari Press.

Marsh, P. (Ed.). (1988). *Eye to eye: How people interact.* Topsfield, MA: Salem House Publishers.

Marzano, R. J. & Marzano, J. S. (2003). The key to classroom management. *Educational Leadership, 61*(1), 6-13.

Mazzocco, M. M. M. & Myers, G. F. (2003). Complexities in identifying and defining mathematics learning disability in the primary school-age years. *Annals of Dyslexia, 53*(1), 218-253.

Meeropol, E. (2001). SBAA fact sheet: Latex (natural rubber) allergy in spina bifida. *Spina Bifida Association of America.* Retrieved January 2, 2010, from www.spinabifidaassociation.org/site/c.liKWL7PLLrF/b.2642343/k.8D2D/Fact_Sheets.htm

Mithen, S. (1996). *The prehistory of the mind: The cognitive origins of art, religion, and science.* London: Thames & Hudson.

Murdock, M. (1987). *Spinning inward: Using guided imagery with children.* Boston: Shambhala.

Myers, M. (2005). Final Paper for Creative Drama.

National Association for the Deaf: www.nad.org.

Noice, H. (1996). The mental processes of professional actors as examined through self-report, experimental investigation, and think-aloud protocol. Empirical Approaches to Literature and Aesthetics. *Advances in Discourse Processes, 52.*

Noice, H. & Noice, T. (2001). Learning dialogue with and without movement. *Memory & Cognition, 29*(6), 820-827.

Noice, H. & Noice, T. (2007). The non-literal enactment effect: Filling in the blanks. *Discourse Processes, 44*(2), 73-89.

Noice, H., Noice, T. & Kennedy, C. (2000). Effects of enactment by professional actors at encoding and retrieval. *Memory, 8* (6), 353-363.

Oatley, K. (2002). Emotions and the story world of fiction. In: Green, M. C., Strange, J. J., & Brock, T. C. (Eds.). *Narrative impact: Social and cognitive foundations.* pp. 39-69. Mahwah, NJ: Lawrence Erlbaum Associates, Publishers.

Olsen, S. (2004). Making sense of Tourette's. *Science, 305*(5689), 1390-1392.

Ornstein, R. (1991). *The evolution of consciousness: Of Darwin, Freud, and cranial fire — the origins of the way we think.* Upper Saddle River, NJ: Prentice-Hall.

Ott, J. (1990). *Light, radiation and you: How to stay healthy.* Greenwich, CT: Devin-Adair.

Parks, S. (1995). Improving workplace performance: Historical and theoretical contexts. *Monthly Labor Review, 118*(5), 18-28.

Pennington, B. F. (2003). Understanding the comorbidity of dyslexia. *Annals of Dyslexia, 53*(1), 15-22.

Pfeiffer, J. E. (1984). *The creative explosion: An inquiry into the origins of art and religion.* New York: Harper & Row.

Pinker, S. (1997). *How the mind works.* New York: W.W. Norton & Company.

Pisano, M. (May 19, 2003). Scientists use MRIs to study ADHD, depression in children. *San Antonio Express-News*, F.1.

Post, Y. (2003). Teaching the secondary language functions of writing, spelling, and reading. *Annals of Dyslexia, 53*(1), 128-148.

Registry of Interpreters for the Deaf: www.rid.org

Restak, R. (2003). *The new brain: How the modern age is rewiring your mind.* New York: Rodale.

Robertson, I. (2002). *Opening the mind's eye: How images and language teach us to see.* New York: St. Martin's Press.

Sacks, O. (1985). *The man who mistook his wife for a hat and other clinical tales.* New York: Summit Books.

Sacks, O. (1989). *Seeing voices: A journey into the world of the deaf.* Berkeley: University of California Press.

Sappolsky, R. M. (1994). *Why zebras don't get ulcers.* New York: W. H. Freeman & Co.

Sawyer, R. K. (1997). *Pretend play as improvisation: Conversation in the preschool classroom.* New Jersey: Lawrence Elrbaum Associates, Publishers.

Scans show clues to ADHD: Tests could help diagnose attention deficit problems. (1999, December). *Kansas City Star.*

Schaefer, C. E. (1993). *The therapeutic powers of play.* Lanham, MD: Jason Aronson, Inc.

Schachter, D. L. (1997). *Searching for memory: The brain, the mind, and the past.* New York: Basic Books.

Schank, R. C., & Berman, T. R. (2002). The pervasive role of stories in knowledge and action. In: Green, M. C., Strange J. J., & Brock, T. C. (Eds.), *Narrative impact: Social and cognitive foundations.* (pp. 287-313). New Jersey: Laurence Erlbaum Associates.

Secretary's Commission on Achieving Necessary Skills (SCANS). (1992). *Learning a living: A blueprint for high performance.* U.S. Department of Labor.

Seligman, M. E. P. (1991). *Learned optimism.* New York: Alfred A. Knopf.

Shaw, P., Eckstrand, K., Sharp, W., Blumenthal, J., Lerch, J. P., Greenstein, D., Clasen, L., Evans, A., Giedd, J., & Rapoport, J. L. (2007) Attention-deficit/hyperactivity disorder is characterized by a delay in cortical maturation. *Proc Natl Acad Sci U S A. 104(49)*: 19649-19654. Retrieved on January 2, 2010 from www.ncbi.nlm.nih.gov/pmc/articles/ PMC2148343/

Shurtleff, M. (1980). *Audition.* New York: Bantam Books.

Siegel, D. J. (1999). *The developing mind: How relationships and the brain interact to shape who we are.* New York: Guilford Press.

Somers, R. (1969). *Personal space: The behavioral basis of design.* Upper Saddle River, NJ: Prentice-Hall, Inc.

Spice, B. (2004, November 30). Autism findings focus on how areas of the brain communicate. *Pittsburgh Post-Gazette*, A.14.

Sternberg, P. & Garcia, N. (2000). *Sociodrama: Who's in your shoes?* Santa Barbara, CA: Praeger.

Talan, J. (March 16, 2004). ADHD grows up: Increasingly, adults are relying on prescriptions and coaches to get their lives in order. *ADHD Screening: Parent-Physician Consultation Services.* Retrieved on January 2, 2010 from www.adhdscreening.com/adult_adhd.htm

Tuma, R.S. (2005). Tourette syndrome: A neural circuit gone awry. *BrainWork: The Neuroscience Newsletter, 15*(1), 3-5.

U.S. Bureau of Labor Statistics (2001). Introduction to *Report on the American workforce 2001.* Retrieved on January 2, 2010, from www.bls.gov/opub/rtaw/rtaw home.htm

U.S. Census Bureau (2001). *Historical Statistics of the United States, Colonial Times to 1970*, Part 1, Series D 152-66.

U.S. Census Bureau. (2002). *Disability status: 2000.* U.S. Department of Health & Human Services. Retrieved on January 2, 2010, from www.census.gov/prod/ 2003pubs/c2kbr-17.pdf

Van der Klift, R., & Kunc, N. (1994). Hell-bent on helping: Benevolence, friendship, and the politics of help. In: Thousand, J., Villa, R., & Nevin, A. (Eds.) *Creativity and collaborative learning: A practical guide to empowering students and teachers.* Baltimore: Paul H. Brooks.

Watson, L. (2000). *Jacobson's organ and the remarkable nature of smell.* New York: W.W. Norton & Company.

Weiss, R. (1995, June 20). The nose knows: Scientists study the mystery of smell. *Washington Post Health*, WH.10.

Westbrook, M. T., Legge, V., & Pennay, M. (1993). Attitudes towards disabilities in a multicultural society. *Social Science & Medicine, 36*(5), 615-624.

Windham, C. (2004, January 23). Brain imaging provides a window on speech and learning problems. *The Wall Street Journal*, A.11.

Winnicott, D.W. (1971). *Playing and reality.* London: Routledge.

Wolf, M. (2007). *Proust and the squid: The story and science of the reading brain.* New York: HarperCollins.

Index

About the Author

Sally Bailey, MFA, MSW, RDT/BCT received her BFA in directing from the University of Texas at Austin where she first started working with access issues in the arts while assisting with the drama program at the Texas School for the Deaf. She earned her MFA in playwriting and directing at Trinity University at the Dallas Theater Center and worked in professional theater, including artistic and management positions at TheatreVirginia in Richmond and The Shakespeare Theater at the Folger in Washington, DC.

In 1987 she discovered drama therapy — the use of drama processes and theater products to help people change, heal, and grow. A registered drama therapist since 1990, she has specialized in working with recovering drug addicts at Second Genesis, a long-term residential rehabilitation facility in the Washington, DC area and was the Arts Access director at the Bethesda Academy of Performing Arts (now Imagination Stage), creating accessible programming for children, teens, and adults with a wide variety of disabilities.

She received her MSW from the University of Baltimore/Maryland in 1998. In 1999 she moved to Manhattan, Kansas to head the drama therapy program at Kansas State University and simultaneously became the director for the Manhattan Parks and Recreation Barrier-Free Theatre. An advocate for the arts and people who have (dis)abilities, she is the author of *Wings to Fly: Bringing Theatre Arts to Students with Special Needs* and *Dreams to Sign*, a book about creating theatre in sign language and voice with hearing and deaf actors for family audiences.

Sally is a past president of the National Association for Drama Therapy and a recipient of NADT's 2006 Gertrud Schattner Award given for distinguished contributions to the field of drama therapy in education, publication, practice, and service. She was presented with the Kansas 2007 Distinguished Service Award in Arts and Disabilities, recognizing outstanding support for the arts and children with disabilities.